McDOWELL

··

AND HIS CRITICS

PHILOSOPHERS AND THEIR CRITICS

General Editor: Ernest Lepore

Philosophy is an interactive enterprise. Much of it is carried out in dialogue as theories and ideas are presented and subsequently refined in the crucible of close scrutiny. The purpose of this series is to reconstruct this vital interplay among thinkers. Each book consists of a temporary assessment of an important living philosopher's work. A collection of essays written by an interdisciplinary group of critics addressing the substantial theses of the philosopher's corpus opens each volume. In the last section, the philosopher responds to his or her critics, clarifies crucial points of the discussion, or updates his or her doctrines.

McDOWELL

AND HIS CRITICS

Edited by

Cynthia Macdonald and Graham Macdonald

Blackwell
Publishing

except for editorial material and organization © 2006 by Cynthia Macdonald and Graham Macdonald; Chapter 2 "Reason and Language" © 2006 by Richard Heck; Chapter 6 "Acting in the Light of the Appearances" © 2006 by Jonathan Dancy.

BLACKWELL PUBLISHING
350 Main Street, Malden, MA 02148-5020, USA
9600 Garsington Road, Oxford OX4 2DQ, UK
550 Swanston Street, Carlton, Victoria 3053, Australia

First published 2006 by Blackwell Publishing Ltd
1   2006

Library of Congress Cataloging-in-Publication Data

McDowell and his critics / edited by Cynthia Macdonald and Graham Macdonald.
    p. cm. — (Philosophers and their critics)
  Includes bibliographical references and index.
  ISBN-13: 978-1-4051-0623-8 (hardback : alk. paper)
  ISBN-10: 1-4051-0623-9 (hardback : alk. paper)
  ISBN-13: 978-1-4051-0624-5 (pbk. : alk. paper)
    ISBN-10: 1-4051-0624-7 (pbk. : alk. paper)
  1. McDowell, John Henry.   2. Philosophy, British—20th century.
I. Macdonald, Cynthia, 1951–   II. Macdonald, Graham.   III. Series.
          B1647.M144M33 2006
            192—dc22
            2006001712

A catalogue record for this title is available from the British Library.

Set in 10 on 12 pt Ehrhardt
by SNP Best-set Typesetter Ltd, Hong Kong
Printed and bound in Singapore
by C.O.S. Printers Pte Ltd

The publisher's policy is to use permanent paper from mills that operate a sustainable forestry policy, and which has been manufactured from pulp processed using acid-free and elementary chlorine-free practices. Furthermore, the publisher ensures that the text paper and cover board used have met acceptable environmental accreditation standards.

For further information on
Blackwell Publishing, visit our website:
www.blackwellpublishing.com

Contents

Notes on Contributors

AKEEL BILGRAMI is the Johnsonian Professor of Philosophy at Columbia University and is the author of *Belief and Meaning* (Blackwell, 1992) and *Self-Knowledge and Resentment* (2006).

SIMON BLACKBURN is currently the Professor of Philosophy at the University of Cambridge and Fellow of Trinity College, Cambridge. He was Fellow and Lecturer in Philosophy at Pembroke College, Oxford, from 1970 until 1990, and from 1990 to 2001 the Edna J. Koury Distinguished Professor of Philosophy at the University of North Carolina, Chapel Hill. From 1984 to 1990 he edited the journal *Mind*. He was elected Fellow of the British Academy in 2001. His books are *Reason and Prediction* (1973), *Spreading the Word* (1984), *Essays in Quasi-Realism* (1993), *The Oxford Dictionary of Philosophy* (1994), *Ruling Passions* (1998), *Think* (1999), *Truth*, edited with Keith Simmons (2001), *Being Good* (2001), *Lust* (2004), and *Truth: A Guide for the Perplexed* (2005).

JONATHAN DANCY is Professor of Philosophy at the University of Reading, United Kingdom, and the University of Texas at Austin. His key publications are *An Introduction to Contemporary Epistemology* (Blackwell, 1985), *Moral Reasons* (Blackwell, 1993), *Practical Reality* (2000), and *Ethics without Principles* (2004).

RICHARD G. HECK, JR. is Professor of Philosophy at Brown University and an Associate Fellow of Arché, the AHRC Research Center for the Philosophy of Logic, Language, Mathematics and Mind. His recent publications include "Truth and Disquotation," *Synthèse* (2004), "Do Demonstratives Have Senses?," *Philosophers' Imprint* 2 (2002), "Cardinality, Counting, and Equinumerosity," *Notre Dame Journal of Formal Logic* 41 (2000), and "Non-Conceptual Content and the 'Space of Reasons'," *Philosophical Review* 109 (2000).

T. H. IRWIN is Susan Linn Sage Professor of Philosophy and Humane Letters, Cornell University. He is the author of *Plato's Gorgias* (translation and notes) (1979), *Aristotle's Nicomachean Ethics* (translation and notes) (2nd edn, 1999), *Aristotle's First Principles* (1988), *Classical Thought* (1989), and *Plato's Ethics* (1995).

CYNTHIA MACDONALD is Professor of Philosophy, Queen's University Belfast, and Adjunct Professor of Philosophy, University of Canterbury, New Zealand. She is author of *Mind–Body Identity Theories* (1989) and *Varieties of Things: Foundations of Contemporary Metaphysics* (Blackwell, 2005), editor of *Philosophy of Psychology* and *Connectionism*, with Graham Macdonald (both Blackwell, 1995), editor of *Knowing Our Own Minds*, with Crispin Wright and Barry C. Smith

(1998), and editor of *Contemporary Readings in the Foundations of Metaphysics*, with Stephen Laurence (Blackwell, 1998).

GRAHAM MACDONALD is Professor of Philosophy, University of Canterbury, New Zealand, and Distinguished International Fellow, Institute of Cognition and Culture, Queen's University Belfast. He co-authored *Semantics and Social Science*, with Philip Pettit (1980), edited *Perception and Identity: Essays Presented to A. J. Ayer, With His Replies to Them* (1979), and co-edited *Fact, Science, and Morality*, with Crispin Wright (Blackwell, 1986), *Philosophy of Psychology* and *Connectionism*, with Cynthia Macdonald (Blackwell, 1995) and *Karl Popper: Critical Appraisals*, with Philip Catton (2004).

PHILIP PETTIT is L. S. Rockefeller Professor of Politics and Human Values at Princeton University, where he teaches in political theory and philosophy. His recent books include *Republicanism* (1997), *A Theory of Freedom* (2001), *The Economy of Esteem*, with Geoffrey Brennan (2004), as well as a collection of his own papers, *Rules, Reasons, and Norms* (2002), and a collection of co-authored papers involving Frank Jackson and Michael Smith, *Mind, Morality and Explanation* (2004).

CAROL ROVANE is Professor of Philosophy at Columbia University. Her key publications include *The Bounds of Agency: An Essay in Revisionary Metaphysics*, and articles on various topics, including the first person, personal identity, rational agency, group agency, consciousness, moral psychology, and ethical relativism.

R. M. SAINSBURY is Professor of Philosophy at the University of Texas at Austin and Susan Stebbing Professor at King's College London. His most recent books are *Departing From Frege* (2002) and *Reference Without Referents* (2005).

MICHAEL SMITH is Professor of Philosophy at Princeton University. He is the author of *The Moral Problem* (Blackwell, 1994), *Ethics and the A Priori: Selected Essays on Moral Psychology and Meta-Ethics* (2004), and *Mind, Morality and Explanation: Selected Collaborations*, with Frank Jackson and Philip Pettit (2004).

Introduction

John McDowell's philosophical work is both seminal and remarkable in a number of ways. The spread of his writing is surely unique; it ranges over interpretative issues in Greek philosophy to contemporary debates in the theory of meaning. His views are highly influential in ethics, epistemology, the philosophy of mind, and the philosophy of language; his writing on Aristotle, Kant, Wittgenstein, and, more recently, Wilfrid Sellars, presents a remarkable engagement with, and sometimes reworking of, the thought of key figures in the history of philosophy. In this introduction we will attempt to summarize his many contributions to philosophy, emphasizing the consistency and unity of McDowell's approach to such diverse issues.

The extraordinary unity in McDowell's thought has its origin in a view of philosophy that McDowell finds in Wittgenstein, one that is opposed to philosophical theorizing, or what McDowell sometimes calls "constructive philosophy." This approach embraces Wittgenstein's dictum that philosophy "leaves everything as it is" (Wittgenstein 1953: 124). The work of philosophy, on this account, is not to supply us with novel explanations of puzzling phenomena, but to release us from the thought that there really is a philosophical problem to be solved here. The general idea is that we are under the illusion that some constructive philosophical work needs to be done because we are tempted to accept some underlying assumptions that generate a tension, a tension provoking philosophical anxiety. We then, erroneously, think that the only way of relieving this anxiety is by producing a philosophical explanation or theory, one that we hope will dispel the anxiety whilst leaving the assumptions in place. The therapeutic method McDowell prefers is to expose and question the assumptions generating the tension: once we clearly see that we are not driven to theorize our way out of the problem, anxiety will subside, and everything will be left "open to view." The option that has been obscured by the intrusive assumptions is made readily visible.

This meta-philosophical view is best appreciated when seen in action. In what follows we begin by looking at a topic that might be thought to least fit the therapeutic approach, the theory of meaning. We start with this not only because it was, chronologically, one of the starting points for McDowell's philosophical work, but also because it is here that we find him resolutely refusing to be drawn into giving a philosophical *explanation* of meaning, an explanation that would provide an account of that relation between meaning symbols and the world that gives symbols their meaning.

McDowell's position on meaning arises out of Davidson's suggestion that a "theory of meaning" for a natural language such as English can be given by a theory of truth for that language. The axioms of the theory would specify the extensions of the semantic primitives in the language (denotations for the case of singular terms, satisfaction conditions for the case of predicates) and combinatorial rules would show how the truth-conditions of complex expressions depend on just such an assignment of extensions to the semantic primitives. The result of doing this for all the semantic primitives and all the possibilities of combination would be an extensional theory of truth for the language, one that would be able to specify for each sentence the truth-condition for that sentence. Davidson relied on the formal apparatus provided by Tarski, taking from Tarski the criterion of adequacy for such a theory: the axioms and rules should deliver as theorems true instances of the biconditional " 'p' is true if and only if p" (known as T-sentences). That is, the denotation assigned to "John" and the extensions assigned to "six," "feet," and "tall" should yield as a theorem: "John is six feet tall" is true if and only if John is six feet tall. Davidson also used the phrase "true-in-L" to relativize the truth-theory to a specific language, avoiding the threat posed by orthographically similar items having a different significance in different languages.

This theory is extensional, so one might wonder how such a theory could be relevant to someone wishing to use it to illuminate the meaning of the sentences of a language, meaning being traditionally construed as intensional. This extensionality may be thought to be a particular problem for one who wishes to respect Frege's intuitions about the difference in meaning, or sense, of coreferring expressions. A Tarski-style theory of truth could be adequate if it delivered theorems such as: "Lewis Carroll is a dead author" is true-in-English if and only if Charles Dodgson is a dead author, given that the mentioned sentence is true if and only if the used sentence is true. Now McDowell does think that Frege's approach to sameness and difference of meaning is fundamentally correct. In particular, he thinks that the Fregean constraint, which states that if a rational thinker can take different attitudes to propositions then that fact should be explicable by the assignment of different meanings to sentences expressing those propositions, must be accepted. So if a thinker can rationally believe that "Lewis Carroll is a dead author" is true whilst not believing that "Charles Dodgson is a dead author" is true, then that difference in attitude must be explicable by the different meanings attaching to "Lewis Carroll" and "Charles Dodgson." How can an extensional theory of truth for a language deliver such differences in sense for coreferring expressions?

To deal with this problem both Davidson and McDowell embed the theory of truth for a natural language in a wider context, that of making sense of the linguistic and other actions of agents who use that language. Making sense of the utterances of speakers becomes part of a wider interpretative task, that of making sense of all of their actions.[1] In this wider context the role played by the adequacy condition for a Tarski-style theory of truth for the language (that it delivers true T-sentences) is that of a *necessary* condition on the acceptability of a theory of meaning for the language. The additional conditions are supplied by whatever is necessary for the correct interpretation and rational explanation of all of the speaker's actions. In the example cited above, it will become obvious from other actions of John's that the expressions "Lewis Carroll" and "Charles Dodgson" are associated with different meanings. That is, an assignment of different meanings to the expressions will make more rational sense of John's actions than will an assignment of the same meanings. The axioms of the appropriate truth-theory will respect this difference by having as an axiom: " 'Lewis Carroll' denotes Lewis Carroll," and not allowing as an axiom: " 'Lewis Carroll' denotes Charles Dodgson."

Earlier we said that the theory of meaning is an area where McDowell's "non-constructive" approach to philosophical method is most under strain, and it should be obvious from the above brief sketch of the project why this should be so. Providing a theory of truth for a natural language adequate to underpin the theory of meaning for that language is a large undertaking, one that has, on the face of it, spawned a great deal of constructive philosophizing. Davidson's own early work in this area is a case in point, especially his work on action sentences. Here his semantic analysis of a sentence like "John cut the bread in the kitchen at midnight" required the semanticist to postulate an ontology of events, so that the sentence could be reparsed as stating that there was an event that was a cutting, by John, in the kitchen, at midnight. Postulating the existence of an ontological category of events in order to save certain semantic inferences seems to be the very paradigm of constructive philosophizing. So how does this fit the picture of McDowell's meta-philosophical position that we have presented, which is one where the impulse to theorize is one that ought to be resisted?

The first thing to note is that the construction of such a theory of meaning is more modest than the more ambitious theoretical project of saying what meaning consists in, or of providing analyses of the meanings of the semantic primitives. There is nothing in the above sketch of how a theory of meaning for a language can be constructed that provides anything in the way of stating what, if any, relation between symbols and world gives the symbols their meaning. Nothing in this picture, so far anyway, relies on the theorist's saying anything about how the semantic primitives acquire the extensions that they are required to have if we are to make most sense of the utterances and actions of those using the language. Any causal relations, say, that "connect" a singular term with its denotation are not considered to be criterial in assigning a reference to that singular term; such causal relations as there are taken to be only evidence for the assignment of a denotation, and so not constitutive of the denotation relation.

It is also of importance that the meaning-theory assumes meaning – the right-hand side of the "T-sentences" *use* a sentence to provide the meaning of the sentence named on the left-hand side. It is not the aim of the project to provide a theory of meaning from "the outside," as it were, by giving an analysis of the concept of meaning in terms that reduce it to something else. Such an aim McDowell characterizes as trying to get a "sideways on" perspective, and he believes it is a characteristic temptation of philosophy to try and attain such a perspective, a temptation to be resisted by seeing that such a perspective is both impossible and unnecessary. We have to learn to be more modest in our ambitions. The more modest theory of meaning sketched above will give us what we need: a theory that, were speakers of a language to be in possession of it, they would know the meanings of the expressions they use.

Commitment to this modest approach differentiates McDowell's position from that of Michael Dummett, whose anti-realism about meaning is seen to result from his commitment to a more robust theory of meaning. For both Dummett and McDowell, an understanding of the expressions we use has to be manifested in relevant behavior. Dummett, though, takes it that instances of language use must be describable, as McDowell puts it, " 'as from outside' content," and so "recognizable for what they are without benefit of understanding the language" (McDowell 1998a: 99). For McDowell, when we attribute intentional content to people's mental states, we do so from "within content," not from some more austere vantage point, some privileged position that eschews the use of intentional terms in describing the behavior of those we then credit with linguistic understanding. Again, the attempt to eliminate such intentional terminology in the description of the relevant behavior is diagnosed as the failure to resist the false attraction of reductionism, here made evident in a commitment to a form of behaviorism.[2]

The commitment to a neo-Fregean construal of sense puts McDowell at odds with those who embrace a Russellian construal of proper names, a construal requiring that a person thinking at one time that Lewis Carroll is a famous author is having the same thought as when they think at another time that Charles Dodgson is a famous author. The identification of these thoughts could lead to the attribution to a person of incompatible attitudes to one proposition, and so fly in the face of the Fregean constraint that the individuation of intentional content must be made on the basis of the rational attitudes a person can take to the content in question. This constraint makes the assignment of different senses to the names mandatory, with the consequence that the thoughts containing the different names are distinct. McDowell's understanding of Frege also distances him from those who think that a commitment to Fregean sense for proper names (and singular terms in general) involves adherence to a descriptive account of reference, an account in which the meaning of a name, say, is given by (some weighted subset of) the descriptions associated with the putative bearer of the name. This view is friendly to the thought that a sentence with a vacuous proper name (one without a bearer) can be straightforwardly false: the content of an assertion of such a sentence is given (partially) by the associated descriptions, and these can be just plainly non-veridical. McDowell prefers to understand singular thoughts, those whose expression involves singular terms, as necessarily succeeding in referring. Thoughts whose expression involves names that do not refer render a thought containing them no longer a singular thought, just as the Russellian supposed; where the Russellian was wrong was in taking the further step of eliminating Fregean sense from the picture.[3]

Singular thoughts bring us into contact with the world in a particularly intimate way. For one thing, as noted above, such thoughts are object-dependent ones; without the objects they are putatively about there is no singular thought to be had. The object-dependence of such thoughts is at variance with an image of the mental as being self-sufficient, as not needing the world "outside" to complete it. This is a "Cartesian" image of self-sufficiency, one in which the mental is seen as being self-standing in the sense that it could be the same no matter what was true of the world beyond the mind. McDowell thinks that such a view is radically mistaken, and is responsible for the assessment of our epistemological position as being particularly precarious. It leads, he thinks, to desperate attempts to regain the world via various epistemological ruses, one notable one being the attempt to resurrect the world on the basis of some mythical "given" in perceptual experience, experience that is then considered to be foundational for our reasoned escape from our subjective prison. The problem here is that the "given," if un-conceptualized, is not fit to play the role of a reason for anything. For McDowell the "space of reasons" is necessarily conceptual: the two, concept and reason, are inextricably linked.[4] If we recognize the futility of this undertaking, but still do not reject the Cartesian image, we are then tempted to make coherence the arbiter of reality. Davidson takes this view because, says McDowell, he rightly rejects the idea that thoughts can be answerable to non-conceptual experience ("impressions").

The solution is to discard the assumption supporting the Cartesian image, an assumption that motivates the dubious epistemological response. We need to realize that we are not forced to choose between the myth of the given and coherentism: we can reject both. This rejection requires a recognition that there are no "intermediaries" between mind and world, that when we perceive a tree in front of us, what we see is not some mental item from which we infer that there is a tree there, but the tree itself. The world comes to us already conceptualized; the world is the totality of facts, facts that are independent of us but essentially "thinkable." Our experience involves the passive actualization of conceptual capacities: "receiving an impression . . . is (or at least can be) a case of having an environmental state of affairs borne in on one" (McDowell 2000: 15). On this view, the facts are available to subjects, and they can "form a rational constraint on their activity of making up their minds" (McDowell 2000: 16). So experience can play the required normative role without construing it, as in the myth of the given, as "outside" our conceptual boundaries, nor as an internal intermediary placed between us and the world.

This picture of perception is presented as one that we would all agree on were it not for the philosophical anxiety produced by the acceptance of the Cartesian image. One source of this anxiety is the thought, encouraged by the argument from illusion, that we may have experiences indistinguishable from veridical experiences, except that these experiences are not veridical. The thought is that our veridical experiences must then also fall short of the world, leaving us with serious epistemological work to do if we are to justify to ourselves that they are indeed veridical. The argument moves from the supposed indistinguishability of the veridical and non-veridical experiences to the claim that they have the same content, so the content cannot be one in which an object is present to the mind. McDowell rejects this identification of the content of the two experiences. On his account, when we have a visual experience as of the tree in front of us, either we are having a fact "borne in on us," or it is as if we have such a fact available to us.[5] This disjunctive account of perception leaves open the possibility that there is no gap between thought and world when we think truly.

One of the thoughts leading us to embrace the Cartesian image of the mind, one connected to the argument from illusion, is the consideration that the person who is suffering from such an illusion is not blameworthy with respect to the beliefs they then come to hold. It is not their fault that they have been misled, we wish to say; it is the world that has failed them. This thought suggests that in this case as far as reason is concerned, the true believer is in the same boat as the false believer; they both have the same reasons for their views. McDowell disputes this, making justification depend on truth, this requiring a revision in the "justified true belief" model of knowledge. That model allows that two people can be equally justified, though one has knowledge because her belief is true, whilst the other, whose belief happens to be false, lacks knowledge. This makes the achievement of knowledge depend on luck – the world has failed to cooperate. The suggestion is that the correct move here is to reject the "interiorization of reason" assumed by this "hybrid" conception of knowledge: the facts provided by the world "actually shape the space of reasons as we find it" (McDowell 1998a: 406). A person may not have the reason she imagines she has, though this may be through no fault of her own.

The rejection of the image of the mind as independent of the "external" world, and of the world as existing outside of the boundary of the conceptual, provides McDowell with space for the idea that we can become acquainted with values, where these are granted the same status as facts, this "fact-hood" being equivalent to the claim that there are moral truths. The ethical domain is thus included in the space of reasons, though one must understand "reason" here as not codifiable, not capable of being captured by a set of general rules known in advance and applied to particular cases where necessary. The moral facts are knowable by a suitably sensitive person, one whose sensitivity has been brought about by proper training, and who exercises something like a perceptual capacity in coming to know moral truths.[6]

The objectivity of moral judgment is comparable to that of judgments of color. In both cases there is an element of the subjective in the relevant concepts. The notion of color cannot be adequately elucidated without bringing into the picture the experience of normal color – perceivers in standard conditions. In the case of moral judgment the response is tied to the properly trained, morally sensitive individual. There is no relativism in this, though when faced with a disagreement over moral matters the best we can do is to engage in critical reflection from within whichever moral outlook we possess. Once again McDowell rejects the possibility of there being an understanding, much less a justification, of moral judgments from outside of a specific moral point of view.[7] We grasp the rationality of the virtuous person's actions by understanding that person's conception of how to live. The non-cognitivist's thought that this must make moral judgments unfit for truth arises, says McDowell, from a scientistic prejudice about what reality consists in. This prejudice arises from the temptation to see reality, nature, exhausted by what natural science tells us there is. Yielding to that temptation gives rise to the scientistic outlook, an outlook that identifies nature with the realm of scientific law, and so one that makes meaning and responsiveness to reason "unnatural."

Eliminating value from nature leaves us with a "disenchanted" view of nature, one bereft of value and meaning. The problem then becomes one of how we resurrect value and meaning with only the material supplied by the scientistic conception of what there is, "first nature." McDowell argues for a partial re-enchantment, one depending on the idea that "second nature" has just as much right to be included in what is deemed to be natural as does law-governed first nature. Second nature arises as the result of our development and maturation as humans, such maturation being dependent upon our biological heritage, a social environment, and relevant training. The acquisition of a language is paradigmatically something acquired in this way; that humans are linguistic creatures is thus part of their second nature, as are the conceptual and rational capacities that come along with language.[8]

The invocation of second nature in this way sets McDowell's position apart from what he calls "bald naturalists," those who recognize as natural only that properly belonging to the domain of science. It leaves McDowell free to see our responsiveness to reasons as being unproblematic, not requiring any special philosophical explanation, an explanation that would be obligatory if we confined our understanding of humans to the material supplied by science. This view is also distinct from what McDowell calls "rampant Platonism," one that severs the connection between being human and the "rules" of rationality and moral precepts. For the rampant Platonist the relevant rules are not grounded in anything recognizably human, and so it is mysterious that they have the normative force that they are required to have. The "oscillation" between rampant Platonism and bald naturalism can be stilled by recognizing the character of second nature, one allowing that rationality is both *sui generis* (so not reducible to concepts figuring only in scientific explanations) and natural (so not mysterious or "spooky").

What we have provided in the above is only a brief sketch of a rich and nuanced philosophical view. It is a view that has developed as much in reaction to contemporary fashion in philosophy (especially to "bald" naturalism) as it has in being influenced by, amongst others, Aristotle, Kant, Wittgenstein, and Sellars. It is thus a view that is particularly unlikely to be without its critics. In this volume we have provided the opportunity for some of those who disagree with aspects of McDowell's philosophical outlook to air their disagreements, and for McDowell to respond to their criticisms. The papers range over most of the topics touched on above, and so provide an in-depth examination of the thought of one of the most original thinkers in philosophy today. We are deeply grateful to all the contributors for their hard work, and to John McDowell for his substantial and detailed responses. We conclude with brief summaries of these papers, constructed with the aid of the contributors themselves.

In "On the Sense and Reference of a Proper Name" (McDowell 1998a: 171–98) McDowell made two main claims: that one should make room for semantic differences between coreferring proper names without supposing that definite descriptions had any role to play; and that, in consequence, one could not allow for intelligible names without bearers. Mark Sainsbury's aim is to endorse the first claim, but reject the second, thus requiring him to dispute McDowell's assumption that the second is a consequence of the first.

The first claim is made good by using homophonic axioms for names, and arguing that such axioms for coreferring names should be distinct. In McDowell's scheme, the axioms have the form exemplified by "'Hesperus' stands for Hesperus"; such axioms require the existence of a bearer of the name, so it seems as if the second claim has been established from the first. Sainsbury maintains that McDowell's axioms could as well have taken the form exemplified by "for all *x*,

'Hesperus' stands for x if and only if x = Hesperus," and that McDowell is in no position to object to this form, since it is classically equivalent to his preferred form. In general, it is claimed, such axioms have all the virtues which attach to the austerity and modesty of McDowell's account, but if quantified axioms are set within negative free logic, they do not entail that the names they address have a bearer. Hence the claim that there could not be intelligible empty names does not follow from McDowell's general position about names (he would require, in addition, a premise rejecting negative free logic). This, claims Sainsbury, is a happy upshot: adopting negative free logic provides all the attractive features of the position set out by McDowell, without the clearly unattractive seeming consequence that there are no intelligible names without bearers. He concludes by arguing that the worry that allowing for empty names would risk creating some sort of chasm between mind and world is baseless.

Richard Heck's paper investigates the significance of the claim that language-use is a rational activity, a claim on which McDowell has himself placed a good deal of weight. Heck argues, first, that the phenomenon of conversational implicature is to be explained in terms of what he calls the "propositional" rationality of speech: the act of saying that p is intentional, and it is so under such propositional descriptions. He then argues that speech is also "verbally" rational: the act of uttering the sentence S is intentional, and it is so under such verbal descriptions. The relation between the propositional and verbal acts is an important question Heck does not try to resolve, but he suggests that neither is really more fundamental than the other.

Heck then uses these conclusions to argue for what he calls the Cognitive Conception of Understanding: an occurrent state of understanding an utterance consists in knowing what the utterance means. Heck argues for that view by arguing against two alternatives, the "Use View" and the "Direct View." The Use View is that understanding a language is knowing how to use it. Heck argues that it is unable to acknowledge the propositional rationality of speech without collapsing into the Cognitive Conception. Heck claims to find the Direct View in McDowell. It holds, very roughly, that understanding is not, in any epistemically relevant way, mediated by perception of words. But then, Heck argues, the Direct View cannot acknowledge the verbal rationality of speech. Heck's paper closes with a preliminary discussion of the question whether the Cognitive Conception does not make thought prior to language in some objectionable way.

The chapter by Akeel Bilgrami attempts to integrate four different themes on which McDowell has written: agency, value, intentionality, and self-knowledge. It is argued that if both agency and intentionality are linked deeply to value, if they are themselves evaluative and normative notions, then we can, without any concessions to Cartesian doctrine, provide a philosophical ground for our intuition that self-knowledge is unlike any other knowledge. We can do so because self-knowledge has the properties of being transparent and authoritative, which other forms of knowledge lack. Bilgrami argues that such an integration has the effect of reducing four longstanding and seemingly miscellaneous problems to one integrated one. The place of freedom in a causally deterministic universe, the place of intentionality in the causal and physical states of the central nervous system, and the asymmetry between first-person and third-person perceptual and inferential knowledge are all at bottom shown to derive from the irreducibility of value to natural facts as viewed by natural science.

Cynthia Macdonald's chapter continues with an examination of the presumed special nature of self-knowledge. She invites the reader to assume that externalism in the philosophy of mind is true (a view that McDowell himself holds), and accordingly, that the ("fully Cartesian") view that the inner realm consists of contentful states (such as the thought that this tiger has stripes) whose contents would remain the same even if there existed nothing beyond the minds of persons, is false. Macdonald then asks: what are the consequences for the (common-sense) belief that subjects are at least sometimes authoritative with regard to knowing what thoughts they are thinking? McDowell's very influential view is that there are *no* consequences for that belief.

Macdonald argues that this is wrong. Even if one rejects the "fully Cartesian" conception of the inner domain, still externalism poses a threat to the view that subjects are at least sometimes authoritative with regard to the contents of their own thoughts. There is thus, she argues, a need for a substantial epistemology of authoritative self-knowledge. Her argument proceeds by considering three types of case that might seem to pose problems for McDowell's view. Macdonald maintains that the first two pose no real threat to the view, but the third does threaten it. She concludes by sketching an account of authoritative self-knowledge that could ground the epistemic asymmetry between self-knowledge and knowledge of others, an account that is consistent with externalism.

It is generally granted on all sides of the philosophical dispute about personal identity that the issue has enormous ethical significance. It is also generally assumed that the issue can and should be settled on strictly metaphysical grounds. In "Personal Identity: Ethical not Metaphysical" Carol Rovane argues that this assumption is mistaken. She offers McDowell's contribution to the dispute as a case-study that illustrates the point.

McDowell marshals considerations concerning the nature of first-person reference – its directness and identification-freedom – in order to argue against the standard neo-Lockean view of personal identity. In response, Rovane shows how a neo-Lockean might countenance forms of personal persistence in which first-person reference is not always direct and identification-free. The strategy of this response is facilitated by moving away from Locke's original emphasis on the nature of personal consciousness and focusing instead on the nature of personal agency. An agent is something with a rational point of view from which to deliberate and act. A group of human beings, Rovane suggests, could together have one rational point of view despite their phenomenological distinctness, and a single human being could host multiple rational points of view within the same consciousness.

If we were to equate personhood with personal agency, then we would be forced, on metaphysical grounds alone, to accept the possibility of such group and multiple persons. But no purely metaphysical consideration forces us to make the equation from which this follows. We might equate personhood with consciousness as Locke did. Or we might equate personhood with a form of animal life as McDowell does. Rovane argues that the only way to decide these matters is by bringing in ethical considerations. Although this is not explicitly acknowledged in most discussions of personal identity, it is implicitly confirmed by much that goes on in them. She closes by exposing the important role that ethical considerations in fact play in the arguments offered by both McDowell and the neo-Lockeans he aims to criticize.

Jonathan Dancy draws analogies between McDowell's views of the relation between experience and belief and views about the relation between belief and action – views which McDowell does not espouse but which one would expect him to accept. He then contends that when one acts in the light of one's beliefs, one's reason is not that one takes things to be this way rather than that, but the way one takes them to be. Applying this to the relation between experience and belief, Dancy argues that though McDowell says that one's reason for belief is an appearance, what he means by this must be that one's reason is that things appear this way rather than that, whereas the truth is that one's reason is the way things appear, not that they so appear. Dancy's main conclusion is that a causal account of reasons for belief is impossible, since things need not be the way they appear to be.

In "External Reasons" Philip Pettit and Michael Smith focus on the debate between John McDowell and Bernard Williams over the possibility of external reasons. Since McDowell claims to offer an alternative to Williams's suggestion that all reasons are internal reasons, Pettit and Smith begin by outlining three claims to which, as they see things, Williams is committed. The first is that an agent A has a reason to act in a certain way in certain circumstances only if an idealized version of herself, Å, would desire that she act in that way in those circumstances, where the idealization in question is fixed by norms of reason: A has a reason to act in a certain way in certain circumstances only if it would be good-from-the-standpoint-of-reason for her to do so. The second claim is that reasons meet a further condition as well. For among those things it would be good-from-the-standpoint-of-reason for A to do are those that A herself, un-idealized, has the capacity to recognize and to which she has the capacity to respond. This more circumscribed class is the class of reasons, according to Williams, because reasons ground the possibility of blame, and blame presupposes the presence of such capacities in those who are candidates for blame. Finally, Williams is committed to the third claim that Hume offers us the best account of what the norms of reason are. What it would be good-from-the-standpoint-of-reason for A to do is what A would desire herself to do if she had and exercised certain Hume-friendly capacities of reason: knew things, was instrumentally rational, and the like. Those who accept all three of Williams's claims hold all reasons to be internal reasons.

What McDowell takes issue with, as Pettit and Smith see things, is Williams's first claim. The category of what it would be good-from-the-standpoint-of-reason to do contrasts with categories that replace "reason" by some other term like "morality," or more specifically by "Humean morality" or "Aristotelian morality" or whatever. What it would be good for A to do in C from such a perspective is what Å desires A to do in C, where Å is well brought up in that perspective. According to Pettit and Smith, McDowell's suggestion is that an agent has an external reason to act in a certain way just in case, if she were well brought up in terms of an Aristotelian morality, she would desire herself to act in that way. But, they argue, if this is the right interpretation of McDowell's position, his account of external reasons would be vulnerable to an objection which Williams himself suggests. For, by the above criteria, it is unclear why we should agree that McDowell directs our attention to a class of external *reasons*, as opposed to considerations concerning what it would be good for an agent to do from the standpoint of Aristotelian morality. Since McDowellian external reasons have nothing to do with *reason* at all, they wonder by what right he calls them "reasons."

Terence Irwin examines McDowell's important earlier paper on the role of eudaimonia in Aristotle's ethics. In particular he discusses McDowell's interpretation of the claim he attributes to Aristotle that "activity in accordance with excellence is *eudaimonia*." McDowell seeks to understand the claim from the left-hand side, so that it explains the character of eudaimonia through an account of virtue. He claims, Irwin argues, that this understanding of Aristotle's position rests on a "derivative" use of prudential concepts; in the course of explaining this derivative use, McDowell introduces his views about reasons and "silencing." Irwin discusses this distinction between the "ordinary" and the "derivative" use of prudential concepts, and he expresses doubts about whether either use, as McDowell explains it, captures Aristotle's claims about virtue and happiness. In conclusion Irwin suggests an alternative understanding of Aristotle's account of prudential concepts.

In his chapter Simon Blackburn ruminates upon the central place that spatial metaphors have played in McDowell's philosophy of mind and of knowledge. These are metaphors concerning what is within the mind, or what it contains, contrasted with what is external to it. The metaphor suggests questions such as how the mind gets as far as facts, whether it "contains" the world or only proxies for the world, and so on, and it is in answer to such questions that McDowell offers his version of Direct Realism. Blackburn argues that these metaphors in fact distort McDowell's discussions, so that features to which McDowell is undoubtedly sensitive, such as the role of causation in observation, nevertheless do not get placed properly.

The metaphor, Blackburn maintains, affects the way in which McDowell thinks of justification, which is conceived primarily as an internal relationship among beliefs, abstracting from the evident way in which it is primarily people who are justified in believing things, and that they achieve this normative status by activities in the world. It also leads to McDowell's "disjunctivism," which, Blackburn argues, only seems to be intelligible, let alone true, if a spatialized conception of a mental state is directing the philosophy. Blackburn urges that what is best in McDowell's thought should provide a way of overcoming the spatial model, and thereby avoid some of the more controversial aspects of his work.

Graham Macdonald questions the distinction McDowell draws between first and second nature. That distinction was first drawn using a conception of "first" nature as that which is law-governed, and thus the proper object of study of natural science. Macdonald, though noting that McDowell broadens this conception to include all explanations provided by science, suggests that a broader, more relaxed idea of a scientific explanation might include second nature in its explanatory domain, and thus render rationality less *sui generis* than McDowell thinks it is. In particular, the suggestion is that there is much that is common to a teleo-semantic approach to our rational capacities and Wittgenstein's grounding of such capacities in training. The teleological approach borrows its explanatory model from evolutionary biology, which sees adapted traits as emerging from a history of natural selection, and so acquiring a function. Macdonald notes that for both Wittgenstein and McDowell a certain history (one of being initiated into a social practice) is essential for a person to be a linguistic animal – to possess a language and the rational capacities that accompany language. Macdonald argues that something like this history is what is required for organisms to possess functional traits. Given a suitably elastic specification of what is required for a trait to be functionally explained, the suggestion is that our rational capacities will be so explained. Whether that explanation is "scientific" or not need not be of any significance, as an answer to that question will be merely stipulative. A consequence of this is that the "science/non-science" distinction, essential to both "bald" naturalists and to McDowell's use of the notion of second nature, cannot do the work required of it.

Cynthia Macdonald and Graham Macdonald

Notes

1   "Understanding linguistic behavior, and hence understanding languages, involves no more than a special case of what understanding behavior, in general, involves" (McDowell 1998a: 6).
2   The debates with Dummett started with "Truth-Conditions, Bivalence, and Verificationism" and continued in "On 'The Reality of the Past'," "Anti-Realism and the Epistemology of Understanding," "In Defence of Modesty," "Mathematical Platonism and Dummettian Anti-realism," and "Another Plea For Modesty," all reprinted in McDowell (1998a).
3   See "On the Sense and Reference of a Proper Name," "*De Re* Senses," and "Singular Thought and the Extent of Inner Space," all reprinted in McDowell (1998a). More recently McDowell has written on Evans's understanding of Frege in "Evans's Frege" (McDowell 2005). McDowell clarifies his position in his "Response to Mark Sainsbury," this vol., ch. 1.

4 McDowell borrows the phrase "the space of reasons" from Wilfrid Sellars. For his critical commentary on Sellars's employment of the locution, see McDowell's Woodbridge lectures, (McDowell 1998c).

5 "Of facts to the effect that things seem thus and so to one, we might say, some are cases of being thus and so within the reaches of one's subjective access to the external world, whereas others are mere appearances" (McDowell 1998a: 241).

6 "The deliverances of a reliable sensitivity are cases of knowledge. The sensitivity is, we might say, a sort of perceptual capacity" (McDowell 1998b: 51).

7 McDowell takes as his model Aristotle, for whom:

> The ethical is a domain of rational requirements, which are there in any case, whether or not we are responsive to them. We are alerted to these demands by acquiring appropriate conceptual capacities. When a decent upbringing initiates us into the relevant way of thinking, our eyes are opened to the very existence of this tract of the space of reasons. . . . We can so much as understand, let alone seek to justify, the thought that reason makes these demands on us only at a standpoint within a system of concepts and conceptions that enables us to think about such demands, that is, only at a standpoint from which demands of this kind seem to be in view. (McDowell 1994: 82)

8 "Acquiring command of a language, which is coming to inhabit the logical space of reasons, is acquiring a second nature. Given that the space of reasons is special in the way Sellars urges, ideas of phenomena that are manifestations of a second nature acquired in acquiring command of a language do not, as such, fit in the logical space of natural-scientific understanding. But there is no reason why that should rule out seeing those phenomena as manifestations of nature, since the nature in question can be a second nature. Actualizations of conceptual capacities, which as such belong in the logical space of reasons, can be natural in a different sense from the one that figures in the admittedly well-drawn contrast with the logical space of reasons." (McDowell 1999: 7)

References

McDowell, J. 1994. *Mind and World*, Cambridge, Mass.: Harvard University Press.

McDowell, J. 1998a. *Meaning, Knowledge, and Reality*, Cambridge, Mass.: Harvard University Press.

McDowell, J. 1998b. *Mind, Value, and Reality*, Cambridge, Mass.: Harvard University Press.

McDowell, J. 1998c. "Having the World in View: Sellars, Kant, and Intentionality," in *The Journal of Philosophy* xcv: 431–91 (the Woodbridge Lectures).

McDowell, J. 1999. "Experiencing the World" and "Responses," in M. Willaschek (ed.), *John McDowell: Reason and Nature*, Munster: Lit Verlag, 1999, 3–17, 93–117.

McDowell, J. 2005. "Evans's Frege," in José Luis Bermudez (ed.), *Thought, Reference, and Experience: Themes from the Philosophy of Gareth Evans*, Oxford: Clarendon Press.

1

Austerity and Openness

R. M. Sainsbury

In "On the Sense and Reference of a Proper Name" (1977), John McDowell makes two striking claims. One is that, without resorting to a description theory of names, we can do justice to Frege's view that names with the same referent may differ in sense. The other is that in order to describe ordinary thought and talk, we need to make use of the notion of *de re* sense, a kind of sense which has its referent essentially and which is unavailable in the absence of a referent. In the early article, the two views are presented as if intimately related. An argument relating the first to the second could be constructed as follows:

> The non-reductive or "austere" account of the sense of names, which allows names with the same referent to differ in sense, describes their semantic contribution on the lines:
>
> > "Hesperus" stands for Hesperus.
>
> Such a description is true only if there is such a thing as Hesperus. An austere account of names associates with every name a sense of a kind which ensures that the name has a referent.

In section I, I argue that the ideal of austerity can be attained in a way which allows for intelligible empty names. In section II, I suggest that there is no tension between allowing intelligible empty names and holding, as McDowell does in *Mind and World* and elsewhere, that the mind is open directly to the world. In section III, I make a similar suggestion concerning the trickier case of demonstratives. The overall conclusion is that McDowell could abandon his belief in *de re* senses (as he understands these) without damage to other aspects of his philosophy.

I

McDowell's first main point is that one can attribute distinct senses to coreferring names without adopting a description theory of names, and he argues for this within the methodology of David-sonian truth-theories. Not all true truth-theories are usable for interpretation. One so usable, an "interpretive" truth-theory, will be sufficient for interpretation in the following sense: if an utterance, u, is an utterance of a sentence, s, and the s-related canonical T-theorem of the truth-theory says that s is true iff p, then the utterer of u thereby said that p.[1] If we can assume that it is one thing to say that Phosphorus is visible and another to say that Hesperus is, we have a reason to prefer a T-theorem:

(1)   "Hesperus is visible" is true iff Hesperus is visible,

to the following:

(2)   "Hesperus is visible" is true iff Phosphorus is visible.

Given the way in which T-theorems are derived from truth-theoretic axioms, this gives us a reason to give axiomatic status to the first rather than the second of the following truths:

(3)   "Hesperus" stands for Hesperus.
(4)   "Hesperus" stands for Phosphorus.

In the same way, we reach the analogous conclusion for axioms for "Phosphorus." This shows that, truth-theoretically, we have a reason to treat coreferring names with different axioms. To the extent that a truth-theory can be regarded as a theory of sense, this shows that we treat coreferring names as having different senses without associating them with any definite descriptions.

As this argument shows, truth-theories are overtly sympathetic to "homophony": the semantic contribution of an object language expression may be properly described by reusing it in the metalanguage. This sympathy should be shared by all semantic theories designed to supply interpretations. It is at least possible that there should be a language containing no redundancy: no pair of distinct expressions count as synonymous. This would mean that it would be impossible to use that language to state or fix the meanings of the expressions it contains except by reusing those very expressions in the homophonic way. If such a language contains "Hesperus," there would be no way of giving a correct semantic description of it within that language, a description fit to lead to interpretation, except by using the expression itself, in some such sentence as (3).

McDowell wards off some misunderstandings concerning what such homophonic sentences achieve, whether they relate to a single word or to a whole sentence. Despite their "austerity," the facts they state are not trivial, if that means known to all reflective persons. A monolingual Spaniard, however reflective, is in no position to know that "Snow is white" is true iff snow is white. However, the homophonic mode of expression of these facts makes the sentences unsuitable for use in a school teaching English. One who does not already understand the sentence "snow is white" will evidently not come to understand it by confronting an authoritative utterance of the sentence " 'Snow is white' is true iff snow is white," though confronting the fact thereby stated, if that could be arranged, would be helpful. The general conclusion ought to be, as Davidson has said, that we shift our attention away from trying to illuminate the meanings of words, trying instead to cast light on the compositional properties of language and on those features of speakers' behavior that constitute evidence for their speaking one language rather than another.

Thus far we have a justification for homophony, or at least for austerity: a semantic theory will not attempt to analyze or decompose the meanings of the object language's words, but will reuse them, or close equivalents, in the metalanguage.[2] In the early article, having recommended the austere homophonic approach to proper names, McDowell turns to consider what he describes as "a complication" besetting such an account: bearerless names (McDowell 1977: 172). Since (3) entails that Hesperus exists, an axiom of this form cannot be given for a name which lacks a bearer. On the other hand (3) is classically equivalent to the following:

(5)   For all x ("Hesperus" stands for x iff x = Hesperus).

The equivalence ensures that a truth-theory with (5) instead of (3) will have just the same T-sentences, and thus be indistinguishable from the point of view of the project of interpretation. It avoids descriptivism, yet the previous arguments apply in just the same way to show (5) to be superior to the equally true:

(6)   For all x ("Hesperus" stands for x iff x = Phosphorus).[3]

Whether or not (5) entails the existence of Hesperus is contentious. Within classical logic, it does; within negative free logic it does not. If there really were a desire to incorporate bearerless names into a semantics of this kind, it could readily be satisfied by making (5) rather than (3) the model for the semantics of names, and adopting negative free logic rather than classical logic. One would then have all the advantages of the first of the two main claims McDowell argues for, without the implausibility of the second; austerity without a ban on sense without a referent.

The free logical model can be completed in more than one way, but according to the completion I envisage every atom with a referring expression which fails to refer is false. This can be effected by a composition axiom along the following lines (for legibility I consider only the monadic case):

(7)   An atomic sentence "Fa" is true iff there is an x such that x is the actual referent of "a" and x satisfies "F"; it is false otherwise.

As with all free logics, there are restrictions on the rule of existential generalization (see e.g. Simons 2001).

Free logical truth-theory makes no concessions to descriptivism about proper names, even though it allows the possibility of a content without a referent. Accordingly, it pulls apart two ideas which risk being merged. In the first sentence of "*De re* senses,"[4] McDowell sets up as a target a supposedly Fregean view according to which there is a kind of:

> content that determines the object by specification, or at least in such a way that the content is available to be thought or expressed whether the object exists or not. (McDowell 1984: 283)

The first disjunct expresses the familiar idea of descriptivism; the second disjunct expresses a view which might loosely be labelled object-independent content. It is easy to see that the free logical approach is not descriptivist, and so is not the target of the first disjunct. The second disjunct is ambiguous between the claim that there are contents which have their objects essentially, a claim accepted by the negative free logician, and the claim that there are no singular contents lacking objects, a claim the negative free logician rejects. I will work through these points in turn.

There are three reasons for which McDowell is committed to the view that free logical axioms along the lines of (5) (for all x ("Hesperus" stands for x iff x = Hesperus)) do not determine an object "by specification" in the undesirable sense. First, such axioms are classically equivalent to McDowell's preferred kind of axiom. Although classical equivalence is obviously in general much weaker than sameness of content, the equivalence makes it hard to see how anyone could suppose that (5) determines an object "by specification" whereas (3) ("Hesperus" stands for Hesperus) does not. Setting (5) in a free logic may be held to affect its content; but it would be implausible to suppose that this would go so far as to transform something which is not a specification (in the relevant sense) to something which is. Secondly, in the earlier paper, McDowell is explicit that the unwanted view is one offering "a blueprint or specification which, if formulated, would be expressed in purely general terms" (1977: 173), thus excluding the kind of "specification" attributable to the free logical model, which is certainly not purely general. Thirdly, the reasons McDowell gives for rejecting specification-determined contents do not extend to a rejection of contents determined by such conditions as *being Hesperus*. For example, he says, entirely convincingly, that we "have the ability to tell that a seen object is the bearer of a familiar name without having the slightest idea *how* one recognizes it" (1977: 165), from which he concludes that one cannot reasonably demand of a semantic theory that it describe the recognitional mechanisms. The free logical model, in making use of such conditions as *being Hesperus*, evidently makes no attempt to provide revealing descriptions of recognitional mechanisms. From a subject's knowledge of the axiom for "Hesperus," whether in free logical or classical form, one can extract no more than that the subject knows what it is to be Hesperus.

Does the free logical approach become a target for McDowell through falling under the second disjunct, offering a "content . . . available to be thought or expressed whether the object exists or not"? Some versions of free logical semantics insist on the rigidity of names, and some of these would endorse this claim by Kaplan:

> a proper name either denotes the same individual with respect to every possible circumstance or else denotes nothing with respect to any possible circumstance. (Kaplan 1973: 510)

The content of a non-empty name is thus not available "whether the object exists or not"; likewise the content of an empty name is not something which allows for the possibility of it being non-empty. On the most natural interpretation of the words in which McDowell introduces object-independent content, the present version of negative free logical semantics does not fall within the target area. The version may consistently hold that there is a semantic category of names, all treated by axioms of the same general kind, which includes both empty and non-empty ones, so that a name's right to belong to the category, and so to be usable in the expression of thoughts, is independent of whether or not some object is its referent.

In the remainder of this section, I consider the role of classical logic in leading McDowell from austerity to the ban on bearerless names. To think of a logic as "correct," in connection with natural language, is to think something on these lines: for every valid first-order argument (validity here being judged by the formal first-order semantics), any natural language argument which it formalizes is valid (validity here being judged intuitively and by informal reasoning). (The converse is not required: that would amount to something like the completeness of first-order logic relative to natural language validity.) It might seem that if we apply this test, we very quickly get a result favorable to the free logical approach. Consider the first-order validity "$a = a$". A natural language instance is, apparently: "Vulcan is identical to Vulcan." Neither McDowell nor the negative free logician regards this as true,[5] so it might seem that we have an agreed counterexample to the test for the correctness of first-order logic. If this were the right moral, our work would be over: McDowell's implicit subscription to classical first-order logic would be shown to be unjustified by his own lights. But the issue is not so straightforward.

The test required that "$a = a$" should count as a formalization of "Vulcan is identical to Vulcan," and this McDowell could dispute, as would anyone who believes in the correctness of first-order logic as a description of natural language. An English expression is fit to be formalized by an "arbitrary name" or individual constant (like "a") in a classical first-order formalization only if it is genuinely a name, and for McDowell that will involve it having a bearer. Since "Vulcan" does not have a bearer, it is not a name, and so cannot be formalized by "a". In attempting to apply the test for the correctness of first-order logic, a test designed to help us forward in our account of the semantics of names, we find ourselves first having to take a stand on the very semantic issue in question. The free logician is happy to see the case as a genuine counterexample because he allows empty names; the classical first-order logician will not see it as a counterexample because he does not. Deadlock.

Can we resolve the deadlock by appeal to the notion of validity in virtue of form? Who can deny that in some sense "Vulcan is identical to Vulcan" is like in form with "$a = a$"? If so, the fact that the first is not a truth is grounds for holding that a correct logic should not count the second as valid, which would immediately count in favor of negative free logic.[6] Likeness of form, it may be said, is to be determined "structurally" and not "semantically," so it cannot be denied on merely semantic grounds; there is no room for McDowell to bring a names-specific view to bear on the relevant question about validity. The problem with this suggestion is that it is not true that the concept of sameness of form is wholly non-semantic. "Walks is walks" is not like in form with "$a = a$" for semantic reasons, not syntactic ones; Paderewski cases lead, by a different route, to a similar conclusion. The syntactic fillings have to have the appropriate semantics; whether this is so for "Vulcan" is precisely what separates the classical and the free logician.

Other attempts to find neutral ground for a decision between classical and negative free logic seem to me no less indecisive. There are two ways in which one might wish to disagree with Leverrier's utterance:

(8)   Vulcan is at least 1,000 miles in diameter.

One might side with Leverrier in thinking that there is such a heavenly body as Vulcan, but dispute his calculations of its diameter; or one might think there is no such heavenly body. Technically, the negative free logician could (but need not) register these options as differently scoped negations:

(9)   Vulcan is not at least 1,000 miles in diameter.
(10)   It is not the case that Vulcan is at least 1,000 miles in diameter.

One could not place any reliance on one's precise opinion being correctly identified by the use of one rather than the other of these sentences. The scope distinctions made available by the logic do not surface reliably in natural language, and some kind of ad hoc explanation is required of why this is. A free logician will take comfort from the fact that the same goes for some scope distinctions endorsed by classical logic. One should not count on a choice between the following to make clear one's position on whether or not there is a unique King of France:

(11)   The King of France is not bald.
(12)   It is not the case that the King of France is bald.

Because the scope distinctions are not reliably detected by ordinary speakers, it is also hard to get any direct evidence relating to the issue which should make for the prime difference between negative free logic and classical logic: the former's restrictions on quantification. For example, the negative free logician who holds that (10) is true will also hold that a proper formalization will not provide a premise which would sustain existential quantification with respect to the position occupied by "Vulcan," just as all agree to the analogous point when the position is that occupied by "the King of France" in (12). But just as one cannot count on English speakers to appreciate the point for (12), perhaps through lack of practice in distinguishing it from (11), so one cannot count on English speakers to appreciate the point for (10), perhaps through lack of practice in distinguishing it from (9).

I think it unlikely that there is a way to choose between classical and negative free logic which does not involve a prior decision about the semantics of names. McDowell's move from austerity to the rejection of the intelligibility of empty names accordingly cries out for supporting argument, for austerity is neutral between classical and free logical approaches. In this context, to assume the correctness of classical logic is in effect to assume that there are no intelligible empty names, whereas we were looking for an argument for this view. If one is going to assume classical logic, and assume that it is applicable to natural language in a straightforward way, the validity of every instance of $\exists x \; x = a$ already settles that natural language contains names whose semantics requires them to have a bearer, and that it contains no other expressions worthy to be called names.

The decision between the logics must be made on the familiar, but admittedly not decisive, grounds of the unnaturalness of not recognizing intelligible empty names, ones introduced through error, deception, or pretense. Because it is so natural to take it that users of such names really do think thoughts thereby, a case needs to be made for the contrary view; otherwise the free logical approach would win by default. A case could be made if intelligible empty names had to be descriptive, but we have seen that they do not. A case could be made if the only austere axioms for names say such things as that "Hesperus" stands for Hesperus, but we have seen that this is not so.

Might thinking of semantic theory as the specification of word-world relations justify the classical logical approach? McDowell's axioms link names to objects, and so are genuinely semantic by the test just mentioned. By contrast, a free logical axiom like:

(13)   for all x ("Vulcan" refers to x iff x = Vulcan)

does not link "Vulcan" to any object, and so, by the envisaged test, does not count as a contribution to semantic theory.[7]

The proposal simply smuggles in its preferred semantics for names, thinly disguised as a general principle of semantics. The basic thought underlying austerity is that one can do no better, in semantic theorizing, than describe an expression's semantics by reusing that expression, with whatever semantic properties it in fact has. If the expression is a name with a bearer, then in using that name to give its semantics one uses it to link it with its bearer; but if a name does not have a bearer, this will not occur. Only a prior commitment to the impossibility of empty names allows one to draw the conclusion that nothing appropriate to semantics will occur.

II

In a number of writings, McDowell has described a philosophical position whose main feature might be expressed by a slogan: the mind is open to the world. Encounters with objects are "glimpses of objective reality" (1994b: 193), rather than an engagement with mediating "proxies" (1984: 292–3); when things go well, what we believe is nothing other than what is the case, and is part of the world (1994a: 9, 27). We should resist a certain dualism of "scheme and world"; and we should recognize that "experience must stand in rational relations to judgment if we are to be able to understand the very possibility of empirical content" (1994a: 125). Which of these major themes, if any, would be compromised by accepting that there are intelligible referring expressions which do not have a bearer and whose content is not given by description? I believe that the answer is: none. I have already shown that the free logical model contains no concession to the kind of descriptivism which McDowell rejects on the grounds that it prevents the mind's full openness. The model also gives no encouragement to two-component views: it is not that it posits an internal content which, in favorable cases, is supplemented by something external. A name with a bearer has a content which it could not have had were there to have been no bearer. A name without a bearer has a content which it could not have had were there to have been a bearer. I suspect that getting these modal facts right is the main task confronting one wishing to separate McDowell's semantic austerity from his rejection of sense without reference for names.

The free logical model is committed to the truth of some interpretation of this claim on behalf of "object-independent" content:

(14)   A content expressible by a sentence containing a proper name may or may not involve an object, the bearer of the name.

The interpretation to which the free logical approach is committed gives wide scope to the modality which is expressed, perhaps obscurely, by the "may or may not," and might be reformulated thus:

It is possible that there is a content expressed by a sentence containing a proper name which has an object as referent; and it is possible that there is a content expressed by a sentence containing a proper name which has no object as referent.

On the free logical approach, both these possibilities are actualities for English, which is seen as containing both empty and non-empty names. The approach is not committed to (14) so interpreted as to render contingent the connection between a non-empty name (given its actual meaning) and its referent, or to render contingent the emptiness of an empty name (given its actual meaning). The free logical semanticist can accept, and embody in her theory, Kripke's insights about rigidity: it is essential to a sentence containing a name with a bearer, holding its meaning constant, that it have a bearer, indeed that it have that very bearer; and essential to a sentence containing a name with no bearer, holding its meaning constant, that it have no bearer. Although not entailed by the free logical model as such, these facts of rigidity are ones that any approach needs to make room for; the free logical model has no problem in doing so.

For names with bearers, the actual bearer is what matters to the evaluation, with respect to any world, of the utterance of any sentence in which the name occurs. For names which in fact lack bearers, this emptiness is to be held constant as an utterance of a sentence containing the name is evaluated with respect to non-actual worlds. Rigidity is essentially the same phenomenon for both empty and non-empty names: reference with respect to an arbitrary world is just actual reference, if any.

This way of putting it is designed to be neutral between two ways of making the notion of rigidity precise. Kripke's original words were:

Let's call something a *rigid designator* if in every possible world it designates the same object. (Kripke 1972/1980: 48)

As he pointed out, this account (as most naturally understood) requires that the names of contingent things designate, with respect to some worlds, things which do not exist in those worlds:

> a rigid designator [has] the same reference in all possible worlds. I . . . don't mean to imply that the thing designated exists in all possible worlds, just that the name refers rigidly to that thing. (Kripke 1972/1980: 77–8)

One might argue for this position by analogy with times. "Aristotle" now refers to Aristotle, even though Aristotle does not now exist. One option for a negative free logical approach is simply to adopt this view. However, it is not entirely unproblematic, and there is an alternative, one which exploits a distinctive feature of free logic. One problem with Kripke's position is that it introduces a non-uniformity in truth with respect to a world of sentences of the form "N does not exist." If N is a name which actually has a referent, and the world is one with respect to which that referent does not exist, the truth of the sentence with respect to that world is a matter of the referent of the name with respect to the world having the property of non-existence with respect to that world. If N is a name which actually lacks a referent, we do not, by hypothesis, want to explain the truth of the sentence in terms which presuppose that N actually does have a referent. I do not say that this is a refutation of the standard Kripkean approach to rigidity,[8] but it motivates looking at the following alternative: for non-empty names, their rigidity consists in their having their actual referent as their referent with respect to any world in which that referent exists, and no referent with respect to any other world. If we consider a world, w, in which Kripke does not exist, the truth of "Kripke does not exist" with respect to w can be explained as follows: "Kripke" does not have a referent with respect to w, so (by (7) above) "Kripke exists" is false with respect to w, so its negation "Kripke does not exist" is true with respect to w. The account is uniform with that of the actual truth of a sentence like "Vulcan does not exist." I suggest that negative free logical semantics should adopt this account of rigidity:

(15)   for all x,y,w ((x refers to y with respect to the actual world and y exists at w) iff x refers to y with respect to w).

A referent with respect to a world always exists in that world. A name which actually refers to a given object has that object as its referent with respect to every world in which that object exists, and has nothing as its referent with respect to worlds in which that object does not exist. A name which is actually empty is empty with respect to every world.

Words intelligibly used on a specific occasion count as expressing "thoughts." In particular, consider the thought expressed by an utterance of "Hesperus is visible." A theorist guided by (15) will not agree that "Whether the object exists or not would . . . be incidental to the availability of the thought" (McDowell 1984: 173). Had Hesperus not existed, what was in fact expressed by those words would not have been expressed by them. Something was expressed which relates to Hesperus and is true at some worlds, times, and places. Had Hesperus not existed, this same thing could not have been expressed.

An objector may protest that a free logical axiom for "Hesperus," unlike a classical axiom, would remain true even if Hesperus had not existed, and hence that a free logical semantics is committed to only that kind of content which is independent of, and indifferent to, the existence of specific objects. In response, we must distinguish between what is possible in some unrestricted sense, which includes the possibility that "Hesperus" should have been used in a language resembling English and have been empty; and a more restricted possibility in which we hold the actual meaning of "Hesperus" constant. The first kind of possibility is not what McDowell is (or should be) worried by: of course there might have been all sorts of languages with some resemblances to and some differences from English. The issue that matters is whether the restricted possibility obtains, a possibility relating to English as actually spoken, and if so whether it leads to a lack of openness. As I see semantic axioms, they are necessary truths, implicitly or explicitly relativized to some actual language. Hence "for all x, 'Hesperus' refers to x iff $x =$ Hesperus" is true even with respect to a world in which Hesperus does not exist. The world-relativized claim is that "Hesperus," as we use it in English, refers to something with respect to w, iff that thing is Hesperus and exists in w, so that if Hesperus does not exist in w, "Hesperus" refers to nothing with respect to w. One can accept this while denying that it reveals a kind of content which is "indifferent to the existence of specific objects," in the way which worried McDowell. The worrying indifference would obtain if the actual world might have contained no Hesperus, yet "Hesperus" have meant just what it actually means. This potentially worrying possibility is not one to which the present semantics is committed. The innocent possibility, which might be mistaken for the worrying one, is simply that there is a possible world lacking the object that our word "Hesperus" actually refers to, and that "Hesperus" has no referent with respect to such a world. If the actual world had been Hesperus-free, then "Hesperus" would not have meant what it actually means; but a specification of the meaning or semantic role of "Hesperus" can properly entail that the word as actually used has no referent with respect to a Hesperus-free possible but non-actual world.

For non-empty names in natural language, arguments for rigidity are familiar from the work of Kripke, Evans, and McDowell himself. It seems to me that the considerations generalize to empty names: there is no world with respect to which "Vulcan is at least 1,000 miles in diameter" is true, even if there is a world with a planet of that diameter between Mercury and the Sun.[9] Moreover, a free logical semantics can, as McDowell would welcome, allow for the possibility of "illusions of content," cases in which people mistakenly suppose that they are using a contentful or intelligible expression. For example, as used in a logic exercise, "John is happy" may have no complete content (there is no possible answer to the question who John is supposed to be), but a student might fail to appreciate this, and delude himself into supposing that there was a genuine content and even that he had grasped it.

III

In discussing names, it is legitimate to bracket the impact of context, and to pretend that for each name, syntactically individuated, there is a single semantic story to be told. We thus overlook the fact that context may determine which Aristotle we are talking about when we use "Aristotle." A similar idealization would not be helpful in an account of demonstratives. In this connection we find a particularly detailed argument by McDowell against alternative views. He urges his preferred conception, according to which a use of a demonstrative which does not have a referent results not in a thought which is false or lacking truth-value, but in no thought at all: there is simply "an absence." Let us consider how these cases might be treated within a free logical model.

The most straightforward idea is that an atomic utterance containing a demonstrative which fails to have a referent would count as false. We adapt the free logical theory to make it speak of utterances rather than sentences. The compositional axiom (7) could be modified to this:

(16)   An utterance of an atomic sentence "Fa" is true iff there is an x such that x is the actual referent of "a" as used on that occasion and x satisfies "F"; it is false otherwise.

Whatever the theory may say about how the referent of a demonstrative on an occasion is determined, and however exactly it deals with the appropriate understanding of austerity for T-sentences relating to utterances containing demonstratives, it seems that anything like (16) will be inconsistent with McDowell's position.

Though the version of free logical semantics I am putting forward goes down this route, it is not the only possible one. In context-free truth-theories, we speak rather casually of "sentences of the (object) language." This does not commit the theorist to treating anything isomorphic to a sentence of the language as also a sentence. If an ant-trail happens to resemble the shape of "All men are mortal," a theorist should not regard his theory as having assigned the trail a truth-condition. The analogous point applied to utterances is that the theorist need not regard as an utterance everything which sounds the same as an utterance: a sound similar to an utterance of "That is a planet," but generated by some odd static in a loudspeaker system, need not be assigned a truth-condition by the theory. The conditions for something genuinely to count as an utterance are presumably typically given in terms of the utterer's intentions. One might insist that for a proper use of a demonstrative there must be an object to which these intentions are suitably related, and so prevent empty uses counting as utterances. Thus even a theory which relies essentially on free logic in its treatment of names might arrive at a position on demonstratives congenial to McDowell. But rather than pursue this version of a free logical treatment of demonstratives, I will revert to the more natural one, according to which uses of atomic sentences containing empty demonstratives come out false.

Consider an utterance of "That is a planet" which, thanks to the use to which "that" is put, involves a reference to Hesperus. There is some temptation to say that what is expressed might have been available had Hesperus never existed. This is because we fasten on to the character (in Kaplan's sense) of the sentence uttered, and rightly see this as available for expression in other contexts, independently of whether that character determines for these other contexts a content, in particular, a referent for the demonstrative. McDowell urges (1984: 288) that we must also be alive to a different way of reckoning. Demonstratives are associated with a *sort* of *de re* sense, something which, in favorable contexts, will determine a *de re* sense, but not in unfavorable contexts:

> Given a context, a sort of *de re* sense may determine a *de re* sense (if one cares to put it like that), or else it . . . may determine nothing. (1984: 288)

If the sort of *de re* sense determines nothing, then:

> there can only be a gap – an absence – at, so to speak, the relevant place in the mind – the place where, given that the sort of *de re* sense in question appears to be instantiated, there appears to be a specific *de re* sense. (1984: 288)

This contrasts with a character which, in some context, fails to determine a content, for the character is available in that very context as a feature of "cognitive space": although only contents are truth evaluable, so that a character which fails to determine a content is not associated with truth-conditions, the character is a something and not a mere absence. It also contrasts with the free logical model, which (on the assumptions we are currently making) delivers a result even further from McDowell's, namely that the utterance or thought is false.[10]

McDowell believes that alternatives to his view will involve us in a conception of demonstrative thought according to which its relation to its objects is indirect, and will thus compromise the mind's openness to the world. He writes:

> if an object thought of demonstratively is present to the mind only by way of something which could have been deployed in thought even if the object had not existed, the object is before the mind only by proxy. Without some seemingly inescapable compulsion, it is hard to believe that anyone would tolerate this indirectness in an account of how demonstrative thinking relates us to objects. (1984: 292–3)

On his preferred view, according to which "contents depend on the existence of the relevant *res*" (1984: 291), there is no such indirectness, for there is no separating the existence of the content and the existence of the object. Indirectness enters the picture once we allow (and presumably only once we allow) a conception of senses according to which they "are expressible whether the objects exist or not" (1984: 292).[11]

Free logical truth-theory need make no mention of senses, but can harmlessly make use of the notion: for senses, to be is to be expressible; the sense of an expression is what is shown by an appropriate axiom for it; expressions have the same sense only if they are assigned the same truth-condition, or contribution to a truth-condition, by the canonical theorems of the theory; and senses are constituents of thoughts. Free logical truth-theory allows that there could be, because there in fact are, senses which are expressible even though there is no object which is their referent. It denies that there could be singular terms with senses whose nature is indifferent to whether they have an object as referent. The last alleged possibility, which corresponds to the most natural interpretation of McDowell's words ("senses are expressible whether the objects exist or not"), would violate the demand for rigidity expressed by (15). Its realization would require a sense which would have been the very sense it actually is even if it had had a different referent, or had had no referent at all. To the extent that the free logical model does justice to (15), it rules out this possibility. Rigidity is sameness across worlds of actual referent (if any), with sense held constant. To allow that one and the same sense has different referents at different worlds is to abandon rigidity. Free logical semantics poses no threat from this direction to the openness of the mind to the world.

The essential point is that free logical semantics can do full justice to the rigidity of reference, and thus prevent the separation of content and object which, McDowell fears, would threaten the mind's direct contact with the world. If this is right, austerity in semantics, and openness in philosophy of mind, do not require what McDowell supposed they did: a ban on sense without a referent. Should one, then, simply recommend that McDowell lift the ban? Will not doing so encourage more thinkers to accept austerity and openness, once these are freed from their entanglement with the ban?

In the case of proper names, I think it is straightforward that the ban should be lifted. Doing so gives by far the most straightforward account of the serious (and non-conniving) uses of empty proper names, like the uses of "Vulcan" before it was discovered that there was no such thing. In the case of demonstratives, however, the situation seems to me more difficult. Whereas, for empty proper names, free logical semanticists can quite well specify, in the austere, and indeed homophonic, way what was expressed by an utterance of, for example, "Vulcan is at least 1,000 miles in diameter," namely, that Vulcan is at least 1,000 miles in diameter, this straightforward device is not available in the case of demonstratives, whether or not they have referents. Typically, the theorist will not be in the same context as that of the target utterance, and so cannot simply reuse the target demonstrative. The methodology of austere truth-theories needs some significant modification in order to deal with this feature, and there are several different approaches. In McDowellian spirit, I will assume that the theory will be guided by how speech is reported. Jill yesterday uttered "That is a planet" and I can today report this event by saying "Gazing earnestly at Hesperus yesterday, Jill said that it was a planet." Reports of this kind involve two parts. In the first part ("Gazing earnestly at Hesperus yesterday"), the reporter sets the scene for the utterance, introducing in his own terms any objects of reference that may be needed (including times); in the second part, the reporter specifies the uttered content, using an anaphoric expression, whose reference is determined by some expression in the first part, in place of the utterer's demonstrative. The anaphor goes as far as possible, under the circumstances, toward meeting the demands of austerity: it reveals nothing about any particular "mode of presentation" that might have been involved in the speaker's act of reference. Though the reporter exercises the capacity to refer to Hesperus as Hesperus, he does not attribute this capacity to the utterer.

This style of speech report readily accommodates certain kinds of error on the part of the speaker, in a way which leaves unaffected the content reported. For example, there is nothing incoherent, or even jarring, about a report like: "Gazing earnestly at a fixed star, Jill said that it was a planet." The question we need to ask, in order to decide whether it would be wise to allow for intelligible empty uses of demonstratives, is whether the error can extend to cases in which there is no object of reference at all. We can coherently envisage a narrative like this: "Jill lay in her hospital bed, still under the influence of the medication. Hallucinating a heavenly body, she said that it was a planet." This passes muster as a report of an empty use of the demonstrative sentence "That is a planet." The nature of the scene-setting part of the report ensures that there is to be no referent for the anaphoric "it," just as there was no referent for Jill's "that." There are various kinds of inference or speculation in which even hallucinating Jill may engage which are most readily explained by attributing to her such a content. There is thus a case to be made for the view that allowing sense without a referent even for demonstratives improves the ease and naturalness with which we can make sense of speech behavior.

McDowell remarks of a somewhat similar case for proper names that a reporter might assert: "This man is saying that Mumbo-Jumbo brings thunder." He goes on: "Such an interpreter is simply playing along with his deluded subject – putting things his way" (1977: 175). In this case, McDowell has to see the reporter as saying something he does not regard as literally correct, for on McDowell's view any use of a genuine proper name, even in oblique contexts, licenses existential generalization, which the reporter in this case does not accept. This makes McDowell's case different from the one we have just considered for demonstratives, in which intuitively, and also according to the free logical model, the reporter says nothing he need retract, or qualify, or fail to take fully seriously. It is not a case of connivance, if to connive involves pretending. The total report is not something that would be accepted by the speaker (assuming that Jill had no awareness of the hallucinatory nature of her condition), so it is not properly described as putting things her way. I conclude that the device that McDowell used to try to make his view about proper names more palatable will not happily extend to demonstratives. Here (as also I believe for empty proper names) we have reports even of empty cases which are accurate and involve the reporter in no kind of error, qualification, or special non-assertive speech-act (connivance). If speech using an empty demonstrative is straightforwardly reportable, the speech must have expressed something, so the words of which it was composed must have expressed something, so even some empty demonstratives have content.

McDowellian austerity in semantics, and openness in philosophy of mind, are positions which, in one form or another, I think we should all adopt. I hope that, by separating them off from the ban on sense without a referent, I will increase their attractiveness.

Notes

1   A T-theorem is any theorem of the form "*s* is true iff *p*." What makes a theorem canonical is supposed to be defined purely syntactically, and is roughly that no T-theorem relating to the same object language sentence can be proved in fewer steps. The idea is to exclude unsuitable T-theorems like "*s* is true iff (*p* and (*q* or not-*q*))." In some presentations of truth-theoretic methodology, e.g. by Larson and Segal (1995), the logic is said to be so weak that, in the present terminology, all T-theorems are canonical. The statement in the text of the way in which T-theories are to be applied in interpretation ignores indexical features of language.

2   Homophony is a special case of austerity. A T-theorem in French which uses "Londres" to describe the behavior of "London" will count as austere even though not homophonic.

3   (5) entails (6), given a general notion of entailment (e.g., one according to which one sentence entails any other whose truth-conditions it includes). It does not follow that the truth-theoretic proof theory will represent this fact. Either the needed additional premises (e.g., "Hesperus = Phosphorus") are to be excluded (perhaps on the grounds that truth-theoretic axioms must be confined to semantic information), or the entailment is by-passed by considering only T-sentences with canonical proofs.

4   On some of McDowell's formulations of the nature of *de re* sense, the best way to put the view I argue for is that free logical semantics allow for *de re* senses. Consider "A *de re* sense would be specific to its *res*" (1984: 287). If this means that a *de re* sense has its referent essentially, this is merely rigidity (for senses rather than expressions), a feature that the version of free logical semantics proposed here is at pains to preserve (section II).

5   There are species of free logician who take such sentences to be true; see Lambert (1991); their views will be congenial neither to McDowell nor to the kind of free logical semanticist envisaged in the present chapter. Nothing hinges on whether the first-order formalization uses arbitrary names (as I assume in this presentation) or not.

6   Negative free logic has "$\forall x\, x = x$" as an axiom, reflecting the logical truth that every object is self-identical. It is not committed to the truth of every instance: instances in which an empty constant replaces "*x*" have no bearing on the self-identity of every *object*. See Burge (1974: 320–1), whose approach is followed here.

7   An axiom of this form for a non-empty name like "Hesperus" does link it to an object, though not as a matter of form or logic.

8   The point is independent of the following difficulty for classical modal logic (no matter which account of rigidity is adopted): if "Kripke does not exist" is true with respect to *w*, then so presumably is "$\neg\exists x\, x = \text{Kripke}$". Given the classical rule of existential generalization, it follows that "$\exists y\,\neg\exists x\, x = y$" is true with respect to *w*. Even Meinongians would not regard this sentence, which says that there is something to which nothing is identical, as true with respect to any world. See Wiggins (1995). The more immediate consequence, that "there is something which does not exist" is true with respect to *w*, is also problematic for non-Meinongians. Negative free logic has none of these troubles, thanks to its restriction on existential generalization.

9   The reasons are familiar from several writers. The earliest expression I have found is by Kaplan (1973).

10 Let a (demonstrative) thought be what is or could be expressed by a (demonstrative) utterance.
11 The demanded directness is consistent with the causal mediation of thought and perception by neural processes, as McDowell explains (1977: 166, n.1).

References

Burge, T. 1974. "Truth and Singular Terms," *Nous* 8: 309–25.
Kaplan, D. 1973. "Bob and Carol and Ted and Alice," in J. Hintikka, J. Moravcsik, and P. Suppes (eds.), *Approaches to Natural Language*, Dordrecht: Reidel, 490–518.
Kripke, S. 1972/1980. *Naming and Necessity*, Oxford: Blackwell.
Lambert, K. 1991. "A Theory of Definite Descriptions," in K. Lambert (ed.), *Philosophical Applications of Free Logic*, Oxford, New York: Oxford University Press, 17–27.
Larson, R. and Segal, G. 1995. *Knowledge of Meaning: An Introduction to Semantic Theory*, Cambridge, Mass.: MIT Press.
McDowell, J. 1977. "On the Sense and Reference of a Proper Name," *Mind* 86: 159–85.
McDowell, J. 1984. "*De re* Senses," *Philosophical Quarterly* 34: 283–94.
McDowell, J. 1994a. *Mind and World*, Cambridge, Mass.: Harvard University Press.
McDowell, J. 1994b. "The Content of Perceptual Experience," *Philosophical Quarterly* 44: 190–205.
Simons, P. 2001. "Calculi of Names: Free and Modal," in E. Morscher and A. Hieke (eds.), *New Essays in Free Logic. In Honour of Karel Lambert*, Dordrecht: Kluwer, 49–65.
Wiggins, D. 1995. "The Kant–Frege–Russell View of Existence: Toward the Rehabilitation of the Second-Level View," in W. Sinnott-Armstrong, D. Raffman, and N. Asher (eds.), *Modality, Morality and Belief. Essays in Honor of Ruth Barcan Marcus*, Cambridge: Cambridge University Press, 93–116.

Response to R. M. Sainsbury

1 In "On the Sense and Reference of a Proper Name" I claim that we could give a semantic theory for a language if we knew how to construct a truth-theory for it that would be austere, in this sense: in saying what it does about expressions in its object language, the theory uses those very expressions or close counterparts of them, as opposed to aiming to analyze or decompose the meanings of those expressions. In particular, I contend that austerity need not require us to be unresponsive to the considerations that induced Frege to introduce the notion of sense.

At the beginning of his fine chapter Sainsbury argues, convincingly as far as this goes, that aiming to respect those Fregean considerations, in an account of a language that centers on an austere truth-theory, leaves it open that the logic of the truth-theory might be a negative free logic. If we frame our truth-theory in a negative free logic, we can make an austere, indeed "homophonic," truth-theory for (some of) English yield theorems on the lines of

"Vulcan is at least 1,000 miles in diameter" is true iff Vulcan is at least 1,000 miles in diameter

by derivations matching those that would yield theorems on the lines of

"Neptune is at least 1,000 miles in diameter" is true iff Neptune is at least 1,000 miles in diameter.

Sainsbury concludes that there is no good inference from the merits of austerity to another thing I urge in that paper: that, to put it in his words, a treatment of proper names should "make use of the notion of *de re* sense, a kind of sense which has its referent essentially and which is unavailable in the absence of a referent."

Sainsbury does not quite accuse me of trying to exploit such an inference. He says only that in my paper "the two views are presented as if intimately related" – which is certainly true. The detailed derivation he considers and rejects is one he himself constructs, not one he actually finds in me. Still, one might wonder what intimate relation I think there is between the two views, if not that one is to be recommended on the basis of the other. I shall return to this question; see section 5 below.

In any case, Sainsbury offers the idea of an austere truth-theory framed in a negative free logic, with that shared shape in theorems for sentences containing proper names whether or not the names have bearers, as affording me a way to hold on to an austere Fregeanism while liberating myself from the "implausibility" of "a ban on sense without a referent" – from "the unnaturalness of not recognizing intelligible empty names."

No doubt unsurprisingly, I shall not seize this opportunity to shed a supposedly unnecessary burden. I think these judgments of implausibility and unnaturalness are tendentious. There is plenty to be said for the idea of *de re* senses independently of austerity. In my view Sainsbury is wrong to suggest that these judgments of implausibility and unnaturalness can exert independent leverage against framing truth-theories in classical logic, which would not yield homophonic specifications of truth-conditions for atomic sentences containing empty names, rather than in negative free logic, which would.

Perhaps more surprisingly, I want to urge that we can begin to understand why the idea of *de re* senses is not implausible or unnatural by seeing how the motivation for it is in effect acknowledged in Sainsbury's own thinking.

2   Sainsbury says it is not compulsory, though it is possible, for proponents of free logical truth-theory to use the Fregean notion of sense. But of course he would not claim that if someone puts forward free logical truth-theories as candidates for being usable in interpreting languages, it is optional for her to connect what a truth-theory of the right kind yields with reasonable theses about the thoughts speakers of a language can express by uttering its sentences, thanks to the fact that the expressions that figure in the sentences have the semantical properties a truth-theory ascribes to them. Indeed that is implicit in the contention of his I have just mentioned, the contention that classical truth-theories should be rejected on the ground that "it is so natural to take it that users of [empty] names really do think thoughts thereby." The point of its being optional to use the Fregean notion of sense cannot be more than that the notion of thoughts that figures in this requirement on truth-theoretical semantics need not be precisely Frege's notion of the sense of a sentence. But there must be a connection with a conception like Frege's, a conception of something expressed in uttering sentences – a conception that promises to pull its weight in making rational sense of speakers.

Now how does this connection go in the case of the sample theorems I displayed above? What are the thought-expressing powers whose attribution to the two sentences corresponds to those theorems about them?

It is a way of capturing the point of Sainsbury's proposal to say he thinks this question should be answered in a parallel way in the two cases. The derivability of the second theorem in a truth-theory suitable for interpreting (some of) English corresponds to the fact that "Neptune is at least

1,000 miles in diameter" can be used to express the thought that Neptune is at least 1,000 miles in diameter. Just so, the corresponding derivability of the first theorem in a negative free logical truth-theory corresponds to the fact that "Vulcan is at least 1,000 miles in diameter" can be used to express the thought that Vulcan is at least 1,000 miles in diameter. This is how we are to avoid the supposed "implausibility."

But if we go a little deeper, it becomes less than compelling that we should set much store by the possibility of saying these matching things about thoughts expressible by sentences with non-empty names and thoughts expressible by sentences with empty names. The sentence containing "Neptune" is enabled, by its composition and the semantic properties of its parts, to express a thought that depends for its truth or falsity on how things stand with a certain object, the referent of the name it contains. It is true that the free logical framework allows us to say that the sentence containing "Vulcan" is enabled, by its composition and the semantic properties of its parts, to express a thought. But this supposed thought is not one that depends for its truth or falsity on how things stand with a certain object, the referent of the name it contains. There is no such object, and the thought that negative free logic allows us to say the sentence is fitted to express is simply determined as false by that fact, independently of the predicative material in the sentence that is supposed to express it. When we put things like this, the thought we are supposed to see as expressible by the sentence containing "Vulcan" seems to be of a strikingly different kind from the thought we can routinely see as expressible by the sentence containing "Neptune."

This reflects back into what needs to be said in terms of the concept of the sense of a name – an at least roughly Fregean concept that seems no more optional than that of a thought. The sense of a name is the difference the name makes to the thoughts expressible by combining it with other expressions in sentences. "Neptune" has a sense that enables sentences in which it is concatenated with predicates to express thoughts that are true or false according to how things stand with its referent, specifically according to whether or not its referent satisfies the predicative material in question. "Vulcan," according to Sainsbury's free logical proposal, has a sense all right, but not one of that kind. Its sense is one that enables sentences in which it is concatenated with predicates to express thoughts that are false anyway, independently of the semantical properties of the pre-dicative material in question. Again, these seem strikingly different kinds of contribution to the thought-expressing powers of sentences.

Sainsbury insists that free logical semantics can hold that names have their semantical proper-ties rigidly. "Neptune" has the sense it has – which enables sentences containing it to express thoughts that are true or false depending on how things stand with its referent – essentially. If the facts had been such as to make Leverrier's hypothesis about the perturbations of Uranus fare as badly as his hypothesis about the perturbations of Mercury, "Neptune" would not have had the sense it has. That sense would not have been a sense any expression could have had. Similarly, "Vulcan" has the sense it has – which enables sentences in which it is combined with predicates to express thoughts that are false anyway, independently of the semantical properties of the predi-cates – essentially. If the facts had been such as to make Leverrier's hypothesis about the perturba-tions of Mercury fare as well as his hypothesis about the perturbations of Uranus, the sense "Vulcan" in fact has would not have been the sense of a name of the planet that on that supposi-tion would have existed. (It makes no difference that the name would have been "Vulcan," as hopefully introduced for the planet Leverrier postulated.)

Do the words "sense that depends for its being the sense it is on the actual existence of an object" mark out a kind of sense? How could the answer be "No," if there are senses that conform to that description at all? But in that case it is Sainsbury's own position that a treatment of names should "make use of the notion of *de re* sense, a kind of sense which has its referent essentially and which is unavailable in the absence of a referent." On Sainsbury's own account "Neptune" has a sense of just that kind. The difference between us is not over whether there is such a kind of sense, but that whereas I want possession of a sense of that kind to be a condition for being a name at all, he wants that kind of sense to characterize only some names, the non-empty ones. (I shall modify this formulation of what I want later; see section 4 below. By then it should be clear that the modification makes no essential difference.)

3 Sainsbury wants us to see empty and non-empty names as belonging together in a single semantic category. He claims that this "gives by far the most straightforward account of the serious (and non-conniving) uses of empty proper names, like the uses of 'Vulcan' before it was discovered that there was no such thing." This applies those judgments of implausibility and unnaturalness to a particular case.

But is there anything natural about a kind of thought that would include both the kind express-ible by atomic sentences containing "Neptune" – thoughts determined as true or false according to how things stand with the referent of a name – and the kind supposedly expressible by atomic sentences containing "Vulcan" – thoughts determined as false by the name's lack of a referent? What holds Sainsbury's single semantic category together is simply that non-empty and empty names are treated alike in free logical truth-theory. He wants that to license a parallel treatment of the thought-expressing powers of sentences containing both kinds of names. As I said, the idea is that just as "Neptune is more than 1,000 miles in diameter" expresses the thought that Neptune is more than 1,000 miles in diameter, so "Vulcan is more than 1,000 miles in diameter" expresses the thought that Vulcan is more than 1,000 miles in diameter. But if there is nothing otherwise natural about the single kind of thought supposedly expressible by atomic sentences containing names, whether non-empty or empty, this appeal to the truth-theory to license matching claims about thoughts seems to go in the wrong direction. Rather than taking it that the sheer possibility of a free logical truth-theory is a recommendation for the idea that there is a single semantic cate-gory here, we should be impressed by the unnaturalness that the supposed single kind of thoughts stands revealed as having, when we go below the level of the statements of thought-expressing powers that immediately correspond to the results of the truth-theory, and we should conclude that the sameness of treatment in free logical truth-theory merely masks an important difference. So much the worse for free logical truth-theory.

Is it natural to treat those non-conniving uses of "Vulcan" in the way the free logical approach enables us to? In fact this does not fit at all well with a plausible account of the thought-expressing intentions of Leverrier while his hypothesis about the perturbations of Mercury was still afloat. If he said (a French equivalent of) "Vulcan is at least 1,000 miles in diameter," he surely meant to be expressing a thought that would be determined as true or false according to whether or not a certain object, the referent he took his name to have, was at least 1,000 miles in diameter. It would not have cohered with his conception of the risks he was running to say what Sainsbury would have us say, that even though he turned out to be wrong about the existence of a referent for the name, he was anyway expressing a thought, one determined as false just by the name's lack of a referent. The only possibility of falsity his thought-expressing intentions would have required him to envisage, for the thought he took himself to be expressing, was a possibility of its turning out, concerning the referent of the name he used, that it was not at least 1,000 miles in diameter. It is quite implausible that his intentions, in so far as they related to expressing a thought at all, whether a true one or a false one, were such as to be satisfied by his having turned out to have satisfied the condition for expressing a false thought that Sainsbury bases on the possibility of free logical truth-theory. Leverrier intended to be running the kind of risk of falsity that is a concomitant of aiming to speak the truth – not a risk of a kind of falsity that would belong with there never having been any chance of speaking the truth by uttering the words one utters.

We might say Leverrier must have envisaged the risk that he would turn out to have expressed a false thought if it turned out not to be the case that Vulcan is at least 1,000 miles in diameter. And on the free logical approach we can say it did indeed turn out not to be the case that Vulcan is at least 1,000 miles in diameter. That would be insisting on staying with thought-specifications ("that" clauses) that immediately correspond to the results of free logical truth-theory. But this yields no reason to disallow inquiring into Leverrier's intentions as specified at the different level I am exploiting. Imagine Leverrier, disabused of his hypothesis about the perturbations of Mercury, having offered to him Sainsbury's way for him to claim to have, all the same, expressed false thoughts when he used the supposed name "Vulcan." He would surely say: "That is not how I meant to be running the risk of turning out to have said something false."

4   Once we have the idea – which Sainsbury himself exploits in his considerations about rigidity – of a kind of sense for names whose contribution to the thoughts expressible by sentences containing their possessors is to determine that those thoughts are true or false depending on how things stand with the referents of the names, the overwhelmingly natural thing to say about Leverrier is that he falsely took "Vulcan" to have a sense of that kind. Any sense we say "Vulcan" actually had, on Leverrier's lips, should not dislodge that from its position as the first thing to say about him.

Of course when we say that Leverrier falsely took "Vulcan" to have a sense of a referent-dependent kind, we are not saying that non-conniving uses of "Vulcan" by Leverrier and his interlocutors were blankly unintelligible – as if they were on a par with gibberish. It is perfectly clear what was going on in such talk. In seriously uttering sentences such as (a French equivalent of) "Vulcan is at least 1,000 miles in diameter," Leverrier was *making as if* to be using a name with a sense of the kind "Neptune" in fact turned out to have. His performances, moreover, had just the sort of background in astronomical facts, and plausible hypotheses about how to account for them, that his uses of the name "Neptune" had before the hypothesis about the perturbations of Uranus was confirmed – apart from the fact that in the case of "Vulcan" the corresponding hypothesis, about the perturbations of Mercury, was going to be disconfirmed. Perhaps we should say on these grounds that "Vulcan," in its non-conniving use, had a kind of sense. But if we do say that, we are envisaging a kind of sense that needs to be understood in terms of the idea of an expression's *purporting* to have a sense of the kind "Neptune" turned out to have and "Vulcan" turned out not to have.[1] This is not the kind of sense Sainsbury's free logical approach credits to "Vulcan."

In "On the Sense and Reference of a Proper Name," I worked with the idea that genuine names have a kind of sense that essentially depends on their having a referent. In view of the concession I have just envisaged making to the claim that "Vulcan" has a kind of sense, I should modify that. If "Vulcan" as used by Leverrier had a kind of sense, it is not a good idea to say baldly that it was not a genuine name. The thesis should be that genuine names either have a referent-dependent sense or have a kind of sense their possession of which consists in their purporting to have a referent-dependent sense.

It should be obvious that this makes no difference to the issue between me and Sainsbury. As I said, a kind of sense such that an expression's possession of a sense of that kind consists in its purporting to have a sense of the referent-dependent kind is not the kind of sense Sainsbury's exploitation of free logic is supposed to allow us to attribute to empty names. It is still right to say, about Leverrier's utterances of sentences containing "Vulcan," that there were no thoughts of the kind that – partly, we can now say, because "Vulcan" had the sense it had – they purported to express, so they could not collect truth-values by virtue of things being or not being as they were said to be. The concession makes no difference to the grounds for saying that this makes better sense of Leverrier than taking the utterances to express false thoughts, as per the free logical approach.

5   The intimate relation I explicitly envisage between austerity and the idea that genuine names have referent-dependent senses,[2] in "On the Sense and Reference of a Proper Name," is that resistance to the latter is "the deepest source" of resistance to the former – the deepest source of the idea that the sense of a name would need to determine its referent by being the sense of a specification.[3]

What I had in mind was a generalization of Russell's argument in "On Denoting."[4] Russell urges a specificatory rather than denotative construal of definite descriptions, on the ground that a denotative construal would require us to suppose no thought is expressed if a definite description to which nothing answers occupies the subject position in a sentence.[5] In the generalization, resistance to the idea of referent-dependent sense, on the ground that it has the supposedly intolerable implication that a subject can fall into an illusion of entertaining a thought, motivates crediting referring expressions with senses of a descriptive or specificatory kind, since such a sense does not depend, for being the sense it is, on the existence of something that satisfies the specification whose sense it is. My idea was that if I could show there is nothing untoward about the supposedly intolerable implication, that would clear away this motivation for descriptive conceptions of reference.

Now Sainsbury offers free logical truth-theory as a way of dropping the "ban on sense without referent" without endorsing a descriptive or specificatory conception of the sense of referring expressions. On this view, resistance to referent-dependent sense should never even have looked like a reason for embracing descriptive theories. And if my main aim was to separate a Fregean attribution of senses to names from a descriptive theory, I had no need to take on the task of trying to undermine resistance to referent-dependent sense.

This is an improvement on the idea, which as I said Sainsbury does not quite commit himself to, that I try to establish a need for referent-dependent sense by inferring it from the claim that austerity can accommodate the Fregean thought that names with the same referent can differ in sense. I thought I had to defend referent-dependent sense in order to protect austerity from what would, if allowed, be a motivation for resisting it. Sainsbury should offer free logical truth-theory not as undermining a supposed inference from austerity to the "ban on sense without referent" but as showing, without any need for the "ban on sense without referent," that this supposed motivation for resisting austerity is illusory.

But this makes no difference to the basic issue. The motivation I consider for a descriptive conception of reference comes from the idea that there should be a kind of thought expressible by atomic sentences containing putative names whether or not the putative names have bearers. Sainsbury purports to disarm this motivation, by claiming that we can accept that there is such a kind of thought without needing to suppose names have descriptive or specificatory senses. The kind of thought is the kind that is supposed to be exemplified equally by the thought that Neptune is at least 1,000 miles in diameter and the thought that Vulcan is at least 1,000 miles in diameter. But, as before, when we look below the level of thought-specifications immediately corresponding to what a free logical truth-theory says about sentences, there does not seem to be anything natural about this supposed kind of thought. It cobbles together two strikingly different kinds of thing: thoughts determined as true or false depending on whether the referents of names used in express-ing them are as they are thought to be, and supposed thoughts determined as false just because names used in expressing them have no referent. The motivation I consider for descriptive theories depends on the idea that there should be a real, natural kind of thought expressible by atomic sentences containing putative names whether or not the putative names have bearers. Invoking his artificial kind, Sainsbury does not really concede that idea. If the idea is genuinely conceded, the result is indeed a powerful motivation for descriptive theories of referring expressions. So, as I thought, protecting austerity does require showing that it need not be conceded.

6   Finally, a remark about conniving, playing along with a subject one takes to have fallen into an illusion of existence. Sainsbury says it is harder to sustain a referent-independent conception of the sense of demonstrative expressions, on occasions of utterance, than it is in the case of proper names, where for most purposes it is harmless to ignore the role of context in determining what is meant. But he nevertheless recommends countenancing referent-independent senses for uses of demonstratives as well. His grounds essentially hinge on the claim that in a case he envisages, the report "Hallucinating a heavenly body, Jill said that it was a planet" cannot involve connivance, making as if to give expression to a thought that according to the reporter does not exist.
     But why not? Sainsbury's argument is that the total report would not be accepted by the person who is its subject, at least so long as she is taken in by the hallucination. But so what? Certainly the first four words of the report convey Jill's situation otherwise than from Jill's point of view. They convey a feature of Jill's situation relevant to such understanding as is available to us of the frame of mind we go on to report her as trying to give expression to. So far their function is like the function of the first five words in another example of Sainsbury's, "Gazing at a fixed star, Jill said that it was a planet." As Sainsbury brings out, this kind of scene-setting is necessary for reporting an expressed thought when the subject's way of expressing it depends on features of the context of her performance that are not available to be exploited by the reporter.[6] In Sainsbury's example, scene-setting of this kind is done by "Hallucinating a heavenly body. . . ." I cannot see how he thinks he can exclude the idea that this scene-setting, unlike that effected by "Gazing at a fixed star, . . . ," sets the scene precisely for a conniving report, one in which the reporter makes as if to credit Jill with giving expression to a thought that the reporter knows, and signals by the scene-setting that she knows, does not exist.

Notes and References

1   See the excellent treatment by David Wiggins, in "Existence and Contingency: A Note," *Philosophy* 78 (2003), esp. at 492, where Wiggins puts "Vulcan," as seriously used by Leverrier, in a category of names "on sufferance or on probation." "Vulcan" was a probationary candidate for being a name of the sort "Neptune" turned out to belong to. Unlike "Neptune," "Vulcan" failed its probation. And what "Vulcan" is now for us, who have no use for it except in saying that Vulcan does not exist, depends on this.
2   For simplicity I shall ignore the modification I have just considered.
3   See p. 184 of "On the Sense and Reference of a Proper Name," as reprinted in my *Meaning, Knowledge, and Reality*, Cambridge, Mass.: Harvard University Press, 1998.
4   Reprinted in R. C. Marsh (ed.), *Logic and Knowledge*, London: George Allen and Unwin, 1956.
5   For some discussion, see my "Truth-Value Gaps," reprinted in *Meaning, Knowledge, and Reality*.

6 Sainsbury says the anaphoric "it" in such a report "goes as far as possible, under the circumstances, towards meeting the demands of austerity: it reveals nothing about any particular 'mode of presentation' that might have been involved in the speaker's act of reference." I think this risks being misleading about the demands of austerity. The point of insisting that austerity is compatible with a Fregean appeal to the idea of sense, by my lights, is that austerity is compatible with claiming that the use of a truth-theory in interpretation can fully capture modes of presentation. That "Hesperus" is said to denote Hesperus, in a truth-theory suitable to be used in interpreting a language, reflects the fact that in thoughts expressed by utterances containing "Hesperus" the planet in question is presented *as Hesperus* (and not, say, as Phosphorus). When we have only these anaphoric reports at our disposal, it is not that we stop short of meeting the demands of austerity. The demands of austerity do not require that we reveal as little as possible about modes of presentation. They require only that we display modes of presentation austerely. It would be better to say that in these anaphoric reports we are forced to *go beyond* the demands of austerity, in being unable to display the relevant mode of presentation at all.

2

Reason and Language

Richard G. Heck, Jr.

When I woke up the other day, I coughed. My coughing was not something I did, but merely something that happened. Some time later, I told my wife that I love her. In contrast to my coughing, that was something I did, and it is important both to me and to my wife that it was not something that merely happened. Of course, there is, in that respect, nothing special about this particular linguistic performance: in general, speaking is something we do, and we are held responsible or given credit for our saying what we do, much as we are held responsible or given credit for other things that we do. And rightly so, since speaking is something we do.

The fact that speech[1] is a form of rational action was emphasized by many of the philosophers in the ordinary language school and is at the center of H. P. Grice's discussions of implicature. Not many philosophers have given the fact much notice in recent years, however, though there are two very notable exceptions: Michael Dummett and John McDowell.

My own interest in the rationality of speech was inspired by Dummett's many discussions of the subject in his writings. Many of the papers that post-date "What is a Theory of Meaning?"[2] are dominated by the question how a recognition of speech's rationality should be incorporated into the theory of meaning. This concern derives, at least in part, I believe, from Dummett's recognition of the force of certain of McDowell's criticisms. The core of these criticisms, which were first elaborated in "Truth-Conditions, Bivalence, and Verificationism" (McDowell 1998f), is that, though Dummett attempts to distance himself from W. V. Quine's behavioristic conception of language-use, Dummett too ultimately represents speech as a non-cognitive enterprise. Dummett effectively concedes this point, at least as regards the view he takes in "What is a Theory of Meaning?" (Dummett 1993c). The idea that understanding a language is a "purely practical ability," which plays such a central role in that paper, is subjected to intense critical scrutiny in "What Do I Know When I Know a Language?" (Dummett 1993b) and does not appear in his later work.[3]

I have attempted to moderate the debate between Dummett and McDowell elsewhere (Heck 2006c), agreeing with McDowell that Dummett has never elaborated a position that satisfactorily acknowledges the rationality of speech. McDowell has argued further that the only way to acknowledge it is to abandon Dummett's characteristic conception of the philosophical significance of the theory of meaning: specifically, to replace his requirement of "full-bloodedness" with an embrace of "modesty" (McDowell 1998c). This further aspect of McDowell's position is one I am not ready to accept. But since the argument is largely a "how else" argument, the only way to evaluate it seems to be to investigate the constraints a due recognition of the rationality of speech does put upon the theory of meaning and to see where that leaves us.

Thus the central question in this chapter concerns what the fact that speech is a rational activity teaches us about human linguistic abilities. Ultimately, I would like to argue that a proper appreciation of the rational structure of linguistic action shows that a mature human speaker's understanding of her language consists, to a good first approximation, in her consciously knowing the truth-conditions of utterances of sentences in that language. I shall not be able to complete that argument here, however. Here, I hope to establish a slightly weaker claim, namely, that a competent human speaker's understanding of her language consists, to a good first approximation, in her consciously knowing what utterances of sentences in that language do, or would,[4] mean. The question whether knowledge of meaning, in the relevant sense, is knowledge of truth-conditions is one I consider elsewhere.[5]

The chapter is organized as follows. The first two sections address some questions about the structure of linguistic action: intuitively, when a normal human speaker utters the sentence "It's cold out," she and her audience know both that she has said that it is cold out and that she has uttered the words "It's cold out." Section I discusses the former aspect of linguistic action, arguing that it is what is most fundamentally responsible for the phenomenon of conversational implicature and, more importantly, that implicature is an inevitable product of speech's rationality, one without which our use of language would not be use of *language* at all. Section II considers the question how our linguistic activity is shaped by our awareness of the words uttered, and raises, but does not resolve, the question how our awareness of what is said and our awareness of the words uttered are related. Together, these two sections motivate the view that semantic competence rests upon semantic knowledge. The next two sections argue for this view by considering and disposing of the available alternatives. Section III argues that competence with a language is not simply the ability to use it; section IV argues that competence is not simply the ability to put one's thoughts into words (to borrow a phrase from McDowell). The final section considers the objection that my view is committed to an overly strong form of the claim that thought is prior to language.

I   Implicature and the Rationality of Speech

Saying that speech is a form of rational (or intentional) action leaves open the question under what descriptions it is intentional. This is a sort of question one can ask about any action. Consider a particular non-linguistic act, say, my squirting my kitten, Joe Joe, with a water pistol. There are many ways to describe what has happened when I do this: I have squirted Joe Joe; I have squirted him, say, in the hind-quarters; I have stopped him from eating the cat bed; I have moved the muscles in my arm in such-and-such a way (which could, in principle, be described physiologically). The action in question – my squirting Joey – is intentional under some, but not all, of these descriptions: squirting him was something I did intentionally; squirting him in the hind-quarters was not, though it might have been (that's just where the water happened to hit him, though on other occasions I might also have tried to hit him there). Moving the muscles in my arm in such-and-such a way was not something I did intentionally and is not the sort of thing I ever do intentionally: of course, if I am to squirt Joe Joe, the muscles in my arm must move somehow; but how exactly they move is not something under my rational control. As for stopping him from eating the bed, that too is something I did, though it was obviously not something I did, as it were, directly, but only something I did by doing something else, namely, by squirting him.

Linguistic actions – such as telling my wife that I love her – are also intentional under some, but not all, descriptions. In the example I used above, what has happened could again be described in many ways, including: telling my wife that I love her; uttering the words "I love you"; moving my tongue and lips in certain ways, physiologically described; making such-and-such a sound, acoustically described. My speech in this case is obviously intentional under the first description, what I shall call the *propositional* description: telling my wife that I love her. Equally obviously, it is not intentional under the physiological description, nor under the acoustical one: neither moving my tongue and lips in that particular way – physiologically described – nor making that particular noise – acoustically described – was something I did intentionally. Of course, if I am to say something, my tongue and lips must move somehow, and some particular sound must emerge, but exactly how my mouth moves, and exactly what sound emerges, are not things under my rational control.

The claim that speech is rational thus amounts, in the first instance, to this: speech is intentional under propositional descriptions, such as "saying that *p*." Let me emphasize that I make this claim not on the basis of a priori reflection but on the basis of empirical observation. That is not to say that it is not a conceptual truth (if such there are) that speech is intentional under propositional descriptions: in fact, I doubt that we would be prepared to call anything "speech" or "the use of language" that was not intentional under propositional descriptions.[6] But I doubt it matters, for present purposes, whether the claim that human speech is propositionally rational, as I shall put it, is a conceptual or merely an empirical truth.

That speech is propositionally rational is obvious, or so it seems to me, so I shall not argue for the claim directly. What I am going to do, though, is argue that the propositional rationality of speech is what ultimately explains the phenomenon Grice called "conversational" implicature. I shall argue, moreover, that once we appreciate how central the propositional rationality of speech is to Grice's own treatment of implicature, we can see that his failure to recognize its centrality is responsible for certain problems with his account. It is worth being clear about these matters for their own sake, since implicature is a pervasive and intrinsically interesting phenomenon, but there is another reason to want a better account of it than Grice offers. As he makes clear in the Prolegomena to his William James Lectures (Grice 1989b), Grice hoped that a proper understanding of implicature would allow us to restore the notion of *literal meaning* to the place from which J. L. Austin and others had sought to remove it. For some time, Grice was widely thought to have won that battle. But in recent years, a number of annoying questions have been raised regarding the extent to which Grice's machinery really can secure the place of literal meaning. I shall not discuss these questions in detail.[7] But there has been – or so it seems to me – a tendency to conclude that such-and-such a phenomenon cannot be explained in terms of implicature when all that has actually been argued is that it cannot be explained in terms of the specific account that Grice offered. I hope that what follows will help to discourage this tendency by making it clear how the spirit of Grice's account can be preserved even while many of its details – some of them characteristic of Grice's own approach to language – are abandoned.

The phenomenon in which Grice was interested is easily enough illustrated. To vary an old and justifiably famous example (Grice 1989a: 33), suppose a professor writes a letter of recommendation for a student, one that says:

To whom it may concern,
Mr Jones is punctual and has excellent penmanship.
Yours sincerely,
Prof. Smith

Obviously, Smith has not *said* that Jones is poorly prepared for graduate study, but his opinion of Jones as a student nonetheless shines through. In general, speakers frequently manage to get something across, to communicate something, by means of a particular linguistic performance, even when they do not, in any reasonable sense, actually *say* it by uttering the words they do. Grice explains how that happens in terms of the conversational maxims of Quality, Quantity, Relevance, and Manner, which are themselves consequences of what he calls the Cooperative Principle: "Make your conversational contribution such as is required, at the stage at which it occurs, by the accepted purpose or direction of the talk exchange in which you are engaged." At the root of the Cooperative Principle is the idea that conversations – talk exchanges, as Grice calls them – are cooperative enterprises governed by some shared purpose "or at least a mutually accepted direction" (Grice 1989a: 26). Now, one might question whether conversations do always have a shared purpose or accepted direction. But a yet more fundamental idea is at work here, namely, that conversation – the use of language – is a rational activity on the part of speakers: if a conversation is governed by a shared purpose, then of course speakers can be expected to act rationally in an attempt to further that shared purpose; but even if there are cases in which conversation has no shared purpose, not even "a mutually accepted direction," that need not prevent speaking from being a rational activity.

Taking it as a basic case, Grice focuses upon conversations whose purpose is the exchange of information: in itself, this move should not be too problematic – at least it should not be unfamiliar – for it is just the obvious conversational analogue of the more familiar tendency of philosophers of language to focus on assertion (or on declarative statements). It is in the presence of this more specific assumption about conversational purpose that Grice's maxims take the forms they do: the maxims specify means toward the shared end of exchanging information; thus, for example, if that is one's purpose, then one certainly should not say anything one believes to be false. The core idea is thus that speech is a rational activity: everything else Grice says is, in effect, by way of elaborating or developing this core idea.

Grice would have us explain Prof. Smith's ability to communicate (without explicitly stating) his opinion of Jones as a student in terms of the conversational maxims: in this case, the professor has not provided the kind, or amount, of information he knows is expected (and so has violated the maxim of Quantity); the reason, or so the reader of the letter is said to presume, is that he has nothing else positive to say about Jones (Grice 1989a: 33). Now, in a sense, I have no problem with this explanation: it is fine as far as it goes, and for most purposes it even goes far enough. Still, though, it seems to me to obscure something important about the phenomenon being explained. In particular, since the explanation appeals directly to the maxim of Quantity, it can easily look as if that maxim is what does the explanatory work. But it isn't. The central idea behind Grice's explanation of such cases is independent of any views about the content of any conversational maxims – if such there are. The really important observation is that, when Smith wrote the letter, he *did something*, namely, say that Jones is punctual and has good penmanship. This is something that, at first glance, it simply makes no sense for him to have done. Smith knows what is expected of his letter; he knows that he is supposed to be providing information that will be helpful to the admissions committee. He has failed, apparently knowingly, to meet those expectations. One can't but ask why. One explanation would be that he has other aims as well: perhaps his mother told him not to say anything if he had nothing nice to say, and he means to obey her injunction; he has said everything positive he can think to say and will say no more. In any event, he has conspicuously declined to say anything *else* positive about Jones, although he surely must know that his doing so would improve Jones's chances for admission: perhaps the reason he has not done so is that he does not think there is anything else positive he could honestly say.

One could spin many such stories. But my point is not to raise questions about the details. My point is that all such stories begin at the same place, namely, with the question why Smith said what he said (or did not say certain sorts of other things): it is in answering this question that we come to appreciate his opinion of Jones as a student. But the question cannot even be asked unless Smith's *saying* what he said was his *doing* what he did, that is, unless his speaking (or, in this case, his writing) was a rational act on his part. It is in that sense that the claim that speech is a form of rational action, and that utterances are intentional under propositional descriptions, is at the foundation of Grice's treatment of implicature.

What I have so far said about implicature omits something Grice regarded as a central element of his view: in particular, I have made no reference to speakers' *communicative intentions*. For example, in telling the story I did about Smith, nowhere did I say that he was trying to communicate to the admissions committee that Jones is a poor candidate: my story makes reference to some of Smith's mental states, and to others' recognition of those states, but not to any communicative intentions Smith may have had. When he tells the story, Grice indicates the sort of explanation he intends by saying that Smith "must . . . be wishing to *impart* information that he is reluctant to write down" (Grice 1989a: 33; my emphasis). But that is just not true. Smith *may* be hoping to communicate such additional information, but I see no reason at all to suppose that he *must* be: he may have been compelled to write the letter and firmly, if vainly, hope his letter will not harm Jones's chances; that may even be part of his reason for refusing to say anything negative about Jones. Nonetheless, Smith's saying what he does (or, in this case, his not having said other things) reveals something about what he believes – in particular, what he thinks of Jones as a student – whether he intends it to do so or not.

In case this example is not convincing, let me offer another one, one that is more important, for Grice's purposes, and so less liable to seem tangential.[8] Consider the word "most." Austin, so far as I know, never discusses this word, but it is easy enough to imagine what sort of thing he might have said about it, namely, that a sentence like:

(1)   Most of the students passed the exam,

is *misused* if all of the students passed the exam, just as "Some of the students passed the exam" would also have been misused under the same circumstances. Grice, presumably, would have wanted to say that the sentence is *true* if all the students passed, though it might indeed be misused in those circumstances, because its use will ordinarily implicate that not all of the students passed. And we know what the explanation of this implicature would be like, too: it would appeal to the maxim of Quantity. If all of the students did pass, uttering:

(2)   All of the students passed the exam,

would ordinarily be more informative. One's uttering (1) thus ordinarily implicates that (2) is false;[9] similarly for other sentences involving "most." That is why it might seem that "most" means: most but not all. But if one utters (1), one does *not* ordinarily do so with the intention to *communicate* that not all the students passed: it is not plausible that one almost always has such an intention when one uses the word "most." A sufficiently reflective speaker will, it is true, recognize that her uttering (1) will usually suggest that (2) is false – and so will on occasion cancel the implicature explicitly – but it does not follow that she typically intends to communicate that (2) is false.

Similar remarks could be made about most of the examples Grice discusses. I conclude that, in many cases, including cases Grice regards as exemplary, one can implicate something even when one does not, in any sense, intend one's audience to acquire information beyond what one literally says.

It will perhaps be objected that a very general conception of implicature, founded not on communicative intentions but on the rationality of speech, whatever its other virtues might be, will utterly fail to capture the notion of *what a speaker means*. What Grice wanted, the objector might say, was not a notion of what someone's act of uttering *S* might indicate to her audience, but of what a speaker might *communicate* by uttering *S*. That is true. And Grice may be right that what is distinctive about cases in which the speaker *means* something she does not literally say is that she has certain sorts of communicative intentions. I am neither endorsing nor denying this part of Grice's view. What I am arguing is that cases in which a speaker means something she does not say, in Grice's characteristic sense, are *special cases of a more general and more fundamental phenomenon*, a phenomenon that is due almost entirely to the rationality of speech. I shall return to this point shortly.

First, I want to draw attention to another feature of Grice's account of implicature. According to his definition (Grice 1989a: 30–1), one conversationally implicates that *p* only when one intends one's audience to take one to have intended to communicate that *p*. One thing that is notable about this definition is the specificity of what is implicated: I am supposed to intend to communicate some *particular* proposition and to expect that you should be able to work out which particular proposition that is. This condition does not always, or even often, obtain (and the finer propositions are individuated, the less often it will obtain). Consider once again Prof. Smith. In explaining the example above, I said that he managed to communicate that Jones is a poor student. But is that what he communicates? Or is it that Jones is poorly prepared for graduate study? Or that he should not be admitted to graduate school? Even if Smith does intend to communicate some such message, I see no reason to suppose that there has to be a *particular* such message he intends to communicate; even if there were, he could not reasonably suppose that his audience could work out which specific message that was.

Grice's discussion of implicature seems to be informed by the following sort of picture: the speaker has something quite specific in mind that she wishes to communicate, but, for some reason, she chooses not to express it literally (that is, to "say" it), but opts instead to communicate it indirectly. Grice writes as if the speaker manages, without speaking literally, to do just what she might have done if she had spoken literally, that is, to communicate a specific proposition. What I have argued is that this is, in general, false. How much this point matters depends upon what one's larger purposes are. There is, however, a case to be made, or so I would argue, that a proper understanding of non-literal speech demands the rejection of the Gricean picture: I strongly suspect that part of what explains the power of non-literal speech is precisely the fact that it usually does not communicate anything *particular*. But I shall not defend that claim here.[10]

Now, just as I do not want to deny that, in some cases of implicature, we have communicative intentions of the sort Grice isolates, I do not mean to deny that, in some cases, we intend to communicate something quite specific *via* implicature. Consider the referential use of a definite description. There at the party, someone in the corner is drinking a bubbly liquid from a tulip-shaped glass, laughing and smiling, and Smith says, "The man drinking champagne is having a good time." On a Russellian analysis, Smith will have spoken falsely if no one in the room is drinking champagne. As Keith Donnellan noted (Donnellan 1966), though, there is a strong intuition that Smith has *said of* the man in question that he is having a good time and so has spoken truly if that man is having a good time, even if he is not drinking champagne.

Saul Kripke was the first to offer a reasonably convincing Gricean treatment of such examples (Kripke 1977), one later developed in detail by Stephen Neale (Neale 1990). Very roughly, the story is as follows. If one says something of the form "The *F* is *G*," there are two kinds of reasons one might have for the claim. One might have a general reason: one might have reason to think that every *F* is *G* and that there is one and only one *F*; then one would have reason to believe that *the F* is *G*. On the other hand, one might have a particular reason: one might have reason to think that *a* is *G* and, as well, that *a* is the one and only *F*; one would then also have reason to believe that the *F* is *G*. So, if someone says "The *F* is *G*," we may ask how he satisfies the maxim of Quality, which demands that he have suffcient justification for his claim. If the context makes it clear that he has a general reason, the use of the description will be attributive; if he has a particular reason, then the use will be referential. So, looking at the sad corpse before us, we conclude that only someone who had snapped could commit such a horrible crime and say, "Smith's murderer is insane"; this use is attributive. Observing the odd behavior of Jones in the dock, we conclude that *he* is insane and, independently convinced that he murdered Smith, say "Smith's murderer is insane"; this use is referential.

I find this sort of treatment convincing, though it remains controversial. I am not going to add to its defense here, however, other than by remarking that examples of referential use are special, because they actually do satisfy Grice's definition of conversational implicature. Ironically, it is because this sort of case *does* have the features Grice claims to characterize *all* cases of conversational implicature, most of which do not actually have those features, that these cases might seem not to be cases of implicature. In this sort of case, we can easily imagine that the speaker intends to communicate something other than what the Russellian analysis delivers as the literal meaning of her utterance; there may well be a particular proposition he intends to communicate, namely, that *that* man is insane, having a good time, or what have you. In this sort of case, one really may intend to communicate something one could also have communicated literally and succeed in doing so: one really does *mean* that *that* man is having a good time.

Note, however, that, even in this sort of case, the speaker can implicate something in the absence of appropriate communicative intentions. Suppose Smith says, in the course of a conversation regarding the dangers of alcohol, "The man drinking champagne is a millionaire." In these circumstances, the assertion that *that* man is a millionaire might be quite irrelevant to the conversational purpose: the point of the remark might be that one doesn't have to be a teetotaler to be financially successful. Still, it may be clear to his audience that Smith has particular grounds for his claim (its not being plausible that he has general ones). If so, he will still implicate that *that* man is a millionaire.

Once again, one might want to say here that Smith will not *mean* that that man is a millionaire. I would not disagree. My point, as earlier, is that this phenomenon – the phenomenon of meaning something one does not literally say – is a special case of a phenomenon for which the propositional rationality of speech is chiefly responsible. The basic notion here, or so I am suggesting, is a weak notion of implicature that does not require one to have any communicative intentions regarding what proposition is implicated: these propositions are ones the audience can conclude the speaker believes on the basis of an inference to the best explanation concerning her specific act of saying what she did; it makes no sense for me to have said that *p* specifically, in this context, unless I believe that *q*; my saying that *p* therefore implicates that *q*, in this weak sense. Meaning something one does not say is a less fundamental notion: meaning, in this sense – and so implicature, in Grice's sense – is implicating something, in my weak sense, *plus* having the appropriate communicative intentions.

The reason to prefer my picture is simple. Even in standard examples of conversational implicature, the condition that the speaker should intend to communicate some proposition p is often not satisfied: in some cases, such as those involving the word "most," the speaker will typically fail to have the right sort of communicative intention; even when she does have some such intention, as in the letter of recommendation example, this intention may not be appropriately specific. Very few of the standard cases of conversational implicature, then, are conversational implicatures as Grice defines that notion. Some other notion is therefore required. And once we have it, it is easy enough to reconstruct Grice's in terms of it.

My view is similar, in a way, to Christopher Gauker's (Gauker 2001). Gauker argues, as I have, that even in paradigm cases of conversational implicature, an implicature can be present even if the speaker did not intend to communicate it to the hearer. But Gauker goes further, claiming that there is no such thing as conversational implicature in Grice's sense: implicatures are, he alleges, *never* a product of inferences the audience makes regarding what the speaker might have wanted to say; rather, they are the result of "situated inferences," inferences made from what is said and aspects of the situation in which it is said. My own view, it should be clear, is different. On Gauker's view, a speaker's psychology is all but irrelevant to what her utterances implicate. I do not accept that claim. On the contrary, my view is that conversational implicature (in my weak sense) is an inevitable product of speech's rationality. If speaking is acting, one's saying what one does is as much a function of one's various beliefs and desires as anything else that one does. Others will therefore frequently be able to draw conclusions about what one believes (or does not believe), or wants (or does not want), from what one says (or does not say), in much the same way, and for much the same reason, that they are able to make such discoveries by considering other things one does (or fails to do).[11]

Similarly, non-literal communication, at least in certain of its forms, is the inevitable result of speakers' *self-conscious recognition* of the rationality of their own and others' speech. Human agents are able to rationalize the acts of others, in the sense that we can discern why people act as they do. We also know that others are capable of rationalizing our own actions, in this same sense, and we can, with some reliability, predict how others will rationalize our acts. We are, therefore, often in a position to act with a reasonable expectation – and perhaps even knowing – that our so acting will be interpreted by others as due, say, to our having a certain belief. So, for example, Smith might write his letter expecting those reading it to conclude that he believes that Jones is a poor student, and that expectation might partly explain why he writes the letter he does. If so, then he may have a communicative intention of the sort Grice identifies. But it is Smith's self-conscious recognition of the rationality of his speech that is fundamental, not his intention to communicate something he does not literally say: it is his knowledge that others recognize his speech as rational that is the source of whatever communicative intentions he may have.

Communicative intentions of the sort Grice identified therefore seem to me to play a much less fundamental role in linguistic action than he supposed. This observation, I think, ultimately undermines his attempt to reconstruct *saying* on the basis of *meaning*. I cannot make that argument in full generality here. But parts of it will surface in what follows.

II Words and the Rationality of Speech

To this point, I have argued that speech – or, more generally, our use of language – is intentional under propositional descriptions, such as: saying that p. So, to return to the example I used earlier, when I tell my wife that I love her, saying that I love her is something I do; my utterance is intentional under that description. But this description of the action is not the only one under which it is intentional. It is also intentional under *verbal* descriptions, such as: uttering the sentence "I love you." [12] This too seems obvious once stated, but here we need to proceed slowly, since it is important to be clear in what sense speech is intentional under verbal descriptions. Let me emphasize, once again, however, that I am not claiming anything a priori: in fact, in this case, it is not too difficult to imagine something much like the use of language that is *not* intentional under verbal descriptions.

What would that be like, to be a "speaker" for whom "speaking" was intentional under propositional descriptions, but not under verbal ones? Well, such an agent would be able to form an intention, say, to tell his wife that he loved her, and then that would just be something he did. Of course, he might make some sort of sound – perhaps a sound speakers of English would hear as "I love you" – but it would be no part of what he (intentionally) *did* that he uttered that sentence. Indeed, such an agent need not even be consciously aware of his uttering a sentence. A sentence would just be produced, much as our own lips and tongues just move when we speak. Indeed, we can imagine that neither our agent, nor any of his fellow speakers, is capable of conscious auditory perception at all. His wife need not consciously recognize the sentence that has been uttered to be able to recognize her husband as having done something that was intentional under a propositional description, as having (for lack of a better word) said that he loves her. Communication between such agents would be like telepathy: it would seem to them as if communication were purely between their minds. [13]

That is not how things are for us. When we speak, we do not just decide to say something and then make a noise of which we are consciously unaware. Nor, when someone says something to us, do we recognize them only as having said something (propositionally described) and not as having uttered certain words. This is apparent from many features of our use of language. For example, we know that we, and others, sometimes misunderstand words: so we know that one can intend to say that Jones was angry but come out with the sentence "Jones was livid," thereby failing to say that Jones was angry, uttering *that* sentence because one wrongly believes that "livid" means *angry*, whereas, in fact, it means *pale*. [14] Other sorts of failures are possible here, too: one might end up saying "That's a nice derangement of epitaphs," when one had wanted to say that the thing in question is a nice arrangement of epithets, not because one thinks "That's a nice derangement of epitaphs" really does mean *that's a nice arrangement of epithets*, but because of some sort of "processing error." In other cases, such an error may be due to a "slip of the tongue." It isn't always clear, in a particular case, what exactly has gone wrong: But we do, in practice, distinguish these sorts of cases pretty well.

Similarly, we are consciously aware that our own understanding of what others have said can be compromised by a failure to understand certain of the words they are using: when we are in that sort of situation, we can ask such things as "What does 'syzygy' mean?" Sometimes, we are unable to determine what someone has said because the reference of a demonstrative or pronoun is unclear: then we can ask to whom, or to what, the relevant expression was supposed to refer. We may recognize the ambiguity in a certain sentence, and ask which of two things the speaker meant when he said "Fighting administrators can be distracting." Occasionally when speaking our own mother tongues, and often when speaking a language not well-known to us, we find ourselves wanting to say something, but not knowing what words would express it: in the latter case, we have recourse to dictionaries; the former sort of case can, as I'm sure we all know, be extremely frustrating. And, finally, even when we know what we want to say, we sometimes put a good deal of effort into determining just how we should say it: sometimes that is a matter of choosing which words we shall use; other times, it is a matter of choosing among different forms of expression (say, between active and passive voice). For a writer, of course, this is all very familiar activity.

None of that would be true for the quasi-telepaths, for they are not aware of themselves as uttering words at all. They could not, for example, have our concept of ambiguity. They might have a related concept. It might be, for example, that it is sometimes unclear to them whether someone has said that it's distracting to fight administrators or that it's easy to be distracted by administrators who are fighting. Then they, like we, would have to appeal to pragmatic factors to decide what had been said. But they would lack any sense of *why* it should be unclear which of these two things had been said, for they would be unaware that one can say both of these things by uttering the same string of words.

These reflections suggest that speech is not only intentional under verbal descriptions but that it is *by* uttering a sentence that we say something. This remark is not intended simply as one about the causal structure of communication. Taken that way, it would apply equally to the quasi-telepaths I discussed above: communication as they have it also depends upon the production and reception of sound; in a purely causal sense, they say things by uttering things, too. What distinguishes us from them is that, in a *rational* (not just a causal) sense, we say things by uttering things. So, for example, if one asks why Smith uttered the sentence "The meeting begins at 4 p.m.," the question may be answered as follows: Smith wanted to say that the meeting began at 4 p.m., and he knew that the sentence "The meeting begins at 4 p.m." meant that the meeting began at 4 p.m. and so that, if he uttered that sentence in that context, he could thereby say that the meeting began at 4 p.m. And so he uttered that very sentence and thereby said when the meeting began. For the quasi-telepaths, on the other hand, no such answer can be given: they do not utter sentences at all (though noises do get made).

To avoid any potential misunderstanding, let me emphasize that, in offering this sort of explanation of Smith's utterance, I do not mean to suggest that Smith must consciously have engaged in any such reasoning. Sometimes we do; more usually, we do not. That fact does not undermine the claim that what explains Smith's uttering what he did is his having the sorts of beliefs and desires mentioned. There is nothing special about language here. Much of what we do is unaccompanied by any conscious awareness of this sort of practical reasoning. If I walk to the refrigerator and open the door, what explains my doing so may be my wanting a beer and my believing that there are beers in the fridge. And if someone asks me why I opened the refrigerator, that is just the sort of thing I might say: I and others explain my actions by adverting to such beliefs and desires; we do so rightly, even if my mind was elsewhere at the time. The point is one that ought to be familiar: the correctness of this sort of rational explanation does not depend upon the agent's awareness of his own practical reasoning (though it may depend upon his having conscious access to his reasons).

A related point holds about comprehension: when Smith speaks to me, I take him to have said that the meeting begins at 4 p.m. because I perceive him to have uttered the sentence "The meeting begins at 4 p.m.," and I know that this sentence means that the meeting begins at 4 p.m. That is not to say that my understanding of Smith's utterance must involve conscious reasoning of this kind. Nor is it to say that one's identification of the sentence uttered must temporally precede one's identification of what is said, nor that it must rest upon grounds independent of one's identification of what is said, or anything of that kind. Rather, the claim is that recognizing what someone says depends upon recognizing the sentence she utters, in a sense that ought to be quite uncontroversial.

Suppose I hear John utter the sentence "I bought a _oat," not clearly hearing the first phoneme of the last word, so that I am unsure whether he uttered "I bought a goat" or "I bought a coat." Given the context, it may be clear enough that John must have meant to say that he bought a goat, not a coat; and frequently, that would be the end of the matter, since we need not care to determine what John in fact said. But maybe we do care what he actually said. Then reason to think he meant to say that he bought a goat certainly would constitute reason to think he meant to utter "I bought a goat" rather than "I bought a coat." That, in turn, may constitute reason to suppose that he *did* utter "I bought a goat" and so that he did say that he bought a goat. But what John *did* say depends upon which sentence he actually uttered, and we, as ordinary speakers, know as much. If I have reason to believe that John actually uttered the sentence "I bought a coat" – perhaps someone taped the conversation and, clearly enough, those are the words on the tape – then I am thereby given reason to suppose that he said that he bought a coat, since, if he did utter that sentence, then that is what he said, whether he meant to say it or not. In that sense, in so far as contextual evidence bears upon what John said, it must fundamentally bear upon what sentence he uttered, even if the evidence itself concerns what it would have made sense for him to say. Similarly, if I do clearly hear John utter the sentence "I bought I coat," then I will thereby hear him as saying that he bought a coat, even if the context makes it completely obvious that what he meant to say was that he has bought a goat. And, of course, when someone utters an ambiguous sentence, we may be clear enough about what words were uttered without knowing what has been said.[15]

We may therefore conclude that our utterances are intentional, and are recognized by others as being intentional, under descriptions of the form: saying that *p* in uttering a sentence *S*.[16] Let us say that our utterances are, therefore, intentional under *semantic* descriptions. The appropriateness of this terminology will be clear if we make explicit a conclusion that was implicit in the preceding discussion, namely, that the rationality of our speech demands explanation in terms of practical reasoning involving such beliefs as that sentence *S*, uttered in a particular context, did or would mean that *p*. That is to say: our use of language – not any *possible* use of language, in particular, not that of the quasi-telepaths, if that is indeed use of language, but nonetheless *our* use of language – depends upon our having conscious beliefs about the meanings of the sentences we utter.[17]

Two points of clarification. First, the word "conscious" is significant. It is notoriously slippery, as well, and I would gladly use an alternative if only I could think of one. I use it mainly in contrast with "tacit." What I am claiming is *not* that our ability to use our language depends upon our tacitly, or unconsciously, knowing a semantic theory for it: that claim is familiar, and one I endorse, but it is not the one for which I have been arguing. On the contrary, I have been arguing that our ability to use and to understand language depends upon our *consciously* knowing what uttered sentences do or would mean, in the sense that such knowledge is available to us *qua* agents of linguistic acts: I have been arguing that the rational explanation of our linguistic actions requires such attitudes to be attributed to us. Second, I have, to this point, been speaking of our conscious semantic beliefs as being of the form: *S* means that *p*. I have been so speaking for ease of exposition. The foregoing establishes nothing about the specific form these beliefs take. My own view, as it happens, is that the real form of these beliefs is something like: *S* is true iff *p*. But I am officially neutral on this issue here.[18]

Now, if I knew what an utterance of an arbitrary sentence of French would mean on any occasion of use, surely I would be able to use and understand French reasonably competently.[19] In that sense, conscious knowledge of the meanings of the sentences of a language suffices for understanding it. What I have argued above is, in effect, that conscious knowledge of the meanings of its sentences is also *necessary* for understanding a language, at least as we humans do: our ability to perform the sorts of linguistic actions of which we are in fact capable requires possession of such knowledge. So conscious knowledge of the meanings of the sentences of a given language is both necessary and sufficient for understanding that language. It is tempting to express this point by saying that, to understand a language, it is both necessary and sufficient that one know what the sentences in that language do or would mean on various occasions of use. That, however, is not quite right. What we have been discussing here is what we might call *occurrent* understanding: the understanding one has of an utterance when it is actually made. And the view for which I am arguing here is that one's occurrent understanding of an utterance consists in one's knowing what the uttered sentence means on that occasion of use. If one accepts that view, then it is tempting to say further that understanding a language consists in knowing what its sentences do or would mean on various occasions of use. Such a state is dispositional: understanding a language is, on this view, being able to determine what uttered sentences mean; better, it consists in the categorical ground of this ability, say, in tacit knowledge of semantic theory. What is distinctive of the view offered here is thus not to be found in its account of our standing ability to speak our language. It is to be found, rather, in its conceiving of our occurrent understanding of an utterance as a cognitive state, consisting in knowledge of what the uttered sentence means. Call that *the cognitive conception of understanding.*

III   The Use View

I take it that, at this point in the dialectic, the cognitive conception is well enough motivated, but it does not follow from what has been argued so far. One might hold, instead, that what understanding an utterance consists in falls short of the sort of semantic knowledge the cognitive conception regards as essential and explains the fact that competent human speakers do typically have semantic knowledge in other terms.

One version of this strategy would be to hold that understanding a language is simply a matter of being able to use it appropriately. Call this the Use View. So, on the Use View, one understands the sentence "snow is white" if one is able to use it appropriately: one's understanding of the sentence does not consist in one's knowing what it means. Indeed, a defender of the Use View might well want to insist, as Scott Soames does (Soames 1988: 189), that understanding does not even require one to possess the *concept* of meaning or truth: if not, then, in general, competent speakers need know neither that "snow is white" means that snow is white nor that it is true iff snow is white. But many competent speakers do possess such concepts, and those who do are in an excellect position to acquire semantic knowledge: if I understand the sentence "snow is white," the verb "to mean," and the significance of quotation-marks, then I can come to know, purely on the basis of reflection, that "snow is white" means that snow is white. Soames thus concludes that semantic knowledge is not what constitutes understanding but something that flows from it.[20]

This way of motivating the Use View goes hand in hand with what is, I think, a common reason for dissatisfaction with the cognitive conception. According to it, what constitutes my understanding of my language is my knowledge of such facts as:

(3)   "Snow is white" means that snow is white.

The source of our knowledge of such facts is – surprise – much disputed, but whatever its source, such "disquotational" knowledge seems insufficiently robust to constitute knowledge of the meaning of the sentence "snow is white." There are many ways to press this point. But one familiar one proceeds by noting that, as the now famous example[21]

(4)   "the borogroves are all mimsy" means that the borogroves are all mimsy,

shows, one can know that (3) is true even if one does not understand the sentence "snow is white." The familiar response is that what we know about (4) is merely that it is *true*: we do not know that "the borogroves are all mimsy" means that the borogroves are all mimsy. On the other hand, we do know that "snow is white" means that snow is white, not just that the sentence " 'snow is white' means that snow is white" is true. And since what constitutes competence, according to the cognitive conception, is knowledge of the proposition expressed by (3), not just knowledge that it is true, the objection lapses: we do not have the relevant knowledge about "the borogroves are all mimsy." But there is a deeper worry, namely, that the difference between (3) and (4) is just that we understand the sentence "snow is white" but do not understand "the borogroves are all mimsy": what is needed to *get* from knowledge that (4) is true to knowledge of what it expresses seems to be an understanding of the sentence "the borogroves are all mimsy." If so, then knowledge of the proposition expressed by (4) *depends upon* and so cannot constitute understanding of that sentence, and the same goes for (3).[22]

There is much to be said about this matter.[23] For present purposes, let me just say this. Even if there is a "trivial" way of knowing such facts as that expressed by (3) – even if one can found knowledge of (3) upon knowledge that it is true and an understanding of the sentence mentioned in it – it simply does not follow that our understanding of "snow is white" cannot consist in knowledge of what is expressed by (3). What does follow is that our understanding "snow is white" cannot consist in our knowing what is expressed by (3) *in that trivial way*, since we can know what is expressed by (3) in the trivial way only if we understand the sentence "snow is white." But for all that, our understanding "snow is white" might consist in our knowing what is expressed by (3) in some other way, in a way that is available without any antecedent understanding of "snow is white." Knowing it in that other way, and so understanding "snow is white," one would then be in a position to come to know what is expressed by (3) in the trivial way, as well. If so, one would have something like a priori knowledge of a fact originally known a posteriori. But there is no contradiction in that.[24]

Let us return, then, to the question whether we should accept the Use View. As I am understanding it, it is the view that one's understanding of one's native language consists in an ability to use it, where the ability to use the language does not itself rest upon possession of conscious knowledge of the meanings of sentences of that language. This view is therefore immune to a familar objection due to Chomsky.[25] Chomsky observes that a monolingual speaker of English might lose her ability to speak and understand it because she was incapacitated by some sort of injury. Once she had recovered from this injury, she might recover her ability to speak and understand English as well, yet have no ability to speak and understand Japanese. So there must be some categorical basis for this ability, in whose presence competence in fact consists. But the Use View can incorporate this corrective. As Chomsky himself notes, a similar remark could be made about the ability to swim (Chomsky 1988). Maybe it is right to say, as Chomsky does, that this ability has a substantial cognitive component. But no one should be tempted by the idea that the ability to swim consists in the possession of certain sorts of conscious knowledge: it is by way of denying *that* claim that one might describe the ability to swim as a practical ability.[26] No defender of the Use View need deny, therefore, that the categorical basis of the ability to use English appropriately should be described in terms of tacit knowledge: The claim is simply that the ability to use a language does not consist in one's *consciously* knowing what its sentences mean. It is, rather, more like the ability to swim.

There are, however, other reasons to be dissatisfied with the Use View.

In some sense, of course, to understand a language is to be able, under suitable circumstances, to use it. But language-use, among human speakers, is a form of rational action whose explanation adverts to beliefs about the meanings of the sentences they utter. The challenge for the Use View, then, is to characterize language-use as something *other than* a form of action that is intentional under semantic descriptions. A central claim of many of McDowell's reflections on language is that there is not going to be such a characterization:[27]

> The essential move is a radical shift from Dummett's conception of language use. . . . For Dummett, language use . . . must be characterizable "as from outside content". This means that particular episodes of language use must be recognizable for what they essentially are without benefit of understanding the language. . . . To embrace modesty, by contrast, is to insist that the outward aspect of linguistic behavior is essentially content-involving. (McDowell, 1998c: 99–100)

What an episode of language-use essentially is, McDowell is claiming, is an action that is intentional under at least a propositional description: in that sense, such an act cannot be characterized "as from outside content"; so to characterize it would be to make it unintelligible as the act of a rational agent (McDowell, 1998a: 112–13). Let me reinforce this conclusion.

The appeal of the Use View, it seems to me, is due in large part to the attractions of a simplistic conception of our use of language, according to which speakers, confronted with facts, come out with sentences in response to them: seeing the rain outside, Kurt says, "Es regnet." One finds such a picture in straightforwardly behavioristic conceptions, such as Quine's, but also in somewhat less behavioristic ones, such as Dummett's and Donald Davidson's: it is with reference to such a picture that one will talk of indications of "assent"; connect use with conditions of verification; or characterize it in terms of what sentences a speaker "holds true."[28] Of course, no one will or should deny that Kurt will sometimes utter the sentence "Es regnet" when it is raining. But he will not always do so, since, in such circumstances, it will often be obvious to all that it is raining, and the maxims of Relevance and Quantity – whatever their source – will counsel him against uttering it. More importantly, he may appropriately utter the sentence in a wide variety of circumstances, in many of which it is not raining. I do not mean by this that he might be lying or joking. Kurt might say that it is raining by uttering the sentence "Es regnet" for many different reasons, some of which require it not to be raining, and he might thereby communicate something about almost anything you please, given an appropriate context.

The conditions under which a sentence is appropriately uttered are extremely various. It is therefore hard to see why the conditions under which a sentence is used – in any sense of "use" that excludes the psychological states of speakers – should be expected to bear any significant relation to that sentence's meaning. Or to put the problem differently: how, on the Use View, is one to explain the appropriateness, or rationality, of Kurt's utterance of "Es regnet" in circumstances in which it is obvious to everyone that it isn't raining? The earlier discussion of implicature was intended to establish that there is no answer to this question that does not invoke the fact that what Kurt is doing when he utters the sentence "Es regnet" is *saying* that it is raining: it is essential to the explanation that both Kurt and his audience should conceive of him as doing just that, that is, as performing an action that is intentional under this propositional description.

A defender of the Use View might reply that such non-conventional forms of communication are of no fundamental significance for our understanding of language: we may abstract from such phenomena in giving our account of understanding. But the sorts of phenomena we have been discussing are, or so I argued earlier, an inevitable consequence of the propositional rationality of speech: so long as speech is a form of action that is intentional under propositional descriptions, something like the phenomenon of conversational implicature – at least conversational implicature, in my weak sense – is an inevitable feature of it. To abstract from these sorts of phenomena in giving one's account of semantic competence is, therefore, to abstract from the propositional rationality of speech. To do that, however, is to abstract from the fact that human beings use language: no form of activity that is not propositionally rational can plausibly be regarded as use of language.

The Use View cannot simply assimilate this observation. To do so would be to regard how a sentence is used as determined, in part, by what it is used to say. We can all agree, of course, that understanding the sentence "snow is white" consists in an ability to use it appropriately if using it appropriately is using it to say that snow is white. But that would utterly trivialize the Use View. If the Use View is not to be utterly trivial, then, it is committed to characterizing the "appropriate use of a sentence" without making any reference to what the sentence is used to say. What I am claiming is that the diversity of our use of language – which is itself an essential feature of our use of language – already makes such a characterization unlikely: how can one explain the appropriateness of an utterance of "Es regnet" made in the complete absence of rain without making any reference to the speaker's knowledge that he is saying that it is raining? I haven't proven that it's impossible to answer that question. But I know of no plausible way to answer it.[29]

I take it that this conclusion, though reached by a very different route, is close to McDowell's: any attempt to characterize particular episodes of language-use "as from outside content" – that is, as something other than as acts that are intentional under propositional descriptions – is to characterize them as something unrecognizable as uses of language.

IV   The Direct View

The propositional rationality of speech is essential to it. Our understanding of language issues (under normal circumstances, of course) in the ability to act in ways that are intentional under propositional descriptions. No account that omits this fact is acceptable. That is what is fundamentally wrong with the Use View. This conclusion, however, leaves us some distance from the view for which I am arguing, that understanding an utterance is knowing what the uttered sentence means on that occasion.

McDowell offers a view that can be construed as an alternative both to the Use View and to the cognitive conception. As noted earlier, McDowell emphasizes that language-use is content-involving. But it is not clear to me whether McDowell understands this point as I would. One of his main points, I do accept, namely, that understanding utterances made in a language one understands is a perceptual capacity (McDowell 1998d: 331ff.): For an ordinary human being who understands a given language, perception of speech that is (or appears to be) in that language really does involve a *perception*, in the strictest sense, of meaning. That is to say, if someone utters the sentence "There are deer in the garden," then it is part of the content of one's experience itself that, say, someone has said that there are deer in the garden. One does not hear only the words: one hears what is said, as well. But McDowell elsewhere suggests that to articulate that insight "we have to entitle ourselves to the idea that acquiring a first language is, not learning a behavioral outlet for antecedent states of mind, but becoming *minded* in a way that the language is anyway able to express" (McDowell 1998c: 105). I myself want no part of that idea, which seems to be optional at this point in the dialectic. I'll return to this remark below and focus here on what I take to be the core of McDowell's suggestion.[30]

McDowell's central idea here is that the ability to use language is the ability to put one's own thoughts into words and, similarly, to recognize the thoughts of others in their words (McDowell 1998c: 97–100). As I have said already, I am not sure whether McDowell intends this view as an alternative to the cognitive conception. But someone might so regard it, so let me consider a version of the view thus intended: on this version of the view, the ability to put one's thoughts into words in no way depends upon one's knowing what one's words do, or would, mean on various occasions of utterance. In light of its similarities to Direct Realist theories of perception, we may call this view the Direct View.[31] Is the Direct View a viable alternative to the cognitive conception?

We must all agree that competent speakers can (barring injury and the like) put their thoughts into words. The disagreement between my view and the Direct View concerns the source of this ability. According to the cognitive conception, we are, of course, able to put our thoughts into words, but that is because we know what our words would mean on various occasions of use:[32] if I want to put my thought that snow is white into words, I can certainly do so, but only because I know that "snow is white" means that snow is white. What is the alternative? I do not know what it could be other than that putting one's thoughts into words is something one *just does*, without deploying one's knowledge (if one has it) of what those words mean. But if so, the Direct View makes us sound too much like the quasi-telepaths. Quasi-telepaths too use language in communication with their fellows. In some sense, a quasi-telepath too can put her thoughts into words and recognize the thoughts of others in their words. Of course, they would not describe themselves that way, since they do not recognize themselves as uttering words. Putting their thoughts into words is thus not something that the quasi-telepaths *do*, though it is nonetheless something that happens.

The Direct View does not, then, present us with an incoherent picture of the use of language.[33] But it does present us with a picture of a use of language that is not ours. What distinguishes us from the quasi-telepaths is precisely that putting our thoughts into words *is* something we do. What is involved in our putting our thoughts into words being something we do, rather than something that merely happens? The difference between us and the quasi-telepaths is most obvious when we consciously choose words to express our thoughts. When we make such a choice, we are deciding which sentence to utter. But with reference to what sorts of considerations are we supposed to be making that decision? The only answer, it seems to me, is that we are deciding on the basis of our knowledge of what those sentences would mean in the context in which they will be uttered. Of course, we do not always make such choices consciously. But the reasons we have for saying what we do when we do not make such choices consciously are no different, in principle, from the reasons we have when we do. My walking to the fridge may not have been preceded by a conscious decision to do so because I wanted a beer and believed there were some beers in the fridge, but that is nonetheless why I walked to the fridge. My uttering "there are beers in the fridge" may not have been preceded by a conscious decision to do so because I wanted to say that there are beers in the fridge and believed that "there are beers in the fridge" means that there are beers in the fridge, but that is nonetheless why I uttered that sentence. My not always being conscious of my reasons for uttering the sentences I do is not to the point: that my utterance of specific words is an intentional act under my rational control, partly explained by my semantic knowledge, is.

These sorts of remarks, I am all too aware, are liable to seem unconvincing: the ability to choose one's words is what partisans of the view I am defending always mention at such points. So let me mention a slightly different sort of phenomenon. Suppose I am standing in a flower shop trying to buy a bouquet to take to a dinner party. I see the one I want and need to tell the florist which one it is. Uttering the words "I'll take that one" won't be sufficient. I need to arrange matters so that she will realize that, when I said "that one," I meant *that* one. In such a case, there is necessarily a gap between the word and its meaning, a gap I cannot fill unless I have a certain semantic intention, namely, the intention to refer to a particular bouquet with my utterance of the demonstrative. A similar story can, of course, be told from the florist's point of view: unless she knows to which bouquet my utterance of "that one" referred, she will not know what I have said.

One might also consider examples involving ambiguity. The point of all of these examples, however, is the same: there are several ways in which our awareness of our words, both when we speak and when we hear others speak, manifests itself. It is part of how we conceive our own actions, and those of others, that we regard what has been said as depending, in a rational and not just in a causal sense, upon what words have been uttered. In short: we are not quasi-telepaths, and the Direct View fails to distinguish us from them.

Now, I said earlier that I find McDowell's claims about our perception of speech appealing: we really do hear what people say and not just the words they utter. One might worry, however, that the cognitive conception cannot incorporate this observation. According to the cognitive conception, understanding an utterance consists in knowledge of what the uttered sentence means on that occasion. But how, one might want to ask, is such knowledge put to use in comprehension? The obvious suggestion is that it underwrites inferences from claims about what words someone has uttered to claims about what she has said. If so, however, then it would seem that the cognitive conception is committed to denying that we hear what other speakers say: if I have to make such an inference in order to know that someone has said that Fred has gone fishing, then what I *hear* must be just the sentence "Fred has gone fishing"; otherwise, no such inference would be necessary. And now, one might add, a similar point holds for speech production: when one speaks, one does not typically have to decide what to say and then also decide how to say it. Rather, one simply says what one means. The cognitive conception, however, would seem committed to regarding one's uttering a sentence as all one can *really* do, one's belief about what the sentence means figuring in practical reasoning regarding what sentence one should utter.

But this argument moves too quickly. As regards speech production, my view, as I have said before, concerns the reasons one has for saying what one does: the fact that we do not ordinarily have to decide what words to utter after we have decided what to say simply does not show that our reasons do not include the belief that those words can, on this occasion, be used to say just that. Nonetheless, however, it does seem to me that there is an important lesson here, namely, that a certain simple model of the rational structure of speech production is incorrect. According to this simple model, uttering a sentence is the most basic form of linguistic action; expressing a proposition, on the other hand, is something one can only do indirectly, *by* uttering a sentence. This is, obviously, the analogue for the case of speech production of the view, for the case of speech comprehension, that one only really hears words, not what is said. Now, I have already said that I find this view of comprehension unsatisfying, and I can well understand why one might find the analogous view in the case of speech production equally unsatisfying. But I do not see why one would suppose that the cognitive conception is committed to the simple model. If the simple model is incorrect, however, the question does need to be asked with what it should be replaced. I confess that I do not know the answer to that question.

Regarding the perceptual case, it is not obvious that one's beliefs about what sentences mean can be deployed in the comprehension of speech only by being used in inferences of the sort mentioned. It is a familiar point, for example, that one's perception of a scene can be affected by one's beliefs:[34] when one realizes that what one thought was a cat is, in fact, a pillow, the scene itself may actually look different. Perhaps one's semantic beliefs regularly affect perceptual content itself, then. There is, however, another possibility, namely, that the most basic informational states deployed in our comprehension of language are not beliefs but something lower level. One might be tempted to suggest that these more basic states are perceptual, but that, I think, would be a mistake. Whatever the most basic informational states deployed in comprehension are, the same states are also deployed in speech production: *modulo* the obvious sorts of context-dependence, a normal speaker hears a sentence uttered by other people as meaning just what she would mean by it were she to utter it herself, and that is because some single piece of information is being deployed both times. This informational state may be a belief, but it could, for all I've said, be of some more basic sort. This possibility does not, it seems to me, pose any real threat to the cognitive conception. The core of the cognitive conception is the claim that understanding an utterance is having information about what the uttered sentence means on that occasion. If having such information is not having a belief, nothing essential will have been lost.

V   Language and Thought: An Objection

McDowell's remark that learning a language is "becoming minded" (McDowell 1998c: 105) is rooted in his desire to reject the view that understanding a language involves tagging concepts one already has with words.[35] One might worry that the cognitive conception will commit us to some such view, in particular, that it implies that language acquisition presupposes an antecedent and therefore language-independent grasp of the thoughts expressed by our sentences. My own view is that we often do antecedently grasp the thoughts expressed by our sentences and then learn what words express them. But it is clear enough that not all of language acquisition is like that. Soames offers the following example. I have many beliefs about Pluto, for example, that it is a distant planet. But I have had no direct contact with Pluto. My beliefs are wholly mediated by representations of the planet, most importantly, by the name "Pluto." Before I became familiar with the name "Pluto," I was not able to entertain thoughts about Pluto, be they that Pluto is a planet or that "Pluto" denotes Pluto. If so, then coming to understand the name cannot have involved connecting it with a concept I antecedently possessed (Soames 1988: 198–9).[36]

All of that must surely be acknowledged. But what follows? Soames wants to conclude that my coming to understand the name "Pluto" cannot have involved my coming to know that "Pluto" denotes Pluto. On the contrary, he says, my knowledge that "Pluto" denotes Pluto *depends upon* my understanding the name, since it is only once I understand it that I can so much as entertain the thought that "Pluto" denotes Pluto. It is thus my understanding that explains my belief, not my belief that explains my understanding. The argument thus leads to a conclusion similar to the one that motivates the Use View.

But all that follows immediately is that our ability to entertain certain thoughts, our coming to grasp certain concepts, may be *coeval* with our coming to understand words or sentences by means of which they can be expressed. In itself, that poses no threat to the cognitive conception. If understanding a sentence S consists in knowing that S means that p, then coming to understand S must at least involve coming to be able to entertain the thought that p. In some cases, this ability may precede our understanding of S; in others, the ability to entertain the thought that p may arise only as a result of the process by which we come to understand the sentence S. All of this I find deeply perplexing, but I do not find it worrying.

We can, and often do, learn what a word means by being told. If I point to one of the curved bits of wood making up the rib of a ship and tell someone, "That is a futtock," she might thereby come to learn what "futtock" means; henceforth, she can use it appropriately. I have certainly taught her how to use the word, but I have done so *by* teaching her what it means. We can see this as follows. The recipient of the explanation – call her Sue – need not have had the concept *futtock* already, but there is no mystery about how my explanation conveys it to her: I've called her attention to a kind of object in such a way that she was led to form a concept of that kind of thing, which concept she takes to be expressed by the word "futtock." Obviously, Sue's acquiring the concept *futtock*, rather than some other concept, is necessary if she is to come to understand (and be able correctly to use) the word "futtock": if she thinks I am pointing to the bit of wood as an example of a big wooden part of a ship and so forms the concept *cuttock* (meaning roughly: any big wooden part of a ship), then she does not understand the word "futtock"; she has to form the right concept. On the other hand, if Sue does form the concept *futtock*, then, although she does so in reaction to my explanation of the word "futtock," her newly formed concept is independent of how she expresses it. Sue might wonder whether she has in fact understood the explanation as it was intended and so wonder whether, as she would put it, "futtock" really means *futtock*. And if she has misunderstood, her new concept may survive: she will not then have any word to express it and might wonder whether there is any word by means of which it can be expressed. The fact that Sue acquired her concept of a futtock in reaction to my explanation of the word "futtock" should thus give us no reason to suppose that her understanding of this word does not consist in her knowing that "futtock" means *futtock*.

This example is, to be sure, different in many ways from the one Soames discusses. His example concerns linguistic deference and, more generally, raises issues connected with individualism, whereas mine does not. But the point of my example is not to prove that there are no problems here: there are plenty. The point of my example is to illustrate how one might come to grasp a concept through one's learning a word but do so in such a way that one's understanding of the word can still consist in one's knowing what concept it expresses. If that is possible, then Soames is simply too quick to conclude from the agreed facts about "Pluto" that our understanding it cannot consist in our knowledge that "Pluto" denotes Pluto. The process of acquiring the name might put us in a position to entertain thoughts about Pluto, including the thought that "Pluto" denotes Pluto, and our acceptance of this thought as true might yet constitute our understanding the name.

The real issue here, it seems to me, is how acquiring the name "Pluto" puts one in a position to entertain thoughts about its referent – how becoming competent with a linguistic expression can lead to possession of a concept. This is a hard problem, and I am not going to solve it here. My goal here is only to show that it is not a *hopeless* problem for defenders of the cognitive conception. What follows is thus a sketch of a view. Do not expect a defense of it.

Suppose Smith says, "It is a distant planet," but that Jones has just entered the conversation and has no idea what the referent or antecedent of Smith's use of "it" might be. Jones, then, cannot understand what Smith has said; that is, he does not know which proposition Smith expressed. But he certainly does know that Smith is talking about some object or other, and he can perfectly well wonder which object that might be. Now, the concept *the object about which Smith is talking* is one Jones can form at this point. If he wishes, he can even introduce a name for this object, saying, "Henceforth, in my language, 'Mysterion' refers to the object about which Smith is talking." And henceforth Jones's language really does contain the name "Mysterion," denoting the object about which Smith was talking, whatever it might be, and Jones *knows* that it denotes the object about which Smith was talking.

As time goes on, Jones might forget how he introduced the name "Mysterion." That need not deprive the name of reference:[37] Jones did not introduce "Mysterion" as an abbreviation of "the object about which Smith was talking" but as a name of the object (whichever it is) about which Smith was talking. So suppose Jones does forget. In his mouth, the name "Mysterion" still refers to the object about which Smith was talking. He no longer knows, of course, that "Mysterion" denotes the object about which Smith was talking on that since forgotten occasion, so his understanding the name cannot consist in his knowing that it does. But he certainly does still know that "Mysterion" denotes Mysterion, and I see no reason, in the description of the example, to doubt that his understanding the name now consists in his knowing precisely that fact: that "Mysterion" denotes Mysterion. Indeed, his understanding the name has, or so I would argue, always consisted in his knowing that "Mysterion" denotes Mysterion.

The case is no different if what Smith says is "Pluto is a distant planet." Then, too, Jones might introduce a name "Mysterion" to refer to the object Smith calls "Pluto."[38] And the case is no different if, instead of introducing a name "Mysterion" into his language, he decides to introduce the name "Pluto."[39] If Jones should forget how he introduced the name, then the following might simultaneously be true: his only contact with "Pluto" is mediated by representations of it, in particular, by uses of the name "Pluto"; he can entertain thoughts about Pluto only as a result of his exposure to sentences containing the name "Pluto"; and yet his competence with the name "Pluto" consists in his knowing that "Pluto" denotes Pluto.

Not that there isn't more that needs saying. But that is enough to show that examples like Soames's yield no knock-down objection to the cognitive conception.[40]

Notes

1   I shall write mostly of speech, since that is the most basic form of language-use, but some of the examples will be of other forms of language-use and I mean to include them within the scope of these remarks.
2   All of these are now collected in Dummett (1993a).
3   Most interestingly, it does not appear in Dummett (1991), although the lectures on which the book was based date from about the same time as "What is a Theory of Meaning?"
4   The point of this qualification has been obscure to some readers: It is intended simply to register the fact that one's linguistic knowledge does not concern only utterances that are actually made.
5   See Heck (2006b). There are many senses in which we are idealizing here. One is that we will not so much as consider phenomena related to compositionality. How precisely these impinge on our subject is a very important, and much neglected, question, but it is one I shall also have to leave for another time: see Heck (2006d) and n.19.
6   This seems also to be the point of Dummett's "barely intelligible fantasy," Dummett (1991: 89–91).
7   For a discussion with which I'm sympathetic, see Stanley (2000).
8   This example is, in one respect, different from the preceding one, in so far as it concerns so-called "generalized" conversational implicatures. The phenomenon in which I'm interested here seems to be more pervasive with generalized implicatures than it is with particularized ones, but it arises in both cases. It's worth considering Grice's various examples with the distinction I'm trying to draw in mind: both example (3), on p. 32, and example (1b), on pp. 33–4, seem not to require the speaker to have any

particular intention to communicate what is implicated. Other examples perhaps do, such as examples (1) and (2), on p. 32.

9 Or, at least, that one has no good reason, or insufficiently good reason, to believe (2), but let us leave this qualification aside.

10 To my mind, this is the central insight of Davidson's work on metaphor (Davidson 1984), though he overshoots the mark when he claims that metaphors are not used to communicate anything at all.

11 My reason for not accepting Gauker's position is as follows. Gauker works hard to show that one *need not* appeal to claims about what the speaker might have meant to say, etc., to determine the relevant implicatures. To argue for this claim, he offers alternative accounts of how one might arrive at these implicatures without appealing to psychological claims about the speaker. But he does not argue, and I do not see how he could argue, that such appeal *must* be out of bounds: I do not see that there could be any reason to deny a speaker the *right* to appeal to whatever she might know about her conversational partners to determine implicatures, including what they might have wished to say. But then I do not see that Gauker has given us any reason to doubt that ordinary speakers *do in fact* appeal to what they know about their conversational partners' psychologies when they calculate implicatures. And, indeed, when reading letters of recommendation, I think of myself as trying to determine what the author believes (or what she meant to say), and I am prepared to deploy everything I know about the author's psychology to determine what she does believe (or meant to say). So much just seems obvious to me. There is no reason we must deny ourselves this way of discovering others' beliefs and limit ourselves to "situated inference."

12 It is, in fact, quite a difficult question just how the verbal intention should be characterized, but the issue can be set aside here.

13 Perhaps such agents would *be* telepaths: no one ever said that telepathy has no medium at all.

14 Precisely what it might be wrongly to believe that a word has a particular meaning is a question I consider in Heck (2006a).

15 One will, of course, typically appeal to contextual factors to determine what has been said in such a case. So, for example, if John utters the sentence "Fighting administrators can be distracting," then I will decide what John has thereby said on the basis of what, in the present context, it would make sense for him to be saying. But, or so I would claim, what John has actually said depends upon which of the two sentences so pronounced he has in fact uttered. That, in turn, depends upon facts about the causal genesis of the sounds he uttered – facts about his linguistic intentions, perhaps, or facts about the logical form assigned to the sentence by his language faculty – and such facts are not always available to me.

16 I do not, at this point, mean to rule out the possibility that the verbal description is the most basic one, intentionally speaking: speech is intentional, on this view, primarily as the utterance of a sentence and only derivatively as the expression of a proposition. I shall return to this issue.

17 As we shall see below, the view to which I shall ultimately commit myself is non-committal about the identity of the informational states involved here. But I shall speak primarily in terms of beliefs. I shall sometimes speak – as is customary in the literature – of *knowledge* of meaning, but that is certainly incorrect. It may be that understanding what someone has said, in a sense that contrasts primarily with misunderstanding what she has said, requires knowledge of what she has said. Indeed, I think it does. But what is at issue here is not the nature of understanding as opposed to misunderstanding but the nature of understanding or misunderstanding as opposed to not understanding at all. Whether a speaker is right or wrong about what an expression means, or whether she has the right sorts of grounds for a true belief, is neither here nor there as far as the explanation of her linguistic actions is concerned. See Heck (2006a) and Pettit (2002) for discussion of some related issues.

18 See Heck (2006b) for discussion of that issue.

19 I say "reasonably" competently, because there could be differences between me and native French speakers, if *all* I knew was what sentences of French meant in context. These differences are connected with issues about compositionality. These complications do not, however, matter for present purposes.

20 Paul Horwich holds a similar view. See Horwich (1998).

21 The example originates in Wiggins (1972).

22 For one version both of the initial reply and the deeper worry, see Dummett (1993c), which contains an extensive discussion of this distinction. As noted, Soames presses a similar point.

23 For further discussion of the status of such sentences as (3) – or, more precisely, of the T-sentences that are analogs of them – see Heck (2004, 2006c).

24 The fact that our discussion should reach this point is reason for confidence: Donnellan deploys much the same sort of machinery in connection with more familiar cases of the contingent a priori. See Donnellan (1977).

25 Chomsky has pressed this objection in several places. For one, see Chomsky (1980: 51ff.).

26 See Chomsky (1980: 102ff., 1986, 270ff.) for discussion of this same point. To a large extent, my purpose here is to explain in what sense it is important that knowledge of language should be conscious. *Contra* both Dummett and Chomsky, I am arguing, there is no reason one cannot accept that claim while also insisting that linguistic competence consists in certain sorts of tacit or unconscious knowledge.

27 Similar points are made in McDowell (1998a, 1998b). As I remarked earlier, on my reading, Dummett actually abandons this view by about 1978, but the interpretive issue is not the important one here.

28 A point not unlike those to follow is made by David Lewis in Lewis (1985). Nonetheless, however, Lewis's own view is, I think, vulnerable to similar criticisms, for which see Heck (2006b).

29 Davidson's own response to this problem would be to invoke the alleged interdependence of meaning and belief. I argue elsewhere (Heck 2006b) that, to deploy that view in the present dialectical context, one must accept that mentality too supervenes on use. Davidson held such a view, but I find it extremely unappealing.

30 I also do not agree with McDowell that these observations (and the rationality of language more generally) must preclude any reductive account of linguistic meaning. That is in part because I reject the assumption that there is no account of the content of thought independent of an account of the content of language. Given that assumption – one McDowell shares with Dummett, who is his target in most of the remarks I'm considering – the conclusion is reasonable, but even then I am not sure it is forced. See Heck (2006c) for my reasons.

31 McDowell himself has often emphasized these similarities, and corresponding similarities between the Use View and sense-datum theories. It is in part for this reason that I believe he probably does intend the Direct View to be an alternative to the cognitive conception. For my own part, however, I believe that here, as elsewhere, he either too quickly dismisses or simply overlooks available alternatives: the cognitive conception, in this case, and theories that take perceptual content to be non-conceptual, in that one. See Heck (2000) for some reflections on the latter question.

32 In earlier drafts, I found myself writing that we are able to put our thoughts into words because we know what words would express our thoughts. In some sense, that is true, but it actually seems to me to get things backwards. To speak, I do indeed need to figure out what sentence, in this context, will express the thought I wish to communicate. But I sometimes find it difficult to do that, and I do not think that impugns my *competence*. The difference is much like that between recognition and recall, in the theory of memory. Indeed, it may well be the same difference: when I am in such circumstances, I am still quite capable of *recognizing* the sentence that would express my thought; I am having trouble *recalling* it. On the other hand, in putting one's thought into words, one does not typically consider candidate sentences and decide which of them expresses one's thought. That is why one can completely fail to notice that the sentence by means of which one did decide to express a thought was ambiguous. It'd be nice to know just what to say here.

33 A similar conclusion seems to be reached in Lepore (1997).

34 Note that the claim is that perception is sometimes so affected. That does not contradict the familiar fact that visual illusions are persistent.

35 In a similar spirit, McDowell writes that the central problem here is "to understand how the mindedness of a community, embodied in its linguistic institutions, comes to realize itself in an individual consciousness" (McDowell 1998c: 107).

36   Note that Soames need not (and should not) claim that I *could not* have been able to entertain such
     thoughts before encountering the name "Pluto," only that I was not. The issue is thus broadly
     empirical.
37   In my own view, it *could* deprive the name of reference, depending on the details of the case: see Gareth
     Evans's discussion of similar sorts of cases in Evans (1982: ch. 3). But that issue is orthogonal to this
     one.
38   Remember that Jones is not introducing the name as an abbreviation for a description. That insulates
     this sketch from objections of the sort Kripke brings against an otherwise similar-sounding proposal
     in Kripke (1980: 68–73).
39   One might observe that my treatment of these examples depends upon keeping it clear whose word we
     are discussing, and not simply talking about *the* word "Pluto." It may well be, in the end, that the threat
     such examples seem to pose to the cognitive conception depends upon our neglecting the difference
     between how someone understands her words and what they mean in a presumed "public language."
40   Thanks to Kent Bach, Robert May, and Brett Sherman for comments on earlier drafts and to Tony
     Corsentino, Michael Rescorla, and Cathy Wearing for discussions about these issues that were particu-
     larly helpful. Conversations over the years with Jason Stanley were, as usual, important to the develop-
     ment of my views. Thanks also to the members of the various classes and seminars at Harvard
     University in which these ideas germinated and grew. A talk based upon an early draft was read to the
     Harvard-MIT Graduate Philosophy Conference in March 2000. Thanks to everyone who attended, but
     especially to Bob Hale, for their reactions. I presented a much later version of this material at the Uni-
     versity of St Andrews in January and February 2004, while I was a British Academy Visiting Professor.
     Thanks to all who attended and participated for their comments and encouragement. Remarks by Daniel
     Nolan, Agustin Rayo, and Crispin Wright were especially helpful. Thanks to the British Academy and
     to Arché, the AHRC Research Centre for the Philosophy of Logic, Language, Mathematics and Mind,
     for their support, which is much appreciated. Special thanks is due Crispin not only for arranging the
     visit but for his support and friendship over the years.

References

Chomsky, N. 1980. *Rules and Representations*, New York: Columbia University Press.
Chomsky, N. 1986. *Knowledge of Language: Its Origin, Nature, and Use*, Westport, Conn.: Praeger.
Chomsky, N. 1988. *Language and Problems of Knowledge*, Cambridge, Mass.: MIT Press.
Davidson, D. 1984. "What Metaphors Mean," in his *Inquiries Into Truth and Interpretation*, Oxford: Claren-
    don Press, 245–62.
Donnellan, K. 1966. "Reference and Definite Descriptions," *Philosophical Review* 75: 281–304.
Donnellan, K. 1977. "The Contingent a priori and Rigid Designators," *Midwest Studies in Philosophy* 2:
    12–27.
Dummett, M. 1991. *The Logical Basis of Metaphysics*, Cambridge, Mass.: Harvard University Press.
Dummett, M. 1993a. *The Seas of Language*, Oxford: Clarendon Press.
Dummett, M. 1993b. "What Do I Know When I Know a Language?", in Dummett (1993a), 94–105.
Dummett, M. 1993c. "What is a Theory of Meaning? (I)," in Dummett (1993a), 1–33.
Evans, G. 1982. *The Varieties of Reference*, Oxford: Clarendon Press.
Gauker, C. 2001. "Situated Inference versus Conversational Implicature," *Nous* 35: 163–89.
Grice, H. 1989a. "Logic and Conversation," in Grice (1989b), 22–40.
Grice, H. 1989b. *Studies in the Ways of Words*, Cambridge, Mass.: Harvard University Press.
Heck, R. 2000. "Non-Conceptual Content and the 'Space of Reasons'," *Philosophical Review* 109: 483–523.
Heck, R. 2004. "Truth and Disquotation," *Synthèse* 142: 317–52.
Heck, R. 2006a. "Idiolects," forthcoming, in A. Byrne and J. Thomson (eds.), *Content and Modality: Themes
    from the Philosophy of Robert Stalnaker*, New York, Oxford University Press.

Heck, R. 2006b. "Meaning and Truth-Conditions," forthcoming, in D. Greimann and G. Siegwart, *Truth and Speech Acts: Studies in the Philosophy of Language*, New York: Routledge.

Heck, R. 2006c. "Use and Meaning," forthcoming, in L. Hahn (ed.), *The Philosophy of Michael Dummett*, Chicago: Open Court.

Heck, R. 2006d. "What is Compositionality?," manuscript.

Horwich, P. 1998. *Meaning*, Oxford: Clarendon Press.

Kripke, S. 1977. "Speaker's Reference and Semantic Reference," *Midwest Studies in Philosophy* 2: 255–76.

Kripke, S. 1980. *Naming and Necessity*, Cambridge, Mass.: Harvard University Press.

Lepore, E. 1997. "Conditions on Understanding Language," *Proceedings of the Aristotelian Society* 97: 41–60.

Lewis, D. 1985. "Radical Interpretation," in *Philosophical Papers Volume 1*, Oxford: Oxford University Press, 108–18.

McDowell, J. 1998a. "Another Plea for Modesty," in McDowell (1998e), 108–31.

McDowell, J. 1998b. "Anti-Realism and the Epistemology of Understanding," in McDowell (1998e), 314–43.

McDowell, J. 1998c. "In Defence of Modesty," in McDowell (1998e), 87–107.

McDowell, J. 1998d. "Meaning, Communication, and Knowledge," in McDowell (1998e), 29–50.

McDowell, J. 1998e. *Meaning, Knowledge, and Reality*, Cambridge, Mass.: Harvard University Press.

McDowell, J. 1998f. "Truth-Conditions, Bivalence, and Verificationism," in McDowell (1998e), 3–28.

Neale, S. 1990. *Descriptions*, Cambridge, Mass.: MIT Press.

Pettit, D. 2002. "Why Knowledge is Unnecessary for Understanding," *Mind* 111: 519–50.

Soames, S. 1988. "Semantics and Semantic Competence," in S. Schiffer and S. Stelle (eds.), *Cognition and Representation*, Boulder, Colo.: Westview Press, 185–207.

Stanley, J. 2000. "Context and Logical Form," *Linguistics and Philosophy* 23: 391–434.

Wiggins, D. 1972. "On Sentence-Sense, Word-Sense, and Differences of Word-Sense," in D. Steinberg and L. Jokobovits (eds.), *Semantics*, Cambridge: Cambridge University Press, 14–34.

Response to Richard G. Heck, Jr.

1   I am not convinced that Heck is fair to Grice.

As he in effect acknowledges, the concept of rationality gets a grip on behavior just to the extent that the concept of being intentional does. We make rational sense of behavior by finding a description under which it is intentional, which requires us to appreciate how the agent's rationality might have been operative in leading her to see *that* – here we fill in that description – as in some way worth doing.

It is surely true, as Heck urges, that making rational sense of someone else's behavior can lead us to attribute certain beliefs to her without taking her behavior to be intentional under any description that includes inducing us, or any audience of her performance, to attribute those beliefs to her. And Heck is surely at liberty to use the concept of implicating in such a way that the agent's performance, or the agent, in such a case implicates that things are as making sense of her performance requires us to suppose she believes they are.

The Gricean notion is different. According to the Gricean notion, a speaker implicates that things are thus and so only if she intends to induce in an audience a belief that she believes that things are thus and so. Grice is interested in a notion of implication in which implicating is essentially intentional under that description, like telling a lie. Contrast asserting a falsehood, which, like implicating on Heck's competing account, may or may not be intentional under that description.

Heck claims that his notion is more fundamental than Grice's. And in one sense that is unquestionable. The intentional activity Grice is interested in is feasible only because speakers know that audiences will try to make rational sense of their activity, and that that will involve attributing beliefs to them. Heck says this knowledge, on the part of a speaker, "that others recognize his speech as rational . . . is the source of whatever communicative intentions he may have." This seems an odd use of the word "source." Communicative intentions (in this Gricean sense) surely have their source in whatever purposes underlie a speaker's goal of getting an audience to form beliefs about her beliefs. But it is true that there can be such intentions only thanks to the known role of belief-attribution in making rational sense of action in general. So it is true that a Gricean implicator intentionally exploits the more general possibility that one can induce beliefs in audiences by an action that need not be intentional under that description. And in that sense the weaker notion is more basic, as Heck says.

But is this a ground for an objection to Grice? Can we say Grice should have focused on a conception of implicating captured by the weaker notion?

In the most obvious case of telling a lie – a kind of action that is essentially intentional under that description – one asserts a falsehood, that is, one performs a kind of action that is not necessarily intentional under that description, but one does so intentionally. (One can also lie by asserting the truth, if one takes what one says to be false. A lie is an assertion contrary to one's mind, not necessarily contrary to the facts. But I shall consider only the kind of lying that consists in intentionally asserting what are in fact falsehoods.) In something like Heck's sense, the notion of asserting a falsehood, not necessarily intentionally, is more basic, because weaker, than the notion of the kind of lying that consists in intentionally asserting a falsehood. If asserting a falsehood – something that may or may not be intentional under that description – were not a possible performance, there could not be intentions to exploit that possibility. But it does not follow that a philosopher ought not to be interested in the kind of lying that consists in intentionally asserting falsehoods, as opposed to being interested in merely asserting falsehoods. And it remains correct to say lying is essentially intentional. I cannot see that Heck's parallel point about weaker and stronger concepts tells any more strongly against Grice's focus on cases in which speakers intentionally induce beliefs in audiences, or against the way he reserves "implicating" as a label for actions of that sort.

I have so far bypassed Heck's point that what is implicated is typically not some particular proposition. It would be wrong to specify what is implicated, in the case of the taciturn testimonial, as the proposition that the student is a poor student, as opposed to the proposition that he is poorly prepared for graduate study, or the proposition that he should not be admitted to graduate school.

Now perhaps some of Grice's formulations suggest something to the contrary. But this seems inessential. Heck's weaker notion is the notion of bringing it about, not necessarily intentionally, that one's audience attributes some belief to one. Working with this notion, we still need to conceive what is implicated by the author of the taciturn testimonial, not as some one particular proposition from among those and perhaps other candidates, but as an unspecific content in the general area indicated by those propositions. What is implicated is that something of that kind is the case, not some particular thing of that kind. And this device, which Heck needs, seems perfectly available to Grice too. A Gricean implicator can intend that her audience take her to have a belief in some general area rather than a belief individuated by its having some particular proposition as its content, so here too what is implicated can be unspecific. There is no obvious connection between communicative intentions, in the Gricean sense, and specificity of content.

2   Heck urges that occurrent understanding of an utterance – which is required alike for comprehending utterances of others and for intentionally making utterances oneself – "consists in one's knowing what the uttered sentence means on that occasion of use." He emphasizes that he is not, at any rate in this chapter, arguing for a cognitive conception of understanding a language considered as a standing state; say, that understanding a language consists in knowledge, which would have to be tacit, of a semantic theory for the language. The knowledge his present thesis concerns is knowledge non-tacitly possessed on occasions of utterance, and perhaps also when one explicitly considers possible utterances,[1] not knowledge tacitly possessed all the time, extending to possible utterances that one is not even contemplating, let alone making or witnessing. For present purposes the standing state can be conceived as the ability, or whatever categorical state of a person underlies the ability, to have that non-tacit occurrent knowledge on occasions when one makes, witnesses, or contemplates utterances.

This is just as well, since it means I need not take issue with the thesis, which Heck endorses but is not here defending, that the standing state – command of a language – is, or at least depends on, tacit knowledge of a semantic theory for the language. For my part I think this is no improvement over conceiving the standing state as the ability to have all those bits of occurrent knowledge. But that is not something I need to argue here.

Heck argues that acts of speech are intentional not only under propositional descriptions (say, telling one's wife she has a bit of spinach on her front teeth) but also under verbal descriptions (say, uttering the words "You have a bit of spinach on your front teeth"). And the two sorts of descriptions are rationally related. In my example, my intention is to utter the words "You have a bit of spinach on your front teeth" *in order to* tell my wife she has a bit of spinach on her front teeth. (Heck has a less prosaic example.)

According to Heck, the cognitive conception of occurrent understanding is motivated, but not established, by these considerations. To establish it, he says, he needs to argue against possible alternatives: the Use View and the Direct View. I find this account of the dialectic of his chapter puzzling. So far as I can see, the Use View is inconsistent with holding that speech-acts are intentional under propositional descriptions, and the Direct View is inconsistent with holding that they are intentional under verbal descriptions. And if that is right those views are already excluded by Heck's reflections about the descriptions under which speech-acts are intentional.

3   Heck sees me as an ally against the Use View, but perhaps (he is uncertain about this) a proponent of the Direct View. But it strikes me as unquestionable that speech-acts are intentional under verbal descriptions, and, as I said, the Direct View seems to be inconsistent with that. I think the Direct View is no less misguided than the Use View. In n.31, Heck says I emphasize similarities between the Direct View and Direct Realist views of perception, and he cites this as a ground for finding it probable that I endorse the Direct View. But I do not discuss the Direct View – the view that "the ability to put one's thought into words in no way depends upon one's knowing what one's words do, or would, mean on various occasions of utterance" – at all, let alone emphasize similarities between it and Direct Realist views of perception. What is true is that I take the epistemology of knowing what others are doing, under propositional descriptions, to be perceptual, and I take perception, quite generally, to be direct – non-inferential – access to what is perceptually known to be the case. But as Heck's own discussion makes clear, there is no good

inference from this to the conclusion that speakers and comprehending hearers are not consciously aware of the words uttered as well as of what propositional performances are being undertaken. Conceding that a comprehending hearer is consciously aware of the words uttered does not commit one to supposing the hearer's knowledge of what is being said must be inferentially based on that awareness.

4   Heck distances himself from my remark that learning a language is becoming minded, as opposed to acquiring a way of giving expression to states of mind one already had. He thinks this claim is "optional at this point in the dialectic." Now no doubt that is correct about the dialectic of his chapter. But this just brings out a divergence between Heck's dialectic and the dialectic of my engagements with Michael Dummett, which is the context in which I make that remark.

The closest Heck comes to my dialectic is to line up some of what I say against Dummett with his own opposition to the Use View. This is, at least potentially, a bit misleading. The Use View holds that "the ability to use [a] language does not itself rest upon possession of conscious knowledge of the meanings of sentences of that language." And that was never Dummett's claim, even in "What is a Theory of Meaning ? (II)," where the idea that command of a language is a practical ability is prominent.[2] Dummett's idea, there and elsewhere, is that it must be possible to say *what it is* to have the knowledge that constitutes understanding sentences – knowledge that surely must come to consciousness when a sentence is uttered or explicitly considered – by crediting speakers with a practical ability whose exercises are specified otherwise than by way of propositional descriptions of speech-acts. The last bit of this involves a kind of correspondence with an aspect of Heck's Use View. But Dummett does not deny that the use of sentences is informed by conscious knowledge of their meaning. Dummett's thought is just that what it is to have that knowledge must be spelled out in other terms.

Against this, I argue that given a characterization of what speakers do in the terms we are restricted to by Dummett's requirement, it could be no better than a hypothesis for a hearer that some speaker is engaging in some speech-act described in propositional terms. I take it that this is what Heck reads as evidence that I favor the Direct View. But my point is to argue against the idea that performing speech-acts susceptible of propositional descriptions *consists in* activity describable in the restricted terms. There is no implication, as in the Direct View, that the restricted terms cannot so much as figure in specifying what comprehending hearers are consciously aware of.

It is Dummett's own doctrine that we must not suppose we can never have anything better than hypotheses about what others mean. (Of course that is sometimes the best we can have.) This brings out a feature of the dialectic of my engagement with Dummett. The engagement turns on my endorsing a fundamental feature of Dummett's thinking. On my reading, his conception of meaning and knowledge of meaning aims at a goal I applaud: steering a course between behaviorism, which downplays the significance of mindedness, and psychologism, which pictures the mental as an autonomous region of reality available to others only by way of inference from its outward manifestations. I argue that in making his restriction on the terms in which it must be possible to say what it is for speakers to know the meanings of sentences in a language, he defeats that admirable goal. It is in this dialectical context that I make the remark Heck distances himself from.

If someone does not agree with Dummett and me on the desirability of the middle course, it is unsurprising if thoughts I represent as compulsory in my dialectical context do not strike him as compulsory.[3] I surmise that something on these lines may fit Heck.

A closer dialectical context for the remark he objects to is another idea I accept from Dummett: that to avoid psychologism we must avoid conceiving language as a code for giving outward expression to thoughts, taken to be what they are independently of this possibility of expressing them. Heck accepts that understanding the speech of others is perception of what they mean. So his thinking is free of the gross psychologism involved in the "hypothesis" conception. But he does not explicitly discuss Dummett's strictures on the code conception, and some of what he says suggests that, apart from special cases like the "Pluto"-Pluto example, he sees nothing wrong with it. If so, it is not surprising that he sees nothing compulsory about a conception of mindedness as acquired with the acquisition of language rather than given an outlet by it. Of course an argument from Dummett's authority cannot show that it is right to reject the code conception. The point for now is just that Heck would need to address the details of *my* dialectic if he were to justify rejecting my remark on the ground that "the" dialectic does not require it.

Notes and References

1 As when one considers what an utterance of some sentence would mean; see Heck's n.4.
2 Heck cites the first "What is a Theory of Meaning?" paper in this connection, but the second is more to the point. See Dummett's self-critical remarks about that paper in the Preface to *The Seas of Language*, Oxford: Clarendon Press, ix–xii.
3 I register this, in effect, in n.28 (p. 97) to "In Defence of Modesty," in *Meaning, Knowledge, and Reality*, Cambridge, Mass.: Harvard University Press, 1998.

3

Some Philosophical Integrations

Akeel Bilgrami

I   Introduction

I would like to pursue some integrating implications of John McDowell's inspiring opposition to the prevalent naturalism of our time. (Because he is careful not to discard the term "naturalism" in describing his own philosophical views, I have been careful to say the "prevalent" naturalism to describe the set of doctrines he opposes, but from now on I will cease being careful and drop the qualification.)

By "integrating," I mean that I will try to link in this essay different themes and issues in the philosophy of mind and value on which McDowell has written, with a view to revealing a certain thematic and argumentative unity that is possible within the range of "anti-naturalist" ideas he has explored. It is not obvious to me – and I would be curious to know – whether he himself thinks that this rather specific integrity is implicitly present in his own thinking on the subject, or whether he thinks that the relations between these elements are more miscellaneous and less radically unified than I present them. The four themes I have in mind to integrate are: (a) the possibility of value in a world of natural facts; (b) the possibility of freedom and agency in a deterministic universe; (c) the possibility of intentionality within the physical and causal states of a central nervous system; and (d) the special nature of the knowledge and the perspective we have on our own thoughts, i.e., the special nature of first-personal or self-knowledge.

In presenting these integrations, I will necessarily have to be quite brief on this range of topics, each of which needs much more extensive treatment. The project here is to deal with each of these elements only as they come together to form a single and highly integrated thematic, not as separate topics intended for the sort of discussion each of them deserve. I will be briefest on the first two integrations (summarized in the next two sections) since they recapitulate material that I have published elsewhere.[1]

II   Of Agency with Value

The first integration is of agency with value. A good starting point in this would be to register McDowell's sympathetic appeal to Kant's location of the very concept of freedom and agency ("spontaneity" to use McDowell's Kantian term) in the realm or "space" (to use McDowell's Sellarsian term) of *Reason*.

This location is easy to lose sight of, when one approaches the subject of freedom in contexts of discussion that are purely metaphysical, that is, in contexts where one simply asks: "How is freedom possible in a deterministic universe?" When the question is underdescribed in this way, despairing answers denying its possibility, as well as stubbornly libertarian answers asserting its existence on the basis of "contra-causal" gaps in the universe, both proceed as if the normative realm of reasons was beside the point. All that is seen as relevant is the question of whether to allow or disallow these gappy states in our causal framework, with intricate and sophisticated analysis of whether things, in particular our doings, "could (or could not) have been otherwise" as determining the right answer.

It helped a little but not enough that with someone like Hume,[2] a more ecumenical (later sometimes describing itself as "compatibilist") answer was offered than the two I have just mentioned. When Hume said that causality *in itself* did not threaten the idea of freedom, only *some* coercive and compulsive causes did, he raised a possibility that he did not himself pursue to its end. He failed to pursue it because he never thoroughly investigated *what it is about* coercive causes that made them coercive, since coerciveness does not seem to be something we can read off from a scrutiny of just the causes themselves. He simply gave examples and left it to our intuition to grasp the difference. And, worse, Hume's own framework for thinking of the examples he himself gave of non-coercive causes of our actions – causes such as our beliefs and desires, and intentional states generally – was so resolutely psychologistic and dispositional that it is hard to see why any determined incompatibilist would see them as allowing for agency and freedom at all.

When, much more recently, P. F. Strawson[3] offered a framework for the discussion of freedom in which our reactive attitudes of *evaluation* were brought on to centre stage, we not only got an answer to the question that Hume did not pursue (to put it crudely and summarily, the answer was: those causes are coercive which cause actions to which we justifiably react with praise and blame, resentment and admiration, guilt and pride, etc.) but it became clear that freedom was in the space of *values* quite generally, whether those exercised in theoretical or in practical and moral reason. Our conclusions based on theoretical reason and our actions based on practical and moral reason are just the sort of things that can be evaluated. To cease being evaluators and to cease making the kinds of judgments and actions which are the justifiable objects of evaluation is just to become the kind of subject that falls outside of our talk of agency and freedom and spontaneity.

Thus Strawson directed us, for the first time in the discussion of the subject, to the insight that the coextensiveness of freedom with the space of deliberative reason (whether theoretical or practical) reaches all the way down to the space of values or evaluation. This normative nature of agency is in fact more radical than Strawson himself quite realized. For his tendency was to rest complacently with thoughts such as that we could not but be the kinds of creatures who had reactive evaluative attitudes. That is just how we are. So, also, he is inclined to rest with the thought that it would just simply be conceptually inappropriate to resent and blame a cat for urinating on the furniture or a piano for being untuned. That is just how things are. But I think these cannot be the resting points. If we are the kinds of creatures who are evaluative that is not some sort of transcendental description of us; it is because our further values tell us that we should be (and continue to be) such creatures. Equally it is not just some kind of conceptual inappropriateness to blame and resent cats and pianos; it is an appropriateness indicated by further values we possess.[4] Thus, as philosophers like to say, it is values all the way down and it is these values that constitute our agency, and it is these very values of ours that underlie our refusal to grant agency to cats and pianos.[5]

It is worth repeating that this integrating of the talk of freedom and the "space of reasons" with the applicability and exercise of evaluative attitudes and reactions allows one to see the "space of reasons" as broadly as it deserves: that is, as including within it not just theoretical but practical and moral reason as well. And, conversely, it allows one to correct a narrowing impression going in the other direction in Strawson's rhetoric and examples, i.e. it allows one to say that when it comes to something as general as agency and freedom, the scope of value need not be restricted to moral reason either. The evaluative reactions we justifiably have to the deliverances of theoretical reasoning place them just as much within the domain of agency and freedom as the responses we have to conclusions of moral and practical deliberation, even if they are not usually accompanied by the emotive states (such as "resentment") which surface most prominently in Strawson's examples.

III   Of Self-Knowledge (and the First-Person Point of View) with Agency

If freedom and value are integrated in this way, it creates the prospect of a second kind of integration having to do with seemingly more distant issues of self-knowledge and of the first-person perspective or point of view, quite generally.

What this idea of agency – as constituted in normative terms by the relevance of the evaluative attitudes – makes possible is a way (if not *the* way) of understanding and accounting for the philosophical basis of our own intuitions regarding the special character of our knowledge of our own intentional states. This special character has two aspects: transparency and authority. I will focus on transparency in this section and turn to authority in the last section, once yet another integration is in place.

Transparency is a property of intentional states, a property not possessed by other sorts of objects of other sorts of knowledge, such as, for instance, the facts and objects in the external environment, knowledge of which requires cognitive acts of looking and seeing. Therefore when one says that self-knowledge is transparent, one is saying that self-knowledge is a cognitively effortless achievement.

When one says that self-knowledge is not (paradigmatically) the product of cognitive acts of seeing, looking, checking, etc., or to put it more explicitly, the product of any *inner version* of such cognitive acts, one has in mind to draw a contrast between knowledge from a first-person point of view and knowledge that comes from a third-person stance that we take upon ourselves. And it is arguable, I think, that the former kind of knowledge is a fall-out of the fact that our intentional states (paradigmatically) have deep analytical links with our agency, with our actions when they are justifiably the objects of the evaluative reactive attitudes. Agents may be rightly taken to believe that they have the first-order intentional states they have, not (paradigmatically) because they undertake or undergo some act of inner scanning, but because the very fact of their agency, *understood in these normative Strawsonian terms*, presupposes that they have these second-order beliefs. The basic idea here is that the evaluative reactive attitudes of blame, praise, resentment, and indignation, which we have seen to constitute the very notion of agency, are only appropriate or justified to the extent that those praised, blamed, and so on are presumed to have self-knowledge of the actions and deliberative conclusions that they are praised and blamed for – which implies in turn that they have self-knowledge of the states of mind which rationalize those actions, states of mind which give those actions the descriptions under which they are justifiably praised and blamed.

When self-knowledge is understood along these lines, the relation between the first-order intentional states and second-order beliefs about them which go into self-knowledge is a *conceptual* link, a link forged by the *background* fact of agency. It is not a *contingent* link forged by the causal-explanatory fact of activated causal-inner perceptual mechanisms in the *foreground*.

This is not necessarily to deny that there *can be* causal mechanisms linking these first- and second-order intentional states. It is only to deny that these causal links, if they exist, may be invoked to provide the causal-perceptual explanations of self-knowledge and its special character that many would like to provide. That is, it is to deny the reliabilist ways of explaining self-knowledge which go along the following lines: causal mechanisms link first-order intentional states with the second-order beliefs about them, and our intuitions about the transparency and authority of self-knowledge are just misleading ways of describing the superlative reliability of these mechanisms. Our intuitions about the special character of self-knowledge (captured in such terms as "transparency" and "authority") would not be all that special, if they were explained along these causal-perceptual lines. What makes it more special than this sort of account allows is the conceptual link between first-order states and second-order beliefs about them, afforded by a normative conception of agency. The idea is not that the conceptual links between the relevant first- and second-order states rule out any possibility of causal links between them. *The idea is rather that even in a world where there were no causal links, so long as there was agency there would be self-knowledge.* For the point is that links forged by causal mechanisms *could* always break down, that being the nature of mechanisms. But, *given agency (normatively understood)*, there is no question of the breakdown in the links between these states of first and second order.

That it is a *normative* conception of agency that makes possible these conceptual and non-contingent links implies that the following tempting thought is not open to us. It is tempting to say: let it be the case that agency is relevant to self-knowledge along these lines, but still in any particular case where someone believes that she has an intentional state, it is explained by a causal mechanism linking the intentional state to the belief about it. And yes, of course, there can be breakdowns of causal mechanisms, but those breakdowns will *coincide* with those cases where there is no agency in play.

This temptation becomes resistible as soon as one realizes that when the notion of agency is understood in normative terms, talk of such "coinciding" is absurd. The normative considerations involved in agency, as I said earlier, are the Strawsonian ones of justifiable reactive attitudes. Causal mechanisms are not sensitive to normative considerations of this sort. It would be absurd to think that such a mechanism would be operative or would break down with an eye to whether reactive attitudes of praise and blame are appropriate and justified. Far from "coinciding," there is a total failure of fit between the causal links being invoked as explanatory and the normative elements, which characterize agency.

The grounding I have just proposed for our intuitions about what marks out self-knowledge among the various knowledges we possess is entirely dependent on the first of the integrations I discussed in section II. And, being so, it affords us a second integration. How is this? The grounding provided depends indispensably, as I said, on a notion of agency that is thoroughly normative. A more purely metaphysical notion of agency and freedom, uninformed by the constitutively evaluative angle provided by the insightful Strawsonian point I relied on in section II, would not have the power to make the *internal conceptual* links between our intentional states and our self-knowledge of these states, which my grounding of our intuitions about self-knowledge appeals to. But with his insight in place, in turn putting in place these internal conceptual links, the grounding *itself integrates* with the prior integration of agency and value. *Three* things now – value, agency, and the special character of self-knowledge – are all of a piece.

If this is right, we can work our way in reverse from the points about the special character of self-knowledge back to value. What the second integration shows is that it is simply not possible to pull apart the special angle we have on ourselves – the first-person point of view – from what Kant, in the third section of his *Groundwork*, called the point of view of agency. And, moreover, if this integration owes to a prior integration of agency and value, then it is not possible to pull apart our evaluative lives (our exercise of norms in our reactions, as well as our actions and thoughts being the justifiable targets of such exercises) from the possession of an angle which each of us has only on ourselves and which no one else can have on us, and which is the basis of our agency.

I will return to the significance of this at the end of the chapter.

IV   Of Intentionality with Value

The special character of the first-person point of view and of self-knowledge, I have said, depends on a normative conception of agency, and so is integrated with a prior integration of agency with value that was first formulated by Strawson. In making this point I have: (1) restricted myself to self-knowledge of *intentional* states; but have (2) lifted the restriction (often found in discussions today of the special character of self-knowledge) to self-ascriptions of occurrent mental states made by their possessors in the present, often referred to by them as the "basic case."[6] This shouldn't be surprising since: (1) considerations of agency and value, unlike the other sorts of considerations philosophers have invoked to account for the special character of self-knowledge, apply more to intentional states such as beliefs and desires than to phenomenal states; but *as a result* (2) they also therefore apply across the board to all beliefs and desires, whether one is actually explicitly self-ascribing them in the present, as in the "basic case," or not.

Some attention needs to be given now to the nature of *what* is self-known (intentional states) in this special way, since other sorts of objects of other sorts of knowledge, are not special in this regard.

Intentional states, according to current naturalistic ways of thinking about them, are dispositions of a complicated sort, linked with one another holistically, and at bottom causal states apt to be caused by certain kinds of inputs and apt to cause certain outputs, when they are so linked. McDowell has written with insight and critical power against such a view of intentionality,[7] invoking arguments first formulated by Davidson[8] that appeal to normative or evaluative considerations, and freeing those arguments from an unnecessary metaphysical context – defined by a specific kind of monism and a specifically Humean notion of cause – in which Davidson presents them.

The next integration I want to pursue here is the integration of *intentional states* with the notion of *value* that is so central to the Davidsonian argument McDowell invokes. Davidson himself does *not* make the integration, but there is no apparent reason why he should resist it, especially now that McDowell has freed his argument along the lines I have just mentioned. So I will argue.

To integrate intentional states with value is to see them as *themselves* being evaluative states – or "commitments," to use a word gaining some recent currency.[9] Desires[10] and beliefs, to stick with the paradigm examples of intentional states, are commitments. A desire is a commitment to do various things, which things being determined by the specific desire it is and its relation to other desires and beliefs. A belief is a commitment to believe various other things, which things being determined by the specific belief it is and by its relation to other beliefs. (I am unembarrassed by the fact that I am using the notion of belief to characterize what a belief qua commitment is, since

I am not trying to give an explicit definition.) Thus a desire that I pursue philosophy is a commitment to do various things, such as think about certain subjects, read and write certain sorts of books . . . ; a belief that there is a computer in front of me is a commitment to believe various things, such as that there is something in front of me . . .

One way of seeing how we can identify the very idea of an intentional state with a certain kind of value or commitment one has, is to see the (more or less) exact way it stands in contrast with the idea of a disposition as that idea is found in the standard naturalistic picture of intentionality mentioned earlier. The contrast is best revealed by an extension of Moore's "open-question" argument which was directed at moral values.

Moore famously argued that a naturalism about moral values which definitionally identifies goodness with a natural property – for instance, social aggregate utility understood in Benthamite terms – amounted to a fallacy because it disregarded the fact that one can raise the following sort of *non*-trivial question: "Here is an action (or rule) which has or promotes the highest social aggregate utility – is it good?" Unlike the question "Here is a bachelor – is he unmarried?", the former question is a non-trivial question, and that reveals in general just the sort of gap between values and the properties of nature that these naturalisms have disregarded. Moore's argument carries over without strain to naturalisms about intentionality, so long as their identification of intentional states with causal, dispositional states is definitional, as for instance with "analytic functionalism." Here, the non-trivial question whose possibility threatens the naturalism (taking a desire, for example) would be: "I have these dispositions to Φ, but *ought* I to Φ?" If this is a genuinely non-trivial question, then that is some sort of proof that the intentional state of desire is not these sorts of disposition but rather an internal ought of some kind.[11] In other words, a "commitment."

But Moorean arguments work only against definitional reductions. Against naturalisms about intentionality based on posited a posteriori identities between intentional states (thought of now as "commitments") and dispositional or physical states, a Fregean supplement to Moore is needed. One must like Frege point out that a person who denies that a posteriori identity is not irrational, merely ignorant of a worldly identity. And then, like Frege, one must ask what accounts for his rationality? The answer will have to invoke, as Frege did, the sense or the meaning or the definition of the terms involved. If that is so, then we must ask if the sense of the value-term "commitment" in the subject's denial of the a posteriori identity, expresses a natural property or a non-natural property. If the former, then the Moorean argument applies all over again because we are back in the terrain of definitions, and that is what Moore's argument was targeting. If the latter, we don't have a naturalistic reduction in the first place. So there is something like a pincer in effect in this argument. One begins with the Moorean hand and if there is a defection on the part of the naturalist to a more contemporary non-definitional version of the doctrine, there is the Fregean hand of the argument which either repudiates this version of it or forces it back to a more traditional definitional naturalism, vulnerable to the initial Moorean hand of the argument. Much more needs to be said about this pincer argument, which I have elsewhere,[12] so here I will only pursue its implications.

This three-punch Moore–Frege–Moore argument is vivid and clean, and it allows for a quite literal identification of intentional states with values (in the internal sense, of a subject's commitments). If there is a great distance between intentional states and dispositions naturalistically understood, it is the very same distance as that between values and the properties of nature.

The contrast between intentional states (qua commitments) and dispositions, which this extension of Moore's argument reveals, makes clear that one may have a commitment (take again, a desire) without doing anything that would count as living up to it, and (this is the point) one may have a commitment even if one lacked the *disposition* to do something that counts as living up to it. If that is right, it would be quite wrong to equate commitments in any simple way with dispositions. By "simple way," I mean equate them with the dispositions to do whatever would count as living up to the commitments.

However this does not mean that *no* sort of dispositions are relevant to characterizing commitments. It would be implausible to say that someone possesses a certain commitment if she lacks not only the first-order disposition to do what would count as a living up to it, but also lacks the following two sorts of higher-order dispositions: (1) the disposition to accept criticism for not doing or not having the disposition to do what it takes to live up to the commitment; and (2) the disposition to try and do better by way of living up to the commitment by, say, cultivating the first-order disposition to do what would count as living up to the commitment. If these higher-order dispositions were also lacking, it would be hard to say what distinguished someone who possesses that commitment from someone who lacked it.

But even if (1) and (2) are dispositions which go into the characterization of intentional states qua commitments, that gives no comfort to the naturalist about intentional states.

For one thing, there is no way to characterize these dispositions in a way that leaves out a mention of commitments. That is, there is no way to specify them independently of the fact that they are dispositions to accept criticism for not having lived up to a commitment or not having the disposition to live up to a commitment, or that they are dispositions to try and do better by way of living up to the commitment by, say, cultivating the disposition to do things which count as living up to the commitment. And the more fundamental point remains that, even if one tried to so characterize them, one would once again run afoul of the Moorean argument given above since the question would arise: I have all the dispositions, of various orders, so characterized, to Φ, but ought I to Φ?

For another thing, and relatedly, these second-order dispositions – unlike the first-order dispositions to do the things that count as living up to the commitment – are not part of the causal nexus that would suit them for a naturalistic understanding along functionalist lines. Let me explain.

It is a familiar point that the term "disposition" has a more and a less minimal characterization. Minimally, dispositions can be seen in terms of counterfactuals without the counterfactuals in any way getting a realist causal grounding along the lines of a familiar scientific realism. Ryle's notion of mental disposition as "inference tickets" was explicit about this mere and minimal understanding of them. To have a commitment could well be to have a disposition in this minimal sense (though not by any means necessarily Ryle's specific sense), and the point is that that would be no concession to the naturalist.

By contrast the less minimal conception of dispositions sees them as having an interesting and substantial causal grounding, as part of the causal nexus that natural science investigates. In short the fully Humean picture of cause and causal explanation, which McDowell thinks it is unnecessary for Davidson to have embraced, is assumed by naturalism to underlie the notion of intentional state when it goes beyond the minimal understanding of it as involving dispositions thought of in purely counterfactual terms.

I have described the causal grounding which takes one beyond the minimal understanding of dispositions as an "interesting and substantial" grounding in causality. This suggests that there is a more minimal understanding of *cause* as well, in terms of which the minimal notion of dispositions can be understood. The difference between commitments and dispositions (non-minimally understood), therefore, can be described as follows. When one views intentional states as dispositions in the non-minimal sense, one expects that citing intentional states in explanations give substantial and interesting explanations. Citing beliefs and desires in this sense is citing states which causally explain actions in a sense redeemable along substantial and interesting lines. On the other hand, when one views intentional states as commitments (as dispositions in the *merest* sense) one says nothing more interesting than that a commitment causes the person who possesses it to try and live up to that commitment. Uninteresting, it would seem, in the style of *virtus dormativa*.

Notice, that this is just the uninterestingness that we found in the higher-order dispositions we granted in the characterization of commitments. To say that, in having a commitment, someone need not have any first-order dispositions to do what would live up to the commitment, to say that he need not have anything more than second-order dispositions to accept criticism for not having lived up to it and to try and do better by way of living up to it, is just to say that the causal power of a commitment is exhausted by the fact that it causes one to try and live up to it. There is no more informative and interesting way to describe its causal power.

It would appear, then, that when the focus is on the causal element, rather than the normative one, commitments do little more than reveal the elements of *goal-directedness* in human minds. Unsurprisingly, under this focus, they say nothing very interesting by way of explanation.

The interest of citing intentional states (when viewed as commitments) therefore lies entirely elsewhere than in giving substantial and interesting answers to the explanatory question: "Why did someone do what she did?" Its interest lies much more in the fact that it raises not explanatory questions about the relations between one's intentional states and one's doings, but rather in the normative questions about the relations between one's intentional states and one's doings – questions such as "Is what she did in accord with her intentional states?", "Did it live up to her commitments?" . . . But notice this kind of question is *not even in view* while we are raising the explanatory question about why someone did what he or she did. And vice versa. This failure of each question to be in view while asking the other is principled and it is echoed – also for reasons of principle – in certain kinds of inter-perspectival "unavailabilities" that I will take up at the very end, once all the integrations I have in mind are established.

To put some of this in other words, what the Moorean argument shows in the end is that there are two radically different questions that one can ask about human behavior. "Why did someone do what she did?" and "Is what she did in accord with her commitments?" For the naturalist, the first question may be answered substantially and interestingly by citing dispositions, naturalistically understood, but the naturalist would be the first to see that it is a pretense to think that one can get the same substance and interest by citing commitments, or by citing dispositions in the minimal sense as one finds then in the higher-order dispositions that go into characterizing commitments. If it is of any interest to mention these latter it is to ask a quite different question of one's doings than the explanatory one – do they live up to one's commitments or not?

Returning, then, to the integrative point I began this section with – the identification of intentionality with value or commitment – a question arises as to why Davidson himself does not quite make the integration, despite his stress on the normative nature of intentionality. He does not *identify* intentional states with normative states such as commitments, in a way that the Moorean argument allows one to do. Instead he insists that they are dispositions and argues that they are "governed" and "guided" by principles of rationality, claiming it is this fact which makes them irreducible to physical states or generally to states which are not so governed.

Thus Davidson's anti-naturalism literally lacks a certain kind of "integrity" because it requires *two distinct* irreducibilities. First, is the irreducibility of intentional states – thought of as dispositions or causal states along Humean lines – to the dispositional (and categorical) states posited by the various natural sciences; and, second, the irreducibility of values to the natural properties posited by the natural sciences. (Davidson clearly must assume this second irreducibility as well as the first since he cannot appeal to values and norms in his argument for anti-naturalism, if he thought them to be reducible.)

What I am calling a more "integrated" anti-naturalism would see *only one* irreducibility, where Davidson sees two. This is because on its view intentional states are *themselves* values of a specific internal sort, a subject's "commitments." So such irreducibility as they have *is* the irreducibility of values – a special case of it.

At the very least, parsimony in the matter of irreducibility would recommend the more integrated approach, but there is much more that recommends it. So a question arises as to why Davidson does not make the identification of intentional states with values or commitments, which the Moore–Frege–Moore argument allows one to make. There are two reasons why he does not find his way to this view, and I will sketch and criticize them, if only to indirectly show some of what I take to be the attractions of the integrated picture I am promoting.

The first reason is this. I have said that once one sees intentional states as themselves being commitments, there is something quite disjoint about the questions, "Why did someone do what she did?" and "Is what she did in accord with her commitments?" Due to a deep and longstanding theoretical strain in his work, Davidson is loath to see these two questions quite as separately as is being suggested here. This is the principle of non-optional charity, by which it is built into the very nature of intentional states and doings that they are by and large rational. What this means is that if he were to go along for a moment with the idea that intentional states are commitments, then he would also insist on seeing them as by and large commitments we live up to in our doings. (Davidson is explicit about this.) And if we do see intentional states along these principled "charitable" lines, then there is no longer the same urgency to keep the two questions apart. And so there is now no longer any pressure to continue to go along with the idea that intentional states are commitments. To put it in other words, if in answer to the first question, we pretend for a moment that there are such things as commitments and say that what causes and causally explains one's doings are one's commitments, and if on the matter raised by the second question, we say that one's doings are by and large in accord with one's commitments, then we wouldn't feel the same pressure to see these two questions as radically disjoint. And so, in turn, if we don't feel that pressure, we can then turn around and say that we don't really see why we should talk about commitments in the first place, since it's just as good to say that the causal states which get cited in answering the first question are dispositions that are, by their nature, by and large rational, i.e., they by and large meet the standards set by the principles of rationality.

The second reason is this. For Davidson, the principles of rationality "govern" and "guide" our intentional states. One way to describe this – if we can put up with the slightly oxymoronic quality of the very idea – is to say that as intentional subjects we have "non-optional commitments" to the rational principles that guide our thinking. And moreover the normative element of commitment is *exhausted* by these few governing commitments. By Davidson's lights these are the *only* commitments we need to say we have. There is no need to go on to clutter the mind with innumerable *further* commitments by saying that each belief and desire is itself also a commitment. Let's call this the "austere" view of commitments.

If either of these reasons were convincing, the integrity being sought in this section is misguided. But it is arguable that there is a flaw in each of them.

Charity, as a principle, needs to be delicately handled. What plausibility it has needs to be carefully stated. It does seem roughly plausible to say that charity, of the sort Davidson wields as a theoretical principle, applies to defining an *intentional subject*. If we allowed that intentional subjects could be massively irrational, one would not be able to quite say why someone is wrong, if he attributes all the beliefs and desires I have to the paperweight lying on my table. It has all my intentional states, but it is just sitting there because it is massively irrational – comprehensively weak-willed, say. Thus, requiring that an intentional subject cannot be massively irrational makes sure that we will not be implausibly generous in what we count as an intentional subject. However, it is one thing to say that charity is necessary to defining intentional subjects, quite another thing to say that it is necessary to defining intentional *states*. The *slippage* from one to the other is quite illicit. Such irrationality as there is, and there is quite a lot in intentional subjects, makes it quite implausible and complacent to appeal to charity in defining intentional states themselves in terms of it. And without charity playing this illicit role, we cannot any longer refuse to feel the pressure of seeing our two questions as radically separate ones, nor appeal to charity in denying the need for the notion of commitments in characterizing intentional states. Or to put it the other way round, thinking of intentional states as commitments prevents us from such a slippage regarding charity.

(I should add as an aside which I will not develop any further here, that such a view of beliefs and desires as themselves being commitments does not have the problems dealing with the fact of fairly widespread irrationality that Davidson has. For Davidson, because the normativity of intentional states enters as something that constitutes the dispositional states that beliefs and desires are, he has to deal in some special way with the fact of irrationality by all that further gerrymandering whereby human minds are divided in order to make it come out that each divided half of the mind is after all constituted as rational, despite the fact of irrationality.[13] No such gerrymandering is required to deal with the fact of irrationality once we see the normative element in intentionality enter by viewing intentional states such as beliefs and desires as themselves normative states or commitments. Now irrationality is just the simple and natural and unstrained idea that human subjects have failed to live up to their commitments.)

On the second point: the austere position (that what we view as our commitments should be restricted to the rational principles and not extended to beliefs and desires themselves) is quite inadequate for doing what Davidson wants it to do, namely, "guiding" our thought. For instance, in the following scenario, it gives quite the wrong instruction. Suppose someone believes that p. And suppose also that when a question is raised, in a fit of distraction, he asserts or assents to something that is inconsistent with p, say "not-p." Now, on the austere view, the only instruction we get in this scenario, is: "Get rid of the belief that p or withdraw the assent to 'not-p'." That is all the relevant principle of rationality can tell us to do. But, given how I have set up the scenario, that is not the instruction one needs. One needs the instruction: "Withdraw the assent to 'not-p'." The austere view cannot deliver this instruction. It is only delivered when we view beliefs themselves as commitments, the very thing denied by the austere view of commitments.

These diagnostic and critical remarks about why Davidson does not take the more integrated view presented in this section are not intended to suggest anything very deeply wrong with his view of intentionality. He is after all an anti-naturalist and a pioneer among them. McDowell and other readers will see immediately that this is a sort of Trotskyite quarrel on marginal matters, rather than on anything fundamental. I raise them in a paper speaking to McDowell's own positions on these subjects because I do think that the integrated view I am presenting has implications – some of which I have tried to draw explicitly, such as those about the quasi-teleologically understood notion of the causal powers of intentional states in terms of goal directedness – which square well with some of McDowell's own criticisms of Davidson on the nature of cause, causal explanation, and his specific brand of monism.

V   Pulling the Strands Together

The various strands of integration should now be pulled together, and some concluding remarks should be made about the importance of these integrations for the special *authority* we have over our intentional states and more generally for an anti-naturalist philosophy of value and mind. What is the relation that the integration of intentionality with value (as proposed in the last section) bears to some of the other integrations suggested earlier?

Earlier (in section III) I had made claims to the special character of self-knowledge by invoking an integration of agency with value. A thoroughgoing normative notion of agency, I had said, would deliver an account of what made self-knowledge special. But I had restricted myself there to just one of the two properties that made self-knowledge special – transparency – saying that I would deal with the other property – authority – after some further integrating spade work. With the integration of intentionality with value in (section IV) that spadework is done, and I turn now to authority.

Authority, if it exists, is a property of second-order beliefs. This special authority we intuitively grant to self-belief has the same effect as transparency does: it makes it doubtful that self-knowledge is like other forms of knowledge, in particular, perceptual knowledge. Should someone want to explain away our intuitions about the authority of self-belief by giving a causal-perceptual account of them, she would have to establish that there is one and only one sort of *cause* of our beliefs about our beliefs and desires: the first-order beliefs and desires themselves. And she would have to say it is this fact which is misleadingly expressed by such terms as "authority." Once again, such a view would leave self-knowledge looking not all that special among the knowledges we have. It would not capture our intuitions about authority. Rather than seek such a unique causal source for our second-order beliefs, therefore, the grounds for our intuition about the authority of self-belief are better sought in more broadly conceptual sources.

But someone may want to question the very intuition that there is authority of this special kind, pointing out that there is much evidence that our avowals and the self-beliefs they express are occasionally false. Don't we often claim to have various beliefs and desires, which our behavior manifestly puts into doubt, showing that we were self-deceived in thinking that we had those beliefs and desires? Someone says he believes that he is healthy. His behavior suggests that he is very anxious and neurotic about his health. Doesn't this make his avowal false? It would seem so.

One can try and save authority by saying that the behavioral evidence only shows that the avowal is not sincerely made and therefore there *is no* genuine second-order *belief.* So since authority holds of self-*belief,* the threat to authority is removed. But this is not always going to work. It is sometimes possible that such behavioral evidence can exist even if the avowal is entirely sincerely made – that is, even if there genuinely is a second-order belief about his first-order belief that he is healthy. In these cases, it may seem that the second-order belief is false, just as perceptual beliefs might be.

But this would only seem so if we had not taken in the integrity I have just argued for, in particular, if we had not taken in the fact that intentional states such as beliefs and desires are themselves commitments. The behavioral evidence does not provide any evidence that the person lacks the commitment which he has sincerely affirmed in his avowal. It only shows that he has not lived up to the commitment in his behavior. His behavior reflects some of his dispositions, which he may not be aware of. And these will conflict with his commitments. If he becomes aware of them, all we need to find in order to attribute the commitment to him, is that he accepts criticism for not living up to his commitments, and tries to do better by way of living up to them, by perhaps cultivating the dispositions to do what it takes to live up to them, and so on. And so, even when he is not aware of his dispositions and his failures, so long as he is prepared – were he to become aware of them – to accept criticism for not having lived up to his commitments and so long as he is prepared to do better by way of living up to them by perhaps cultivating the necessary first-order dispositions, that is sufficient to attribute the commitment to him. If he meets these conditions for having the commitment (i.e., if he has these forms of preparedness, which I had described earlier as "second-order dispositions"), his behavior can no longer be seen as evidence for his second-order belief about his commitment being false, but only of him not having lived up to that commitment.

Here is another way of putting the point. If what I said in the last section holds, when our protagonist avows a belief in his health, he is avowing a commitment. Two things must be established to conclude that there is authority: his avowal must be sincere (otherwise there is nothing – there is no second-order belief – to be authoritative); and the conditions for his having the commitment must be met. Let us assume that the avowal is sincere, despite the behavioral evidence, because if it were not there would be no question, as I said, of something being either authoritatively true or being false, that is, there would be no dispute. Now, what are the conditions for the sincerity of his avowal, given the behavioral evidence which suggest anxiety on his part about his health? The answer here is revealing: there are no conditions which would establish the sincerity of his avowal *which would not also be the conditions which establish that he has the commitment he is avowing*. The conditions for having the commitment, I said, would be his preparedness (were he to become aware that he is not living up to his commitment) to accept criticism for not having lived up to it and his preparedness to try and do better by way of living up to it. These preparednesses, I am now saying, are the *very conditions* which would establish that his avowal of the commitment is sincere. What else could establish its sincerity?

It is simply impossible then to embrace the integration I have proposed in the last section and view intentional states as commitments, while denying that we have authority regarding our own intentional states. And it is because we implicitly really do view them as commitments that we have strong intuitions about authority in our knowledge of our own intentional states. (I myself doubt that anything short of this view will capture the intuition, but it would be dogmatic to put this in any other terms than a doubt, without saying much more than I can here.)

McDowell remarks in one of his papers[14] that "we know our own intentions because we *form* them." This is intended to contrast, one assumes, with the idea that one knows them because one has some sort of inner perception of them. Can we generalize McDowell's point here to our knowledge of our intentional states other than intentions, such as beliefs and desires? Immediately, one will hear the protest, familiar from remarks made in Bernard William's well-known essay "Deciding to Believe,"[15] that much of the time we do not *form* beliefs at all in any deliberative sense. Though that is true, the generalization of the insight in McDowell's remark to belief consists not in thinking implausibly that we form beliefs in that deliberative sense, but rather more subtly in the fact that beliefs like intentions fall within the fully normative realm. If beliefs are commitments, there is a question as to whether we *succeed or fail to live up to them*, just as there is a question as to whether we succeed or fail to live up to our intentions. If we did not integrate beliefs with value or commitment as was done in the last section, it would not be so obvious that McDowell's point *would* be generalizable.

Much more could be said to bring together the relations between these integrations, but let me conclude by making one large point about the importance of the very task of seeking integrations of this kind within a broad anti-naturalism.

Naturalist views of mind and value go deep in our philosophical and scientific culture. They are often presented as the most obvious truths, denying which places one in some stubborn, pre-modern cast of mind. After all, in the newest and most sophisticated dress, naturalists are not really any longer explicitly asserting crude reductions of mind and value to matter and measurable utilities. They are asserting far weaker identities or dependencies of value and mind on the states of nature posited by the natural sciences, dependencies which they capture in labels such as "non-reductive materialism" and "supervenience." The air of plausibility that might seem to emerge with these weaker claims also makes it seem as if the anti-naturalist is some sort of extremist or reactionary for opposing them.

Since, I have assimilated (literally identified) the anti-naturalism about intentionality or mind with the anti-naturalism about value, I will restrict my attention to the latter. The point of these claims to weaker dependencies of values on facts (as they are studied and posited by natural science) is to question the self-standing nature of values. Consider one of the weakest of the claimed dependencies. It is apparently the idea that it is implausible to have all the facts of nature fixed (as the fundamental natural sciences fix them) while one allows for variability among values. One should at least be able to predict from some global fixing of facts what the values will be, in the following weak form. If certain values are attributed in a world by the exercise of interpretation, and it is then recorded that they are accompanied by a global range of facts as fixed by natural science in that world, then in another world with the same facts, one should be able to fix the same values. It is said that anti-naturalisms which deny this are incoherent.

But once one understands anti-naturalism in the *integrated* sense I am seeking, such a claim to dependency might just be unassessable. If the integrities I am seeking are there to be found, then talk of the domain of values being (globally) dependent on the domain of facts seems to be not quite so easily assertible or deniable.

Recall that we have integrated the domain of values with the perspective of agency, which in turn has been integrated with the first-person point of view that only we have on ourselves (i.e., the perspective that makes our self-knowledge quite unlike the knowledge that others might have of us which *is* in a sense akin to perceptual knowledge where we take a third-person stance upon our own minds).[16] Therefore, while in the domain of value one *is* in the perspective of agency and in the first-person perspective. While in this perspective, we cannot so much as state the phenomena as we need to state it in order to describe what the dependency is a dependency on, for that requires being in a third-person perspective from which agency is not available. In other words, while looking at things from the perspective of agency, we cannot take the perspective of a perceiver, a "third" person, to describe the "facts" that values are dependent on and on the basis of which one can make the global predictions. Spinoza famously pointed out that one could not possibly predict while deliberating. But this insight is not an isolated one; it is, *au fond*, an insight about why values *are* self-standing. That is to say – and this is the point of crucial importance – once the integrities have been established, the very *thesis* of the irreducibility of value is not something apart from the *thesis* of the unavailability of the perceiver's or spectator's or predictor's point of view while one is in the agent's point of view, exercising values, deliberating about one's commitments (what *ought* I to do, not what am I disposed to do), and so on. Being able to even state the dependency claim requires one to be able to straddle these perspectives. And it is this straddling that is precisely not possible, if Spinoza is right. One perspective cancels the other out.[17]

Here is an analogy. Think of what I am calling the first-person point of view in terms analogous to the performative aspect of promising. We may of course talk of promises, even our own, in the third person, but in doing so we will be describing things which are essentially performative. We cannot then in our talk of them claim that they are supervenient on descriptive facts. It is not as if one can deny the supervenience thesis either. By refusing to assert it, one is not forced into denying supervenience and saying what seems absurd: that two worlds may be exactly alike in descriptive facts but not in performative facts. That is what I mean by saying that the thesis might be unassessable. Supervenience is not a thesis that is made for, made to fit, the performative aspect of promising. Whatever it fits, it does not fit the performative aspect. That is exactly analogous to the point about the supervenience of values or of intentionality (thought of as values or commitments) on non-evaluative facts.

Now, of course, this claim about the irrelevance of the supervenience thesis to values and intentionality only holds so long as we think of values in terms of the exercise of our first-person point of view in questions such as "What ought I to do or think?" – in other words values and intentionality as they (to use my own term) "integrate" with agency. Without this integration, the naturalist, presenting himself in this more sober guise, can express puzzlement about why one is bringing in questions of first- and third-person perspectives at all while the subject is his claim regarding the weak dependence of values on natural facts: "Only a claim about value is being made," he will protest. "Why are we, in the midst of making this claim, suddenly being told to consider the Spinozist claim about the unavailability of third-person descriptions while in the first-person perspective?" Without the integration of value (at any rate some values, such as internal oughts or commitments – see n.16) with the first-person perspective, there is no obvious answer to this protest. But with that integration in place, the protest is silenced because the relevant evaluative facts (facts about our deliberative intentional life, which is a life trafficking in commitments, about what ought to be done and thought) *are* first-personal facts. While in the realm of these facts, the facts described from a third-person perspective are not in view – just as supervenient bases of descriptive elements are irrelevant to the *performative* aspect of promising.

It might be thought that this is not plausible, since even when one is deliberating in the first-person mode about what one *ought* to do as an *evaluator* and when one decides what *to* do as an *agent*, one is deploying third-personal knowledge. Thus, if I deliberate about whether I ought to help the poor and decide affirmatively and form the intention to do so, I do deploy the third-personal observational knowledge of facts of nature such as that this or that person or persons needs aid or food, and so on. For the doubts I am raising about supervenience, I don't have to deny this, though I can point out that to see someone as being in need is to observe a fact that is laden with value in the sense that I perceive it to be making certain evaluative or imperatival demands on me. To perceive the world along those lines is *not* to perceive it along lines that are third personal. It is essentially to see the world with a sense of first-personal *engagement*.[18] So it is not as if the first-person point of view is a Cartesian or solipsist point of view that leaves the *world* out.[19] It is rather that it sees the world in a way that implicates and involves the agent's engagement with it. By contrast, when one perceives it from the third-person point of view, one might register such things as the caloric intake of the subjects involved and a prediction of their undernourishment or death and so on. But then, from this, there will have to be a *switch* of perspectives to the agential one of engagement in which one perceives the facts quite differently, as really making normative demands on one, which then in turn leads to forming of decisions and intentions – in this case, to help the poor. And the worry I am expressing is that if it really is a *switch* of perspectives, then there is something obscure in the idea that the former kind of facts are supervenient on the latter kind of facts precisely because of the Spinozist point of the unavailability of these perspectives to one another. When perspectives are unavailable to one another and there is no richer perspective to go to (since one is always in one or the other perspective), it is an oddity, a conceptual oddity, to even try and establish that facts, which are essentially facts of the one perspective, have the requisite naturalist dependency on facts in the other.[20]

One may of course deny the irreducibility of value in the first place. But to do so would require disputing the Moore–Frege–Moore argument we mentioned earlier, and the theorists who invoke the global dependencies do not (do not usually, at any rate) feel the need to do that. Indeed, Moore himself was the first to formulate the dependency under the name of the "supervenience" of values on the facts of nature.[21] So the point in these concluding remarks is not so much to *argue* for the view that values are irreducible. That depends on the validity of the combined Moore–Frege–Moore argument presented earlier. The point is rather to stress the significance of the integrations. The significance is that they seem to put into question the very assessability of the more sober naturalist strategy, i.e., the strategy which concedes that values are irreducible, and then goes on to claim the kinds of weaker naturalism that these claims to dependency offer. They put it into question by making clear that the irreducibility of value is deeply implicated with the *unique* perspective of agency, and of the special character of self-knowledge and the first-person point of view. The relevant naturalist dependency, however, requires a kind of *inter*-perspectival availability which the irreducibility of value (once understood in its integrated relations to these other things) makes impossible.

It is not mere parsimony, then, which is gained by the integration of the four themes I said I would seek, at the beginning of the chapter. The integration helps us to see the full force of McDowell's anti-naturalism.[22]

Notes and References

1   See particularly "Self-Knowledge and Resentment," in C. Macdonald, B. Smith, and C. Wright (eds.), *Knowing Our Own Minds*, Oxford: Oxford University Press, 1998. I have dealt with each of the elements discussed here at much greater length in *Self-Knowledge and Resentment*, Cambridge, Mass.: Harvard University Press, 2005.

2   D. Hume, *A Treatise of Human Nature*, Oxford: Oxford University Press, 1978, bk. II, pt.III, chs 1 and 2.

3   P. F. Strawson, "Freedom and Resentment," *Proceedings of the British Academy* (1962). Reprinted in *Freedom and Resentment and Other Essays*, London: Methuen, 1974.

4   There are literally a score of refinements and qualifications to be made of such a claim, and I have tried to provide them in the works mentioned in n.1. I suspect that this last somewhat voluntaristic modification (and some others that I have made in that work) to Strawson's views of agency would not be congenial to McDowell's thinking, which may be inclined to leave things just where Strawson did.

5   When I say "all the way down," I mean it. I don't mean that there will be increasingly higher-order values justifying lower-order ones. Perhaps a better expression would be "all the way round" because there is no hierarchy or descent. There is rather mutual reinforcement of values.

6   Both Tyler Burge and Christopher Peacocke, for instance, begin with such a "basic" case of self-ascription in the presence of a conscious thought. See, for instance, Burge's "Individualism and

Self-Knowledge," *Journal of Philosophy* 85 (1988), and Peacocke, *Being Known*, Oxford: Oxford University Press, 1999.

7   See his "Functionalism and Anomalous Monism," in E. LePore and B. Mclaughlin (eds.), *Perspectives on Actions and Events*, Oxford: Blackwell, 1986.

8   For these arguments and for a number of other elements in Davidson, mentioned in this section, see his "Mental Events" and various other seminal papers gathered in his *Essays and Actions and Events*, Oxford: Oxford University Press, 1980.

9   The currency of the term brings with it various elements, which I think are not required at all to understand the notion of commitment. For example, most who talk of commitments, think that they are commitments in the sense that one will defend them against those who raise a question about them. That strikes me as being of no great relevance to commitments. If someone challenged my belief that the earth is not flat, or that I have a hand, to take Moore's example, I will not take him seriously. In fact for many challenges to my beliefs from others which are based on what I take to be not very serious grounds, I will not defend my commitments. This does not mean that one should not respond when there is counter-*evidence*, whether it is provided by others or by one's own inquiries and encounters. Responding to *others* with a defense, therefore, is not what is essential or defining of commitments. In general, this kind of social element is not what is of primary and defining relevance to commitments. Thus efforts to give a plethora of social constraints to elaborate the nature of commitments as is found in some accounts of intentionality may well be beside the point or, at any rate, beside the main point.

10 There is no denying, of course, that we use the term "desire" to speak not merely of fully intentional states, which I am calling commitments, but of urges, such as a desire for a cigarette. I will be restricting my use of the term to the former.

11 That is to say, if the answer to the question is affirmative, it is an "ought"; if it is negative, it is an "ought-not." But the general point is that the fact that the question can be raised at all in a non-trivial way is proof that there is a gap between dispositions and desires (intentionalistically understood as commitments – oughts and ought-nots).

12 See my contribution to Mario De Caro and David Macarthur (eds.), *Naturalism in Question*, Cambridge, Mass.: Harvard University Press, 2003, for responses to possible objections to the argument.

13 Davidson struggles with the widespread fact of irrationality and proposes the divided mind thesis in his essay "The Paradoxes of Irrationality," in Richard Wollheim and James Hopkins (eds.), *Philosophical Essays on Freud*, Cambridge: Cambridge University Press, 1982.

14 "Meaning and Intentionality in Wittgenstein's Later Philosophy," in his *Mind, Value, and Reality*, Cambridge, Mass.: Harvard University Press, 1998.

15 Published in his *Problems of the Self*, Cambridge: Cambridge University Press, 1973.

16 Of course, to think of values in this way as being of a piece with the first-person point of view is to give up on certain hyper-objectivist conceptions of value that certain positions describing themselves as "Kantian" have adopted. In a paper on Bernard Williams ("Might There be External Reasons?" in the volume *Mind, Value, and Reality*, referred to earlier), McDowell, despite some of his criticisms of Williams's Humean psychologism about values, is also critical of many of Williams's objectivist critics and opponents, who would divorce values from our perspective on them. There is much to be discussed here, but for the purposes of this paper, I will simply admit that when I make these integrating claims regarding value and the first-person point of view, I am restricting myself to value-commitments and am excluding certain highly objectivist conceptions of value from the claim. Perhaps the most clear example of a position being excluded is the objectivist position taken by Derek Parfit in recent papers. See his "Reason and Motivation," *Proceedings of the Aristotelian Society* (1997).

17 I say more on this Spinozist point and its implications for anti-naturalism and intentionality in my "Psychoanalysis as Technology," forthcoming in a volume of essays, Erik Olsson (ed.), Cambridge: Cambridge University Press, title to be announced later.

18 I say more about this theme of viewing the world with a sense of engagement in my contribution to a forthcoming volume of essays on "Transitional Justice," Jon Elster (ed.), title and other details to be announced.

19 Nor does it leave the body of the first-person out. By "world" here I mean to include the body of the agent himself as well as the environment he perceives with a sense of his own engagement with it. There is no reason to think, in fact there are good reasons not to think, that the first-person point of view leaves the subject or agent as disembodied. There is nothing Cartesian about the first-person point of view.

20 Stephen White, who has independently taken this view of things, thinks that the view is best expressed as a form of Kuhnian incommensurability. I have some qualms about that way of putting the point. The fact is that incommensurability of that sort was intended to attach to scientific theories, and scientific theories are *fragments* of a *third*-person discourse and point of view on the world, whereas the point here is about the unavailability of the first- and third-personal discourses and points of view to one another. Because they are fragments within a third-personal discourse, it is hard to be actually convinced that there *are* cases of the complete and principled unavailability of one scientific theory to another. Surely, we want to say, there is always scope to retreat to some minimal belief or set of beliefs that both theories share, and then deliberate from there on. Surely, we want to say, there is always an open possibility that one theory will be able to offer the other theory at least some internal argument to bring it around. But none of these deflationary and skeptical responses are possible in the case of inter-perspectival unavailability that holds for the first- and third-person points of view. Here there really is no question of finding a common ground and there is no other perspective to go to. So my own inclination is to resist too much talk of incommensurability – at any rate to insist that if we fall into that talk, then the notion of incommensurability should be restricted to whole discourses, to the discourse of facts as the natural sciences study them, and the discourse of value or (what is the same thing, once my integrations have been made) to first-personal, agential descriptions and third-personal descriptions. In other words, talk of incommensurability is fine, but only so long as we make clear that it applies not to what it was initially thought to apply to when it was introduced by Kuhn and Feyerabend, but to something much broader and more general and basic than they had in mind.

21 Whatever Moore had in mind by that formulation had better not be, if I am right, in the service of these weaker forms of naturalism.

22 While writing and revising this paper, I have benefited from helpful comments from and discussions with Annalisa Coliva, Isaac Levi, John McDowell, Carol Rovane, Stephen White, and Crispin Wright.

Response to Akeel Bilgrami

1 I appreciate Bilgrami's integrating aspirations on my behalf. There is something obviously attractive about the idea that various things I think form a unity, rather than just a collection of thoughts that are – I hope – consistent. But I have reservations about the specifics of the integration he aims at.

2 I agree with a point Bilgrami makes toward the end of his section II: moves aimed at alleviating anxieties about the place of freedom or agency in the world should not be restricted to worries about morality, or even worries about the practical in general. Freedom figures in deciding what to think no less than in deciding how to act.

But I think Bilgrami overestimates the Strawsonian point he appeals to. On its own it cannot entitle us to bypass metaphysical questions about agency, by all means in that extended sense.

Bilgrami thinks the familiar anxieties about freedom depend on forgetting that the very idea of agency belongs in a normative setting. But that is not so. On the contrary, a conception of agency in normative terms, no doubt sometimes only in an inchoate form, is exactly what drives the anxieties. We can capture them in this question: how can responsiveness to reasons – here the normative setting for the concept of freedom is explicit – make a difference to what happens in the world? This question seems urgent because a modern world view makes it tempting to suppose everything that happens is part of the workings of an impersonally describable causal nexus.

The most that the Strawsonian connection between freedom and certain reactive attitudes could do toward helping with this puzzlement would be encouraging us to suppose there must be a mistake in the idea that the question expresses a real problem. To allay the anxiety expressed by the question, we would still need to expose the mistake.

And when he goes beyond Strawson as he does, so far from exposing the mistake, Bilgrami puts at even more risk than Strawson does the prospect of an assurance that there is one.

Strawson leaves it looking like a mere brute fact that we have those reactive attitudes in some cases (for instance toward normal human beings who do us wrong), and not in others (for instance toward pianos that are out of tune). He discourages the question whether this discrimination is warranted. Strawson says nothing to dislodge anyone from this thought: though it is natural for us to feel resentment, say, toward normal adult human beings who wrong us, a correct metaphysics reveals that such attitudes are out of place.

Bilgrami for his part says there is nothing "transcendental" about our proneness to reactive attitudes. He says we are that way because we value being that way. He seems not to mind the implication that being that way is in some sense optional for us (in n.4 he calls the position "voluntaristic"). If someone is stuck in the familiar metaphysical puzzlement, how could this help? To such a person, it will seem to be an admission that our values require of us attitudes and thoughts that are revealed as ill-founded, by an apparently compelling conception of a way in which it is in principle possible to account for everything that happens. Nothing has been done to undermine the appearance of compellingness. If it is a choice on our part to adopt these attitudes and thoughts, such a person will think it is one we should not make.

3 Bilgrami makes it seem that there is no need to respect a metaphysical puzzlement about freedom. He contrives this partly by the suggestion I have been objecting to, that one can feel the puzzlement only by failing to register the normative character of the concept of agency. But even when the puzzlement is expressed by a question on the lines of "How is it possible for responsiveness to reasons to make a difference to what happens?", so that the normative context needed by the concept of agency is explicit, Bilgrami might still seem equipped to dismiss the question. Here I am thinking of the sharp contrast he draws in his section IV between explanatory and normative questions. "Make a difference," in the question, indicates a concern with explanatory questions. But it is responsiveness to reasons that we are asking about, and that indicates that our concern is with intentional items. And Bilgrami says intentional items cannot figure in "substantial and interesting answers" to explanatory questions.

But this contrast is overstated. Bilgrami wants to reject the idea that intentional items are "part of the causal nexus that natural science investigates," and I sympathize. But he proceeds as if that requires him to deny that intentional items are part of any explanatory nexus at all, and this strikes me as throwing out a baby with the bathwater. That we believe and desire what we do makes a difference to what we do. So our beliefs and desires make a difference to some of what happens. Explanations of action, invoking intentional items on the part of agents, answer explanatory questions. And Davidson has made it overwhelmingly plausible that the understanding we acquire from such an explanation is causal understanding. Responsiveness to reasons does make a difference to what happens – a causal difference, according to Davidson. And one can be forgiven for finding it puzzling how that can be so, given how tempting it is to suppose everything that happens is embraced within "the causal nexus that natural science investigates." This puzzlement cannot be suppressed by distinguishing explanatory and normative questions.

In recommending his sharp contrast, Bilgrami suggests that intentional items can yield only *virtus dormitiva* answers to explanatory questions. He tries to exemplify this by considering cases in which a commitment is said to lead someone to try to live up to that very commitment. Now I have no problem with conceiving intentional items as commitments. (I shall say more about this below.) But I cannot see that it warrants Bilgrami's idea that citing intentional items cannot address explanatory concerns. I think Bilgrami's schematic handling of the conception of intentional items as commitments has led him astray here. It is far from obvious that we cannot achieve substantive understanding of a bit of behavior by seeing it as an attempt to live up to a commitment. And the point is even clearer with more specific concepts of kinds of intentional item. "Why did she thumb her nose at him?" "Because she believed he had insulted her." This answer is potentially explanatory. It has none of the uselessness of *virtus dormitiva* explanations. And the point is unaffected if we agree with Bilgrami that the belief invoked in such an explanation, and perhaps a desire that is taken for granted in it, are commitments.

4 I am puzzled by some features of Bilgrami's Moore–Frege–Moore argument.

He describes the Moore leg as "some sort of proof that the intentional state of desire is not [a] disposition but rather an internal ought of some kind." But the Moore-like open question he exploits is "I have these dispositions to O, but *ought* I to O?" An argument that turns on this question *assumes* that we are concerned with an "internal ought." It could not prove that we should be. The Moore leg of Bilgrami's argument shows, rather, that *if* we regard desires as "internal oughts," we are debarred from definitionally identifying them with dispositions, conceived as items that would figure in a description of "the causal nexus that natural science investigates."

As Bilgrami presents the second leg of the argument, it supplements the first leg's rejection of definitional identifications, by ruling out a posteriori identifications. The second leg is supposed to work by presenting the identifier with a dilemma. In using the conceptual apparatus with which she picks out an intentional item, when she claims that it can be identified a posteriori with some natural item, does the theorist take herself to be capturing the item through a natural feature of it? ("Natural" here is to be glossed in terms of placement in "the causal nexus that natural science investigates.") If so, she runs afoul of the first leg. This relies on the idea I have just queried, that the first leg shows that intentional items must be conceived as "internal oughts" – as opposed to spelling out a consequence of conceiving them so, which was all I could find in it. But at this point I want to focus on the other horn of the dilemma. If the theorist disclaims an intention to exploit a natural feature of an item when she picks it out in intentional terms, Bilgrami says, then "we don't have a naturalistic reduction in the first place." This is supposed to force such a theorist back to the first horn and so back to the Moore leg of the argument. But what is the point of claiming that the naturalizing identification holds only a posteriori? Surely the point is that the claim enables the theorist to concede that the conceptual apparatus with which we pick out intentional items as such is not naturalistic in the relevant sense, while maintaining that the items that satisfy those concepts also satisfy concepts that place the items in a naturalistically conceived causal nexus. In this way of thinking there is no intention to propose a naturalistic reduction, and for all Bilgrami says the second horn of the dilemma is a comfortable resting place. It is where Davidson places himself.

As I said, I have no problem with conceiving intentional states as commitments, in something like the sense Bilgrami spells out. I see nothing in Davidson's basic outlook that should induce him to resist the idea either. In the part of his paper in which Bilgrami is discussing a failure to integrate that he finds in Davidson, Bilgrami is not working with texts of Davidson's, but responding to conversations with him. I suspect Davidson may have been led to resist the idea that intentional items are commitments by Bilgrami's representing it as carrying the implication that we cannot attribute a substantial explanatory role to intentional items. Davidson certainly has reason to resist that supposed consequence, and, as I have indicated, I think this resistance is well placed. But as I have urged, there is no such implication.

It is true that I think Davidson's monism is a mistake. But I do not see how Bilgrami's Moore–Frege–Moore argument could show that it is. There is indeed a residual naturalism, in the sense of the outlook Bilgrami and I agree in resisting, in that part of Davidson's thinking. But the way to eradicate it is not, as Bilgrami suggests, to drop the very idea that intentional items belong to a causal nexus – to restrict invocations of intentional items to contexts in which our concern is normative as opposed to explanatory.[1] The right move is to drop the idea that for intentional items to belong to any causal nexus at all is for them to belong to "the causal nexus that natural science investigates," in a way that would need to be spelled out by redescribing them in non-intentional terms. That is the idea that drives Davidson's argument for his non-reductive monism. When Davidson argues that the understanding provided by ordinary explanations of action is causal understanding, he says enough to display intentional items as belonging to a causal nexus in their own right. To recognize that they are causally efficacious, we do not need to suppose that they can be redescribed in natural-scientific terms, so as to stand revealed as belonging to something we could conceive as *the* causal nexus.[2]

The naturalistic picture of *the* causal nexus that underlies Davidson's monism stands in tension with the idea that intentional items are causally efficacious in their own right. We should not drop the idea that intentional items are causally efficacious at all, as Bilgrami urges when he argues that intentional items are not suitable for addressing explanatory questions. Rather, we should extract the idea that intentional items are causally efficicacious from the setting Davidson puts it in, the monistic picture of *the* causal nexus.

Removed from that setting, a Davidsonian picture of the causal character of ordinary action explanation can be helpful in response to anxieties about freedom. Consider the gap Bilgrami points to in Hume's attempt to disarm such anxieties. As Bilgrami says, Hume invokes an unexplained distinction between coercive and non-coercive causes. Now Davidson gives us the means to make a principled distinction in this area. The difference between causes that impugn freedom and causes that do not is that the causes that do not impugn freedom are rational causes, causes whose operation is constituted by actions aimed at furthering the projects of their agents in the light of how they see the situations in which they act. Unlike Bilgrami's appeal to reactive attitudes, this does not merely ignore a perfectly intelligible difficulty, but addresses it.

All this leaves conceiving intentional states as commitments, so far as I can see, at best harmless, not the key thought that Bilgrami represents it as being. The idea does no positive work in enabling us to improve our thinking about freedom.

5   Like Bilgrami, I believe there is a deep connection between freedom and self-knowledge. But the connection that I think matters for understanding self-knowledge is not the one Bilgrami invokes.

Self-awareness is an essential feature of activities, cognitive or practical, in which one exercises the ability to take charge of one's life, to be in rational control of it. And this should have a central place in an understanding of self-consciousness in general.

In a remark Bilgrami cites approvingly, I was pointing to a case of this kind of self-awareness. He reports me as saying we know our intentions by forming them. But what I said was that that would be more nearly right than saying we know our intentions by inner observation – not that it would be right.[3] And it would not be right about intentions in general. There are intentions that we do not form, but just find ourselves acting on. Consider, say, casual conversation. One says what one says intentionally, but the intention that animates a burst of speech is not an intention one has formed, in any natural sense. To form an intention is to decide to do something, and there is often no decision behind intentional action.

Bilgrami talks about generalizing my remark to other intentional states, in the face of, for instance, the fact that most beliefs are not deliberately adopted. He suggests that if we conceive intentional states as commitments, items that "fall within the fully normative realm," we can see that the remark has general application. I find this claim mysterious. As I have said, I have no problem with the idea that intentional states are commitments. I do not see how it could enable us to assimilate a person's knowledge of a belief or intention that she just finds herself with to her knowledge of a belief or intention that she has adopted, necessarily self-consciously, in an act of making up her mind. Contrary to Bilgrami's claim, the idea of knowing intentions by forming them does not generalize even to all intentions, let alone to all intentional states.

What would be needed, in order to situate the point I was getting at in a satisfactory account of self-knowledge in general, is not a generalization but a different kind of move. We would need to explain how being minded a certain way at all, not necessarily as a result of making up one's mind, is intelligible only against the background of the ability to make up one's mind. And we would need an explanation of how we can move out from what I said is the central case of self-consciousness – self-awareness in exercises of the capacity to be in rational control of one's life – to an understanding of self-consciousness in areas of one's mindedness that are not exercises, or results of exercises, of that special capacity.[4]

Those remarks do no more than describe a shape that a helpful characterization of intentional self-knowledge might take. Much more would need to be said in filling in the details. But I think my sketch of the shape is already enough to bring out a contrast with Bilgrami.

In my sketch, the thought that the concept of freedom needs a normative setting is explicated in terms of the idea that agents – practical and cognitive – have a special capacity, the capacity to be in rational control of features of their lives. That is what it means to say the realm of freedom is the space of reasons.

Now this is not to offer normative talk as a substitute for metaphysics. Normative talk – talk of responsiveness to reasons – figures here in a claim, about what is special to free agents, that there is no reason not to classify as metaphysical.

Bilgrami, by contrast, appeals to Strawson's linking of freedom with reactive attitudes as a way to avoid metaphysics. The picture of self-knowledge he offers centers on this thought (he says it is "the basic idea here"): "the evaluative reactive attitudes . . . which we have seen to constitute the very idea of agency are only appropriate or justified to the extent that those praised, blamed and so on are presumed to have self-knowledge of the actions and deliberative conclusions that they are praised and blamed for – which implies in turn that they have self-knowledge of the states of mind which rationalize those actions, states of mind which give those actions the descriptions under which they are justifiably praised and blamed." So if someone finds the special character of self-knowledge puzzling, she is to be told we must presume that agents have self-knowledge if we are to sustain our reactive attitudes. This will be obviously unhelpful if the person who needs philosophical help about self-knowledge is also puzzled about how the reactive attitudes can be well-placed; see section 2 above. But even independently of that, if someone finds it mysterious how self-knowledge can have its special character, how can it help to be assured that our reactive attitudes, and the practices of praise and blame they sustain, require us to presume that we and others have such knowledge? Such a person might reasonably say: "I know that, but my problem is that I still find it hard to see how such knowledge – which I agree there not only is but must be – is possible." To deal with this, we would need to uncover a mistake underlying the appearance that the special character of self-knowledge is problematic. It is no help to insist that giving up the idea of such knowledge is not an option, or at least no more of an option than abandoning our reactive attitudes.

6   Why does Bilgrami believe he needs to combat supervenience theses? I think he underestimates how weak they are. They need not be even vestigially naturalistic, in the sense in which "naturalism" labels the way of thinking he wants to attack. In this respect they contrast with, say, Davidson's monism.

Bilgrami says proponents of supervenience theses aim "to question the self-standing nature of values." But as he himself notes, Moore has no problem affirming the supervenience of values on natural facts, but insists that values are self-standing, under the guise of arguing that the good is non-natural.

Bilgrami must think Moore can be set aside as a special case. I am not sure if he is trying to justify that idea when he writes that supervenience theses – perhaps not including Moore's? – imply an ability to "predict from some global fixing of facts what the values will be." Such wording might seem to threaten the autonomy of evaluative thinking. But Bilgrami's own gloss makes it clear that what the ability to predict comes to here is that we would be able to say how values stand in some possible world if we had a prior determination of values in a different possible world in which the arrangement of non-evaluative facts is the same. There is nothing here to threaten the obvious point that the prior determination, the basis of the prediction, would require evaluative thinking, which as far as the supervenience thesis goes can be just as autonomous, just as undetermined by non-evaluative facts, as Bilgrami wants.

Bilgrami puts great weight on the agentive character of evaluating. And it is surely right that it makes no sense to affirm, or deny, that *actions* are supervenient on facts that might be in view from a perspective other than that of the agent. Actions, performances, are not the right kind of topic for a supervenience thesis. But the fact that evaluating is something we do cannot undermine the fact that an evaluator makes a claim, says that things are thus and so: for instance, that some action is despicable or heroic. So there is something for a supervenience thesis to be about. What supervenes on non-evaluative facts is not the action of evaluating, but the kind of thing that is said to be so, sometimes truly, when someone evaluates something. Given an action that is, say, despicable, and another exactly like it in all non-evaluative respects, the second must be despicable too. I cannot see that Bilgrami gives any reason not to accept that claim, and others like it, as innocuous.

I have been urging that Bilgrami's eagerness to exclude supervenience theses, not as false but as senseless, is not well-motivated. And I think the apparatus he uses to argue for the exclusion leads him astray in a way that can be separated from the fate of supervenience theses. His argument relies on the claim that we must segregate the perspectives of first-personal and third-personal thinking. But this threatens a proper understanding of first-personal thinking. First-personal thinking positively requires to be undertaken under a conception of it as involving a distinctive angle on facts conceived as third-personally statable. I do not mean that, for instance, in deliberating whether to send money to Oxfam I need to contemplate third-personally characterizable facts about famine and so forth. Bilgrami acknowledges that, but disarms the concession by remarking that the third-personally accessible facts have to be seen from a perspective of engagement. I do not want to object to that. What I mean is rather that the capacity of the first-person pronoun, or other devices to the same effect, to make references at all depends on the fact that a first-personal thinker conceives the referent of her self-references as a particular person, an element in the third-personally describable world. By insisting on the uncombinability of the perspectives, Bilgrami threatens to make it unintelligible how a subject's uses of "I" can refer.[5]

Notes and References

1   I have been saying "items" rather than "states," since Davidson's focus is on events rather than states. There are reasons why this is a good thing, but it would take us too far afield to go into the matter. See J. Hornsby, *Simple Mindedness: In Defense of Naive Naturalism in the Philosophy of Mind*, Cambridge, Mass.: Harvard University Press, 1997, e.g. at 134–5.
2   For a fine treatment of the issues here, see J. Hornsby, "Agency and Causal Explanation," reprinted in her *Simple Mindedness*, 129–53.
3   See *Mind, Value, and Reality*, Cambridge, Mass.: Harvard University Press, 1998, 319.
4   "Mindedness" here covers how things are with a subject in respect of mental phenomena belonging to kinds that come within the scope of the capacity to make up one's mind, though, as I am insisting, not all instances of such kinds result from exercises of that capacity. A different kind of extension would be needed to accommodate self-consciousness in respect of, for instance, sensations. Bilgrami sets that region of self-knowledge aside, and I am following him in this.
5   For more on this, see G. Evans, *The Varieties of Reference*, Oxford: Clarendon Press, 1982, ch. 7. See also my "Referring to Oneself," in L. E. Hahn (ed.), *The Philosophy of P. F. Strawson*, Chicago: Open Court, 1998, 129–45.

4

Self-Knowledge and Inner Space

Cynthia Macdonald

In the past three decades, externalism in the philosophy of mind has become an entrenched position. The view has been variously formulated, but a central claim involved in it is that some intentional states, ones such as my thinking that that tiger has stripes, have contents that are individuation-dependent, and so dependent for their very existence on factors beyond the minds of their subjects. Suppose that externalism, thus described, is true, and accordingly, that the "fully Cartesian" conception of the inner realm as consisting of contentful states whose contents would remain invariant even if there existed nothing beyond the minds of persons, is false. Then it seems that a subject could be mistaken about the natures and contents of her own intentional states, even to the extent that she might have the illusion of entertaining a thought with a given content when there is no such thought to be entertained. What are the consequences of this view for the belief that there is an asymmetry between self-knowledge and knowledge of others, in that subjects are at least sometimes authoritative[1] with regard to knowing what thoughts they are thinking?

John McDowell (1986) holds that there are *no* consequences for that view. On the contrary, he claims, it is only if one buys into the "fully Cartesian" conception of the inner that one might be tempted to think that the supposed asymmetry between self-knowledge and knowledge of others is problematic and needs explaining. If one rejects that conception, then there is nothing problematic about the asymmetry, even given externalism. In short, it is the "fully Cartesian" conception of the inner realm, and not externalism, that is the source of the illusion that there is a problem about privileged self-knowledge that needs addressing.

I think that this is wrong. Even if one rejects the "fully Cartesian" picture, the asymmetry between self-knowledge and knowledge of others is something that needs explaining in the light of externalism. In what follows, I want to make a case for this. I begin, in section I below, by setting out the problem that externalism seems to pose for the view that subjects have authoritative self-knowledge of certain of their thoughts. Then, in section II, I discuss the central features of the "fully Cartesian" picture, whose rejection seems forced by the acceptance of externalism. In section III I argue that even if one accepts externalism and rejects the "fully Cartesian" conception, externalism presents a real problem for the view that there is authoritative self-knowledge, and so there is a need to develop an account of what that authority consists in. Finally, in section IV, I identify one clear sense in which subjects can be said to be authoritative with regard to knowledge of their thoughts in the light of externalism, and the sorts of feature an account of this knowledge might exploit.

I   Externalism and Authoritative Self-Knowledge

Externalism in the philosophy of mind is a doctrine whose roots stem from the work of Hilary Putnam (1975) and Tyler Burge (1979, 1982, 1985, 1986, 1988). Briefly, it is the view that certain intentional states of persons have contents that are "world-involving" in that they depend on the existence of objects and/or other factors beyond the minds of their subjects.[2] Suppose that I am currently consciously thinking that that tiger has stripes, and that this thought falls into the class of thoughts to which externalism applies. My capacity to think it depends on the existence, in the world around me, of tigers. I could not think a thought with this content in a world in which there were no tigers. I might have the illusion of thinking such a thought; but this would be merely an illusion.

McDowell is an externalist, particularly with regard to singular thoughts, ones of the form, "That F is/has G," such as the thought that that tiger has stripes.[3] He also endorses a specific type of externalism, according to which the contents of subjects' thoughts are Fregean modes of presentation. For McDowell, there are three items about which we can speak when we speak of a subject's entertaining a singular thought (such as a demonstrative one). First, there is the thinking, the current conscious (inner) mental event or occurrence in the subject. Second, there is what one is thinking about, what we might call the *object* of the thought. In the case of a true thought, this is a state of affairs or fact, or a truth-value. Third, there is the content of one's thought, or *how* what is thought about is presented. On this view, the content of one's thought, in the case of a singular thought, is what one thinks: a singular proposition, whose constituents are Fregean modes of presentation. In the case of a true thought, McDowell claims, "*what* one thinks *is* the case" (1994: 27).[4] If externalism is true of singular thoughts, one can have them only in cases where the objects thought about (*what* one is thinking about) exist. Further – and this is a point to which we shall return – the point of introducing a class of object-dependent thoughts, with "the Fregean fineness of grain needed for them to serve in perspicuous accounts of how minds are laid out, lies in the way it liberates us from Cartesian problems" (1986: 146). McDowell's commitment to singular-thought externalism is thus motivated by his rejection of a "fully Cartesian" picture of the inner realm. Hostility to this picture lies at the core of his philosophy.

What problem does externalism seem to pose for the view that subjects have authoritative self-knowledge? It seems to imply that subjects can be mistaken not only about whether the thoughts they are actually thinking are true of the world around them, but also about whether they are thinking certain thoughts it seems to them that they are thinking. More generally, it seems to imply that others can be better placed than a subject to know whether that subject is thinking thoughts of the kind that she takes herself to be thinking, irrespective of whether she *is* thinking those thoughts.

Three sorts of case seem to present problems for the view that subjects have authoritative self-knowledge of the contents of such thoughts. The first concerns situations in which a subject may take herself to be entertaining a thought of a certain kind but is not, because to do so would require the presence of a particular object in her visual field where none exists. Consider, for example, a subject who lives in an environment in which there are tigers and who attempts to think a thought of the type "that tiger has stripes" in a situation in which there is no suitably situated tiger. Although she may have thought token thoughts of that type in the past in contexts in which tigers were visually present to be demonstrated, she fails in this case to think a token thought of that type.

This kind of case threatens authoritative self-knowledge because it is one where the subject mistakenly takes herself to be thinking a thought that is not, in her situation, available for her to think; and another may be better placed than her to know this. It contrasts with a second sort of case. Suppose that a subject is attempting to think a thought of the type "that tiger has stripes," not just in a situation in which there is no suitably situated tiger present in her visual field, but in a world (Twin Earth) in which there are no tigers at all but only pligers – creatures which look, feel, and behave like tigers but have a different biological constitution. In this case there is no *tiger* content – real or apparent – in the inner realm to constitute the content of her thought. In this case, unlike in the first one, it is not even possible for the subject to entertain singular token *tiger* thoughts on other occasions; and another, who has better knowledge of the facts of biology and knows that the world in which they are living is not Earth but Twin Earth, might be in a better position than the subject is to know this.

Both of these cases contrast with a third type of case, where a subject *rightly* takes herself to be thinking a thought with a certain content but where she nonetheless lacks authoritative self-knowledge of that thought. Thus, consider a situation in which someone knows the facts about biology and Twin Earth, where there are pligers but no tigers, and knows that she has not, unbeknownst to her, been transported to Twin Earth. This person seems to be in a better position to know that the singular *tiger* thoughts of another, who is ignorant of the facts about chemistry and Twin Earth, are indeed *tiger* thoughts. Here externalism seems to jettison authoritative self-knowledge, not because there is no thought of the kind available for the subject to think, but because another may be in a better position than the subject to know that the object demonstrated is indeed a tiger.

One familiar way of attempting to rescue the conviction that subjects are at least sometimes authoritative with regard to knowing the natures and contents of their own thoughts in the face of externalism is to distinguish epistemological issues about content from semantic–cum–metaphysical ones (cf. Burge 1985, 1988). It is one thing to know that the thoughts one is currently consciously thinking are *tiger* thoughts, and another to know what makes *tiger* thoughts *tiger* (as opposed to *pliger*) thoughts. Consider, by way of analogy, cases of perceptual knowledge. I can know that that tiger visually present in front of me has stripes without knowing what individuates tigers from other animals. Similarly, the thought might continue, I can know that the thought I am thinking is a *tiger* thought without knowing what makes it a *tiger*, rather than a *pliger*, thought.

However, this claim, even if correct, doesn't solve the problem that is pressing here. The doubt that externalism raises is not just about whether that view is compatible with self-knowledge. It is about whether the view is compatible with *authoritative* self-knowledge, the kind of knowledge that lies at the heart of the supposed asymmetry between self-knowledge and knowledge of others. The analogy with perceptual knowledge cannot help here, principally because the intuition that needs defending is not that a subject can know her own thought contents even when she does not know what individuates them as the contents they are. It is, ironically, that her knowledge is authoritative, *despite* the fact that she does not know what individuates her thought contents as the contents they are. The puzzle that externalism presents is that, *unlike* perception, where knowing what makes a tiger the biological creature it is may put a subject in a better position than another to know that the animal visually present is a tiger, the authoritative status of self-knowledge does not seem to be threatened by ignorance of the individuation conditions of one's own thought contents.

So, even if self-knowledge is analogous to perception in the way suggested (namely, that one can know that one is thinking a thought with a certain content without knowing what makes that content the content it is), appeal to the perceptual analogy does not help to show how externalism might be compatible with authoritative self-knowledge. Moreover, the appeal to perception is itself problematic. Many have argued that the perceptual analogy is misguided altogether because self-knowledge is fundamentally unlike observation or perception (Burge 1996, 1998; Peacocke 1996, 1998; Shoemaker 1994). Specifically, it has been argued (Shoemaker 1994) that, in perception, the objects of perceptual knowledge can exist independently of their being perceived, and independently of there being creatures capable of perceptual experience. But this independence condition is not met in the case of self-knowledge.[5] It is in the nature of intentional states that they are capable of being known by their subjects, and known in a certain way. The ability to think intentional contents is inseparable from being able to employ them in inferences, including practical ones, involving other contents. One needs to be able not only to engage in such inferences, but also to at least sometimes know what inferences one is engaging in, since part of what it is to be a reasoning creature is to be capable of critically reviewing and evaluating one's reasonings as reasonings. One cannot exercise this ability without being able to distinguish contents from one another. But this seems to require that subjects be capable of full knowledge of at least certain of their thought contents, and with this, knowledge of their individuation conditions.[6]

Some take this conclusion to show that externalism is incompatible with authoritative self-knowledge because it has the consequence that such knowledge of certain contents entails knowledge of the empirical factors that individuate them, which is absurd (McKinsey 1991). Others argue that since the individuation conditions of contents are constitutive of them, the appropriate comparison in the case of perceptual knowledge is not with the case of knowing that, say, the animal visually present is a tiger. Rather, it is with the case of knowing that, say, the person visually present is sunburned. One might know that something visually present is a tiger without knowing what makes a tiger the animal that it is. But one cannot know that something visually present is sunburned without knowing that it has been burned by the sun.[7]

If this second point is right, fundamental differences between perception and self-knowledge imply that authoritative self-knowledge is actually incompatible with externalism. Evidently, the problems that externalism presents for the view that there is authoritative self-knowledge run very deep. They are not ones that are easily solved by comparison with cases of perceptual knowledge.

II   The "Fully Cartesian" Conception

The attempt discussed above to defuse the threat from externalism to the view that subjects at least sometimes have authoritative knowledge of their own thought contents looks initially as though it does not involve commitment to any problematic Cartesian assumptions. It simply attempts to extend the application of features of perceptual knowledge to cases of self-knowledge. However, McDowell argues that the presumption that externalism poses a threat to authoritative self-knowledge *already presumes* what he calls a "fully Cartesian" conception of the inner realm. Once this is recognised, and the conception's grip on those who accept the presumption is dislodged, no attempt is needed to "rescue" authoritative self-knowledge from the apparent threat. What is this "fully Cartesian" conception, and how does it invade the thinking of those who view authoritative self-knowledge as threatened by externalism?

The fully Cartesian picture is a conception of subjectivity that begins with the assumption that, irrespective of whether one might be in doubt about what lies beyond the mind, one cannot be in doubt about what lies within it. One cannot be in doubt about how things seem to one to be. One's "intellectual" seemings, so to speak, are a special case of how things are; special because they are *inner facts*; facts about how things seem to one to be.[8]

Further, these facts are not just indubitable; they are infallibly knowable. If, attending to my apparent perception that that tiger has stripes, I think that it seems to me that that tiger has stripes, I know that it seems to me that that tiger has stripes. Although I can be mistaken about how things are in the world beyond my mind, I cannot be mistaken about how things are in the world that lies within it. I cannot be mistaken about the fact that it seems to me that that visually present tiger has stripes. This implies that although I can get it wrong whether the contents of my seemings are answered to in the world that lies beyond my mind, I cannot get it wrong what the contents of these seemings are.

This picture, McDowell claims, falls short of the "fully Cartesian" conception, and he has no objection to it. His reason is that, so far as it is committed to subjects' infallible knowledge of facts about how things seem, it is compatible with a "disjunctive" account of such facts.

> Short of the fully Cartesian picture, the infallibly knowable fact – its seeming to one that things are thus and so – can be taken disjunctively, as constituted either by the fact that things are manifestly thus and so or by the fact that that merely seems to be the case. On this account, the idea of things being thus and so figures straightforwardly in our understanding of the infallibly knowable appearance; there is no problem about how experience can be understood to have a representational directedness towards external reality. (1986: 150)

This less-than-fully – or, what might be called "quasi-Cartesian" – picture is capable of accommodating the idea that there is authoritative self-knowledge and along with it an asymmetry between self-knowledge and knowledge of others. Why? Because the infallibly knowable facts of the inner realm are facts about how things seem to their subjects to be, and in itself there is nothing objectionable about the idea that subjects may have a way of knowing these facts that is not subject to the sorts of error that is characteristic of knowledge of facts that lie beyond the inner realm.

At the same time, this quasi-Cartesian picture is compatible with externalism, precisely because the infallibly knowable facts that constitute the inner realm can be understood disjunctively, as constituted *either* by the fact that things are manifestly thus and so to the subject *or* by the fact that things merely seem to be thus and so.

> Of facts to the effect that things seem thus and so to one, we might say, some are cases of things being thus and so within the reach of one's subjective access to the external world, whereas others are mere appearances. (1986: 150)

Because of this, the externalist consequence that another might sometimes be in a better position than a subject to know that subject's mental states can also be accommodated. Specifically, someone might be in a better position than me to know, of the infallibly knowable fact about how things seem to me to be, which disjunct obtains: whether it is a case of knowing how things are within the reach of my subjective access to the external world, or whether it is a case of knowing how things merely seem to me to be.

> short of the fully Cartesian picture, there is nothing ontologically or epistemologically dramatic about the authority which it is natural to accord to a person about how things seem to him. This authority is consistent with the interpenetration of the inner and the outer, which makes it possible for you to

know the layout of my subjectivity better than I do in a certain respect, if you know which of those two disjuncts obtains and I do not. In this framework, the authority which my capacity for "introspective" knowledge secures for me cannot seem to threaten the very possibility of access on your part to the facts within its scope. (1986: 154)

If this is the quasi-Cartesian picture of the inner, what more is involved in the "fully Cartesian" one? Evidently, the latter takes the further step of assuming the realm of inner facts to be *autonomous* with respect to the outer realm. It takes how things seem to be "self-standing" infallibly knowable facts about how things are in the inner realm. It does not make it obligatory to understand the facts about how things seem disjunctively. It takes facts in the outer realm to be only "extrinsically" or "externally" related to facts in the inner realm.

As this final way of characterizing the additional assumption made by the fully Cartesian conception brings out particularly clearly, that conception is incompatible with externalism. It is incompatible because, if externalism is true, certain contents are not extrinsically or externally related to factors in the outer realm: those factors serve to individuate those contents as the contents they are. McDowell thinks that we should reject the fully Cartesian conception because it risks severing the inner from the outer realms, and, with this, risks the very possibility of having contentful thoughts at all.

III   Externalism and Authoritative Self-Knowledge

Suppose that we reject the fully Cartesian picture of the inner for the reasons given. Is it possible to consistently combine externalism with the quasi-Cartesian conception in a way that preserves the two important claims that (a) there is "interpenetration between inner and outer" (1986: 154) and (b) subjects are authoritative with respect to knowing their own thought contents? Further, does this combination allow one to take a "quietist" attitude toward authoritative self-knowledge, one which deems it unnecessary to give a substantive account of how it is that subjects are at least sometimes in a better position than others to know the contents of their own thoughts? McDowell believes so. As he puts it:

By itself, there is nothing dangerous about the idea that how things seem to one is a fact, knowable in a way that is immune to the sources of error attending one's capacity to find out about the world around one. We can think of this "introspective" knowledge as a by-product of our perceptual capacities, available on the basis of a minimal self-consciousness in their exercise. (1986: 154)

In another context, he continues:

"How is it possible that . . . ?" . . . is indeed a good way to express philosophical difficulties of a familiar kind, and some such difficulties may be worth tackling. . . . If a question of that shape is to express a determinate philosophical difficulty, it must be asked from a frame of mind in which there is at least a risk of its looking as though whatever the question is asked about is *not* possible. So one's first move, if someone tries to interest one in a "How is it possible?" question, should be to ask: why exactly does it look to you, and why should it look to me, as if such-and-such a thing (e.g., baseless authority about oneself) is *not* possible? (1998b: 58)

And McDowell is a quietist. He believes that there is no need for a substantial epistemology of authoritative self-knowledge, and that only somebody already in the grip of the fully Cartesian conception could think that the authoritative status of self-knowledge presents a problem that needs solving. His reason is that it is only if one views the realm of the inner as autonomous with respect to the outer that one can no longer view authoritative self-knowledge as a simple by-product of the exercise of one's ordinary cognitive capacities, capacities directed toward a world to which others have access. One then seems forced to appeal to the idea of a kind of inner observation, an inner vision, in order to account for such authority.

But is this right? The case rests on whether the quasi – or not quite fully – Cartesian conception has the resources to accommodate authoritative self-knowledge compatibly with externalism. This is a conception of the subjective domain that tries to respect features that seem essential to the states that fall within it, namely, representational directedness toward the world and accessibility to introspection, without taking the further step of construing that domain as autonomous. The question, then, is whether those features are capable of grounding authoritative self-knowledge consistently with externalism.

McDowell thinks that they can because they allow one to take the knowable facts about the inner – facts to the effect that things seem thus and so to oneself – to be infallibly knowable, where such infallibility is part of the *acceptable* Cartesian conception. They are so knowable because, once the inner is viewed as interpenetrable by the outer, they can be taken disjunctively. I can infallibly know that it seems to me that that tiger has stripes. What I infallibly know when I know this is *either* that it is manifestly the case that that tiger has stripes, *or* that it merely seems to me that that tiger has stripes. This is true not only of my knowledge of how things seem to me to be in the world beyond me, and in particular, of my perceptual seemings, but also of how things seem to me to be in the inner realm, the world within me. It must be true of how my own mental states – states that are the by-products of the exercise of outwardly directed cognitive capacities like perception – seem to me to be.

So, suppose that I am currently consciously thinking that that tiger has stripes. What is the infallibly knowable *inner* fact, taken non-disjunctively, that I know when introspecting, when thinking *about* this thought? Is it that it seems to me that I am currently consciously thinking that that tiger has stripes? This seems right, if the analogy with McDowell's account of how to take facts about how things seem to me to be in the outer world – the world beyond me – is to go through. Taken *disjunctively*, then, what I infallibly know when I know that it seems to me that I am currently consciously thinking that that tiger has stripes is *either* this: that it is manifestly the case that I am currently consciously thinking that that tiger has stripes, *or* it is this: that it merely seems to me that I am thinking that that tiger has stripes. Put another way: of facts to the effect that it seems to me that I am thinking that that tiger has stripes, some are cases of genuinely thinking that that tiger has stripes within the reach of my subjective access to facts in the inner realm, and others are mere appearances. Subjective access to facts in the inner realm is, for McDowell, the exercise of a kind of "minimal self-consciousness" that is a by-product of the exercise of my outward-directed cognitive capacities.

But consider now the first type of case that might be thought to pose problems for authoritative self-knowledge given externalism mentioned earlier, in Section I. Suppose that I am in a situation in which I mistakenly take myself to be thinking a thought of the form "that tiger has stripes," mistakenly, because there is no suitably situated tiger in my visual field for me to demonstrate, and so no thought available for me to think. The problem externalism seems to pose here is that another may be better placed than me to know this. More specifically, another may be in a better position to know, not *which* of the two disjuncts – (1) it is manifestly the case that I am thinking that that tiger has stripes or (2) it merely seems to me that I am thinking that that tiger has stripes

– obtains, but *whether* there is any such disjunct available for me to know at all. If my thought contents are not *tiger* ones, then I cannot undergo even an apparent thought with this content, and so neither (1) nor (2) is available for me to think. And another might be in a better position than I am to know this.

McDowell might acknowledge this but point out that the mere fact that there is no suitably situated tiger present in my visual field is not sufficient on its own to rob me of the ability to think any thought with a *tiger* content. So long as there are tigers in my world, and I am able to demonstrate them in singular thoughts in contexts other than the one that I am currently in, the absence of a suitably situated tiger in this particular situation will make it impossible for me to think this particular token *tiger* thought, but it will not prevent my thinking such token thoughts on other occasions. Further, in order for it to seem to me that I am thinking that that tiger has stripes, it may suffice that there be a *sort* or *type* of *tiger* content that I can employ in other contentful token thoughts, one of which I wrongly suppose myself to be thinking in the present situation. Thus, he says:

> Particular *de re* senses, each specific to its *res*, can be grouped into sorts. Different *de re* senses (modes of presentation) can present their different *res* in the same sort of way: for instance, by exploiting their perceptual presence. And the univocity of a context-sensitive expression can be registered by associating it with a single sort of *de re* sense. . . . Given a context, a sort of *de re* sense may determine a *de re* sense (if one cares to put it like that), or else it . . . may determine nothing. And in the latter sort of case, according to this way of thinking, there can only be a gap – an absence – at, so to speak, the relevant place in the mind – the place where, given that the sort of *de re* sense in question appears to be instantiated, there appears to be a specific *de re* sense. (1986: 288)

One might say that what gives the appearance to a subject that she is thinking a particular token *tiger* thought is precisely that there *is* available to her a *sort* of *de re* sense, the *tiger* sort, which she mistakenly thinks in this situation is instantiated in a particular place in her mind.

This response is unlikely to convince someone who thinks that the case envisaged compromises authoritative self-knowledge. The reason is that it concedes that another might be in a better position than the subject, not to know what thoughts she is thinking (i.e., which disjunct is in question), but to know that there are no contents available for her – however it may seem to her – to think. But perhaps this foists on McDowell a position he does not and need not hold. It supposes that authoritative self-knowledge requires, not just that a subject be in a better position than another to know what it seems to her that she is thinking when she is indeed thinking it, but that she be in a better position than another to know, in a situation in which she fails altogether to think a particular thought, that it only seems to her that she is thinking a thought with a particular content *because* there is no such thought content available for her to think. That is to say, it supposes that she must also be in a better position than others to know that there is "a gap – an absence – at, so to speak the relevant place in the mind – the place where, given that the sort of *de re* sense in question appears to be instantiated, there appears to be a specific *de re* sense."

McDowell might object that the asymmetry between self-knowledge and knowledge of others only applies in cases where there is a thought content available for the subject to think. With respect to that content, he might insist, a subject is in a better position to know what it seems to her that she is thinking than is another. Despite this, knowledge of the externistically constrained individuation conditions of content may put another in a better position than the subject to know which disjunct is in question. Equally, in a particular situation in which neither of the disjuncts is available at all for the subject to think, it may be that another is in a better position than the subject to know this. But again, this does not compromise a subject's authority with respect to knowing what thought she is thinking, since in that case there is no thought available with respect to which she can be knowledgeable, let alone authoritatively knowledgeable.

A similar response can be made to the second sort of case mentioned earlier. Suppose that I am attempting to think a thought of the type, *that tiger has stripes*, not just in a situation in which there is no suitably situated tiger present in my visual field, but in a world in which there are no tigers at all but only pligers. In this case there is no *tiger* content – real or apparent – in the inner realm to constitute either disjunct (1) or disjunct (2). Not only is there no particular *de re* sense, but there is no *sort* of *de re* sense, so I am not even able, as in the first case envisaged above, to entertain singular token *tiger* thoughts on other occasions. As Evans puts the point:

> those who hold that a person may wrongly think he has a thought of the form "*a* is *F*" need [not] be committed to the view that such a subject has a thought of the form "I am thinking that *a* is *F*." All that is being credited to such a subject is the intention of thinking a thought of a certain particular kind, and the belief that he is thinking such a thought. Obviously if there is no thought of the appropriate kind available, then there is no possibility, either for the subject or for anyone else, of giving the content of the thought he wishes, but fails, to entertain. (1982: 46)

When Evans says "and the belief that he is thinking such a thought," he cannot and does not mean "and the belief that he is thinking that *a* is *F*." Nor can he mean "and the belief that he is thinking a thought of the form, '*a* is *F*,'" if this requires thinking a thought of the "*a* is *F*" kind, since a world in which there are no *a*s is a world in which (to use McDowell's terminology) there are no specific *de re a*-senses *and* a world in which there is no *de re a*-sense sort. To say this is not necessarily to say that nothing is going on in the inner realm of the subject at all. Words, images, and/or various subsidiary thoughts with genuine content might be passing through his mind. What is not going on in his mind, however, is a thinking of a genuine singular thought with the content, *a* is *F*. Nor is he mistakenly supposing that a sort of *de re* sense is instantiated in a place in his mind where there is only, so to speak, a gap, since there is no such sort.

The objection that this case suggests is that, if externalism is true, another might be in a better position than the subject to know that although it might be for him exactly as if he were thinking a thought of the type "that tiger has stripes," he fails to think a thought of the type he supposes himself to be thinking, because there is no object in his world of the kind required for him to think a thought of that type in his world. And if he cannot think such a thought, he cannot think a thought of the type, "It seems to me that I am thinking that that tiger has stripes," since there is no such content available for him to think.

In short, the objection is that externalism seems to rob subjects of infallible self-knowledge. In order for a subject to know infallibly that it seems to her that she is thinking a thought of the type, "that tiger has stripes," there needs to be a *tiger* content embedded in the content of her thought. This is so even if it only seems to her that she is having a thought with that content. If externalism is true of such contents, a subject can think them without having knowledge of their individuation conditions. So another, who knows what would be required for there to be genuine singular thoughts of the type "that tiger has stripes," and who knows that such a requirement is not met, can undermine that subject's claim to infallibly know that it seems to her that she is currently consciously thinking a thought of the type "that tiger has stripes."

But, again, it is open to McDowell here to deny that there is a problem of authoritative self-knowledge in this second kind of case for his view to deal with, on the following grounds. That another may sometimes be in a better position than a subject to know whether there is a fact – real or apparent – of the relevant kind for her to know doesn't compromise a subject's authority with regard to knowing what the contents of her apparent thoughts are, the case envisaged notwithstanding. For, in this case, there are no thought contents of the relevant kind available for the subject to know, let alone authoritatively know. So another cannot be better placed than the subject to know the nature and contents of the thoughts she is thinking. Furthermore, what another *is* better placed to know in a situation such as this – namely, that there is no thought available, real or apparent, of the kind the subject takes there to be for her to think – is not something that any subject *could* be authoritative about, given externalism. So there simply is no problem of authoritative self-knowledge, given externalism, here to solve.

This will be counterintuitive to anyone sympathetic to the Cartesian conception of subjectivity, since, if it is true, subjects really can be very confused both in supposing in particular cases that they are thinking certain thoughts at all – in supposing that there are certain places in their minds where sorts of *de re* senses are instantiated – and in supposing that there are sorts of *de re* senses to be so instantiated. Part of the attraction of the Cartesian conception is that it might have the resources to avoid having to accept it. Still, McDowell argues persuasively that the cost of endorsing this aspect of the Cartesian conception is to forfeit the "interpenetration of inner and outer" and so to commit to the *fully* Cartesian picture. Since it is no part of McDowell's view to embrace this picture, but it *is* part of his view to embrace the quasi-Cartesian conception, where this allows for infallible self-knowledge, I shall take it that he construes the latter as permitting infallible self-knowledge only in cases where there are thoughts available of the kind a subject takes there to be for her to think. That is, I shall take McDowell's view to be that only in cases of object-dependent thoughts where there are suitably situated objects for subjects to think about can subjects have authoritative (i.e., infallible) self-knowledge, not just about whether it seems to them that things in the world beyond the mind are thus-and-so, but about whether it seems to them that things in the inner realm are thus-and-so.

In short, then, McDowell's position seems to be this. If there *is* an inner fact – a singular thought – available for a subject to know, she is capable not only of knowing it, but of knowing it infallibly, even if externalism is true. This is simply because to grasp a thought is to grasp it in terms of its content, so that a subject cannot think a thought by grasping a content other than the one it has. If she were to grasp her thought by means of a content other than the one it has, she would be thinking a different singular thought altogether. If there *isn't* an inner fact of this kind available for a subject to know, then she not only cannot know it infallibly but cannot know it at all, if externalism is true. She may be thinking a thought of another kind, say, a descriptive thought, or words or images might be going through her mind. But she will not be thinking a genuine singular thought, and so will not be thinking a thought that she can know, let alone know infallibly. Either way, externalism doesn't compromise authoritative self-knowledge and the quasi-Cartesian view of subjectivity that presumes it.

If this is right, then neither the first nor the second kind of case establishes that there is any problem about authoritative self-knowledge that needs explaining in the light of externalism. Let us turn, then, to the third and final kind of case mentioned earlier, in section I. Here there are object-dependent thoughts available for a subject to think, so that she is capable of thinking, in the presence of a suitably situated tiger, a genuine singular thought of the type, "It seems to me that I am thinking that that tiger has stripes." In this case the problem posed by externalism is that another may be better placed than the subject to know that that subject is indeed thinking a thought with this content because that other knows the facts of biology and Twin Earth, and knows that the subject has not, unbeknownst to her, been transported to Twin Earth. Does this kind of case compromise authoritative self-knowledge and with it the quasi-Cartesian conception?

What the subject infallibly knows in a case like this, taken disjunctively, is either this: it is manifestly the case that I am currently consciously thinking that that tiger has stripes, or this: it merely seems to me that I am currently consciously thinking that that tiger has stripes. Not only can she think this thought and know that she is thinking it, but she can also know (if she knows the externistically constrained individuation conditions of the content of her thought) which of the two disjuncts obtains. But she may not know this, and further, another may be in a better position than she is to know it. McDowell says that one reason why this may be is that another may know "the layout of [her] subjectivity" better than she herself does. In the case envisaged here, what another knows and the subject herself does not is that she has not, unbeknownst to her, been transported to Twin Earth, where there are pligers but no tigers. This fact is one about which the subject knows nothing, and so it does not occupy a place in her subjective "layout."

As we have seen, McDowell takes the authority another may have as a result of externalism to be compatible with the quasi-Cartesian conception and so with authoritative self-knowledge because what the subject infallibly knows is a fact, construed disjunctively – either it is manifestly the case that she is thinking that that tiger has stripes or it merely seems to her that she is thinking that that tiger has stripes; whereas what another knows authoritatively is which of the disjuncts is in question – in this case, that she is indeed thinking that that tiger has stripes. Since the facts with respect to which the two are authoritative are different, the authority that externalism might purchase for another is consistent with the authority that the quasi-Cartesian conception purchases for the subject.

The situation, however, is not as straightforward and unproblematic as this response suggests. It is true that in this case the fact that the subject might infallibly know is different from the fact that another may be better placed than the subject to know, so that the authority of one is consistent with the authority of the other. But the other may not *just* be better placed to know which of the two disjuncts is in question. He may *also* be better placed than the subject to know whether there is a fact, construed disjunctively, available of the kind the subject takes there to be, and, crucially, what that fact is. The authority which externalism purchases for another extends, not just to knowledge of which disjunct obtains, but also to knowledge of the fact, construed disjunctively, itself. And it purchases this for another precisely because that other may be better placed than the subject to know the facts about biology and Twin Earth, and to know that, unbeknownst to the subject, she has not been transported to Twin Earth.[9] This will remain the case *even if* both the other and the subject know that externalism is true. Another may be better placed than the subject to know this: that it is indeed the case either that she is manifestly thinking that that tiger has stripes or that it merely seems to her that she is thinking that that tiger has stripes. And this – I submit – encroaches on a subject's authority precisely because externalism is true of such thoughts.

So, inasmuch as McDowell's attempt to reconcile externalism with authoritative self-knowledge and the quasi-Cartesian conception trades on the claim that the fact about which a subject has authoritative self-knowledge is not the same fact as the one that another may know authoritatively, he is right to say that authoritative self-knowledge

> is consistent with the interpenetration of the inner and the outer, which makes it possible for you to know the layout of my subjectivity better than I do in a certain respect, if you know which of those two disjuncts obtains and I do not. (1986: 154)

This is not, however, all the authoritative knowledge another may have with regard to a subject's thoughts. If externalism is true, another may be better placed than a subject to know that there are indeed two disjuncts, one of which constitutes her thinking that it seems to her that she is thinking that that tiger has stripes. And this undermines the claim, which even the quasi-Cartesian conception endorses, that subjects are authoritative with regard to knowing what thoughts it seems to them that they are thinking. The disjunctive maneuver, while preserving the openness of mind to world that forces rejection of the fully Cartesian conception, does not preserve the authoritative position subjects have with regard to knowing what thoughts it seems to them that they are thinking. Once externalism is in place and the fully Cartesian position is rejected, a subject's authoritative position with regard to knowing what thoughts it seems to her that she thinks is jettisoned. Inasmuch as this is so, McDowell has no defense for his claim that "there is nothing ontologically or epistemologically dramatic about the authority which it is natural to accord to a person about how things seem to him," given externalism.

IV   A Suggestion

I said earlier that McDowell is a quietist about the phenomenon of authoritative self-knowledge. He has no difficulty accepting the view that there are inner facts, and that these facts are knowable by their subjects in ways that are immune to the sources of error that attend knowledge of facts about the outer realm. But, in the absence of commitment to the "fully Cartesian" conception of the inner, he does not see that there is anything particularly dramatic or in need of explanation with regard to such knowledge. And so he does not see that there is any pressing need for it to be supported by a substantial epistemology.

I have argued that externalism with regard to nature of certain mental contents does pose a threat to the claim that subjects have authoritative self-knowledge, since others can be better placed than they are to know the facts, construed disjunctively, that constitute their apparent thinkings. In the light of externalism, it is deeply puzzling how it could be that

how things seem to one is a fact, knowable in a way that is immune to the sources of error attending one's capacity to find out about the world around one. (1986: 154)

The problem is to see how it could be that subjects have *any* kind of authoritative self-knowledge of thoughts whose contents are externistically individuated.

I think that the appropriate conclusion to draw from this discussion is that if externalism is true, then subjects do not have authoritative self-knowledge of those thought contents for which it is true. When it seems to me that I am currently consciously thinking that that tiger has stripes, and I am indeed thinking this, the inner fact to the effect that I am thinking that that tiger has stripes is not one that I authoritatively know. It is not, in this sense: another can be better placed than I am to know whether there is a *tiger* content to constitute that inner fact.

However, there is something important and right about the view that subjects do sometimes have authoritative self-knowledge, and that there is an asymmetry between self-knowledge and knowledge of others that flows from this. Further, it is something that the Cartesian conception of the epistemology of self-knowledge can help us to see. According to it, at least some contents of subjects' minds are directly or immediately available to their subjects when they are employing them in thoughts of certain kinds. The kinds of thoughts in question here are the *cogito*-type ones

– ones in which subjects are currently consciously thinking about their thoughts while thinking them. The kind of epistemic access subjects have to the contents of their thoughts in such cases, in being direct and immediate, contrasts with the epistemic access others have to those contents. When I am currently consciously thinking, and thinking about a thought with a given externalistically individuated content, another may be in a better position than I am to know what content is available for me to think, and so to think about. But that other is not in a better position to grasp, and so to know, the particular content that constitutes the subject matter of the thought about which I am thinking. Put slightly differently, another may be in a better position than I am to know whether there is a *sort* of *de re* sense available to determine, given the context, a specific *de re* sense in the appropriate place in my mind. And another may be better placed than I am to know what, given the context, that *sort* of *de re* sense might be. But that other is not in a better position to know, in a particular context, the specific *de re* sense that constitutes the subject matter of my thought, when I am both thinking, and thinking about it. When *I* am both thinking it and thinking about it, I have, whereas another does not, a special kind of epistemic access to the content of that thought. Being in that position gives me an epistemic purchase on it that no other has.

What this shows is that there is another direction in which we could – and I think should – be going. When I am currently consciously thinking, say, that I am thinking that that tiger has stripes, while thinking that very thought, the contents of that thought are manifested to me in a peculiarly direct way. My awareness of these contents is not evidence-based. It is not based on inference from anything else. It is not based on my awareness of anything else. Attention alone brings these contents to the forefront of my awareness.

Elsewhere (Macdonald 1995, 1998), I have argued that we can get a firmer grip on this special kind of epistemic access by focusing our attention on cases of knowledge where notions like "direct epistemic access" and "immediate access" have a natural home. One place where they have a natural home is in perception. Consider properties other than contentful intentional ones where the notion of direct epistemic access is generally thought to apply. I know that the table visually present before me is brown, and that it is rectangular, and this knowledge is plausibly understood as being direct, although not baseless. One explanation of how I can know directly that the table is an instance of this particular shape property, or an instance of this particular colour property, is that the instance is presented to me *as* an instance of that property through my sense of sight. I perceive the instance *as* an instance of that property, and so no evidence is needed to come to know that it is an instance of that property.

This is not true of other properties. Water, for example, is an instance of the chemical structural property H_2O, but this instance is not manifested to me *as* an instance of that property through one of my senses. In short, certain properties seem to be ones to which we have direct epistemic access because they are observable; whether objects are instances of them can be determined just by unaided observation of those objects.

This is not to say that one can know which observable property is being manifested to oneself on any one occasion just by being presented with an instance of it. One must be capable of recognizing another instance of that property as of that property when presented with it on another occasion, and this requires one to have mastery of the concept of the relevant property. This means that the notion of direct epistemic access is intensional: for one to have direct epistemic access to a color property such as the property, *brown*, it is not sufficient that one sees an instance of that property. One must see it *as* an instance of that property.

Certain features of observable properties characterize their epistemic directness in a way that marks them off from other properties. One is that they are epistemically basic or fundamental to knowledge of objects that instance them. The point is not that grasp of the observable properties of objects necessarily constitutes knowledge of their true nature. Rather, it is that such properties are those by which objects that instance them are typically known in the first instance. Knowing an object through instances of certain properties and not others favors certain ones epistemically.

Another, crucial, feature of observable properties is that they *are* in general as they appear to be when instances of them are presented to normal perceivers in normal circumstances. Again, this is not a point about the natures of the objects that instance the properties but about the properties themselves. The nature of water may be such as to have the chemical constitution H_2O, but this is compatible with water's instancing certain observable properties that are such that *they* are as they appear to be to normal subjects in normal circumstances.

The point of focusing on the example of observable properties in perception is not to argue that self-knowledge is just like perceptual knowledge. There are clearly important, and fundamental, differences between these two sorts of knowledge. Intentional properties – properties like *thinks that that tiger has stripes* – are importantly different from observable ones. And introspection, as a means by which information about one's own states of mind is made available to oneself, is not perception. For one thing, there is a kind of phenomenology to perception of observable properties which is lacking in the case of self-knowledge of one's intentional states.

So I am not arguing here that self-knowledge is just like perception. Although I am making use of an observational analogy in order to articulate a position on authoritative self-knowledge, I am not doing so in what might seem to be the obvious way, namely, by appeal to something like an "inner sense." Rather, I am appealing to more abstract and general features of observation of external things, specifically, features of observable properties, which help to explain our direct and immediate access to them. Because these features are abstract and general, they are not tied to cases of observation alone. Those who appeal to such phenomena as "intellectual experience" or "intellectual intuition" in their accounts of authoritative self-knowledge may well appeal to such features.[10] My claim is that these two features of observable properties (not: of objects that have these properties) – that they are epistemically basic and that they are in general as they appear when instances of them are presented to normal subjects in normal circumstances – apply to intentional properties in the *cogito*-type cases in a way that can help us to see why subjects, but not others, have direct epistemic access to certain of their thoughts and so have authoritative self-knowledge of the contents that they are thinking. Thinking about those contents while thinking them puts subjects into direct epistemic contact with the contents themselves.

Consider, then, the first feature – that observable properties are epistemically basic or fundamental to knowledge of objects that instance them. When one thinks about one's own intentional state while undergoing it, from the point of view of the reflective thought, one's grasp of the thought reflected upon is first and foremost a grasp of it as a state of a certain contentful type. When I think that I am thinking that that tiger has stripes, my reflective grasp of that thought is as a thought with the content: *that that tiger has stripes*. The point is not that that state cannot be known by means of other properties (intentional or non-intentional); if physicalism is true, every contentful mental state is identical with a physical state – a state with physical properties – and that state is capable of being thought about in physical terms. The point is, rather, that when I *do* think about an intentional state of mine while undergoing that state, I typically think about it as a state with a given content – *that that tiger has stripes*.

Consider now the second feature: that such properties are in general as they appear to be to their subjects. This feature also applies to intentional properties in the *cogito*-type cases. The reason is that the contentful type by which I grasp my thought when thinking about it while thinking it can only succeed in grasping it if I redeploy the same contentful type in thinking about it that is employed in thinking it.[11] One cannot have a thought of a certain contentful type, succeed in grasping it while thinking about it, and misidentify it. Since to grasp a thought is to grasp its content, to attempt to grasp it by means of a thought of a different contentful type would be to fail altogether to think about that thought.

So one can have authoritative self-knowledge because, in the *cogito*-type cases, one can have direct epistemic access to one's own thoughts in a way in which others cannot. Grasping one's thoughts in terms of their contents, and those contents being in general as they appear to be when they are thought about in this way, gives one authoritative knowledge of them.

How is this reconcilable with externalism? Externalism tells us that the contents of our thoughts are individuation-dependent on factors in the environment. So it is possible that, on a given occasion, unbeknownst to me, I may be thinking a *pliger* thought rather than a *tiger* thought. But if this is so, I cannot have authoritative knowledge about the contents of my own thoughts.

But I can have authoritative knowledge, when I am thinking thoughts with the contents that they do indeed have, of the contents that I'm thinking. This is because when I am currently consciously thinking about them while thinking them, I grasp these contents in an epistemically basic and favored way. Another can be better placed to know whether there are contents available for me to think. But since they do not occupy the epistemically favored position with regard to my thoughts that I do when I am thinking them, they are not better placed to know the contents that I am thinking.

So, externalists about thought content can agree that, in a certain important sense, externalism rules out authoritative self-knowledge, and rules it out irrespective of commitment to the "fully Cartesian" conception of the inner. But there is another sense in which it is right to say that externalism does not impugn authority, and this sense is critically important to preserving the common-sense intuition that there is an asymmetry between self-knowledge and knowledge of others. Ironically, it is the Cartesian conception of a subject's epistemic relation to her own thoughts in the *cogito*-type cases that can help us to see why it *is* right to say this.

Notes

1 By "authoritative" I mean here "better placed," whether or not this includes infallibility.

2 Note that I do not say "beyond the bodies of their subjects." For one thing, one can have singular thoughts about parts of one's body, say, one's nose. But I also want to leave it open whether externalism might be true of such phenomenal states as sensations; and to do so I need to allow that the physical factors that exist within the bodies of persons might help to individuate such states.

3 See McDowell (1986). He includes in this class of singular thoughts ones involving proper names. See McDowell (1977).

4 Dodd (1995) has termed this McDowell's identity-theory of truth.

5 But cf. Macdonald (1999) who criticizes this argument.

6 But see Tyler Burge, who claims that, if externalism is true, certain contents – those that are individuation-dependent on factors beyond the minds of persons – are ones that subjects employ in thought and practical inferences without knowing what makes those contents the contents they are. His point is that full mastery of contents is an unreasonable requirement to place on thinkers, since most rational and competent thinkers and speakers regularly fail to meet it. Note, though, that his claim is not that one can have full mastery of a content without knowing what makes it the content it is.

7   See, for example, Howard Robinson (1994: ch. 5). He claims that consciousness of perceptual content
     involves consciousness of all of its relata: "from the perspective of reflective consciousness, content is
     constitutive of the mental state: it is like perceiving a family rather than like perceiving a father, in that
     all the relata must be included in the grasp and not merely exist outside the scope of the awareness."
     He concludes that externalism is incompatible with the identity-theory of the mental and the physical,
     since "awareness of a state as mental involves awareness of its content, but no awareness of a brain state
     per se will involve awareness of any external object standing in a causal relation to it. Considered as a
     state of which we can be reflectively conscious, therefore, a mental state cannot be identical to a brain
     state" (all quotations from p. 146). I think that Robinson begs the question against the identity-theorist
     by assuming that intentional states cannot be relationally individuated without being relationally *con-*
     stituted. See Cynthia Macdonald (1989: ch. 5).
8   "Intellectual seemings" is a term used by Burge (1996) and Bealer (1999).
9   This may look like it has the form of a familiar Cartesian skeptical argument. However, the point here
     is not that a subject's knowledge is compromised; it is that her authority is compromised.
10   See, for example, George Bealer (1999), in his theory of the a priori, and Tyler Burge (1996).
11   For more on conceptual redeployment, see Peacocke (1996).

References

Bealer, G. 1999. "A Theory of the A Priori," in J. Tomberlin (ed.), *Philosophical Perspectives*, vol. 13,
     Cambridge, Mass.: Blackwell, 29–55.
Burge, T. 1979. "Individualism and the Mental," *Midwest Studies in Philosophy*, vol. IV, Minneapolis:
     University of Minnesota Press, 73–121.
Burge, T. 1982. "Other Bodies," in A. Woodfield (ed.), *Thought and Object*, Oxford: Clarendon Press,
     97–120.
Burge, T. 1985. "Cartesian Error and the Objectivity of Perception," in R. Grimm and D. Merrill (eds.),
     Contents of Thought, Arizona: University of Arizona Press, 86–98.
Burge, T. 1986. "Individualism and Psychology," *The Philosophical Review* 94: 3–45.
Burge, T. 1988. "Individualism and Self-Knowledge," *The Journal of Philosophy* 85: 649–63.
Burge, T. 1996. "Our Entitlement to Self-Knowledge," *Proceedings of the Aristotelian Society* 96: 91–116.
Burge, T. 1998. "Reason and the First Person," in C. Wright, B. Smith, and C. Macdonald (eds.), *Knowing
     Our Own Minds*, Oxford: Oxford University Press, 243–70.
Dodd, J. 1995. "McDowell and Identity-theories of Truth," *Analysis* 55: 160–5.
Evans, G. 1982. *The Varieties of Reference*, Oxford: Clarendon Press.
Macdonald, C. 1989. *Mind–Body Identity-Theories*, London: Routledge.
Macdonald, C. 1995. "Externalism and First-Person Authority," *Synthèse* 104: 99–122.
Macdonald, C. 1998. "Externalism and Authoritative Self-Knowledge," in C. Wright, B. Smith, and C.
     Macdonald (eds.), *Knowing Our Own Minds*, Oxford: Oxford University Press.
Macdonald, C. 1999. "Shoemaker on Self-Knowledge and Inner Sense," *Philosophy and Phenomenological
     Research* 59: 711–38.
McDowell, J. 1977. "On the Sense and Reference of a Proper Name," *Mind* 86: 159–85. Reprinted in
     McDowell 1998.
McDowell, J. 1984. "*De Re* Senses," *Philosophical Quarterly* 34/136: 283–94. Reprinted in McDowell
     1998a.
McDowell, J. 1986. "Singular Thought and the Extent of Inner Space," in P. Pettit and J. McDowell (eds.),
     Subject, Thought, and Context, Oxford: Clarendon Press, 137–68. Reprinted in McDowell 1998a.
McDowell, J. 1994. *Mind and World*, Cambridge, Mass.: Harvard University Press.
McDowell, J. 1998a. *Meaning, Knowledge, and Reality*, Cambridge, Mass.: Harvard University Press.

McDowell, J. 1998b. "Response to Crispin Wright," in C. Wright, B. Smith, and C. Macdonald (eds.), *Knowing Our Own Minds*, Oxford: Oxford University Press, 48–62.

McKinsey, M. 1991. "Anti-Individualism and Privileged Access," *Analysis* 51: 9–16.

Peacocke, C. 1996. "Entitlement, Self-Knowledge and Conceptual Redeployment," *Proceedings of the Aristotelian Society* 96: 117–58.

Peacocke, C. 1998. "Conscious Attitudes, Attention, and Self-Knowledge," in C. Wright, B. Smith, and C. Macdonald (eds.), *Knowing Our Own Minds*, Oxford: Oxford University Press, 63–98.

Putnam, H. 1975. "The Meaning of 'Meaning'," in K. Gunderson (ed.), *Language, Mind, and Knowledge. Minnesota Studies in the Philosophy of Science*, vol. 7, Minneapolis: University of Minnesota Press, 1979. Reprinted in *Mind, Language, and Reality*, vol. II, Cambridge, Mass.: Cambridge University Press, 1975, 215–71.

Robinson, H. 1994. *Perception*, London: Routledge.

Shoemaker, S. 1994. "Self-Knowledge and Inner Sense," *Philosophy and Phenomenological Research* 54: 249–314.

Response to Cynthia Macdonald

1 Macdonald mostly discusses some material of mine in which I consider implications of a couple of varieties of externalism. As she notes, the passage she cites to document my so-called "quietism"[1] is not from the same context. But she writes as if the "quietism" passage were meant to address a supposed problem about the consistency of self-knowledge with externalism. This is a juxtaposition that strikes me as unfortunate.

My point in the "quietism" passage is about what would be required for there to be a problem about the asymmetry between some knowledge one can have of states and occurrences in one's own mind and any knowledge others can have of those states and occurrences. Suppose someone asks: "How is it possible that one can speak authoritatively about how things are with one, without needing to base one's pronouncements on investigation, or indeed on anything?" I claim that until we have been told why it should seem impossible that self-knowledge should be special in that way, the question does not present a determinate problem.

It is only under protest that I allow "quietism" as a label for this line of thought. "Quietism" might mean a refusal to concern oneself with certain problems. But my point is not to acknowledge that there is a problem about self-knowledge while refusing to address it. My point is to express a skepticism about whether a problem has been posed.

In the paper Macdonald quotes from, I argue that Crispin Wright's attempt, in particular, to find something problematic in the asymmetry between self-knowledge and knowledge others might have about oneself is unconvincing. Of course someone might try to do better. A blanket denial that there could be a good "How possible?" question about the asymmetry would be merely dogmatic. My so-called "quietism" amounts to a challenge to formulate a good "How possible?" question about the asymmetry, and an alert to the fact that philosophers typically do not take the trouble to show that their supposed problems really are problems.

Externalism is not even on the scene here. The question is whether the asymmetry between self-knowledge and knowledge on the part of others sets an explanatory task for philosophers, and my so-called "quietism" is a skepticism about that. Wright, who is my target here, does not claim it is externalism that makes the asymmetry problematic.

2   If I were forced to address the question whether externalism brings a problem about the asymmetry into view, I would, as it happens, be similarly skeptical. But this would not be an application of some general quietism. It would need to be defended by specific thoughts about the supposed problem. And though in the essay Macdonald discusses I come as close to considering that question as I do anywhere, what I do there is at best obliquely related to it.

This makes for a problem about Macdonald's paper. She reads the material she considers as if it were meant to argue that externalism raises no problem about the special character of self-knowledge. But in fact that question is off-stage in the paper she considers.

My aim in that paper is to suggest that a conception of singular thought as object-dependent points the way to improving on a Cartesian conception of the "inner." There is more than one thing that is unsatisfactory about a Cartesian conception of the "inner." My target is the way the Cartesian conception represents us as confined in our own "inner" worlds, so that our access to the "outer" world, and the access of others to our "inner" world, come to look problematic. My target is not an implication of the Cartesian conception for whether externalism can be made out to be consistent with the asymmetry between self-knowledge and knowledge on the part of others.

The material Macdonald considers comes from a section in which I try to capture the flavor of the Cartesian conception, in the first instance as applied to perceptual experience.

In ancient skepticism appearances are said not to be open to question, but the concept of truth is not applied in connection with how things appear to a subject. How things appear to a subject is not counted as a case of how things are. Following a suggestion by M. F. Burnyeat, I approach what is distinctive about the Cartesian conception of the "inner" by way of how it diverges from that.

The first step away is to extend the concept of truth to statements about how things appear to subjects. With this step, appearances are seen as facts, and the ancient idea that appearances are not open to question becomes the idea that a subject's pronouncements about how things appear to her reflect an infallible capacity to get those facts right. The result is a conception of a range of facts about how it is with a subject that are infallibly knowable by the subject. These facts can naturally be conceived as "inner." And this idea of a region of infallibly knowable "inner" facts might seem already Cartesian.

But for a Cartesian picture of perceptual experience we need a second step. We need to suppose that the "inner" region of reality that is newly recognized with the first step is exhausted by the facts brought into view by that step: facts infallibly knowable by the subject, to the effect that things appear a certain way to her. Only with this second step do we arrive at the picture of a region of reality whose layout is through and through available to an infallible cognitive capacity.

This second step is not required by the first. To show that we can stop at the result of the first step, I invoke a disjunctive conception of appearances, in the sense of facts to the effect that things appear a certain way to a subject. A fact to the effect that things look a certain way to a subject – to focus on visual appearances in particular – is either the fact that things are that way making itself visually manifest to the subject, or the fact that it merely looks to the subject as if that is the case. Those are two different possible configurations in the subject's "inner" world. The infallible capacity that comes into view when we take the first step does not provide knowledge of which disjunct obtains. So we can take the first step, and equip ourselves with the idea of a realm of "inner" reality knowable in a special way by its subject, without going all the way to the Cartesian picture, in which "inner" facts are all knowable by their subject with the certainty of the *cogito*.

I go on to exploit an analogy between the disjunctive conception of perceptual appearances and a disjunctive conception of situations in which it at least seems to one that one is entertaining an object-dependent thought. Here too one cannot be wrong about the seeming. But here too such situations come in two kinds, those in which one is entertaining an object-dependent thought and those in which that merely seems to be so. As before, those are two different possible configurations of a subjectivity. A subject can take herself to be entertaining an object-dependent thought when, because the supposed object does not exist, there is no such thought to be entertained, so the appearance that she is entertaining an object-dependent thought is a *mere* appearance. We can put that by saying the two different possible configurations can be indistinguishable from the subject's point of view. But the parallel indistinguishability in the case of appearances does not imply that a visual experience (say) cannot *be* seeing that things are thus and so – as opposed to something that, along with circumstances external to it, enters into the constitution of a case of seeing that things are thus and so. Just so, the indistinguishability in this case does not imply that object-dependence cannot be an intrinsic feature of a configuration in a mind. It does not imply that object-dependence is merely a feature of a way of attributing states that have their character independently of extra-mental objects.

In both these areas, what I urge amounts to a defense of the idea that configurations of subjectivity can be externalistically constituted. Perceiving that such-and-such is the case requires that such-and-such be the case, and having an object-dependent thought requires that the object exist. In both areas, moreover, I claim that the states in question come within the scope of a distinctively self-related kind of knowledge, at least under less specific characterizations: as cases of at least seeming to perceive that such-and-such is the case and at least seeming to entertain an object-dependent thought. I do not consider whether they come within the scope of a special self-knowledge under their more specific, externalistically determined characterizations also. If that question arose, I would urge that they do. It seems plausible that that is an implication of the claim I do make, that under those more specific characterizations they are configurations of subjectivity. But it is not to my purpose to defend the implication directly, and I do nothing in that direction in the paper Macdonald discusses. My purpose there is fulfilled by arguing that indistinguishability from the subject's point of view between actually perceiving, or actually entertaining an object-dependent thought, and merely seeming to perceive, or to entertain an object-dependent thought, does not imply that actually perceiving, or actually entertaining an object-dependent thought, is anything but an intrinsic character of an "inner" state.

I offer no general picture of self-knowledge here. In a passage Macdonald quotes, I recommend that we should regard the capacity to know how things perceptually appear to one as a concomitant of a self-consciously possessed capacity to perceive how things are. Knowledge of how things appear to one is, unsurprisingly, immune to the risks of error that attend the capacity to acquire knowledge of the environment through perception. This thought is obviously specific to perceptual appearances. It does not carry over to the capacity to know, on occasion, that it at least seems to one that one is entertaining a singular thought. That capacity is a particular case of the capacity to know what one is, or at least seems to be, thinking. That is something I do not discuss, but simply take for granted.

3   In the case of perceptual appearances, the only special capacity for self-knowledge that I have occasion to make anything of is an infallible capacity for knowledge of how things appear to one. That is what results from the ancient idea that appearances are not open to question, when how things appear to a subject comes to be conceived as a case of how things are.

To repeat, this step yields an innocuous, not yet Cartesian, picture of an "inner" region of reality, populated by facts within the scope of this infallible capacity for knowledge. The point of the disjunctive conception of appearances is that it enables us to recognize further truths, in that region of the "inner" world, that are not infallibly knowable by the subject. Someone else may be better placed than the subject to know which of the two disjuncts obtains. I may take myself to see that things are thus and so in a situation in which someone else, who is in a position to know that things are not thus and so, knows, as I do not, that it merely looks to me as if things are thus and so.

Self-knowledge has a special authority. And Macdonald glosses this authority by saying that a self-knower is "better placed" than others (n.1). Given what I have just said, this has the effect of ruling out, from the start, any possibility that one's knowledge that one is, say, seeing that such-and-such is the case as opposed to merely seeming to, or that one is entertaining a singular thought as opposed to merely seeming to, can have the special authority of self-knowledge. When she offers her gloss, Macdonald purports to leave it open whether the authority of self-knowledge, understood in the way she is explaining, requires infallibility. But the gloss implies that in the picture I rehearsed in section 2, it is only the results of the not yet Cartesian infallible capacity to know how things at least seem to one that can exemplify that special authority. In keeping with this, when she speculates about what I would need to say in response to her questions, Macdonald takes it that I would have to find something a subject can know infallibly, to be the content of self-knowledge in cases where some aspect of how things are with a subject is not infallibly knowable by that subject because it is externalistically determined.

This is tendentious. In section 2 I remarked that it is plausible that configurations of subjectivity should be, just as such, within the scope of self-knowledge. My point there was that that was not something I set out to defend in the paper Macdonald discusses. But if the suggestion is right, Macdonald's gloss on the authority of self-knowledge would blankly exclude my claim that those externalistically determined state-attributions are specifications of configurations of subjectivity, further specifications of how things intrinsically are in the "inner" realm. Her gloss cannot be common ground between us, on the basis of which she can pose problems for my thinking. The gloss has to be wrong by my lights.

Suppose I see that things are thus and so, and suppose I know that I do. Clearly the capacity that is operative in my having this knowledge has exactly the fallibility of my capacity to acquire the knowledge I acquire by seeing that things are thus and so. In a different case, the same capacity may lead me to think I see that things are thus and so when it merely looks to me as if things are thus and so – as someone else, better placed than I am, may know.

Why should it seem to follow that when I know that I see that things are thus and so, my knowledge cannot have the distinctive character of self-knowledge? What is special about self-knowledge is how it differs from knowledge of the same facts that others can have. Knowledge on the part of others has to be mediated by awareness of one's behavior, facial expressions, and so forth. What I have just acknowledged is that a subject is fallible as to whether her experience constitutes seeing that things are thus and so, with a fallibility that matches her fallibility as to whether things are as she thinks she sees they are. But of course that does not imply that to know that she is seeing that things are thus and so she needs to advert to the sort of "outer" manifestations others need to advert to. A subject's knowledge that she is seeing how things are contrasts with the knowledge others can have that she is seeing how things are in just the right way. It is irrelevant that the capacity that issues in such knowledge is fallible. The special authority of self-knowledge consists in its not needing a basis, not in its being such that others cannot be better placed to know the facts in question.

Similarly with knowledge that one is entertaining a singular thought. Suppose, at the zoo, I express a thought by saying "That tiger looks undernourished." If the perceptual presence of a tiger to me were an illusion, I would merely seem to be entertaining a thought of the kind I take myself to be entertaining, and someone else might be better placed than I am to know that that is so. The capacity that issues in my knowing that I am entertaining such a thought is fallible. But suppose the presence of the tiger is not an illusion, and I do know that I am entertaining such a thought. Here again, the fact that I am not better placed than anyone else to know that I am entertaining such a thought does not imply that my knowledge has the character that someone else's knowledge of the same fact would have. My knowledge is not mediated by "outer" manifestations. This knowledge too is special, in comparison with knowledge others might have, in not needing a basis. The asymmetry between the first person and the second or third is not threatened.

4 That deals, in effect, with the first of Macdonald's three problems about combining externalism with self-knowledge.

The second involves attempting "tiger" thoughts – thoughts in specifying whose content our word "tiger" can correctly be used – when such thoughts are unavailable because one is on Twin Earth, where there are no·tigers. And the third involves someone else being better placed to know that one's "tiger" thoughts are "tiger" thoughts, because this other person knows, as one does not, that one is not on Twin Earth.

As far as I can see, these cases pose no real problems for the consistency of externalism with self-knowledge.

In the case that poses the second supposed problem, the only way I can make sense of the subject's even attempting "tiger" thoughts – assuming an externalistic account of "tiger" thoughts – is to assume she learned to think on Earth, where there are tigers, and has been unknowingly transported to Twin Earth. But in that case, why must her attempts at "tiger" thoughts fail to be "tiger" thoughts, as opposed to succeeding in being "tiger" thoughts, though, as such, they are not true of any animals she might come across in her present environment?

It is true that someone else might have knowledge this subject does not have. She will think she can explain her use of "tiger" by, say, pointing at some of the animals in her environment and saying something like "My word 'tiger' is true of animals of the kind these animals belong to." And someone who knows that she is on Twin Earth will be in a position to know that that does not capture what she means by "tiger." But it does not follow that she does not know, with the authority of self-knowledge, what she is thinking when she thinks a "tiger" thought. She can use the word "tiger," expressing her Earth-acquired conceptual capacity, to say what she is thinking. And, as before, this knowledge is not mediated by awareness of "outer" manifestations of her meaning what she says she means, so the asymmetry between self-knowledge and other-knowledge is preserved. The knowledge she lacks is irrelevant.

As for the case that poses the third supposed problem, here too it is not clear that the problem is real. Consider a subject who has never encountered Twin Earth thought experiments. That leaves her knowledge of what she is thinking when she thinks "tiger" thoughts unthreatened. If she had been brought up on Twin Earth, the words she might use to express her knowledge of what she is thinking when she thinks "tiger" thoughts would have determined the thoughts as being about pligers, and she has not considered that possibility and ruled it out. But she was not brought up on Twin Earth, and the words, with the meaning they have acquired in her upbringing on Earth, serve perfectly well to express her knowledge that the thoughts are about tigers.

Macdonald asks us to contemplate someone who knows, as the subject does not, that that alternative way things might have been – her word "tiger" being true, not of tigers, but of pligers – is not actual. But is it so clear that the subject does not know that? Since she does not have the idea of Twin Earth or the idea of pligers, she is not in a position to express any knowledge of hers in those terms. But she does know that the animals she means by "tigers" are *tigers*, not animals of some other kind. In knowing that, she knows something that implies that they are not pligers, even though she lacks the conceptual resources to formulate this implication. And this knowledge of what she means by "tigers" is knowledge for which, unlike anyone else, she needs no basis. So it stands in the required contrast with knowledge of what she means that others might have.

Note

1   From p. 58 of my "Response to Crispin Wright," in C. Wright, B. Smith, and C. Macdonald (eds.), *Knowing Our Own Minds*, Oxford: Oxford University Press, 1998.

5

Personal Identity, Ethical not Metaphysical

Carol Rovane

When Locke begat the philosophical dispute about personal identity, he argued for a distinction between personal identity and human (animal) identity on the basis of a thought experiment. He asked us to imagine that the consciousnesses of a prince and a cobbler are switched, each into the other's body, and to work out where the *persons* of the prince and the cobbler would then be. He took it to be obvious that each would be where his consciousness went rather than remain with his original body.

Broadly speaking, there are three main lines of response to Locke now in currency. Proponents of his distinction tend to argue for it on the basis of what they take to be uncontroversial metaphysical assumptions about the nature of mind (most often they assume that psychological facts supervene on non-psychological facts, such as functional facts, neurophysiological facts, or physical facts in the narrow sense associated with physical theory). Opponents of his distinction tend to argue that it involves some sort of incoherence. And a smallish minority advocates a more cautious line, according to which we would first need a full-fledged scientific account of the nature and basis of consciousness before we could reasonably take a stand, either for or against Locke's distinction. (In contrast, the various proponents and opponents of the distinction believe that no amount of scientific investigation will ever undermine their respective arguments.)

Despite their obvious differences, these three main lines of response to Locke have something in common. They presume that the issue of personal identity is a purely metaphysical issue that can be settled independently of ethical considerations. This is not because the issue is generally regarded as being devoid of ethical significance. On the contrary. Many philosophers regard it as having great ethical significance. But they presume that, in the proper order of investigation, metaphysics must be prior to ethics. Their thought is that we won't have earned the right to our view about the ethical significance of personal identity until after we have arrived at a correct metaphysical account of it. One of the themes of this chapter is that such a value-neutral approach to the issue of personal identity isn't available.

I say it is a theme, because I don't have the space here to give a full defense of it.[1] Instead, I propose to illustrate it by taking John McDowell's responses to the issue of personal identity as a case study.

In section I I will review his critical discussion of Derek Parfit's account of personal identity,[2] and explain why it appears to me that the purely metaphysical considerations that he raises against Parfit fall short of a refutation. Parfit agrees with Locke that the same person could survive in a new and different animal body. He goes on to make an even more controversial claim, that a person could have something as good as survival without identity – with two or more future selves. McDowell rejects both of these claims on a combination of phenomenological and transcendental grounds. I will show that Parfit need not oppose McDowell on these grounds in order to defend his claims.

Obviously, the possibility that Parfit raises, of something as good as survival without identity, would depart in crucial ways from life as we know it. But McDowell forces us to consider in detail how much it would depart from the phenomenology of personal consciousness as we know it. Or, to put the point in another way, he forces us to consider in detail how much the phenomenology of personal consciousness as we know it owes to the way in which it is situated in animal life. That is why so much would be lost in the possibilities that Locke and Parfit have raised, where the life of a given person can diverge from the life of a given animal.

Being forced by McDowell to think about this has made me realize that my own sympathy for Parfit's suggestions derives from a preoccupation with an aspect of personhood that Parfit does not himself make central in his own account, namely, *personal agency*. The reason why I think we could have something as good as survival without identity is not because I think that personal consciousness as we know it would be preserved in such a case. It is because I think that we could frame and carry out personal projects that would be appropriate to the case and, in doing so, we could achieve a real continuity of personal point of view – even into a branching future.

This last claim goes together with an even more radical suggestion that I've defended elsewhere.[3] It is a revisionist suggestion that flows from sustained reflection on the familiar and important conception of the person as a reflective rational agent. If I'm right, then it follows from that conception that there could, in principle, be group persons who are composed of many human beings and, also, multiple persons within a human being. This gives us a novel way of interpreting Locke's distinction between personal and animal identity that does not depend at all on his idea – which Parfit takes over and McDowell challenges – that the same personal consciousness could be transferred from one animal body to another. It depends rather on the ways in which human agency can be exercised from points of view that are neither determined by their bodily points of view, nor, for that matter, by their phenomenological points of view. Such agency is exercised, rather, from a rational point of view. And that is something that needs to be understood in wholly normative terms, as opposed to biological or phenomenological terms.

There is no doubt in my mind that McDowell would be just as opposed to this way of defending Locke's distinction as to any other way. In his view, personal agency is just as situated in animal life as is personal consciousness. But he has yet to offer a detailed account of why this is so. His remarks about personal agency are usually brief addenda to much longer accounts of consciousness and experience, with an indication that it should be given parallel treatment. At the end of section II I will try to follow out what I expect his line of thought would be as best as I can and then explain why here too – as is the case with his objections to Parfit – I don't think that the purely metaphysical considerations he would bring to bear amount to a refutation.

There is a parity here. The metaphysical considerations that move Parfit and me to embrace our versions of Locke's distinction between personal and animal identity would not amount to a refutation of McDowell either. Indeed, his overall philosophical vision supplies just about the most subtle, systematic, and powerful reasons that I know for rejecting Locke's distinction in favor of the "animalist" view of personal identity. But, all the same, I don't think they absolutely compel us to embrace that view, any more than Parfit's metaphysical considerations compel us to embrace the opposing view.

For reasons I can't fully rehearse here, I think this is par for the course in the philosophical dispute about personal identity.[4] The opposed parties are locked in a metaphysical stalemate. That is one reason why I recommend that we turn to ethical considerations – in order to tip the metaphysical balance as it were.

In the concluding section, I will show that ethical considerations already *are* intruding in what McDowell and Parfit take to be a purely metaphysical dispute between them. Indeed, it seems to me that their ethical differences are, quite literally, sustaining their disagreement about personal identity. Since their ethical differences are profound, I don't think that bringing them in will necessarily help to resolve their disagreement. But it will help us to better understand the real terms of their debate. I will close by indicating what sorts of ethical considerations incline me to take the view I do of personal identity, which countenances the possibility of group and multiple persons. I will also try to identify some of the ethical, as opposed to purely metaphysical, sources of McDowell's probable opposition to it.

I   McDowell's Criticisms of Parfit

Parfit claims that the existence of a person consists in "nothing but" the existence of certain sorts of psychological events standing in certain sorts of psychological relations. Part of the point of insisting that there is nothing more to the existence of a person is to flag that there is no such thing as a soul or ego that houses the psychological events and relations which, according to Parfit, constitute the life of a person. Another part of the point is to allow for Locke's distinction between personal and animal identity. Parfit's idea is that a person continues to exist so long as the requisite psychological relations hold over time. Nothing else – such as their holding within the same brain or body – is required for the continued existence of that person. Locke's distinction follows, so long as it is possible for such psychological relations to reach across animal bodies. Parfit thinks they can, largely because he thinks of psychological facts as supervening on non-psychological facts which are, in principle, duplicatable. Thus, insofar as my current psychological state supervenes on my current brain state, I can survive in a new and different animal body so long as that same brain state can be duplicated within that animal body. Why does Parfit think that I, the very same person, could be said to exist in this condition? Because the resulting person would remember my past, complete my projects and, more generally, approach the world from the point of view that I take to be mine, including regarding itself *as me*. This, you might say, is Parfit's interpretation of Locke's notion of "sameness of consciousness" – which, both philosophers agree, is a necessary and sufficient condition for sameness of person, regardless of any changes of bodily circumstance.

One objection that is widely regarded as fatal to the Lockean position is the so-called "duplication objection." But Parfit doesn't regard it as fatal. Instead, he takes it as an occasion for revising some of our common-sense ideas and, even, some of our more theoretical ideas about personal identity. I don't think it is possible to fully understand his thesis of psychological reductionism independently of his response to this objection. The objection claims that personal identity cannot be analyzed in terms of psychological relations because personal identity is necessarily a one-to-one relation, whereas psychological relations are not necessarily one-to-one. In other words, two or more persons can bear psychological relations to the same past events and, yet, they cannot both be identical to a single past person. Because this is so, there is a prima facie difficulty about analyzing identity in terms of psychological relations. Parfit's response can be boiled down to the claim: so much the worse for personal identity. When we think of the future and wish to survive, it is psychological relations to our future selves that really "matter" to us. If it should turn out that two future persons will bear psychological relations to the present "me," then I shall have all that matters to my survival, except in duplicate. Of course, if I want to persist uniquely, I won't have everything I want. But Parfit's point is that losing one's identity through psychological duplication wouldn't be like ordinary death. It's not as though there would be no one who could remember my present and past, or no one to carry out my projects.

McDowell raises many just complaints against Parfit, most of which I won't discuss because I want to move directly to what I see as the heart of their disagreement.[5] It concerns the nature of first-person thought and reference.

In order to see what McDowell is driving at, let's start by considering first-person thought as we normally find it, in "non-branching" lives where personal survival involves strict identity over time. In such lives, first-person reference reaches across time, backward via memory and forward via anticipation and intention. And the pronoun "I" refers uniquely to the same thing throughout, a single, abiding person. It also expresses this identity. That is to say, when my memories present themselves in the first-person mode, as memories of what I have done or experienced, part of my thought is that *I* – the person now remembering – am *also* the person who did and experienced those things. This is built into the very concept of memory. It is a conceptual truth that the past I remember is *mine* and no one else's.

According to McDowell, this conceptual truth goes together with a feature of first-person reference that Gareth Evans labelled "identification-freedom."[6] In first-person modes of thought, the identity of the person being referred to is already settled, without the need for any identifying work. Thus, memories do not report that *someone* did something, and then leave one to work out *who* did it. The identity of the person who did it is already *given* with the first-person mode in which memories present themselves, namely, *oneself.* But a question arises: how is it possible for first-person thought to reach out, even across time, to the right referent – myself – without my having to do any identifying work? McDowell takes over and elaborates Evan's answer to this question. The capacity for first-person thought belongs by nature to human beings, as part of their biological endowment. The same holds for memory. The specific function of memory, for a particular human being, is to retain information about its own past. This function requires that the contents of memories be first personal. It also permits first-person reference to be identification-free. Given the situatedness of memories in a particular animal's life, no question can arise about *whose* life is being remembered. It is guaranteed to be the life of the particular human animal in which the memories are situated.

Aside from accounting for the conceptual truth linking memory with personal identity, and aside from explaining how and why first-person reference can be "identification-free," McDowell's way of situating first-person thought in animal life has an additional advantage. It allows us to make sense of the possibility of errors of memory. Since "remember" is a success verb, there can't be errors of memory strictly speaking. But there can be errors in which we wrongly take ourselves to remember things – cases of merely apparent memory. And it is an old objection against Locke that his account of personal identity does not provide us with adequate conceptual resources with which to distinguish cases of merely apparent memory from veridical memory. For that purpose, we would need to conceive a person's history in terms of something besides what the person takes to be its history – something "outside" the person's consciousness. McDowell provides this by equating personal identity with animal identity. The history of the person is the history of a particular human being, whose inward impressions of that history are not necessarily veridical, even though they normally are.

It follows from McDowell's account of the first person that Parfit's duplication scenarios do not involve memory at all; rather, they involve an *illusion* of memory. If the function of memory is, as McDowell describes, to provide first-person information about a particular animal's history, then a duplicate of me cannot remember my past. And this is so regardless of whether the duplicate is a true duplicate living alongside the "real" me in my original body, or whether the duplicate is the unique survivor of my biological death.

I think McDowell is probably right about the phenomenology of human memory. When we take ourselves to remember something, we automatically take ourselves to be remembering our *own* pasts in a sense that involves strict identity over time. But I don't think Parfit's view absolutely requires him to challenge this phenomenological point. In fact, the point isn't challenged in most descriptions of duplication scenarios. We are typically asked to imagine, in the first person, that the supervenience base of *my* current psychological state is reproduced in another body. Insofar as my current state includes having the impression of being identical with the person whose past experiences and actions I now remember, my duplicate is bound to share that impression – which is bound to be erroneous.

However, this needn't prevent me from embracing a branching future in the spirit that Parfit recommends, as something that would be as good as ordinary survival except without identity. All I need to do is to figure out a way in which my duplicates can *compensate* for the illusions that will arise in such a future. They will need to bear in mind that what they seem to remember did not happen to *them* in the sense that implies identity. (In all other respects, their apparent memories will, of course, reliably inform them about real past events.[7])

It must be admitted that ordinary language doesn't provide us with the tools we would need in order to describe – and, indeed, to live – the sorts of "branching" lives that Parfit is asking us to envisage. For example, duplicates would need another term besides the ordinary term "memory" in order to correctly describe their relation to the past events that present themselves in their apparent memories. Sydney Shoemaker introduced the technical term "quasi-memory" for this purpose, and I have proposed to supplement his innovation with a quasi-first-personal pronoun, "I*."[8] These technical terms would enable a duplicate to correctly describe the intimate connection that it bears to its past, by saying "I quasi-remember that I* did such-and-such." "I*" would have forward-looking uses as well, not on the part of duplicates but on the part of the antecedent person who exists before duplication and who anticipates a branching future. Such a person could, for example, form the quasi-intention that I* will do such-and-such, with the understanding that the quasi-intention would be carried out by one or another of its future selves.

When we first try to imagine what it would be like to form and act on quasi-intentions, we are naturally struck by two related problems. One is a problem of individuation: how could a person who anticipates branching direct separate quasi-intentions at different future selves? The other is a problem of motivation: since all of the future selves would quasi-remember all of the same quasi-intentions, why should they be moved by the ones directed at them rather than by the other quasi-intentions that they also quasi-remember? I believe that the problem of individuation could easily be solved by appropriate temporal, spatial, and other descriptive qualifications on uses of "I*." I also believe that, once the problem of individuation is solved, the problem of motivation should go away. It should be no more difficult than the problem that we have to solve in our non-branching lives when we form intentions to do different things at different times. Suppose I intend to do something at 3 p.m. today, but I have also formed intentions about what to do at 4 p.m., 5 p.m., . . . tomorrow, next week, next year, and so on. At 3 p.m. today I will probably remember all of these other intentions. How can I count on myself to act on the right one? Clearly, there is no causal mechanism by which I can ensure this.[9] If I do what I originally intended to do at 3 p.m. it will be because there is good reason, which I will then recognize, to do so. The same would hold true of duplicate selves. They will act on the quasi-intentions that were specifically directed at them, provided that there is good reason, which they will then recognize, to do so. They might, of course, choose a different course. But changes of mind are always possible, even in non-branching lives.[10]

I want to draw attention to the fact that references to the past and the future with "I*" would not be identification-free in the way that McDowell claims for ordinary first-person reference with "I." "I*" has a variable reference, depending on the context in which it is being used – whether it is before or after branching, and whether it is in the context of a forward-looking or a backward-looking attitude. And its reference would have to be nailed down in the ways I just described above in connection with the problem of individuation, through appropriate temporal, spatial, and descriptive qualifications. The fact that reference with "I*" would be identification-dependent in these ways should not be surprising. As McDowell himself insists, the conditions for identification-free reference with "I" are not in place in the cases we're trying to imagine. But this does no harm to the positive point that "I*" is a tool that, along with notions like quasi-memory and quasi-intention, could be used by persons in order to cope successfully with the sort of branching existence that Parfit is asking us to envisage.

McDowell might respond by insisting that I haven't taken into account the whole range of metaphysical considerations that he can invoke in favor of the opposed animalist view of personal identity. In addition to the issues I've discussed so far concerning the first person, there are also much larger issues to contend with. They concern nothing less than transcendental questions about the very possibility of experience, and the contribution of experience to intentionality in general.[11] McDowell's transcendental goal is to portray experience as a form of direct contact with things without compromising the fact that the contents of experience are fully conceptualized and, hence, have an irreducibly normative dimension which is intelligible only from within the space of reasons. This raises something of a puzzle: how can experience put the mind in touch with things which themselves stand outside the space of reasons while, at the same time, have content that is intelligible only from within that space? I won't try to do justice to McDowell's solution to this puzzle. I only want to emphasize that his solution requires us to think of subjects of experience as animals. He rightly points out that, in all animal life – including non-rational animals – the function of the senses is to put animals in direct touch with various things in their environments that they need to cope with. The difference in the human case is that sensory capacities must work in tandem with conceptual capacities, so that things can be perceived from within the space of reasons – and, thereby, become topics for rational reflection as well as objects of experience.

It seems to me that Parfit can accept a great deal of McDowell's account of experience without giving up his version of Locke's distinction between personal and animal identity. He can allow that persons require animal embodiment at all times of their existence, because without such embodiment they could not be subjects of experience at all. And, yet, he can also insist that the life of a given person can, over time, diverge from the life of a given animal.

The matter would be different if McDowell were claiming that consciousness is tied to animal life in such a way as to rule out the illusions that he sees in Parfit's duplication scenarios – if it were impossible to produce, in another animal body, so much as the impression of being me and remembering my past. Perhaps those who wish to leave the dispute about personal identity for science to settle believe that science might eventually show us that these illusions are impossible. So let me put my point conditionally: *if* we are willing to allow that these illusions are possible, then I think it is also possible to embrace a future that involves them in the ways I've been suggesting in this section. I do not see that this conditional claim is undermined by the broader transcendental considerations that incline McDowell to embrace the animalist view of personal identity.

II Group and Multiple Persons

Perhaps it could be fairly said against Parfit that his way of conceiving personal survival does not really do justice to Locke's original idea that sameness of person consists in sameness of consciousness. Perhaps the cognitive work I described in the last section, by which persons could hold themselves together over time across different animal bodies, would get in the way of their sustaining a single phenomenological point of view over time. Perhaps the sorts of "psychological contuinuity" that they could achieve would be better viewed as a form of rational and practical continuity than as a form of consciousness per se. If all this is so, then Locke was wrong to suppose that the same consciousness could be transferred from one animal body to another. But all the same, he might not have been wrong to think that personal identity is distinct from animal identity. That depends upon how close the connection is between personal identity and personal consciousness.

In this section, I will argue that there need not be any such connection at all. If we are prepared to conceive persons as reflective rational agents, then we shall see that the condition of their identity is not the condition in which there is a single consciousness. A single agent can incorporate many distinct consciousnesses, and a single consciousness can be the site of many distinct agents. So, even if consciousness is necessarily tied to animal life in the deepest possible way, it doesn't follow that the life of a person is. There can be multiple persons within a single being and, also, group persons composed of many human beings.[12]

The first step of my argument notes that persons – qua reflective rational agents – are subject to certain normative requirements of rationality. Moreover, they are also *committed* to satisfying those requirements in the following sense: they grasp, and are responsive to, their normative force.

The most general requirement of rationality is that a person should arrive at and act upon all-things-considered judgments about what it would be best to do in the light of all of its beliefs, desires, and other attitudes. Such judgments presuppose a variety of rational activities that together comprise a person's deliberations, such as the following: resolving contradictions among one's beliefs; working out the implications of one's beliefs and other attitudes; and ranking one's preferences in a transitive ordering. Each of these rational activities is directed at meeting a specific normative requirement of rationality – the requirements of consistency, closure, and transitivity of preferences, respectively. But they all have a common purpose, which is to contribute to the overarching rational goal of arriving at and acting upon all-things-considered judgments.[13] I'm going to call the state that would be achieved if a person were to succeed in this endeavor, of arriving at and acting upon all-things-considered judgments, the state of *overall rational unity*. And I'm going to suppose that there is one overarching normative requirement of rationality on persons that incorporates all of the other, more specific requirements like consistency, closure, etc. – namely, the normative requirement to achieve overall rational unity.

The next step of my argument notes that the normative requirements of rationality contain an implicit reference to *personal identity*. For the requirement to achieve overall rational unity *defines* what it is for an *individual* person to be fully or ideally rational. (This can be seen from the fact that there is no failure of rationality when a group of persons fails to meet this ideal, but only when an individual fails to meet it. So, for example, if I have inconsistent beliefs, I am guilty of rational failure; but my beliefs may be inconsistent with yours without there being any rational failure on either of our parts.) One promising way to approach the problem of personal identity, then, is to investigate the condition in which the normative requirement to achieve overall rational unity applies – or, what comes to the same thing, the condition in which a *commitment* to meeting it arises.

It is overwhelmingly plausible that the capacity for reflective rationality belongs to the native biological endowment of human beings. This might seem automatically to entail an animalist conclusion. For, given what I have just said, human beings cannot exercise their rational capacities without aiming for rational unity. And it is hard to see how they could do that without, implicitly, having the very commitment that I am claiming characterizes the individual person.

Here is why an animalist conclusion doesn't follow. Although rational capacities must always be directed at achieving rational unity *somewhere*, they needn't be directed at achieving rational unity within the biological boundaries by which nature marks one human being off from another. Human beings can exercise their native rational capacities in order to achieve different levels of rational unity within different boundaries. They can exercise their rational capacities together so as to achieve rational unity within groups that are larger than a single human being, and they can also exercise their rational capacities in more restricted ways so as to achieve rational unity within parts that are smaller than a single human being. (Here, I obviously don't mean bodily parts, but temporal parts – and these may be scattered temporal parts.) When this happens, it is not individual human beings but, rather, groups and parts of them that function as individual agents. If we follow Locke in assuming that persons are rational agents, then we must conclude that such groups and parts of human beings would qualify as individual persons in their own rights. These claims are bound to meet with skepticism. Unfortunately, I can't give a full defense of them here. What I can do is indicate the kinds of considerations that support them and, in doing so, further elaborate their meaning.

I'll start with the case of group persons. It is well known that when human beings engage in group activities, their joint efforts can take on the characteristics of individual rationality. Think, for example, of marital partners who deliberate together about how to manage their homes and families and other joint concerns. They may in the course of such joint deliberations do as a pair all of the things that individuals characteristically do in order to be rational: they may pool their information, resolve conflicts between them, rank their preferences together, and even arrive at all-things-considered judgments together about what they should think and do together – where the "all" in question comprises all of their pooled deliberative considerations. The same can also happen in a less thoroughgoing way when colleagues co-author papers, or when teams of scientists design and run experiments together, or when corporations set up and follow corporate plans. We tend to assume that such joint endeavors leave human beings intact as individual persons in their own rights. Insofar as that is so, it should be possible to engage those human beings separately in conversation, argument, and other distinctively interpersonal relations. But sometimes this is not possible. Sometimes marital partners won't speak for themselves. Their commitment to deliberating together is so thoroughgoing and so effective that everything they say and do reflects their joint deliberations and never reflects their separate points of view. The same can happen to co-authors, team members, and bureaucrats. The kind of case I have in mind is not one in which human participants simply wish to give voice to the larger viewpoint of the groups to which they belong. The kind of case I have in mind is one in which the human constituents of the group are not committed to having separate viewpoints of their own. That is, these human beings are not committed to achieving overall rational unity separately within their individual lives. Yet it is not because they lack rational capacities. It is because those rational capacities are directed in a different way, so as to help fulfill a larger commitment on the part of a whole group to achieve overall rational unity within it.

If this seems implausible, think about two different attitudes you might bring to a philosophy department meeting. You might bring your own separate viewpoint to the table with the aim of convincing your colleagues to agree with you. This attitude takes for granted the status of each colleague as an individual person in its own right with its own separate point of view. The attitude also *perpetuates* that status. For the effect of adopting it will be that you maintain the separateness of your point of view by deliberating on your own, with the aim of achieving rational unity just within your own self. Even when you are moved by what your colleagues say, the reason why is not that you want to resolve disagreements with them, or do anything else that would help you to achieve rational unity as a group. You will be moved by your colleagues only insofar as what they say bears on your personal project of achieving such unity by yourself – by showing you that you have internal reasons, from your own point of view, to accept what they are saying. But you might bring a quite different attitude to a department meeting, one that would not perpetuate your separateness from your colleagues. You might bring to the table all you have thought of with respect to the issues the department faces, with a view to pooling your thoughts with your colleagues' thoughts, so that you can together discover the all-things-considered significance of the whole group's thinking. If your colleagues do the same, then it won't be true that each of you is committed to achieving overall rational unity on your own; you will be jointly committed to achieving such unity within the department. And, for this reason, it will be possible for others to engage the department itself in conversation, argument, and other distinctively interpersonal relations. The department could be asked, for example, why did you do such and such, and there will be a coherent answer that reflects the department's joint deliberations. I'm not saying that departments of philosophy typically have the commitment that would render them sufficiently unified to be engaged in this way. But I am saying it is possible. It is possible for human-size philosophy professors to undertake a commitment to achieve rational unity together. And, if they were to live up to that commitment, then the lines that divide one person off from another, would have shifted. They would no longer follow the biological divisions that mark off different human animals, or the phenomenological divisions that mark off different centers of consciousness. They would follow nothing else than the commitment to rational unity that is characteristic of the individual person.

It might be objected that my own descriptions of group persons belie my claim that a commitment to unity within a group can obliterate the lines that divide their human participants as separate rational agents with their own rational points. I referred, for example, to two different attitudes that an individual philosophy professor might bring to a department meeting. One would maintain its internal rational unity and, thereby, the separateness of its point of view, while the other would contribute to the overall unity of the department and, thereby, help to constitute the department's more inclusive point of view. I also described two marital partners as each being committed to engaging in joint deliberations. My language may have given the impression that the unity of the group person is in each case actively maintained through individual commitments and efforts on the part of its human members, the philosophy professors and marital partners, respectively. And that seems to imply that the human members themselves must remain individual persons in their own rights even in the context of a group endeavor, since otherwise they could not possibly maintain group unity through their *individual* commitments and efforts. But my language was misleading. What is true is that a group person may *initially* be brought into existence through the individual decisions and actions of smaller persons, typically of human size. But if these initial efforts have been successful, then a group person will have been brought into existence. Thereafter, at least some of the intentional episodes that occur within the human organisms involved will be episodes in the life of a group person rather than in the separate lives of human-size persons. Going back to the case of a philosophy department, when I bring to the table the aim of joining in a departmental deliberation, then, insofar as my aim is shared by others and is efficacious, the result will be that the subsequent deliberations around the table are carried out from a new, emergent group point of view that can't be equated with my point of view or any other human-size point of view.

Let me now outline the considerations that I think support the idea that multiple persons are possible.

These considerations are really generalizations from the case of group persons. In other words, I propose to model *all* cases of rational unity on the unity of a group. My suggestion is that rational unity doesn't *just happen* as the inevitable product of some natural process, such as the natural biological development of a human being. Rational unity is something that is *deliberately achieved* for the sake of some *further end*. There are things that a philosophy department can do as a unified group person that no human-size person can do on its own. And that may constitute a *reason* why such human-size persons might initially decide to pool their efforts in a joint endeavor. If they implement their decision, they no longer maintain separate rational points of view. So, what perpetuates the group person once it has been brought into existence is not separate commitments on the part of its human constituents; it is up to the group itself to maintain its existence by continuing to strive for overall rational unity within it. When we view the unity of a human-size person along these lines, we must see it as deliberately achieved for the sake of some further end that couldn't be achieved without it.

The appropriate contrast here is with an impulsive human being who doesn't strive for rational unity – who doesn't deliberate at all but simply follows current desires unreflectively and uncritically. Since the capacity to deliberate belongs to human nature, perhaps it would be correct to say that such a human being is acting against its nature. But that doesn't harm my point, which is that when human beings do exercise their rational capacities, they are *generating* rational unity through their intentional efforts. And it is part of this same point that these capacities can be directed at the achievement of rational unity within different boundaries. An initially impulsive human being might come to strive for rational unity within each day, or week, or month, or year, or even a whole lifetime. The last goal was celebrated by Plato as part of the just life and by Aristotle as part of the virtuous life. In a less high-minded way, we now typically pursue the project of living a unified human life for the sake of other more specific projects such as lifelong personal relationships (friendships, marriages, families) and, also, careers. But what I want to emphasize is that these are *projects* and they are *optional*. It is possible for human beings to strive for much *less* rational unity than these projects require and still be striving for rational unity. And, sometimes, the result may be relatively independent spheres of rational unity with a significant degree of segregation.

Such segregation is evident in degree in the lives of many human beings whom we find it possible to treat for the most part as roughly human-size persons. We may find, for example, that when we visit the institution where our friend works, the friend "becomes" a bureaucrat who cannot recognize the demands of friendship at all. What this means is that our friend's life actually takes up a bit less than the whole human being we are faced with, the rest of which literally belongs to the life of the institution. According to the account of personal identity that I've been elaborating, this would not aptly be characterized as "role playing." It would be better character- ized as a fragmentation of the human being into relatively independent spheres of rational activity, so as to generate separate rational points of view that can be separately engaged. Of course, group endeavors do not necessarily result in such fragmentation; in principle, they can completely absorb the human lives that they involve (this may actually happen in the armed forces and certain very intense marriages). But when a group endeavor does *not* completely absorb the human lives that it involves, there is a consequent split in those lives.[14] And I propose to conceive multiple persons along precisely these lines. The only difference is that the separate rational points of view of mul- tiple persons need not be imposed by involvements in group projects but, rather, by involvements in other sorts of projects that it is not possible for a single human being to pursue in a wholehearted and unified way. When a human being's projects are numerous, and when they have nothing to do with one another, this may make it pointless to strive to achieve overall rational unity within that human life. And it may be a rational response to let go of the commitment to achieving such overall rational unity within that human life and to strive instead for as many pockets of rational unity as are required for the pursuit of those relatively independent projects. So, just as a group person may dissolve itself for the sake of human-size projects that would otherwise have to be forsaken for the sake of the group's overall unity, a human-size person may dissolve itself for the sake of even smaller projects that would otherwise have to be forsaken for the sake of the human being's overall unity. In such conditions, we will find the emergence of multiple persons within that human being, each of whom can be treated as a person in its own right.

I'm not suggesting that this is typically how persons come into existence, through the break- down of some larger unity. I think it usually occurs in the reverse direction, when it is noticed that there is something worth doing for the sake of which more unity needs to be achieved. That is certainly how group persons would typically come to be. And I'm suggesting that the same holds for human-size persons.

In conclusion, it is not human nature alone, but intentional activity and the undertaking of appropriate projects, which yields the commitment to rational unity that is characteristic of the individual person, and which transforms a human being into a human-size person. There is no law of nature that precludes a less ambitious transformation into multiple persons instead. To a certain extent, this happens when human-size persons give over portions of their lives to group endeavors. And, to a certain extent, this happens in all human lives. Qua reflective rational agents, human beings are less separate from one another, and less whole within themselves, than is ordi- narily assumed. What individuality human beings manage to achieve, qua reflective rational agents, is, truly, an achievement. So it is with every case of rational unity, whether it be in whole human beings, or in groups of them, or in parts of them.

I would expect McDowell to oppose my arguments in this section by invoking transcendental considerations similar to those I briefly mentioned at the end of the last section, when I was con- sidering how he might respond to Parfit's arguments – only in this case his focus would be on the possibility of agency rather than experience. As before, I won't try to do justice to his transcen- dental vision, but merely indicate why he sees it as inviting the animalist view of personal identity.

The goal of agency is always to effect change. As McDowell sees it, such changes always need to be thought of as changes in the world. This is so even when agents are changing their own minds – something that they might be wrongly tempted to conceive in Cartesian terms, as a dis- embodied process. For their minds, too, belong to the world. And the only way in which an agent can affect the world is through bodily movement. The fact that rational agents act for reasons – and, therefore, from within the space of reasons – does not alter the fact that the case of bodily movement is basic. It is impossible to effect change for reasons without initiating bodily movements. This means that rational agents need bodies. They also need motor capacities by which to move their bodies – the same sorts of motor capacities by which non-rational animals are able to move their bodies.

I haven't dwelled on what I take to be transcendental about this view of rational action. As I understand it, McDowell's transcendental project is to characterize how the mind meets the world – more specifically, how subjects who inhabit the space of reasons can make contact with the very objects of their thoughts. One direction of this contact is passive: the mind receives through experience impressions of how the world is. The other direction is active: the mind effects changes in the world through intended bodily movement. In both cases, McDowell claims that we cannot make sense of the sort of contact that is at issue without seeing it as contact between a suitably endowed animal and its environment.

I am certainly not arguing for the possibility of disembodied agency. Indeed, I have expressly assumed that the rational and practical capacities which are necessary for personal agency belong by nature to human beings. But it doesn't follow that the point of view from which a person deliberates and acts is the same thing as the bodily point of view from which an animal perceives and moves. For the point of view from which a person deliberates and acts is a rational point of view. And, for all the reasons I gave above, the boundaries of a rational point of view are not set by the boundaries of an animal's body, nor of its whole lifespan. This is so despite the fact that the capacities that are necessary for personal agency belong to human nature. And it will remain so even if the case of bodily movement is basic in the ways that McDowell claims.

III   How Ethical Considerations Might Enter

McDowell sees all attempts to distinguish personal identity from animal identity as involving a kind of Cartesian mistake. This mistake is to regard the "inner" perspective of the first-person point of view as something separable from animal existence. We can fall into this mistake without going so far as to embrace substance dualism or the possibility of disembodied existence. We fall into it whenever we try to transcend the limitations that are naturally imposed by animal nature. And this, surely, is something that all proponents of Locke's distinction try to do in one way or another.

When McDowell identifies this mistake, he portrays it as a metaphysical mistake. Yet, even within his metaphysical perspective, he is prepared to grant something *like* the possibilities that Locke, Parfit, and I have raised. It is clear from his critical discussion of Parfit that he is prepared to grant that a person could have the impression of remembering a past associated with a different body than it presently has – and, also, that two (or more) persons could have the impression of remembering the same such past. He has also granted (in conversation) that the rational and practical energies of human beings could be exerted to achieve rational unity within different boundaries – in groups of human beings and parts of human beings as well as in whole human beings. The question is, how can he compel us to view these possibilities in the way that he recommends? How can he compel us *not* to view them as cases in which the life of a given person comes apart from the life of a given animal? The burden of what I've said so far in this chapter is that if he wants to do so, he must bring in additional considerations beyond the purely metaphysical ones I've been discussing so far.

It is significant that he does precisely that at the end of his paper on Parfit. He points out that there is an ethical dimension of personhood that Parfit cannot preserve within the framework of psychological reductionism, which concerns the nature and basis of prudential self-concern.

McDowell holds that an individual person feels – and ought to feel – prudential concern for its own well-being. As he portrays it, the basis of self-concern is entirely different from the basis of our concern for others. Sometimes, our concern for others is grounded in an impartial perspective from which we recognize that we ought to be equally concerned for the well-being of everyone. But, according to McDowell, the reason why persons should be concerned for their own well-being is not tied to this impartial perspective. It is not as though the dictates of prudence amount to nothing more than an instruction to take one's own well-being into account along with, and on a par with, everyone else's. There is something essentially *partialist* about self-concern. Of course, my concern for others can also be partialist, insofar as it has a basis in something that sets certain others apart from the rest – such as that I live among them, or am engaged in common projects with them, or hold values in common with them. But these bases of concern for others might not last. And when they don't last, I lose my reasons for the concern itself. We might be tempted to think of our partialist concern for others in such a way that it could and should last through all such psychological changes, no matter how transforming they might be. I am dubious about whether this attitude is coherent. But, according to McDowell, it certainly isn't incoherent in the case of self-concern. The reason why I should be especially concerned for my own future well-being is simply that it's *mine*. As such, it holds even when I anticipate very substantial psychological change, and believe that I will later reject the projects and values I now hold to be most important. Some philosophers, including Parfit and Sidgwick, would challenge the coherence of this attitude in much the way that I doubt the coherence of its interpersonal counterpart. The mere idea that a particular future will be *mine* shouldn't, according to them, move me to be especially concerned about it. It simply isn't a reason. The only thing that could count as a reason would be something general. And then its justificatory force would reach beyond my own case, as is true of the reasons I just canvassed above (impartial concern for everyone, or shared projects and values). It is a serious challenge to preserve the idea that our reasons for self-directed concern truly are reasons even though they are not generalizable to others. McDowell proposes to meet the challenge by appealing to a biologically based drive for self-preservation that human beings have in common with other, nonrational, animals. In human beings, this drive translates into reasons for action that are consciously aimed at self-preservation. And these reasons bring in train a rational concern for the quality of one's life as well. On this way of conceiving the basis of prudential self-concern, it is essentially concerned with the quality of one's *own* life – conceived, of course, in biological terms, as the life of an animal. That is why the demands of prudence can coherently speak to us even when we anticipate substantial psychological change. And that is what makes it essentially unlike the sorts of concerns we have for others.[15]

If we want to see prudential self-concern as essentially unlike concern for others, I don't see any alternative to McDowell's account of it. Moreover, if we were to accept it, we could not possibly avoid an animalist conclusion in the dispute about personal identity. A person, qua locus of this sort of prudential self-concern is, necessarily, a suitably endowed animal. This is a very important reason why McDowell takes the attitudes he does toward the possibilities that have led others to embrace Locke's distinction between personal identity and animal identity. If we view them as cases where the life of a person diverges from the life of an animal, then we shall be conceiving the individual person in terms that *remove* this natural basis of prudential self-concern.

It is not as though proponents of Locke's distinction do not recognize this. Parfit thinks we ought not to be moved by special concern for ourselves; we ought instead to recognize a universal demand to be impartially concerned with all well-being no matter whose it is. This moral aspiration does not absolutely require him to give up animalism in favor of psychological reductionism. But, all the same, he sees psychological reductionism as a metaphysical framework that facilitates the achievement of impartiality – because it makes the facts that separate one person from another seem less deep than they seem within the animalist framework.

Here I should like to make two observations. One is diagnostic and one is methodological.

We can diagnose why McDowell and Parfit take such different attitudes toward the same metaphysical possibilities in terms of the fact that each brings different ethical commitments to bear in his metaphysical responses. I think it would be a real form of intellectual progress if they were to make this an explicit part of their metaphysical arguments. If they were to do so, they could no longer rest with accusing each other of metaphysical mistakes. They would have to see that each is making a *recommendation*. McDowell is recommending that we embrace the animalist view of personal identity in order to preserve an ethical conception of the person as a proper locus of a special sort of prudential self-concern. Parfit is recommending that we reject the animalist view in order to escape that ethical conception.

The methodological point is that this is an appropriate form of argument. It is right and proper that the attitude we take toward the metaphysical possibilities raised by Locke, Parfit, and myself should be guided by a sense of what is ethically at stake.[16]

My own reasons for recognizing the possibilities of group and multiple persons are avowedly ethical. Like Parfit, I am happy to give up the idea that prudential self-concern is essentially unlike concern for others. But this is not because I share his moral aspiration of complete impartiality. I think our ethical responses ought to proceed from our particular points of view, and be guided by our personal commitments. But I think this guidance ought to take account of more considerations than that provided by prudential concern in McDowell's sense. I don't mean that they should be impersonal considerations. But even as we approach matters from a personal point of view, rather than be concerned with how a particular human life is going, we should focus on the fact that we exist for the sake of the things that we can do as agents of the size we are – with the degree of internal unity and separateness from others that we have achieved for those purposes. And we should be open to the fact that there might be things that it would be more worth doing that would require us to achieve rational unity within different boundaries – larger or smaller – than those that presently circumscribe our individual rational activities. To recognize that there are things more worth doing may well be to recognize a normative demand that is in tension with the more purely prudential concerns that McDowell focuses on when discussing personal identity.[17]

Of course, it is not foreclosed that we might discover that what is *most* worthwhile is to lead a unified *human* life. Perhaps it is right to value the sorts of things we can do with that level of rational unity – such as life-partnerships, lifelong careers, and so on – more than what we could do by integrating into group persons or fragmenting into multiple persons. But, it is important to see that this evaluative attitude does not tell against my metaphysical position which allows for the possibility of multiple and group persons. The relative worth of human-scale projects is a reason to *choose* human-size existence over the alternatives of group and multiple personhood. It is not a reason to reject the claim that these alternatives are open to us as genuine forms of personal existence.

So, if McDowell wants to oppose this conclusion, he will need to appeal to other ethical considerations, besides the value of a unified human existence. His conception of prudential self-concern is one such consideration. And there is another one that he has raised in conversation which I'll briefly mention. It concerns personal responsibility.

As I've said, McDowell admits that it is within the power of human beings to act together so as to achieve rational unity within groups and, also, to forgo such unity within individual human lives. But he also thinks it is important to see the lines of personal responsibility as following individual human lives. To think this is to have a reason to link personal identity with animal identity after all. It is a reason that many would find natural. But it is symptomatic of an outlook that I think it is important to revise.[18]

The outlook I have in mind is akin to methodological individualism in the social sciences. According to this outlook, what I would describe as group agency could always be redescribed as actions undertaken by human beings from their individual human points of view. I have already explained in section II why I think such redescriptions would be false to the facts in many cases. Sometimes, what is done by groups really is done by groups and not by individual human beings. But it has to be admitted that this is not an entirely comfortable fact. We often feel helpless in the face of wrongdoing by corporations, institutions, and other group agents. We worry that we can't effectively punish them, because they can't suffer in the ways that individual human beings can. And, because this is so, we also worry that the threat of punishment will never deter them. Furthermore, we might also worry that attempting to address a group-size point of view about what a group-size agent did will, inevitably, be ineffective. The worry here is that groups are not responsive to criticism and are incapable of moral development. All of these worries might lead us to focus our moral responses on the individual human beings who participate in group actions rather than on the group itself. Here there seems much more scope for influence. For example, we might try to prevent group wrongs by threatening appropriately severe punishment on any human individuals who participate in them. But this sort of coercive practice has notoriously failed in contexts where the commitments that prompted group action were deemed important enough – as in the case of revolutionary causes.

As an aside, I should explain that it is distorting to take corporations as the paradigmatic case of group agency. They exist only for the sake of profits. Not only is it the case that this is an impoverished conception of what it is most worth doing; but, also, it is an end that more properly belongs to the human participants in corporate activities than to the corporations themselves. So it is perfectly sound to hold individual human beings responsible for much corporate wrongdoing, and we probably don't do it enough. What would not be sound would be to assume that this is what we must always do.

The topic of corporate responsibility and other forms of group responsibility is very difficult. In my view, our ethical thinking would be improved if we took care to distinguish the cases in which group actions really do proceed from points of view that are *not* of human size. One reason why it is important to acknowledge their points of view is to facilitate their moral development, by demanding an account of the reasons for which they act and subjecting those reasons to public critical scrutiny. A less ambitious reason is simple realism. We will never manage to respond appropriately to the reality of group agency until we identify the points of view from which it is being exercised.

All of these reflections on responsibility are compatible with the evaluative attitude I mentioned earlier, according to which human individuality should be valued above all. In addition to the fact that a unified human life affords the pursuit of things really worth doing, like lifelong relationships and careers, it also seems to be a fact that we want to hold human beings individually responsible for their whole lives. Let me repeat that these sorts of evaluative considerations speak against forming group and multiple persons, but they don't speak against the value of recognizing their possibility. We should keep these possibilities in view, partly because there might be things worth doing that would give us reason to realize them. But we should also keep them in view so that we don't overlook the ways in which they might already be realized. If we were to allow individualist prejudices to prevent us from recognizing real cases of group and multiple personhood, our moral responses to what such persons do will be inappropriately aimed at the wrong targets (individual human beings).[19]

No doubt, there are wider ethical considerations that McDowell would want to bring to bear against my view than the specific ones I've been considering, concerning prudential self-concern and individual responsibility. It is bound to be the case that the naturalism of his metaphysical outlook is matched by a suitable naturalism in ethics. And I think this is the deeper place to look for an objection to the possibilities of group and multiple persons – in the moral importance of the sort of naturalism to which McDowell recommends us. However, I haven't yet found my way to that conclusion. So let me close by drawing attention to a contrast between the ways in which he and I see personal life as *emerging* from human nature.

It is part of my argument that all cases of rational unity are an achievement and not a metaphysical given. The capacities needed for personal life belong to human nature, but persons themselves emerge only with the exercise of those capacities. Put in this way McDowell would not disagree. He too sees personal life as emerging from human nature and not automatically given with it. He invokes the idea of second nature in order to flag the role that socialization plays in forming the person. Such formation reflects the forces of culture and history on what is biologically given to human beings. It is not an exaggeration to say that the very idea of an individual, along with the idea that the individual is a locus of ethical distinction and importance, is a product of these forces. The same could be said of the particular development of that idea that I am offering. Perhaps it required the actual emergence of things like corporate agency and dissociative identity disorder to put the possibilities of group and multiple personhood into philosophical view. That is one sense in which these possibilities are emerging from human nature – through culture and history. But what is equally important to recognize, in my view, is the way in which *each individual person* must also emerge from human nature, not only as a result of the cultural and historical forces at work in socialization, but also as an *explicitly* intended outcome. The identity of a person – qua reflective rational agent with a distinct rational point of view – is in that sense *non*-natural.[20]

McDowell's writing on personal identity has provided a more subtle and interesting challenge to how I (and others in the Lockean tradition) have thought about the subject than anything I have encountered so far. Some of the things I have said in this last section in response to the challenge need more development and fortification than I can provide in a short paper. But, even if they do not persuade the animalist in all details, I think a modest claim can be made for the governing methodological orientation that I have tried to promote in the chapter as a whole. Even if the ethical considerations – from prudence and from responsibility – that McDowell invokes to support his view of personal identity are compelling, they are *ethical* considerations. So, the larger theme of the chapter, that it is ethical considerations which should be driving the metaphysics of persons, and which should be rescuing us from the metaphysical stalemate that I identified as afflicting the debate between Parfit and McDowell, still represents a better methodological approach to this subject than is found in Parfit and McDowell's own writing.

Notes and References

1   In chapter 2 of *The Bounds of Agency*, Princeton: Princeton University Press, 1998, I argue for an ethical approach on methodological grounds. I argue first that both sides of the philosophical dispute about personal identity are supported by common sense. This means that, no matter which side we defend, we will be defending a revision of some aspect of common sense. But, furthermore, both sides can elaborate coherent positions. And this means that we cannot defend one side by ruling out the other. At least we cannot do so on the grounds that have characteristically been employed in the philosophical dispute about personal identity – i.e. demonstrating incompatibility with common sense and/or demonstrating incoherence. So we are left with a methodological difficulty. How can we justify taking one side or the other in the dispute, given that doing so requires a revision of common sense and, also, the rejection of an alternative which is perfectly coherent? I propose that we can do so by turning to ethical considerations that meet the following desiderata: these considerations must not beg the question in the dispute about personal identity; they must be uncontroversial enough that they can be accepted by all sides in the dispute; they must be important enough that all sides should be committed to them. See n.19 for an account of the specific ethical consideration that, I think, meets these desiderata.

2   See J. McDowell, "Reductionism and the First Person," in J. Dancy (ed.), *Reading Parfit*, Oxford: Blackwell, 1997, and D. Parfit, *Reasons and Persons*, Oxford: Clarendon Press, 1984.

3   See *The Bounds of Agency*, op. cit.

4   See n.1 for a brief indication of why this is so.

5   He notes, for example, that Parfit cannot establish psychological reductionism just by establishing that there is no soul or ego in which psychological events and relations inhere. For there might well be some other substance in which they inhere and which, for this reason, can rightly be said to constitute the person. The obvious candidate is, of course, the human being – which would entail the "animalist" account of personal identity that McDowell favors (though he doesn't like the label). He also notes that Parfit's claim – that the existence of a person is not all or nothing – provides no special support for psychological reductionism, since the claim holds on the animalist account as well. Finally, he notes that Parfit's reductionist goal of describing persons in wholly impersonal terms is neither feasible nor attractive. With this last complaint we come closer to the real crux of their disagreement, which concerns the nature of the first person.

6   See G. Evans, *Varieties of Reference*, Oxford: Clarendon Press, 1982, ch. 7.

7   The "reliability" in question has to do with the following idea: the process by which these apparent memories come about specifically and successfully aims at preserving information about the real past of a real person. See J. Perry, "Memory and the Problem of Circularity," in J. Perry (ed.), *Personal Identity*, Berkeley, Calif.: University of California Press, 1975, for an account of why such a process could replicate the function of ordinary memory in such a way as to provide for a distinction between veridical and non-veridical apparent memories – without appealing, as McDowell does, to the animalist view of personal identity.

8   See S. Shoemaker, "Persons and their Pasts," *American Philosophical Quarterly* 7 (1970), and my "Branching Self-Consciousness," *Philosophical Review* (1990).

9   That's too strong. Sometimes there are causal mechanisms by which we can ensure our future conformity to our present intentions. That's what Odysseus did when he tied himself to the mast, in order not to follow the Sirens' call. But, of course, being tied to the mast is not a good model for the execution of intentions. What Odysseus really did was ensure that he could not act at all when the time came to execute his intention to resist the Sirens. But, normally, the future execution of our longterm intentions will involve the exercise of our agency in the future. And that means that we will be free – then – to choose whether or not to execute them. That's what I mean to get across by the claim that there is no causal mechanism by which we can ensure future conformity to present intentions. Such a causal

mechanism would undermine our status in the future as *agents* who are deliberately carrying out those intentions.

10 Another problem that is sometimes raised in connection with branching concerns competition between the duplicate selves. Who, it is asked, will get the spouse and who will get the house? It is certainly conceivable that a person with one spouse and one house might unexpectedly be confronted with a branching fate in which that question would pose real and painful difficulties. But if the person had been in a position to anticipate its branching future, it ought to have taken measures to avoid such difficulties. That is, it ought to have avoided projects like conventional marriage which are predicated on not branching. This is something I take it to be within the power of persons to do. I also take it to be within their power to frame projects that would be suited to a branching future. See my "Branching Self-Consciousness," op. cit., for further discussion of this and related matters.

11 See his *Mind and World*, Cambridge Mass.: Harvard University Press, 1994, for his most sustained treatment of these transcendental questions. See also his Woodbridge Lectures, "Having the World in View: Sellars, Kant, and Intentionality," *Journal of Philosophy* (1998), for a more complete treatment of the topic of experience as a form of direct contact with objects – which he there calls "intuitions."

12 What follows here is a brief account of the longer arguments given in *The Bounds of Agency*, op. cit. It substantially overlaps with other summaries I've given of those arguments in "A Nonnaturalist Account of Persons," in M. deCaro (ed.), *Naturalism in Question*, Cambridge, Mass.: Harvard University Press, forthcoming, and "Rationality and Persons," in A. Mele (ed.), *Oxford Handbook on Rationality*, New York: Oxford University Press, 2003.

13 If it is not evident to you that the more specific normative requirements of rationality do contribute to this overarching rational goal, try to imagine what it would be like to arrive at all-things-considered judgments without satisfying them. If you refused to resolve contradictions among your beliefs, for example, there might be no such thing as what it was best for you to do in the light of your beliefs. One belief might direct you to perform a certain action while its contrary (which you also believe) directed you not to perform it. Similar problems would arise if you refused to work out the relevant implications of your attitudes, or to rank your preferences transitively. You would be refusing to consider all things in the sense required for deliberation; you would be refusing to consider their rational import.

14 I shouldn't exaggerate the consequent split. There may be very substantial harmony of evaluative outlook between a group and its participants, in the form of shared ideas about what the most important goods are. Sometimes, these same goods can simultaneously be pursued in different ways by group persons and persons of roughly human size. This can justify and yield a consequent division of labor between a single-group person and many persons of less than human size, all of whom supervene on the same human beings. Whether this division of labor really yields a group *person*, as opposed to a group *endeavor* carried out by many human-size persons, depends upon whether the division extends to deliberative activities. For that is what invites us to think of the group as having its own point of view, as I discussed above. My point here is that this may constitute a "split" in human lives – in the form of deliberative and practical independence of parts, one of which belongs to a group person while the rest do not – which does not bring in train any particular tension or conflict.

15 I have misleadingly portrayed the contrast between concern for self and for others as being starker than it needs to be on McDowell's account. There is no reason why animal nature shouldn't provide a biological basis for certain forms of concern for others, assuming that there are biological functions that would be served by it. Some obvious examples might be the protection of offspring and/or members of one's biological group (the pride, the pack, etc.). The real contrast that needs to be drawn, therefore, is between such biologically based concerns and the more purely rational concerns to which Parfit and Sidgwick want to confine us. There is a rational perspective from which special concern for one's own life and members of one's biological group should not persist in the face of value conflicts – or, if it should, it should be on the basis of impartial considerations that would extend further than oneself and one's group. The contrast I speak of in the text, between a certain form of prudential self-concern and concern for others, would be more accurately described in these terms.

16 To repeat, I do not take myself to have demonstrated this in the chapter. See nn. 1 and 19 for further elaboration of the point and references to a fuller discussion.

17 One should not take away the impression from my discussion here that McDowell places prudential self-concern at the center of ethical reflection. He is very clear that there are many different sorts of virtue, of which prudence is only one.

18 Actually, there are two directions of revision. One concerns our understanding of group responsibility, which I go on to discuss immediately in the text that follows. The other concerns our responses to disorders of identity such as dissociative identity disorder. See my "A Nonnaturalist Account of Personal Identity," op. cit., for an account of how we might want to revise our understanding of these phenomena in the light of the possibility of multiple personhood – including the clinical goal of integration.

19 The topic of prejudice raises another important ethical consideration that is central to the arguments I give in *The Bounds of Agency* for the possibility of group and multiple personhood. There – as in this chapter – the arguments proceed from the premise that a person is a reflective rational agent. Here, I have merely stated that this is an important and familiar conception of the person that all parties to the philosophical dispute about personal identity take for granted; whereas there I defend the conception on explicitly ethical grounds. Unlike the ethical issues I've just been discussing, these grounds are not tied to my avowedly revisionist conclusions about the possibility of group and multiple persons. They have to do with an ethical dimension of personhood that all sides in the philosophical dispute about personal identity can and should acknowledge. That is why it can serve the methodological purpose I described in n.1. It meets all three desiderata I mentioned there: it does not beg the question in the dispute about personal identity; it is sufficiently uncontroversial that both sides can accept it; it is sufficiently important that both sides should accept it. Let me now say a bit about this last matter, concerning why the conception of the person as a reflective rational agent is ethically important.

Reflective rational agents are the sorts of things that can treat one another specifically *as persons*, by engaging one another in rational ways, such as conversation, argument, and criticism. It is in the nature of the case that the beings that can treat one another as persons will recognize this fact about one another. One pernicious form that prejudice against persons has historically taken is this: to deny that something *is* a person while, at the same time, recognizing that it is possible to treat it *as* a person. Such prejudice is almost always hypocritical. So long as we have entered into distinctively interpersonal engagements with another – even if this takes the form of lies and threats – it is necessarily hypocritical to deny personhood to that being. Yet there are reasons why some have been tempted to such hypocrisy. For the recognition of another's personhood brings with it certain ethical pressures. It matters to persons how they are treated by other persons. It also matters to persons that any differential treatment that is meted out to them be justified. The ethical pressure comes with recognizing that the choice we make with regard to how we treat other persons will matter to them in these ways. Whatever we choose to do, our choice will have ethical significance simply because it will matter to those who will be affected by it. A common motive for hypocritical prejudice is to escape this ethical pressure – to indulge in exploitative and oppressive treatment of certain persons without having to admit that something of ethical significance has been done that needs to be justified. We can see clear signs of such hypocrisy in the historical treatment of women and of African slaves. And one important form that political and civil progress has taken in the last centuries is to expose that hypocrisy – by requiring us to explicitly recognize the personhood of all whom we can engage as persons and to act accordingly.

This progress has gone hand in hand with granting certain rights that are commonly supposed to attach to personhood. The prospect of extending those rights to group and multiple persons is certainly alarming. But the answer is not to deny their personhood in the characteristically hypocritical way that has marred the history of interpersonal relations. Metaphysical prejudice is no more forgivable than gender- and race-based prejudice. If we don't want to grant rights to all of the persons we recognize as such, then we need to clarify our thinking about rights. We need to decide whether they attach to all rational agents, or only to some of them, or whether they attach to rational agents at all – as opposed to human beings, or animals in general, or perhaps, even, all living things.

But the point I really want to underscore here is that, in addition to all of the ethical advances that I think would follow upon recognizing the possibility of group and multiple persons, the argument for these possibilities proceeds from an unassailable ethical premise, which is that we ought not to deny the personhood of anything it is possible to treat *as* a person.

20   The contrast between McDowell's and my thoughts on this point is subtle. As I've made clear, I don't want to challenge his idea of second nature. Human possibilities are only partly afforded by first nature (biological endowment); they are also afforded by what history and culture give to human beings through socialization. Everything to do with second nature depends on the individual exercise of agency. There could be no history, culture, or socialization without it. But it is also possible for the forces of history, culture, and socialization to work in a way that is not explicitly intended by individuals. The emergence of capitalist society was not intended, nor the emergence of the particular virtues for which it provided a social context. But, if I am right, we cannot say the same about the existence of individual rational agents. Their existence comes about as the result of intentional activity that is expressly aimed at that. Here is another aspect of the same contrast: as I have portrayed the facts that constitute personal identity, they are directly within our intentional control in a way that the forces of history, culture, and socialization are not.

Response to Carol Rovane

1   Locke's account of personal identity centers on the thesis that a person is "a thinking intelligent being, that has reason and reflection, and can consider itself as itself, the same thinking thing, in different times and places."[1]

To get from there to a distinction between what it is for persons to persist and what it is for human beings to persist, he needs a premise to the effect that this capacity, the one he makes definitive of being a person, can be separated – even in a case in which it is a human being who gives expression to exercises of it – from the capacities the continued exercise of enough of which is what continuing to be alive comes to for a human being. The capacity to think, considered as including the capacity to consider oneself as oneself, would need to be exercisable in separation from the capacities whose actualization constitutes a human life. That idea is palpably Cartesian. And to Locke's credit, he is explicitly agnostic about a cognate idea, that "that thinking thing that is in us" is immaterial (III.27.27). This implies an agnosticism about whether his basic thought, that a person is a kind of thing that can "consider itself as itself," is well captured by the distinction between the identity of persons, even those whose incarnation is human (a qualification needed in case there are any others), and the identity of human beings.

To give up the extra assumption, and hence to give up the distinction between the identity of persons and the identity of human beings, would not be to abandon Locke's account of what a person is. It would merely be to stop thinking that, from the fact that what is distinctive of persons is the capacity to conceive oneself as oneself "in different times and places," one can conclude that persons are a kind of continuant whose persistence conditions are other than those of human beings (or whatever other kinds of persons there may be). The capacity to conceive oneself as oneself would need to be understood, instead, as the person-constituting member of a set of capacities the exercise of enough of which is what being alive comes to for a human being. If there are persons who are not human beings, the special capacity would be the person-constituting member of a set of capacities the exercise of enough of which is what being alive comes to for an individual of some other kind, perhaps a Martian.

On a view of this sort, if a prince's consciousness could be made to animate what used to be the body of a cobbler, the human life that would continue in that body would be the life of the prince, not, as Locke has it, the life of the cobbler. Locke's different way with the thought experiment reflects the extra assumption, which can be expressed – from the other direction, so to speak – by saying that what the continuation of a human life consists in does not include self-consciousness and the capacities that go with it. So Locke's way with the thought experiment comes within the scope of the agnosticism I mentioned. If we resolve Locke's agnosticism by saying the brain is the organic basis of the special capacity by which Locke defines persons, and if we make Locke's thought experiment concrete by supposing there might be a way to keep the prince's brain functioning in what was the cobbler's body, we should conceive what happens as a body transplant for the human being – and person – who is the prince, not as a brain – and personal consciousness – transplant for the human being who is the cobbler.[2]

As Rovane presents things, the separation between persistence conditions for persons and persistence conditions for human beings is essential to "the Lockean position." By implication, her final paragraph excludes me from "the Lockean tradition." But, as I have explained, the distinction is implied by Locke's central thought only in conjunction with an assumption he himself signals as extra, and disputable. A charitable reading of Locke would focus on the central thought, and would not hold him to the Cartesian assumption – optional for him in any case – that makes it look as if the continued existence of a person could be something other than the continuation of a certain individual life, of a special kind by all means. My so-called "animalism" is nothing but the Lockean conception of what a person is, freed from Locke's extra assumption so that the continuation of a certain individual life can emerge as a condition for a person to continue to exist.

2   Locke's formula shows no sign that he aims to exploit a characterization of the special capacity he says is distinctive of persons in a psychologically reductive account of personal identity – a specification of a mode of relatedness between temporally separated psychological states that would be intelligible independently of the idea of the continued existence of an individual of the kind he is explaining. On the contrary, his formula openly uses the idea of the sameness over time of individuals of the kind in question, in a way that would stand condemned as circular if he were aiming at a reduction. To repeat, what he says is that a person is a thinking thing that "can consider itself as itself, the same thinking thing, in different times and places."

And it is not just that the idea of reducing personal identity to temporal relations intelligible independently of personal identity lacks the cachet of having been put forward by Locke – who is, as Rovane says, the progenitor of philosophical interest in the topic. In "Reductionism and the First Person," I exploit considerations that Rovane does not take issue with, in order to argue that there is anyway no reason to believe in the availability of materials for such a reduction.

The supposed case for reduction centers on the fact that we can understand concepts such as that of quasi-memory. The concept of quasi-memory is like the concept of memory – retained knowledge of a past that was one's own – except that we lift the requirement that the recalled past occurrences took place in the life of the subject who recalls them. But I argue, following Evans, that the concept of quasi-memory is intelligible only as one whose compliants are either ordinary memories (cases of recalling occurrences from one's own past), or illusions of ordinary memory (illusions of recalling occurrences from one's own past). The concept of quasi-memory is not intelligible independently of the concept of a past that is the subject's own. The concept of one's own past – and hence the concept of the sameness over time of individuals of a kind one belongs to – is needed for making sense of quasi-memory, even though when we characterize some conceivable cases of quasi-memory we need to use the concept of one's own past only in specifying the content of an illusion. So the concept of quasi-memory is not material for reductively explaining the concept of the identity over time of self-conscious subjects.

In section 1 I argued that reductionism about personal identity has no precedent in Locke. And in this section I have sketched an argument against the most familiar attempt to supply the kind of conceptual apparatus a reduction would need. So far, there does not seem to be the "metaphysical stalemate" Rovane claims to find between a reductionist approach to personal identity and the approach I have recommended. If our topic is personal identity, reductionism has nothing going for it.

3   Well, perhaps our topic should not be personal identity? Parfit claims that the future existence of someone who will stand to me in a complex relation in which a central element is that he quasi-remembers occurrences in my life would be "about as good as ordinary survival," even though the relation does not suffice for identity.[3] He thinks it is irrational to care especially about the existence (and welfare) of a future person who will be identical with me. He thinks the considerations that might rationally ground an interest in my own future would equally ground a concern for future individuals who stand in that relation, not constituting identity, to me. So personal identity does not matter.

This figures in Rovane's presentation as Parfit's "so much the worse for personal identity" response to the "duplication" objection – the objection that the relation between temporally separate psychological states that is supposed to yield a reductive account of personal identity could link my present psychological state to those of two or more different future individuals, who cannot both, or all, be identical with me.

But why should I accept that the prospect of there being someone who stands to me in that complex psychological relation, though in the envisaged future the individual person I am will no longer exist, includes, as Rovane puts it, "all that matters to my survival"? In caring about my survival, I care that the individual life I am leading should continue. Why should I accept that the existence in the future of a subject, perhaps more than one subject, with the illusion of being me should be enough to satisfy whatever is rational in that concern?

How does Parfit make it look rationally arbitrary to prefer the continued existence of the individual I am to the future existence of a subject or subjects who will stand in that relation of "psychological continuity" to me? Only by assuming that the continued existence of the individual I am would consist in the fact that that relation holds between me and an individual existing in the future, plus the fact that this case of the relation is sustained by a kind of causal connectedness that excludes duplication. On this picture, the real focus of the future-related concern that, in my ordinary thinking, takes the form of a concern for survival is that there should be at least one future individual who will stand in that psychological relation to me, and it looks like mere prejudice to care whether the underlying causation is such as to exclude duplication or such as to allow it.

Now it should be obvious that this part of Parfit's thinking does not supply a consideration independent of the idea I have attacked, the idea that a concept of "psychological continuity" suitable for a reduction of personal identity is available. If that idea collapses, as I have argued it does, there is no ground for saying the real focus of the future-related concern that ordinarily presents itself as my concern to survive is that there should be at least one future individual who stands to me in some relation describable without appealing to the concept of personal identity. And now the apparent arbitrariness disappears. The real focus of the concern is precisely that the individual I am should continue to exist, and it is simply not true that all that matters to me about that prospect can be secured by the existence of someone in the future who is acknowledged not to be identical with me. That the envisaged future individual will have a quasi-memory impression of having lived my life makes no difference. The most we can say is that since he will inherit my projects and pursue them, his existence might be a consolation, in the face of the prospect that my concern to survive is going to be disappointed. But that falls massively short of supplying all that matters to my survival. A consolation gives comfort when one is not going to have what one wants.

Rovane registers, in a way, a strand in my "Reductionism and the First Person" in which I try to make this point. But she casts the material she considers in this area as my beginning to appeal to ethical considerations to control reflection about personal identity – just the sort of thing she urges is needed to tip the scale in a "metaphysical stalemate." Taking me to be, in effect, acceding to her methodological recommendation to resort to ethical considerations in order to resolve a metaphysical deadlock, she responds that the guidance by our personal commitments that is appropriate for our ethical responses "ought to take account of more considerations than that provided by prudential concern in McDowell's sense."

It is hard to see how, in implying that this constitutes an objection to something I think, she could fail to give the impression that she is representing me as placing prudential self-concern at the center of ethical reflection, though she disclaims this intention in n.17.

But anyway, she is wrong to cast my point as an appeal to an ethical consideration in order to resolve a metaphysical stand-off. My point is that the "as good as ordinary survival" claim has no standing. The "as good as ordinary survival" claim is supposed to warrant replacing personal identity with a different relation, in our conception of what shapes the rationality of concern with the future. But the claim depends essentially on the supposed availability of a relation of "psychological continuity," describable independently of the concept of personal identity, so that it could figure in a reduction of the concept of personal identity (supposing anyone were to go on being interested in that concept). And I have discredited this metaphysical support for the "as good as ordinary survival" claim, exploiting considerations that, to repeat, Rovane does not take issue with. There is still no "metaphysical stalemate" here. It makes no difference if we expand reductionism to include the thesis that personal identity does not matter; the expanded position still has nothing going for it.

Rovane has devoted enormous ingenuity to devising analogues to first-personal thinking that would be suitable for beings who multiply by splitting, like amebas. But without the "as good as ordinary survival" claim, it should be clear that this does not pertain to Locke's topic any more closely than, say, the fact that one can make a drink from what one gets by roasting and grinding acorns pertains to the topic of coffee. Perhaps the acorn stuff would be better than nothing, but it is not coffee, and I doubt that even the best such brew is about as good.

4 The heart of Rovane's own thinking is her proposal that what is essential to being a person is the "overall rational unity" that is a requirement for rational agency. She argues that this requires us to recognize the possibility, at least, of persons who are larger than individual human beings and persons who are smaller: group personal agents and multiple personal agents embodied in single human bodies. This may seem to threaten my view that the continued existence of a person is the continuation of a certain individual life. There is a potential problem for me here, independently of the suggestion I have been responding to, that my objection to Parfit leaves us in a "metaphysical stalemate."

I shall start with group persons.

If a group achieves enough togetherness to exercise agency as a group, over a period of time, perhaps we should, on just those grounds, conceive it as a living individual whose life extends over that period of time. I claimed that the continued existence of a person requires the continuation of an individual life. I never restricted the required individual life to the life of an individual human being. There was always a need to leave room for the possibility that, say, Martians or dolphins might be persons in the Lockean sense.[4] So one line I could take, in defending my so-called "animalism" against Rovane's appeal to group persons, would be to stress that the idea that does the work, in the position that is only awkwardly so called, is not the idea of an individual constituted as such by mere biology but the idea of a kind of continuity recognizable as the continuation of an individual life. And perhaps the unity over time of a group agent can be a case of that.[5]

But independently of that possibility, I want to question an assumption that pervades Rovane's discussion of the idea of group agents: the assumption that if a group of human beings achieved the kind of practical unity she considers, and so constituted itself as a person, that would require that the human beings who make up the group are not persons, in the sense of unified rational agents, as well. If that assumption is wrong, there is nothing to prevent me from accepting that there might be groups so practically unified as to be persons, while still insisting that the primary case of personhood is the individual human being. If a group person would be made up of human beings who are still persons, it seems reasonable to say the application of the concept of a person to the group would be secondary. And then even if the group's unity does not suffice for crediting it with a life of its own, as the special kind of individual it is, the only modification I need is to restrict the thesis that a person's continuing to exist is the continuation of an individual life to persons in the primary application of the term. That is a modification I can take in my stride.

Why does Rovane think the achievement of group personhood would require the human beings who make up the group not to be persons? It would require them to be moved, in their capacity as elements of a group agent, by purposes intelligible only in terms of interests, aspirations, and so forth that belong to the group, as opposed to acting in pursuit of goals that could be intelligibly attributed to them as human individuals considered in abstraction from the group. But why should this feature of the purposes that inform their actions seem to conflict with their having, and indeed needing to have, as the human individuals they are, the unity required for agency?

Consider, say, the viola player in a string quartet that plays so single-mindedly that it is plausible to say it performs as a single agent.[6] If the group's action is to have that kind of unity, the viola player's playing must be successfully intentional under a description on the lines of "playing the viola part so as to fit perfectly into the performance we are engaged in." That description does not make sense in abstraction from a performance the group is engaged in. But it is an individual human being whose activity must be intentional under that description. It is an individual human being who needs to move her fingers and arms in such a way that the description applies to what she does. That requires her movements to be responsive to auditory and visual experience of what the other members are doing, enjoyed from her own individual human point of view. She is still an individual human agent – just one whose purposes, during performances at any rate, are those of the group.

In envisaging group agents whose members are not individual agents, Rovane must be envisaging an immersion in group activity that goes beyond the sort of thing I have just described. Perhaps we are to suppose something like this: after a perfect performance our viola player says, in all honesty: "It was as if an agent other than my individual self was in control of my fingering and bowing. There was no need for me to intervene, as it were, in what was happening, in a way determined by responding to my experience of what the others were doing."

Well, perhaps there are levels of perfection in certain group activities that are achievable only if the individual members can acquire this kind of depersonalization in the phenomenology of performance. But even here, the depersonalized phenomenology characterizes the performing experience of the individual human members of the group. The human persons who, together, gave the perfect performance do not disappear from the scene. It would be wildly unjust to use the fact that their phenomenology of performance was depersonalized in that way as a pretext for refusing to give them credit, as the human persons they are, for the perfection of the group's playing.

And this kind of case is quite special. Consider Rovane's case in which a philosophy department achieves the status of a group agent. Suppose a spokesperson for the department, after a conversation in which she was assigned to communicate its views to a student or an administrator, said something on these lines: "It was as if the group was in control of the words that emerged from my mouth. There was no need for me, as a human individual, to embody intentions of my own in my speech, in response to my experience of the moves made by the other party to the conversation." That would surely be merely creepy – if not dishonest, then pathological, not to be held up as exemplifying a valuable possibility for a mode of personhood that transcends what I am insisting is the primary case.

This note of something pathological needs to be sounded also when we move to considering multiple agents embodied in a single human body. I have been urging that I need not object to the very idea of group persons; I can insist that the idea does not threaten the claim that the primary application for the concept of a person is to individual human beings. Just so with multiple personal agents embodied in a single human body.

Perhaps the only possible way of dealing with certain sorts of intolerable stress is to abdicate one's human personhood in favor of multiple agents, who take turns to be the agents of the actions involving the single human body in which all these agents are embodied. In such a case it would be harsh and unhelpful to issue an injunction – to whom? – on the lines of "Pull yourself together." What was a human person has tried to remove herself from the scene, and it would be unfeeling to refuse to let her do that, and cajole her (though she is not even present to be cajoled, if we allow that she has done what she set out to do) to recapture a practical unity that would encompass all the bodily actions that involve that body.[7]

But that makes no difference to the fact that the situation is essentially pathological. It is one thing to say that in such a case we ought to acknowledge multiple agents, rather than – what would be merely cruel – proceeding as if we were dealing with a still present human person who is merely incompetent or spineless, in a project supposedly incumbent on all human beings, that of achieving overall practical unity throughout a human life. It would be quite another thing to represent becoming multiple agents as just one among several possibilities, all on a level, for achieving agentive unity, as if a practical unity on the part of a whole human being were not part of the content of the primary application, the normal application, of the concept of a person. And it is not just that the suggestion gets no support from what is called for in a properly sympathetic response to a way of dealing with intolerable stress. I think the suggestion is positively repulsive, in the possibility it opens up for unpathological agents, not under intolerable stress, to cop out of responsibility for evil-doing by deciding to become a multiplicity of agents none of whom is the one who perpetrated the evil.

Of course that is an ethical thought. So was my thought about the creepiness of a spokesperson who disclaims individual responsibility for how she speaks. So was my thought about the injustice of refusing to give credit to the members of a string quartet that succeeds in playing as a group agent. I agree that reflection about the identity of persons should be shaped by ethical consider-ations. But the position of these ethical considerations in *this* dialectic gives no support to Rovane's picture, in which ethical considerations settle a metaphysical stalemate about reductionism. We have left reductionism behind. And the role of ethical considerations here gives no support to the implication of Rovane's title, that we should take the topic of personal identity to be ethical and not metaphysical. Why should we have to choose between those classifications? Why not both?

Notes and References

1   P. H. Nidditch (ed.), *An Essay Concerning Human Understanding*, Oxford: Clarendon Press, 1975, III. 27.9.
2   So taken, the thought experiment yields a conceivable case in which, in one clear sense, "the same person could survive in a new and different animal body." (Not all of the body would be new, but it would be natural to speak of the prince being given a new body.) And I have nothing against the thought experi-ment taken this way. So Rovane is wrong to say I reject that claim about a possibility for survival. My opposition to Parfitian reductionism does not turn on rejection or acceptance of that claim. (The label "animalism" may mislead Rovane here. It leads her to underestimate how Lockean my thinking is.)
3   The quoted phrase is from Parfit, *Reasons and Persons*, Oxford: Clarendon Press, 1984, 261.
4   See p. 367 of "Reductionism and the First Person," as reprinted in *Mind, Value, and Reality*, Cambridge, Mass.: Harvard University Press, 1998.
5   Rovane routinely overstates the significance of biology for me. For instance she says I hold that "the capacity for first-person thought belongs by nature to human beings, as part of their biological endow-ment." But that would be right only if we were born able to think "I"-thoughts, or acquired the ability in merely biological maturation. What is part of our biological endowment is the capacity to acquire the capacity to think "I"-thoughts.
6   I have been helped by conversation with Rovane about this example, which seems more lifelike than the case of a philosophy department.
7   Here again I have benefited from conversation with Rovane.

6

Acting in the Light of the Appearances

Jonathan Dancy

I

In this paper I consider relations between the views expressed in *Mind and World* and what one might say about certain issues in the philosophy of action. *Mind and World* is about the relation between experience and belief. Our experiences are reasons for, or give us reasons for, one belief rather than another. What is more, when we believe, our reason is, or can be, the nature of our experience. Experience can favor one belief rather than another, and it can explain why we so believe, if we do. McDowell wants to understand how this can be. I, by contrast, have been interested in the relation between belief and action. Our beliefs, it may seem, are reasons for, or give us reasons for, one action rather than another. What is more, when we act, our reason is, or can be, what we believe. Beliefs can favor one action rather than another, and they can explain why we so act, if we do. I want to understand how this can be.

John McDowell has had a significant influence on me over the years, both as a person and as a philosopher – an influence which I am keen to acknowledge, with which I am very happy, and for which I am most grateful. I view the sorts of things that I want to say about the relation between reasons and action as almost entirely McDowellian in spirit. It will turn out, however, that it is not so easy to take the views expressed in *Mind and World* and simply apply them in the philosophy of action, and the present chapter is an attempt to bring the difficulties to light.

McDowell wants to say that experience need not fall short of the facts. In veridical cases we should understand experience as a fact making itself manifest. If the experience, or what we experience, is our reason for adopting a belief, then our reason for adopting that belief is the fact itself. Our reason, in veridical cases, is not some psychological surrogate for that fact. It is the fact presented, experienced, or manifest, not something standing proxy for it. Nor is it this (other) fact: that we experienced that fact.

Similarly I want to say that when we act our reason for acting is what we believe, how we take things to be, which in successful cases is how they are. Our reason is not that we so believe, nor is it some psychological correlate for the thing believed, perhaps our so believing. (Always taking it that there is a distinction between my so believing and the fact that I so believe.) When, in a successful case, I act for the reason that she is in the room, my reason is her presence, not that I believe that she is present, nor my believing that she is present.

When I say here that my reason is her presence I could equally well have said that my reason is that she is present. But we should be sure to retain the sense that my reason does not fall short of the facts, in the sense that my reason is the way things are: her presence, or her being present.

Let us now turn to unsuccessful cases: what are we to say about them? In the case of the relation between experience and belief, what we are trying to do is to ensure that our access to the facts in successful cases is not shown to be indirect by what has to be said about the unsuccessful ones; and we have the further aim of showing that, when we explain a belief by appeal to an illusion or mere appearance, what we say does nothing to unsettle the thought that in successful cases the *explanans* is a fact or state of affairs, not some surrogate for such worldly things.[1] McDowell achieves these aims by judicious use of a disjunctive conception of "its appearing that *p*." When our experience is a mere appearance, it is still an appearance. Some appearances are facts making themselves manifest, and others are mere appearances. In the latter case, of course, our access to the facts is not direct, since there is no fact accessed. But this does nothing to unsettle the claim that when things are going swimmingly we are in direct contact with some feature of our surroundings. Further, the explanation of belief runs smoothly in either case. Mere appearances have the same explanatory powers as do those appearances that are manifestations of facts. The reason why we believe may be a mere appearance just as easily as an unmere one, even though in the latter case that reason is a fact and in the former it is not. In either case our reason is the appearances, how things appear.

Accordingly, when we turn to the philosophy of action, we should say that the idea that in successful cases our reason for action is the fact that *p* should not be unsettled by what we say about unsuccessful ones. When I act for the reason that *p*, my reason is still that *p*, even when I am mistaken about its being the case that *p*; my reason is not that I believe that *p*, nor is it my believing that *p*. But where we mistakenly believe that *p*, our reason for action cannot be the fact that *p*; there is no such fact, or state of affairs. It must be something else, but what? Perhaps we could say that in these cases our reason must be how things appear to us, in the more general sense of how they seem to us to be, or how we take them to be, but cannot (of course) be how they are. If we can say this, it would seem that the experience–belief relation can be taken as a model for the belief–action relation. Sadly, however, things are not so simple.

There are two general obstacles, which need to be brought out at the beginning. The first of these is that as we move from the experience–belief relation to the belief–action relation, we have to broaden the notion of appearance, if we are going to use it at all, and it is not clear that it will survive the broadening process. Not all beliefs that *p* can sensibly be thought of as appearances that *p*. Someone who decides, on the balance of such evidence as is available, that the housing market will remain stable for a while can hardly be said to be someone to whom this fact, should it be a fact, is making itself manifest. It could not even be said that he is a person for whom it is *as if* the housing market will remain stable. Such thoughts are fine for the explication of experience, but not for the explication of all correct judgment whatever. So in what follows I will be careful to speak of the relation between belief and action, not between appearance and action (despite my title). This should not be taken to mean that it is impossible to act in the light of appearances – only that not everything in the light of which we can act can properly be called an appearance, conceived as an experience.

The second obstacle is that when we were dealing with perceptual experience, it seemed sensible to say that there are only two possibilities. The first is that a fact is making itself manifest; the second is that we are dealing with a mere appearance. But when we turn to thinking about belief more generally, this bipartite distinction seems less inviting. It may be that there are cases in which facts make themselves manifest to us in a non-perceptual way; McDowell would think of these as instances of non-perceptual knowledge. But there will certainly be other cases where our belief is true but is not knowledge: cases, that is, that stand between knowledge and error. For McDowell, where there is knowledge the world is transparent to the mind; the mind's eye penetrates directly to the fact. Opacity reigns elsewhere – even when our belief is correct and things are as we take them to be.

The sort of tripartite account that we need here (knowledge, true belief, error) is analogous to one that McDowell himself provides in ethics. The virtuous person is the person for whom opposing reasons are silenced. This person therefore experiences no contrary inclinations, and so is not vulnerable to weakness of will, nor to accidie. Virtuous people are in the perfect situation, as it were.[2] But not all those who act for moral reasons are virtuous. It is possible to have a moral belief and act in the light of it, without opposing reasons being silenced at all. McDowell tends to think of such agents as less than perfect; their motivational structure is vulnerable to opposing desires, since such desires have not been silenced as reasons. This shows that the structure of their motivation is not the same as that of the virtuous; it is effectively Humean rather than purely cognitive. So we have three possibilities. There is the virtuous person; there is the Humean who does the right thing despite contrary motivations; and there is the Humean who, despite true beliefs about his duties here, fails to act accordingly.[3]

If there are three elements (knowledge, true belief, error), still McDowell would take the important division to be that between transparency and opacity. He would say that we should not allow ourselves to be persuaded that knowledge is impossible by thinking about the nature of mere true belief. The "highest common factor" approach thinks of mere true belief as similar to error in its general structure, and McDowell has no complaint about that. What he objects to is any suggestion that we should think of the third element, knowledge, in similar terms. Admitting the possibility of an intermediate state should not disturb him.[4]

But I am going to suggest that on the philosophy of action side there are going to be difficulties deriving from the relation between true and false belief, difficulties that are not resolved by allowing the existence of the supposedly perfect case.[5]

II

I start by introducing a distinction between two ways in which we use the notion of a reason to explain an action. This is the distinction between the reasons why we act and the reasons for which we act. The reasons for which we act are the considerations in the light of which we do what we do. These are the features which we take to tell in favor of so acting; they will figure prominently in our deliberation, and they will normally be the ones we specify when asked why we did what we did. It is in their light that we act. The reasons why we do what we do, however, constitute a broader class. Maybe we should think of that class as including the reasons for which we act; certainly ordinary usage would sanction such a picture, for in many cases we would happily identify the reason for which he acted with the reason (or a reason, at least) why he acted. But some "reasons-why" are not "reasons-for-which." A glaring example is that of the shy person who decides not to go to the party because he might meet there lots of people who he doesn't know. The reason for which he decides not to go to the party is just that: that there might be lots of unfamiliar people there. But the reason why he didn't go to the party is that he is shy. In fact, that he is shy is not only the reason why he didn't go to the party, but also the reason why he stayed away for the reason that he did. We might, after all, ask how anyone could take the possibility of meeting unfamiliar people as a reason not to go to the party; that's what parties are for, we might say. And the answer to *that* question is that he is shy; shy people take as reasons against an action considerations which for the less socially challenged are reasons in favor of it. *This* reason-why excludes the reasons for which he stayed away.

So understood, reasons-why can be psychological states, such as his being afflicted by embarrassment, or traits, such as shyness, or facts about such things, such as that he was embarrassed or that he is shy. And as such they are well set up to be causes of decisions and actions (though of course it depends on whether we want our causes to be states or facts, or neither). And this appears to open the door to saying that when someone acts for the reason that p, the reason why he acts may be, or at least include, that he believes that p. The reason why he acted might be that he believed that p even where the reason for which he acted was that p, not that he believed that p.

It is common to hear people arguing that where the agent falsely believed that p, the reason why he acted cannot have been that p, and must have been that he believed that p. But even if one allows this, one should not be led thereby to admit on similar grounds that his reason for acting, the reason for which he acted, cannot have been that p, and must have been merely that he believed that p. One can act for the reason that p even when it is not the case that p. It would be a mistake to say that since he is (or might have been) wrong about whether p, his reason for acting must have been something else that he was not (or could not have been) wrong about.

In general, and normally, one's reason for acting is that p, not that one believes that p, or that it appears that p, or any other such surrogate. Think of the man who believes that there are pink rats in his boots. He might call the pest-control officer. If he does this, his reason for doing it will be that there are pink rats in his boots. But he might seek medical help instead. If he does that, his reason for doing it will be that he thinks there are pink rats in his boots, not that there are. There is, therefore, a big difference between acting for the reason that p and acting for the reason that one believes that p, and the difference counts all in favor of saying that the ordinary case is the simpler case in which one's reason is the (supposed) fact, not that one so supposes.

The same point can be made about appearance. There is a difference between acting for the reason that p and acting for the reason that it appears that p. Someone who knows perfectly well that it is not the case that p may still act for the reason that it appears that p. For instance, a detective might arrest a woman who he does not believe to be guilty, doing this merely for the reason that the appearances are against her. If so, his reason is not that she is guilty, nor that he believes that she is guilty, but that it *appears* that she is guilty. This is a different reason from the other two.

Everything I have said so far is consistent with the idea that when it is not the case that p, but my reason for acting was that p, the reason why I acted was that I believed that p. It might be that, in such cases at least, my reason for acting is not among the reasons why I acted. If this suggestion is incoherent, that will be for different reasons.

We seem to have established that it is only in rare cases that my reason for a belief or an action is either "that I believe that things are thus-and-so" or "that things appear thus-and-so." Such things, we have said, are rarely among the reasons for which people believe or act, or believe. But stay: I can act for the reason that p when it appears that p. If I do so, that p is how things appear to me, and that p is my reason for acting or believing. So, even if my reason is not that things so appear, my reason could still be the way they appear. I can act or believe in the light of how things appear to me. And this is true whether we use the narrow sense of "appear" which is restricted to experience, or the broad sense in which it is close to "how things seem" more generally. I can indeed do this. We merely need to be clear that when I do so, my reason for acting is not that they so appear, but something else. Reasons-statements are intensional, description-sensitive. We should be wary of substitutions.

III

McDowell's general aim, as I have said, is to establish that what we say about unsuccessful cases should not be allowed to distort our understanding of the successful ones. This aim operates equally in three different areas. In epistemology, we want to say that the possibility of illusion does not show that our access to facts about our surroundings is essentially indirect. In the philosophy of mind, we want to say that the possibility of error does not show that what we believe necessarily falls short of what is the case. Finally, in the explanation of belief a fact itself can function as *explanans*, though a mere appearance can have the same explanatory power as that of a manifest fact. It is this latter claim that I am mainly concerned with at the moment – or rather with its ana-logue in the explanation of action. The general idea is that a mere belief can explain an action by standing as the reason why the agent so acted. Where the agent is mistaken, there is still his belief that *p*; and this belief enjoys just the same explanatory power as does the fact. There is, after all, a belief both times, though only one is a *mere* belief. Even a mere belief can be the reason why the agent acted. The reason why he did it was the way he took things to be (though not, of course, the way they were). This might have been how they actually were, and is what explains his action.

So now we have it that a mere belief can enjoy the same explanatory power as a fact. What sort of explanation is involved? Is there any reason why it should not be causal? I was present at the 2002 East Coast meeting of the APA, where there was a celebratory discussion of Donald Davidson's work, to mark his eightieth birthday. In his contribution to this discussion McDowell said of Davidson's "Actions, Reasons and Causes" that it "*fixes* it that intentional explanation is causal explanation" (his words, my italics, his stress). So McDowell thinks that intentional expla-nation, reasons-explanation, not only *could* be causal, but in fact that it *must* be causal. The way the agent takes things to be, then, can be the cause of an action; in virtue of that, it can explain the action; and the explanation would work by giving the reason why the agent did it.

Let me leave on one side[6] McDowell's extraordinarily strong commitment to the achievements of "Actions, Reasons and Causes" and work only with the thought that intentional explanation *could* be causal (for which see *Mind and World* 1984, 71 n.2). For this to be the case, we must be able to identify in each case something capable of functioning as a cause. Has McDowell the resources required? Intentional explanation is explanation in terms of reasons. But are these reasons reasons-why or reasons-for-which? Well, not all reasons-why explanations are intentional. The reason why the radiator gives no heat any more is that the valve is jammed shut. Which then are the intentional ones? Only those that appeal to the psychological, perhaps. But appealing to the psychological is not enough for intentionality either. The reason why he didn't come to the party was that he was shy. This is no doubt a potentially causal explanation, and it is a reasons-why explanation. But is it an intentional one? I don't think so. We can explain someone's blushing by appeal to his shyness in a similar sort of way, without his blushing being conceived as an action, let alone an intentional one. A more promising suggestion is that the intentional reasons-why explanations are those that can be converted into a reasons-for-which explanation. We can ordinar-ily do this,[7] at least for reasons-why explanations that appeal to such things as "that he believed that *p*" as *explanantia*. If the reason why he did it was that he believed that *p*, ordinarily his reason for doing it was that *p* (even if it was not the case that *p*). But not always. There are those cases where his reason for doing it was not that *p*, but rather that he believed that *p* (pink rats). There are also cases where, though the reason why he acted was that he believed that *p*, still *p*-related considerations were not among his reasons at all. For instance, the reason why he doesn't bother to pay much attention to the feelings of others is that he thinks he is the center of the universe. But that he is so transcendentally important need not be among his reasons at all; we don't ordinarily neglect or ignore things for reasons any more than we forget them for reasons.

If intentional explanations are reasons-for-which explanations, what is the nature of the *explanans* in a case where things are not as the agent supposed? It looks as if there will be no difficulty in finding an *explanans* for the associated reasons-why explanation: it will be how the agent took things to be – which is different from his so taking them, and different again from the fact that he took them to be so. But if the explanation is to be causal, our *explanans* will have to be something that is the case. For surely all causal explanations are, as I have put it elsewhere, factive. By this I mean that the truth of the causal statement entails that both cause and effect were in fact the case, or did happen, or obtained (depending on one's causal metaphysics). In our reasons-for-which explanation, I would say, how the agent took things to be is not something that could be a cause if in fact they were not so. There are potential causal *explanantia* around, of course: these include that he so took them, and his so taking them. But these are different beasts.

But isn't it possible that the way the agent took things to be is the way they are? Yes, indeed it is, and in such cases there is no difficulty in supposing that the way he took things to be, his belief in that sense, causes the action; but we were dealing with a case where things are not as they were taken to be. To find a cause in the unsuccessful case we are thrown away from the way they were taken to be, and have to look somewhere else.

Does this matter? I think that it does. The question is whether intentional explanation can be causal. McDowell's thought was that it can be causal, because in the unsuccessful cases we can find something other than a manifest fact that enjoys the same explanatory powers as manifest facts do. The thing that plays that role is an appearance, which is not a nothing even if it is illusory. We have been trying to say similar things about acting in the light of belief. But it seemed that intentional explanations are reasons-for-which explanations. And when the agent is mistaken, he acts in the light of something that is not the case. The reason for which he acts is still that p, even when it is not the case that p. But something that is not the case cannot be a cause.

Of course there is still the enormous temptation to insist at this stage that in cases where the agent is mistaken, his reason cannot be that p, and must be something that is the case, such as that he believes that p. But we have seen that agents' reasons are not normally that they believe that p. So the enormous temptation must be resisted. What is driving this insistence is the sense that all explanation (and not just causal explanation) is factive, in the sense I gave above. Something that is not the case cannot explain something that is the case. My own view, however, is that this is little better than prejudice. In the next section I try to show why.

IV

I offer here three reasons for abandoning the view that intentional explanation is factive. In doing so, I am doing little more than stressing things that have already emerged along the way.

First, we should remember the purpose of rational explanation. This is to reveal the favorable light in which the action presented itself to the agent. It is not required for this purpose that the action should actually have been the (rosy) way the agent took it to be. Nor is it required that that way is in fact a rosy way. One can be comprehensibly (and comprehensively, I would say), mistaken about whether a given feature is in fact a positive one rather than a negative one. All that is required for explanation of this sort is that we come to see how the agent could have found something about the action that led him to think it worthwhile. It is not required that the agent be right on any point. Rational explanation differs in this respect from causal explanation. The purpose of causal explanation, I take it (though it may be hard to show this), requires that only something that is the case can explain *in that way* something else that is the case. We should not suppose that because causal explanation requires this, *all* explanation requires it.

Second, there is no reason to suppose, when an agent offers as his reason for doing what he did something about which he is quite wrong, that he is therefore also wrong about whether it was his reason. If he was wrong about it, this does nothing to show that his reason must have been something else that he was not wrong about. In particular, it does nothing to show that it was something essentially concerned with himself – "that I believe that *p*" – something perhaps with quite a different subject matter from the one we started with. There is just no pressure to insist that where an agent acts for a reason, his reason must be something about which he is not mistaken.

Third, consider the following argument:

1. When an agent falsely believes that *p*, we cannot say that his reason for action was that *p*, and must say that it was that he believed that *p*.
2. The true/false distinction should not affect the form of the relevant explanation.
3. So even when the agent's belief is true, his reason must be that he believes that *p*, not just that *p*.

We have already decided that the conclusion of this argument is false, on the grounds that there is a difference between acting for the reason that there are pink rats in one's boots, and acting for the reason that one thinks that there are pink rats in one's boots. I have used a rather different example elsewhere.[8] Suppose I believe that a cliff is crumbly, and suppose that, so believing, it is more likely that I will be afflicted by nervousness while climbing it, with the result that my grip falters and I fall. Knowing this, I decide not to climb. What is my reason? It is *not* that the cliff is crumbly, but genuinely that I believe it to be crumbly. For ask yourself under what conditions I conceive of my reason as ceasing; the answer is that the reason vanishes, not when the cliff ceases to be crumbly, but when I cease to believe it to be crumbly. Even if the cliff ceases to be crumbly somehow, I still have the same reason not to climb it, so long as I continue to believe it crumbly. So my reason is *that I believe* that the cliff is crumbly. But this is a quite unusual case, and the case is unusual in a way that shows that the normal case is quite different.[9] Normally, one's reason for not climbing is not some fact about oneself but a fact about the cliff.

So the conclusion of the argument is false. But, it seems, the argument itself is valid. What are we to do, then? Taking it that the second premise is hardly challengeable, I suppose that we must deny the first premise. But denying the first premise is pretty well all that is involved in holding that rational explanation is not factive.

These are my three reasons for thinking that rational explanation is not itself factive. And I have a sort of persuasion to add to them. This is that if rational explanation were factive, and factive in the same sense in which knowledge is factive, we would know it would be immediately incoherent to add "but not-*p*" to "his reason for acting was that *p*." But it is not incoherent to do this. Consider: "his reason for doing this was that it would increase his pension, a matter about which he was sadly mistaken." Is this like "he knows that it is raining, but sadly he is mistaken"? I don't think so. To make sense of the latter, we have to hear the "knows" in scare quotes, as it were; to make sense of the former, no such device is required.

One can say all these things while allowing that rational explanations are often expressed in ways that render them factive. For instance, I tend to allow that if we use the word "because" in place of "for the reason that" we end up with something factive. We cannot say "he stayed in because it was raining," and add to this "but it wasn't." But all that this shows is that some of the ways of expressing rational explanations are factive, while others are not. And I take this to show that the sort of explanation offered is not a factive sort. We cannot take something that is factive and turn it non-factive by expressing it in a different way, but we can do the opposite.

So an agent can act for a reason that is not the case, as we have supposed all along. And something that is not the case cannot be a cause, I would suppose. The temptation, of course, is to revert to a reasons-why explanation; these do indeed always specify as *explanans* something that is the case. But reasons-why explanations are not intentional explanations unless they can be successfully converted into reasons-for-which explanations. Reasons-for-which explanations normally specify what the agent believed rather than that he so believed, or his so believing, as the reasons for which the agent acted. In all such cases, even though the explanation given is correct, it is possible that the *explanans* is not the case. If so, it seems that intentional explanation *cannot* be causal. And it is no use saying that even if such explanations are not causal in unsuccessful cases, they might still be causal in successful ones, where things are as the agent supposes. For the *style* of explanation does not change as we move from one sort of case to the other. As Bernard Williams once said, we should not allow the distinction between true and false to alter the nature of the relevant explanation. So if intentional explanations are not causal on one side of the true/false distinction, they are not causal at all.

I would say, then, that McDowell's (supposed) willingness to appeal to appearances as *explanantia* shows that he is not really thinking of reasons-for-which explanations at all. He was thinking of reasons-why explanations, which I agree may plausibly be conceived as both factive and causal. And even to understand the reasons-why explanations as he wishes to do, McDowell has to hear "the reason why he did this was the way he took things to be" as specifying something capable of being a cause, and "the way he took things to be" is only capable of this if we convert it into something like "that he so took them" or "his so taking them." My conclusion is that the explanations which he holds to be causal are not intentional explanations at all.[10]

V

In the preceding argument I have been assuming something that can reasonably be challenged. I speak of reasons-why and reasons-for-which explanations, and assume in so doing that the *explanans* in each case is the feature specified as the reason. It is only because of this that I am driven to the conclusion that the *explanans* in reasons-for-which explanations need not be the case. To repeat: someone can act for the reason that p when it is not the case that p; we do not need to find something else that is the case (that he believes that p, perhaps) to be his reason. But can I be so sure that the *explanans* is indeed the feature specified as the reason? Couldn't the *explanans* be that he acted for that reason? When I say that he acted for the reason that p, I do explain his action. But it does not follow from this that what explains is the reason for which he acted, rather than the whole thing that I say in giving my explanation. Why should the *explanans* be this or that part of the "explanatory statement" rather than the whole? So if the explanation of his doing it is that he did it for this reason, we have recovered something that is the case to act as our *explanans*, and there is no longer any excuse for treating our explanation as non-factive.

Wayne Davis, who made this point to me, puts it thus:

> I believe we need to distinguish the claim that actions can be explained by reference to reasons from the claim that the reasons are what explain the action. . . . We can certainly explain a person's action by saying that certain normative reasons were the reasons for which he acted. The statement that my reason for saving was that my son will need money for college does explain why I saved. But it does not follow, and is not true, that my reason explains my action. For my reason was that my son will need money for college. That something will be true in the future cannot explain the fact that I did something in the past. It is even more obvious that the reasons themselves do not explain anything when they are false, even though actions can be explained by observing that they were done for such reasons. . . . The claim that motivating reasons are things that explain actions is undermined by the fact that motivating reasons are intentional objects. To think of reasons themselves as explanatory is to treat instances of "that p" as referential terms.[11]

This point is important, I think, but not right. When we think about an explanation, we think about relations between three things: that which explains, that which is explained, and the explanation-relation in which they stand. There is also the action of explaining, which is something else again. In the causal case we explain the effect by appeal to the cause as *explanans*, and the explanation-relation is the causal relation. In the action case we explain the action by appeal to the reason as *explanans*, and the explanation-relation is that of being "done in the light of." Further, the *explanans* cannot include the *explanandum*.[12] So the *explanans* cannot actually *be* that the action was done for this reason. This includes that the action was done. It must be, then, that the *explanans* is the reason for which the action was done, not its having been done for that reason. In explaining the action, we say that it was done for that reason, but it would be a mistake to conclude from this that the explanation we give is the *explanans*. *We* explain the action by citing *what* explains it, and what explains it in this case is the reason for which it was done. Or so I would claim.

Davis offers two considerations in support of his claim that though we explain by reference to reasons, it is not the reasons that explain. The first point is that something in the future cannot explain something in the past. I am tempted to respond to this by saying that it is now the case that his son will need money later; it is now the case that his need for money is not immediate. But actually I would do better just to deny that how things will be cannot explain an action; we commonly cite the future in giving our reasons for action, and the only reason not to take this practice at face value is an antecedent presumption that the sort of explanation involved should be able to be causal. Remember that we sometimes refrain from an action on the grounds that it would be wrong; it is not promising to think of the fact that the action would be wrong if we were to do it (which is *not* a fact about a particular action that happened not to get done, since there are no such actions) as a cause of the action's non-existence.

Davis's second point is that to think of reasons as explanatory is to treat instances of "that p" in referential terms. But this seems to me to be just a mistake. Or rather, it would be a mistake to treat all "occurrences" of "that p" as referential, but it is not a mistake that either I or anyone else needs to make. (When I ensure that p, there is no "that p" that I am ensuring.) However, I do think that the reason why someone acted can be something that is the case; our reasons need not fall short of the facts. This does not show that all reasons are objects, of any sort. Davis says that motivating reasons are intentional objects, as opposed presumably to ones of a more solid nature. I would rather say that statements of motivating reasons introduce a contained intensional context, since the specification of a reason is description-sensitive. But this does nothing to show that motivating reasons are objects of any sort.

VI

In section III of this chapter I suggested (much though I would like to suppose otherwise) that in the theory of reasons for action we cannot say the sorts of things that McDowell uses the concept of appearance to say about believing in the light of one's experience. Acting in the light of one's beliefs cannot be understood as causal when a belief is false, because the reason for which we act is neither that we so believe nor our so believing. When we act in the light of what we believe, and are wrong, our reason is bleakly something that is not the case, and it cannot be converted without distortion into something that is the case. This being so, we cannot claim that a mere appearance can have the same explanatory power as that enjoyed by a manifest fact or state of affairs, if the explanation concerned is to be causal.

That whole discussion, however, was predicated on the desire to find structures in the explanation of action by appeal to belief that are similar to those which McDowell finds in the explanation of belief by appeal to experience. What emerged was that we cannot say, of the reasons–action relation, what McDowell does say of the experience–belief relation. I turn in this final section to ask whether this fact, should it be a fact, has any tendency to undermine what McDowell says about the relation between experience and belief.

Now of course there is one crucial difference between the two cases. That is that in the case of the relation between experience and belief, the two are understood as having, or at least as able to have, the same content. Talking in terms of appearances, it appears to the agent that p, and the result is that the agent takes it, believes that p. Nothing like this was available when we were thinking about action. On the other hand, the distinction between reasons-why and reasons-for-which would seem to be as applicable to the explanation of belief as to the explanation of action. Some reasons why people have the beliefs they do are not reasons for which they have them. Such reasons-why may include those people's sense of their own inadequacy, or the fact that they were educated at Oxford, or the fact that they have never traveled very much (these three things might even go together). These things are not necessarily among the reasons for which they form the beliefs they do. Further, some of the reasons for which we hold the beliefs we do are things that are not in fact the case. This is true even when the reasons are such things as "I am presently enjoying an experience of such-and-such a sort." One can be mistaken about that, just as about most other things. But in such cases there is at least the experience itself, which is not a nothing. There is how things appear, and there are many beliefs that we want to explain by appeal to experience in the sense of how things sensibly seem. (Or perhaps how the agent takes them sensibly to seem.)

As McDowell sees it, when things are going well, our belief is to be explained causally, by appeal to the manifest fact as cause (and as reason, of course). A manifest fact is an appearance, in the sense that how things are is how they seem. When things are not going well there is still an appearance; this time it is a mere appearance, but McDowell wants to insist that its being mere does not prevent it from having the same explanatory power as does the manifest fact. So our beliefs can be explained by appeal to the appearances, whether mere or not. Could such explanation be causal? If there is causation there must be a cause, and a nothing cannot be a cause. But an experience, whether mere or not, is not a nothing. This is to be the picture. Does it resolve our puzzles? Somehow I doubt it. The difficulties we found in the case of the belief-action relation seem to recur here, so long as we think of the experience as the reason for which we form the belief. But we do so think; for we form our beliefs in the light of our experience. The way things *appear* is our reason for supposing them so to *be*. It is a reason-for-which, not merely a reason-why. But how are we to understand "the way things appear"? Is this capable of being a cause? If not, this will be because the reason for which we believe is not necessarily itself something that is the case. There is something that is the case in the offing, namely, that things so appear, or their so appearing; but these things are not our reason, it seems.

Is that so clear? In the action case, we were able to show that there is a difference between acting in the light of how we believe things to be and acting for the reason that we so believe. We might have expressed this in terms of appearance, saying that there is a difference between acting in the light of appearances and acting for the reason that things so appear. But perhaps there is no such difference when we stick to the narrow sense of "appear" in which an appearance is always an experience. Someone for whom his experience is a reason is someone for whom how things appear is his reason for believing; he believes it because it is manifestly so. And this "because" can perfectly well be "for the reason that."

But what about the unsuccessful case? In fact it seems that there are two ways of being unsuccessful. First is the case where things seem so but are not so. There is no problem here for McDowell, so long as our reason is that things appear so, or their so appearing. Second is the case where the agent mistakes the way things seem, misreads the appearances themselves. Is McDowell in a position to deny this last possibility? If not, won't he have to allow that the reason for which we believe is something that is not the case? The reason will be the way things appear, or perhaps that they so appear, when they don't in fact appear that way at all.

In the action case, the difficulties we faced in attempting to use McDowellian structures derived from the need to keep the concept of belief out of the specification of the reason. There are cases where that one believes something is exactly one's reason for acting, but they are special and rare. But with the belief case, it is important to retain the centrality of the notion of an experience. Surely the reason why we have many of the beliefs we do is the nature of our experience. But is it *our* reason, a reason-for-which we believe as we do? There are cases where we believe that q because of the way things look, though they do not look as if q. What I mean by this is that the way the sky looks may explain our belief that it has rained recently, when we would not want to say that the fact that it has recently rained is given in experience. (It "looks as if it has just rained" only in a weak sense.) There are other cases where we believe that p because that is how it looks; the belief that p is the natural product of the p-experience, we might say. The question I am edging towards is whether in this sort of case we would wish to say that we believe that p *in the light of* its appearing that p. When it sensibly seems to me that p, and I believe accordingly, do I believe for a reason, or is it just that I respond instinctively, or is it something else again? I have a reason to believe it, true enough; but am I believing it *for that reason*? We might say "I believed it because it was manifestly so." But someone who takes it to be manifestly so is *already* a believer, most of the time; so saying "I believed it because it was manifestly so" looks more like a justification than an intentional explanation.

Even in this latter case, however, if it is really possible to misread the appearances, it is also possible to believe for a reason that is not the case. And if that is possible, the attempt to understand the reasons-explanation as causal must be subverted. Mere appearances may inherit the explanatory powers of self-manifesting states of affairs, but misread appearances cannot do so.

So: can one believe for the reason that things so appear when in fact they do not so appear, or for the reason that they do not so appear when in fact they do? All experiences have conceptual content, for McDowell. Can one ascribe the wrong content to an experience? Can one say, for instance, that one had taken it that one's experience was an experience that p, but that on reflection one realizes that it was an experience that q? In such a case, one might later come to think that the experience in fact justified beliefs for which at the time one did not recognize that one had justification. An example: when tuning my double bass I am sometimes in doubt as to whether a string is sounding sharp or flat. I know how it is sounding, but whether that is a flat way or a sharp way is not always easy to determine. Listening more carefully, I decide that it is sounding sharp. Presumably what I am doing here is attributing a content to an experience – but it is one about which I was earlier undecided (though the experience continues unchanged), and about which I might be wrong. I don't mean by that that though it may be sounding flat, the string might not actually be flat (in the sense of too slack); that, we presume, is impossible for other reasons.

To suppose this possible, one does not have to suppose that what appears is something other than the world itself – a mental image, say, whose own nature could be misapprehended. Nor does one have to suppose that experience has non-conceptual content for one to be wrong about. If one doesn't make these two "mistakes," what else renders the misreading of experience an impossibility?

VII

I have tried to suggest that there are difficulties in understanding intentional explanation of action as causal, no matter how flexible one is with the notion of causal explanation. My main reason for saying this is that intentional explanation is not intrinsically factive. This simply assumes that a causal explanation must be factive. But McDowell has views about intentional explanation which I have not so far mentioned, and one might think that these put him in a position to dispute my presumption of a link between the causal and the factive. In his paper "Functionalism and Anomalous Monism"[13] he suggests in Davidsonian style that intentional explanation is different from the sort of explanation we find in the natural sciences. The idea is that explanation in the natural sciences operates by subsumption under law, while explanation of action (and of belief and meaning) operates by approximation to an ideal. When we explain someone's action, we attempt to show them as having been rational in doing what they did (so far as possible). To be rational in what one does is a matter of responding appropriately to the situation as one conceives it to be. Response is a causal notion; so here we have rationality and causality combined.

Explanation by approximation to an ideal may still be either factive or non-factive. How is the ideal conceived? For Davidson, I take it, rational perfection is partly a matter of internal coherence – but not only of that. He writes "In our need to make him make sense, we will try for a theory that finds him consistent, a believer of truths, and a lover of the good (all by our own lights, it goes without saying)."[14] Here being a believer of truths and a lover of the good is not a matter of internal coherence. It is not that rational perfection requires one to love what one believes to be good; or rather, this may be required but it is not enough, for one is also required to love what *is* good. This is a much wider sort of rational ideal. Now one might say that "explanations in which things are made intelligible by being revealed to be, or to approximate to being, as they rationally ought to be"[15] are not factive, since how things ought to be is not a "factive" matter. But, even if true, that is not really to the point. There is a distinction between the question what is the *explanandum* and what are the *explanantia*, and the question what is the nature of the explanation of the former offered by appeal to the latter. The "things" that are to be made intelligible by being shown to be as they rationally ought to be are the agent's beliefs, intentions, emotions, and actions. The explanation of those things is normative in the sense that it attempts to show that those things are as they ought to be; this is the explanation's distinctive style. But to admit, indeed applaud, all this is not even to address the question whether the *explanantia* in such explanations need to be the case. It is, I maintain, perfectly consistent with McDowell's stress on the characteristically normative nature of rational explanation to insist that we explain an action or a belief by showing what the agent's reasons were for so acting or believing, in a sense which allows that the agent may have acted for those reasons even if they were not the case.[16]

Notes and References

1   So by "fact" I do not mean "true proposition." As I see it, the notion of a fact hovers uneasily between that of a state of affairs, something incapable of being true, on the one hand, and that of a truth (or true proposition). In the present chapter, however, I am thinking of facts as states of affairs or aspects of the situation.

2   Their situation need not be entirely perfect, I would say, since they need not be omniscient; as morally perfect, they need only know those things ignorance of which is evidence of moral imperfection (in the situation).

3   In my *Moral Reasons*, Oxford: Blackwell, 1993, ch. 2.1, and again, in *Practical Reality*, Oxford: Clarendon Press, 2000, 81, 93–4, I claimed that there are weaknesses in this tripartite picture, which I expressed by saying that it is hybrid. My point here is only that in this area McDowell recognizes a sort of successful case that is less than perfect. His distinctive account of the perfect case should not blind us to the possibility of someone acting rightly, hitting the moral target, but not being perfect in that sense.

4   There is one thing to say at this point, though. This is that if our aim is to ensure that our beliefs need not fall short of the facts, we want to ensure this not only for knowledge, but also for the intermediate state of "merely true" beliefs. If I believe that the housing market will remain stable for a while, and my belief is true, what I believe need not fall short of the facts. But to show that, it doesn't seem that we need to appeal to the supposed perfect state in which the fact manifests itself to us.

5   It may be that McDowell would only be willing to think of an agent's reason being a fact in cases where the agent knows things to be so, not in cases where the agent has mere true belief. But this would give the wrong account of almost all the reasons for which we act, if I am right in what I say below.

6   I give my reasons for thinking much less well of the arguments of "Actions, Reasons and Causes," in *Practical Reality*, 161–3.

7   But only ordinarily. If he blushed because he thought she had caught him looking through the keyhole, he could not be said to have blushed for that reason, or in the light of that consideration.

8   *Practical Reality*, ch. 6.1.

9   This argument is peculiar, because it involves arguing that a theoretical account is not generally applicable by appeal to a case which it perfectly suits – an argument from example rather than from counter-example.

10   One might wonder whether it might not help to think of the matter disjunctively. I consider this issue directly in ch. 7.1 of *Practical Reality*, where I argue that disjunctivism is no remedy.

11   W. Davis "Reasons and Psychological Causes," *Philosophical Studies*, forthcoming.

12   As Roger Teichman pointed out to me, this general remark needs some qualification; someone can be laying bricks because he is building a house. This is a case where we explain an action by showing the larger context of which it is a part. But that sort of part/whole relation is quite different from the relation between the reason for which the action was done and the action's being done for that reason.

13   First published in E. LePore and B. McLaughlin (eds.), *Actions and Events: Perspectives on the Philosophy of Donald Davidson*, Oxford: Blackwell, 1985, 387–98; reprinted in McDowell, *Mind, Value, and Reality*, Cambridge, Mass.: Harvard University Press, 1998, 325–40.

14 *Essays on Actions and Events*, Oxford: Oxford University Press, 1980, 222.

15 A quotation from McDowell's "Functionalism and Anomalous Monism," in his *Mind, Value, and Reality*, 325–40.

16 I have been helped by discussions with Simon Glendinning and Philip Stratton-Lake, and am especially grateful to Maura Tumulty for very helpful comments on an earlier version.

Response to Jonathan Dancy

1 Dancy wants to say that a fact can be a person's reason for acting. One acts in the light of how one takes things to be, and how one takes things to be can be how things are. In his intriguing chapter he considers whether he can find support for this thesis in a parallel with what I wanted to say in *Mind and World* about the relation between experience and belief. The answer turns out to be "No," and at the end of his chapter Dancy suggests that the failure of parallelism may cast doubt on some of what I say about that relation.

I agree that my line about experience and belief cannot be exploited as a parallel for Dancy's line about action. But I do not entirely share Dancy's reasons for this claim, and I do not think he draws the right conclusion from it. I do not believe my view about experience and belief is threatened by considerations about the parallel, or lack of one, with Dancy's view about reasons for acting.

2 Even to get a candidate for something that might be parallel to his thesis that facts can be reasons for acting, Dancy needs to distort what I say about experience and belief.

The parallel would have to be that when one forms a belief on the basis of the kind of experience that constitutes being perceptually open to a fact, it is the fact itself that is one's reason for believing what one does. In his third paragraph, Dancy attributes just that claim to me, including a denial that one's reason is – what would be a different fact – that one experiences the fact that makes one's belief true. But this is simply wrong. When I believe, on the basis of my visual experience, that there is a hummingbird at the feeder, my reason for believing that is precisely that I see it to be so – that I experience, visually, its being so – or at least seem to. If I am asked to give my reason for believing that there is a hummingbird at the feeder, it would be absurd to respond by simply restating what I believe, and the absurdity is not lessened if in doing so I would be stating a fact. If my experience is a case of seeing how things are, the fact itself exerts a rational influence on me, but only by being experienced, and a sheer statement of the fact makes no sense as a specification of my reason for my belief.

When an experience makes it possible to know a fact in the direct way indicated by saying, for instance, that one sees that things are thus and so, I say, as Dancy notes, that the experience is the fact making itself manifest to one. And according to me an experience is, or at least provides, a reason for believing that things are as they appear to be. But even if we go for "is" rather than "provides," this does not warrant leaving out any allusion to one's experience in a specification of one's reason for believing what one does. That would imply the absurdity I am resisting, that merely restating what one believes might be an appropriate response to an inquiry into one's reason for believing it. The circumstance of a fact's making itself manifest to a subject cannot be equated with the fact itself, in contrast with any fact about the subject, as in what Dancy says in his purported statement of my view.

When I say that experience need not fall short of the fact, I am insisting that experience can be such as to exclude any possibility that things are not as they are experienced to be. That is a way of formulating a truism whose application to visual experience in particular is that if one sees things to be thus and so, then things are thus and so. It is not a way of saying that the fact itself, as opposed to the fact that one experiences its obtaining, is one's reason for believing what one believes. No doubt seeing that things are thus and so would not be happily described as a psychological surrogate for things being thus and so, but that does not imply that it can be simply identified with things being thus and so.

So when one specifies the reason for which someone holds a perceptual belief, one cannot, in my view, omit the person's experience and go straight to the fact experienced. But in the action case Dancy wants worldly facts themselves, as opposed to any facts about agents, to be the reasons for which agents act, when they act in the light of how they take things to be and how they take things to be is how things are. The proposed parallel is a non-starter, before we even begin considering Dancy's reasons for holding that it does not help him defend his thesis about action.

3   In his section VII, Dancy raises a question about whether, in cases in which the fact that things are thus and so is given in experience, or it at least appears that that is so, it is right to say one believes that things are thus and so *for a reason*.

It is true that we need care in this area. It is easy to hear the "reason for which" locution, and its variants, as implying that a belief so explained has been adopted in a rational act of making up one's mind. That would falsify the unreflective way in which perceptually grounded beliefs normally impose themselves on one.

But I do not think this goes very deep.

Dancy says "'I believed it because it was manifestly so' looks more like a justification than an intentional explanation." Well, perhaps we can stipulate a restrictive use of "intentional explanation," according to which that label fits only if what is explained is a rational act or the result of one, as opposed to the unreflective onset of a mental posture or the resulting posture. As Dancy notes, to say that something was manifestly so to me already implies that I believed it. That it was manifestly so cannot have been a consideration I took into account in making up my mind as to whether it was so.

But it would be wrong to infer that "I believed it because it was manifestly so" cannot be explanatory at all. Such a statement, or a specific counterpart such as "I believed it because I saw it to be so," can make a belief intelligible by depicting it as the outcome of my rational responsiveness to the situation I found myself in. And at a certain level of abstraction, that fits what is done by intentional explanation of belief, on the restrictive conception, as well. I think the class of explanations that matters, for any purposes that are relevant here, is not intentional explanation in the restrictive sense, which excludes "I believed it because it was manifestly so," but explanations that reveal beliefs as the result of rationality at work, which can include "I believed it because it was manifestly so." It seems reasonable to use the "reasons for which" locution and the like so as to fit this wider class.

4   In the picture Dancy recommends, the reason for which someone does something is the consideration in the light of which she acts. If I call an exterminator on the ground that, as I suppose, there are carpenter ants in my garage roof, my reason for calling the exterminator is that there are carpenter ants in my garage roof.

"McDowell's reason is that there are carpenter ants in his garage roof" is neutral as to whether or not there are carpenter ants in my garage roof.[1] There is a temptation to say that if there are not carpenter ants in my garage roof, then my reason must be, not that there are carpenter ants in my garage roof, but that I believe that there are. Dancy persuasively resists this. That I believe something *can* be the consideration in the light of which I act, as when (his example) I seek psychiatric help on the ground that I believe that there are pink rats in my boots. But that is not the appropriate form for the case in which, taking it that there are carpenter ants in my garage roof, I call an exterminator. The consideration in the light of which I act is that there are carpenter ants in my garage roof, not that I believe there are.

The reason for which I act, then, is how I take things to be, whether or not things are the way I take them to be – not my taking them to be that way, or the fact that I take them to be that way. But if things are the way I take them to be, how I take things to be is how things are, and how things are is a fact. So something that is a fact can be my reason for acting.

5   In this example, all that is required for my reason for acting to be a fact, in the sense Dancy defends, is that there are carpenter ants in my garage roof. There is no requirement that my supposing there are carpenter ants in my garage roof is a case of knowledge. At one point (n.5) Dancy wonders if I would impose a knowledge requirement for a person's reason to be a fact, and he is explicit that he does not; he says "this would give the wrong account of almost all the reasons for which we act." So even if I am only accidentally right in supposing there are carpenter ants in my garage roof, the example is, for Dancy, as good a case as any of my reason's being the fact that there are carpenter ants in the garage roof.

Here we have a lack of parallelism, between my line about experience and belief and Dancy's line about reasons for acting, that Dancy makes something of. But as I said at the beginning, I do not think he draws the right conclusion.

In my account of how experience relates to belief, the important distinction is between cases in which experience makes knowledge available and all others, including cases in which experience induces beliefs that happen to be true. If what is responsible for my visual experience is a *trompe l'œil* representation that perfectly depicts the scene it obscures from my sight, and deceives me into thinking I am visually confronting just such a scene, it would be absurd to suppose my experience-based belief that, say, there is a red cube in front of me, true though it is, can be explained by saying that the fact that there is a red cube in front of me – obscured from me as it is by the interposed representation – is rationally responsible, by way of my experience, for my believing that there is a red cube in front of me. That is what would be the case if the fact were making itself manifest to me in my visual experience. Dancy's view about reasons for action provides for no analogous distinction. As I have stressed, truth, whether or not knowledgeably possessed, suffices for facts to come into the picture in the way Dancy wants.

There is nothing objectionable about this, so far as it goes. The construction Dancy works with – "So-and-so's reason for doing such-and-such is that . . ." or variants of this – puts what fills the blank in a kind of *oratio obliqua* position. (Latin has an *oratio obliqua* variety of "because" clause, with the verb in the subjunctive, and that is a good match for Dancy's construction.) If what fills the blank is something true, there can be no objection to saying that the person's reason is something that is the case – a fact. This is analogous to saying that what someone believes is a fact, if her belief is true. Insisting on a knowledge requirement for a person's reason to be something that is the case would be as unwarranted as saying that what someone believes cannot be something that is the case unless her belief is knowledgeable.

So far so good. But knowing only that someone acted in the light of something she truly took to be the case, without knowing whether her taking it to be the case was knowledgeable, does not settle all the questions we might have about the relation of the relevant fact to her rationality in action. Consider a pair of examples. In both, I suppose there are carpenter ants in my garage roof because someone I take to be an expert tells me so. In the first case the supposed expert is lying. He thinks the piles of sawdust he claims to be basing his assessment on are left over from a do-it-yourself project, but he wants to direct business to his cousin the exterminator. In fact his lying statement is true; the piles of sawdust do indicate the presence of carpenter ants. In the second case the expert is giving expression to knowledge, which I acquire at second hand.[2] In both cases my reason for calling the exterminator is, in the sense Dancy defends, the fact that there are carpenter ants in my garage roof. But in the first case, in which it is an accident that my belief is true, it would be absurd to say that the fact itself exerted a rational influence on my will. And that seems a perfectly appropriate thing to say in the second case.

Here we have a partial analogy with what I claimed about experience and belief. There, facts have a rational impact on belief through experience only in cases in which experience makes knowledge available. Here, facts have a rational impact on the will only if they are known to obtain. And once we see that in one of my two cases but not the other the fact itself can be said to play a role in the operations of my practical reason (to put the same thought in different terms), Dancy's less demanding conception of facts being reasons, which fits just as well in both cases, looks disappointingly thin. There is an interesting discrimination that Dancy's conception does not provide resources for making.

To repeat, I am not suggesting there is anything wrong with the sense Dancy makes of the claim that my reason is that there are carpenter ants in my garage roof, which is, in both cases, a fact. But it seems that cases in which something with the shape Dancy considers is true split into two sorts: those in which my reason is something that is, as it happens, a fact, and those in which the fact itself exerts a rational influence on my will. And now the distinction between cases of this last sort and all others, grouping those in which my reason merely happens to be a fact together with those in which my reason is something that is not so at all, looks – to put it mildly – at least as interesting as the distinction Dancy focuses on.

It is true that there is a kind of intelligibility that my calling the exterminator is shown to have by saying my reason is that there are carpenter ants in my garage roof, whether or not my conviction that there are carpenter ants in my garage roof is a case of knowledge. (I think if we are indifferent to whether or not knowledge is present, the intelligibility we are left with does not even require that the conviction be true.) Analogously, there is a kind of intelligibility that my belief that there is a hummingbird at the feeder is shown to have by saying my reason is that my visual experience appears to reveal to me that that is how things are, and this explanation is indifferent to whether or not my experience is a case of seeing how things are.

But I think Dancy makes too much of this shared intelligibility, common between cases in which there is knowledge and cases in which there is not. This shared intelligibility does not exhaust the available rational explanations.

Seeing that things are a certain way is a kind of reason for belief I sometimes have. If I merely seem to see that things are a certain way, I merely seem to have a reason for belief of that kind. I do not have a reason for belief of that kind. The explanatory power of appearances in general is common as between cases in which one has a reason of that kind and cases in which one merely seems to. But if one sees how things are, that fact has an extra explanatory power. It can explain beliefs in a way that displays them as cases of the sort of standing in the space of reasons that knowledge is.

Analogously, if I call the exterminator because the fact that there are carpenter ants in my garage roof weighs with me, in the sense I have sketched, the action has a special intelligibility, that of a rational response to a fact. This kind of intelligibility is not shared with a case in which, because my conviction that there are carpenter ants in the garage roof only happens to be true, we cannot say that the fact itself weighs with me. (As I said, I think the fact that the conviction is true does not separate the intelligibility in this last case from that of a matching action in a case in which the conviction is not even true.)

What differentiates explanations here is not the distinction between true and false, so there is no violation of the principle Dancy invokes from Bernard Williams. What makes the difference is the distinction between knowledge and its absence.

6   In passing, in his section I, Dancy lines up the distinction between knowledge and mere true belief, in the case of reasons for acting, with the picture I give, following Aristotle, of the distinction between virtue and continence. And he suggests that the motivational structure of a continent person, in my picture, is "Humean," in contrast with a virtuous person, whose reason for acting is how he (rightly) sees the situation he finds himself in. I have two problems with this.

First, a continent person does not have mere true belief. He does not just luck into a true view of what matters about a situation. A virtuous person has a capacity to know what matters about situations that call for virtuous action, and a continent person has a flawed approximation to that capacity. It would not be right to say without qualification that his correct conception of a situation is not knowledgeable.

Second, it is wrong to say that on my putatively Aristotelian view the motivation of a continent person is "Humean."

A virtuous person's correct view of a situation that calls for exercise of a virtue is such as to engross all his motivational energy. In that view of the situation, the attractions of alternative actions do not appear as reasons to pursue the alternatives. The attractions of the alternatives are deprived of the capacity to confer any kind of rationality on competing inclinations. A merely continent person can achieve only an approximation to such a view, defective in that it does not neutralize the rationally motivating potential of attractions possessed by alternative courses of action. Accordingly, to manage a continent action requires something like strength of will, over and above that approximation to the virtuous person's view of the situation, to ensure that one does not act on a competing motivation. With a virtuous person the view itself suffices for action, because the view excludes competing motivations.

There are certainly different motivational structures here. But when Dancy says my picture makes a continent person's motivation "Humean," his suggestion is that according to me there needs to be an extra conative or desiderative element, over and above how the situation is seen, in a specification of the reason for which a continent person acts. And that is not what my view implies. According to me, a continent person acts in the light of a view of the situation that – apart from not being fully achieved, so as to exclude competing motivations – matches a virtuous person's view. The strength of will that he needs, over and above that approximation to the correct view of the situation, is not well seen as an extra element in his reason for acting as he does. His motivational pull towards acting as he does is completely accounted for by how he, in a way, sees the situation. That the seeing is imperfect in the way it is makes no difference to this.[3]

7   I have not yet said anything about whether explanations in terms of reasons for which people do things are causal.

Dancy doubts that these explanations even *can* be causal, let alone that, as I said on the occasion he recalls, Davidson has shown that they *are*.[4] His ground is that "So-and-so did such-and-such for the reason that . . ." is not factive. Even if a fact is the sort of thing that can be a cause, a supposed fact is not. And (Williams's principle) the nature of the explanations supplied by saying something of that form should not differ between cases where what fills the blank is true and cases where it is false.

Of course I acknowledge that Dancy's favored form is not factive. But I think this is a distraction. Dancy's argument would be telling if what settled whether an explanation is causal had to be whether the form of words that gives the explanation includes words that mention or specify a cause. But a different conception is possible, according to which an explanation is causal if the understanding it supplies is causal understanding. And Dancy's argument does not show that the understanding these explanations supply cannot be causal understanding, even granting that when the explanations are given in this form they do not mention or specify causes.

Consider a subclass of reasons-why (as opposed to reasons-for-which) explanations, of the form "So-and-so did such-and-such because she believed that . . . ," picked out by this stipulation: an explanation that belongs to the subclass provides the same understanding as would be provided by the corresponding explanation of the form "So-and-so did such-and-such for the reason that. . . ." (So "He sought medical help because he believed there were pink rats in his boots," in Dancy's example, does not belong to the subclass, whereas "He called the pest-control officer because he believed there were pink rats in his boots" does.) What kind of understanding is provided by reasons-why explanations that belong to this subclass? Dancy's argument leaves us at liberty to suppose it is causal understanding. These explanations invoke a belief – which is the sort of thing that can be a cause – both in the case in which the agent's reason, in Dancy's regimentation, is a fact and in the case in which it is only a supposed fact. But *ex hypothesi* the understanding provided by these explanations is the same as the understanding provided by the corresponding explanation in the "for the reason that" form.[5]

The counterpart explanations are reasons-why explanations, not reasons-for-which explanations. There is no conflict with Dancy's doctrine that the belief that serves as the *explanans* in one of these counterpart explanations is not the agent's reason for acting.

Is there anything wrong with this response? I am defending the claim that the understanding supplied by reasons-for-which explanations can be causal, by pointing to counterpart reasons-why explanations that can, unlike reasons-for-which explanations, be taken to invoke something that can be a cause. It might seem that a defense on these lines could be legitimate only if the counterpart explanations, concerning which it cannot be ruled out that they invoke causes, did their explanatory work independently of any understanding of the idea of acting for reasons. But that would involve a mistake about the pretensions of the thesis that the understanding is causal.

I can bring out what the mistake is by noting its presence in a passage in *Practical Reality*, in which Dancy expresses his skepticism about Davidson's argument that the understanding is causal. (He cites the passage in a note in this chapter.) Dancy thinks Davidson's idea is "that to characterize the relation between reason and action as causal is to make a move *beyond* saying that these features were one's reason for action and those were not," and he puts one of the thoughts that he thinks might underlie this idea as being that "the truth that these things were my reasons and those were not . . . holds in virtue of *another* truth."[6] But Davidson's claim is not that we can analyze the relation between reason and action in independent causal terms, which would operate at some deeper level than that at which we speak of people doing things for reasons. His claim is that the best account of what we are doing *when we speak of people doing things for reasons* is that we are supplying understanding that is itself already causal – causal understanding of a special sort, of course.[7]

Just so, I single out my distinguished subclass of reasons-why explanations in terms of an unanalyzed appeal to the understanding supplied by the counterpart "for the reason that" explanations. As Dancy puts it, "the 'in the light of' relation . . . is what it is, and not another thing."[8] This is perfectly consistent with supposing that what we are supplied with, when we are told about instances of "the 'in the light of' relation," is a species of causal understanding. It is, at least, suggestive in this direction to note how natural it is to characterize reasons-for-which explanations, as I had occasion to do in section 3, by saying they are explanations that reveal their *explananda* as the *result* of rationality at work.

I do not believe any decisively new considerations come into view, so far as the possibility of taking explanations to be causal is concerned, when we consider explaining beliefs in terms of experience. I am skeptical of Dancy's suggestion that it can merely seem to someone that things appear to her a certain way.[9] But suppose it can. We already have, innocently by the lights of Williams's principle, an explanatory difference between "Because so-and-so sees (hears, etc.) that things are thus and so" and "Because it looks (sounds, etc.) to so-and-so as if things are thus and so." (See the end of section 5 above.) It raises no new issues to add a third case, if it makes sense: "Because it (merely) seems to so-and-so that it looks (sounds, etc.) to her as if things are thus and so." This will share a rational-explanatory force that is possessed by statements of the first two forms, the capacity to make the belief that things are thus and so rationally intelligible. Dancy says misread appearances cannot inherit the explanatory powers of self-manifesting states of affairs. But why should that matter? What does inherit those powers – though not all of them, as I have insisted (section 5 above) – in this sort of case, if the case makes sense at all, is not the misread appearance but the appearance that the misread appearance is the way it is erroneously taken to be.

Notes and References

1   If I put this in the first person, saying "My reason is that there are carpenter ants in my garage roof," I do in a sense commit myself to there being carpenter ants in my garage roof. But even here, I can intelligibly add "though I may be mistaken about that." Compare Dancy's case, in his section IV: "His reason was that it would increase his pension, a matter about which he was sadly mistaken." However, I have avoided the first-person form in making the point in the text, because the sense in which the first-person form would commit me to the presence of the ants is potentially confusing.

2   I borrow the structure of the pair of examples, and the point I use them to make, from a forthcoming paper by Jennifer Hornsby, which was called, in the version I heard, "Knowledge and Reasons for Acting."

3   Dancy alludes in a note (n.3) to his arguments, elsewhere, that any account of reasons for acting that allows both "Humean" and non-"Humean" cases is objectionably hybrid. It is true that I do, in other contexts, allow cases of both sorts. But my point in the text is that my account of continence should not itself raise the question whether I represent some reasons for acting as "Humean." I confess I have never understood Dancy's objections to hybridness in an account of reasons for acting. But the issue is not important here, as Dancy indicates by relegating it to a note.

4   I would grant that "shown" may be too strong, though the claim seemed appropriate to the occasion of an eighty-fifth birthday tribute. "Made plausible" might be better. This would leave me just as much in the target area of Dancy's objections.

5 As far as I can see, Wayne Davis's point, in the passage Dancy quotes, could be put by saying that in reasons-for-which explanations in Dancy's canonical form we cannot find *explanantia* – unless we count as an *explanans* what someone who gives such an explanation says, which blurs the distinction Dancy thinks he can insist on. To me this seems quite correct. It is not, as Dancy implies, that there is an *explanans* – as distinct from what is said in giving the explanation – in such an explanation, and *it* is not the sort of thing that can be a cause. There is no "it." This encourages the thought that it should be possible to construct explanations that offer the same understanding and do contain *explanantia*.

6 Dancy, *Practical Reality*, Oxford: Clarendon Press, 2000, 161, my emphasis.

7 I think a similar mistake about Davidson's claim figures in G. E. M. Anscombe's argument against him at p. 2 of "Practical Inference," in R. Hursthouse, G. Lawrence, and W. Quinn (eds.), *Virtues and Reasons: Philippa Foot and Moral Theory*, Oxford: Clarendon Press, 1995.

8 Dancy, *Practical Reality*, 162. (By Dancy's own lights this "relation" is not exactly a relation, on a certain strict interpretation. But this does not matter to the point.)

9 I am not sure what to say about his tuning example. A first thought is that he may not leave enough room for a concept of sounding the way a string sounds when it is flat, a concept that is not the same as the concept of sounding flat. The former concept may apply to an experience without "flat" figuring in a specification of its content, and the subject of the experience may wonder whether it does and be wrong in the answer she comes up with. But as I suggest in the text, I do not need to settle the issue that the case raises.

7

External Reasons

Philip Pettit and Michael Smith

Bernard Williams began a fruitful debate about the nature of reasons in his seminal paper "Internal and External Reasons" (Williams 1980) and the sequel "Internal Reasons and the Obscurity of Blame" (Williams 1989). Williams famously argued that all reasons are internal, in the sense he defined, and that there are therefore no external reasons, in the sense that contrasts with internal reasons as he defines them. On close examination, external reason claims turn out to be disguised claims about what it would be good for someone to do, not claims about what they have reason to do. So, at any rate, Williams argued.[1]

One of the most significant contributions to the debate that Williams began is John McDowell's "Might There Be External Reasons?" Although his title modestly hides the fact, he suggests not just that there might be external reasons, but that there are external reasons, and that moral reasons are among them (McDowell 1995). What the title acknowledges is simply that, as McDowell sees things, more would need to be said in defense of the claim that there exist the sorts of external reasons he envisages than he says in "Might There Be External Reasons?" Williams's main response to McDowell (Williams 1995), at least as we understand it, is to express a kind of exasperation. He reiterates the point that there is a huge gulf between reason claims and claims about what it would be good for someone to do. According to Williams, the external reason claims that McDowell defines are simply more claims of the latter kind, not the former. Williams thus seems to think that McDowell has missed his main point. But is there a distinctive class of external reason claims, different from the class of claims about what it would be good for someone to do? If so, has McDowell properly characterized that class? These are the questions with which we will be concerned in this chapter.

Our chapter is in three main sections. Because Williams's claim that all reasons are internal is so difficult to interpret, we spend the long first section regimenting his claim. This requires us to go beyond anything Williams explicitly says in the text, so, where appropriate, we note alternative readings. In the second section we evaluate Williams's claim, as regimented. In the third section we describe and evaluate McDowell's conception of external reasons in the light of our discussion of Williams. Since we find McDowell's conception of external reasons equally difficult to interpret, much of this final section is spent clarifying and regimenting what he says. But the virtue of the clarification is, we think, evident. For, once clarified, it becomes plain that Williams is right that McDowell's external reason claims turn out just to be disguised claims about what it would be good for someone to do, not claims about what they have reason to do.

I   Williams's Analysis of Internal Reasons

It is now familiar that there is a distinction between normative and motivating reasons (Woods 1972; Smith 1994: ch. 4). Roughly speaking, motivating reasons explain what an agent does, whereas normative reasons are considerations to which we appeal in constructing a justification of an agent's conduct: considerations a sensitivity to which makes an agent immune to rational criticism.

This distinction between motivating and normative reasons needs to be handled with some care, however. On the one hand, when certain motivating reasons explain what an agent does they do so by allowing us to see a minimally rational pattern in her conduct. It thus follows that motivating reasons cannot be divorced entirely from considerations of rationality. On the other hand, when someone has a normative reason, this must be the sort of consideration that could figure in an explanation of her conduct, if not on that occasion, at least on others. Normative reasons thus cannot be divorced entirely from considerations of explanation. Even so, there is, we think, a quite decisive consideration in favor of making a sharp distinction between the two kinds of reason. An agent may have a motivating reason to ϕ without having any normative reason at all to ϕ – indeed, she might think, quite correctly, that all the normative reasons that there are tell against her ϕ-ing – and she may also have a normative reason to ϕ without having any motivating reason to ϕ. Any account of the nature of motivating and normative reasons must therefore preserve at least these two stark possibilities.

In these now familiar terms, Williams's aim in "Internal and External Reasons" is to describe the broad class of normative reasons. According to Williams's famous formula, an agent, A, has an internal reason to ϕ only if she would be motivated to ϕ if she were to engage in deliberative reasoning. Moreover, according to Williams, all normative reasons for action – from here on we will take the qualification "normative" as read – are internal reasons. The only sort of consideration to which we can appeal in providing a rational justification of an agent's conduct, then, is the fact that she would be motivated if she were to deliberate. But, famous though his formula may be, we think it is far from clear what it really means. Our initial task is thus to regiment Williams's formula. As we said earlier, at various points this will require us to go beyond anything that Williams explicitly says. Our aim in such cases is simply to come up with the most plausible interpretation of the formula.

Pro tanto *reasons*

An initial clarification concerns the target concept that Williams is trying to define. We have already seen that he is trying to define the broad class of normative reasons. Importantly, however, Williams is not trying to define what an agent has reason to do in the overall, or all-in, or overriding sense (Williams 1980: 104). Rather he is trying to define what an agent has reason to do in the sense in which an agent's reasons, so defined, might conflict with, and perhaps even be outweighed by, other reasons that she has. In terms that are perhaps more familiar, Williams is concerned to define what an agent has a *pro tanto* reason to do, not what she has all-things-considered reason to do. This means that Williams's talk about motivation has to be understood in a corresponding way. When he talks about what an agent would be motivated to do he means what the agent would have a desire to do – a desire that may not result in any action on his behalf. Just as the reasons in question may be outweighed by other more important reasons to act in some alternative way, so the desires in question may be overridden by other, stronger, desires to act in the alternative way.

Deliberative reasoning

A second, and more difficult, clarification concerns an ambiguity in the phrase "deliberative reasoning" as it occurs in Williams's formula. The general idea is, we take it, plain enough. Williams thinks that what an agent has reason to do is a matter of what she would be motivated to do if her motivations were corrected by engaging in certain reasoning processes, that is, processes whose perfect realization means that those processes conform to certain principles of reason. This is why the reasons themselves are considerations capable of providing rational justifications. But what exactly are these reasoning processes?

According to one very natural interpretation, deliberative reasoning is reasoning whose aim is to figure out what we have reason to do. More specifically, it is the activity of rational belief-formation where the aim is to form beliefs whose content is: that we have reason to do such-and-such. But, natural though it might be, we do not think that this can be what Williams has in mind; or, at any rate, it cannot be all that he has in mind.

Williams's formula is supposed to provide us with an account of what it is that we believe when we believe that we have a reason to act in a certain way. This emerges when he asks, rhetorically:

> *What* is it that one comes to believe when he comes to believe that there is a reason for him to φ, if it is not the proposition, or something that entails the proposition, that if he deliberated rationally, he would be motivated to act appropriately? (Williams 1980: 109; emphasis in original)

Yet if we interpret deliberative reasoning in the way just suggested, and try to use that to explicate what it is that we believe when we believe that we have a reason, then we are reduced to saying the following. When we believe that we have a reason to φ what we believe is that φ-ing has that property, call it F, such that to believe rationally that a way of acting is F is to be motivated to act in that way. It is hard to believe that this convoluted characterization of a reason provides us with the sort of purchase on what it is that we believe when we believe that we have a reason to φ that Williams is after (Williams 1980: 109–10). But in any case there is a substantive reason for thinking that Williams does not endorse this characterization.

Consider the following passage:

> Does believing that a particular consideration is a reason to act in a particular way provide, or indeed constitute, a motivation to act? . . . Let us grant that it does – this claim indeed seems plausible, so long at least as the connexion between such beliefs and the disposition to act is not tightened to that unnecessary degree which excludes akrasia. (Williams 1980: 107)

Williams tells us here that, as he sees things, the belief that one has a reason is not a belief which brings motivation with it: the belief and the motivation are not necessarily connected. The belief that one has a reason does "provide" a reason – by which we take it that he means that the belief is capable of producing a distinct motivation – but only on the assumption that the agent isn't akratic. But in that case it cannot be that what we believe when we believe that we have a reason to φ is that φ-ing has that property possessed by certain ways of acting of being such that, when we come rationally to believe that that property is possessed by a way of acting, we are motivated to act in that way. For it simply isn't true that when we come rationally to believe that that property is possessed by φ-ing – that we have a reason to φ – we are motivated to φ. We are only motivated to act in that way provided we aren't akratic (see also Pettit and Smith 1993a).

The upshot is that we cannot interpret the phrase "deliberative reasoning" in Williams's formula as meaning simply the activity of forming rational beliefs about what we have reason to do. An alternative suggestion, and the one that we think Williams must have in mind, is that deliberative reasoning is the quite general activity of forming desires under the pressure of principles of reason. The basic idea behind this alternative suggestion is that each of us begins with a certain stock of desires – Williams calls this our "subjective motivational set" or "S" – and that what we each have reason to do is a matter of what we would be motivated to do – that is, what we would desire that we do – if our S were added to and subtracted from under the pressure of all of the principles of reason that there are. The thought is, presumably, that there are certain capacities whose possession and exercise enable us to ensure that our desires conform to these principles of reason. What we imagine when we imagine someone having engaged in deliberative reasoning, in the relevant sense of the phrase "deliberative reasoning," is thus that they have and exercise all of these capacities.

In order to spell this story out in full detail we must therefore describe the various capacities, and this in turn requires us to provide a catalog of each and every principle of reason that governs the formation of our desires. The crucial question to ask, if this alternative suggestion is along the right lines, is thus what these principles of reason might be. Suppose that A desires to drink a gin and tonic and that she believes that the stuff before her is gin. If we assume that there is a rational principle requiring agents who desire an end to desire what they believe to be the means to that end, that is, if we assume that the means–ends principle is a principle of reason, then, we may suppose (since if A were to engage in deliberative reasoning in this sense she would be motivated to drink the stuff before her mixed with tonic – let's just stipulate that this is so) that we should conclude, *pro tem*, that she has a reason to drink the stuff before her mixed with tonic. In Williams's terms, this is a case in which, under the pressure of principles of reason, the agent *adds to* her subjective motivational set. Specifically, she adds the instrumental desire.

With this example in mind we can now see the attraction of interpreting the phrase "deliberative reasoning" in the alternative way suggested. For not only does this interpretation guarantee the presence of a motivation – we simply stipulate away the possibility of irrationally ("akratically"?) failing to desire the believed means to a desired end by requiring that the agent has and exercises the capacity to desire accordingly – it also provides us with the more independent purchase on what it is that we believe when we believe that we have a reason, that Williams is after. When A believes that she has a reason to drink the stuff before her mixed with tonic what she believes is, *inter alia*, that she would be motivated to drink the stuff before her mixed with tonic if her desires and beliefs conformed to the means–end principle. Equipped with this more independent purchase on what it is that we believe when we believe that we have a reason, we can also see the plausibility in supposing that someone who believes that a particular consideration is a reason to act in a particular way will be motivated so to act, at least absent akrasia. For someone who believes that she would be motivated to drink the stuff before her mixed with tonic if her desires and beliefs conformed to the means–end principle, but who isn't motivated to drink the stuff before her mixed with tonic, seems to suffer from a kind of incoherence in her psychology, a kind of incoherence not unlike the incoherence in the psychology of an akratic. (Compare someone who believes that her belief set would be more coherent if she believed that p, but who doesn't believe that p. She too seems to suffer from a kind of incoherence in her psychology.) In this way we can see how reason itself might underwrite our being motivated to do what we believe we have reason to do: all that is required is the exercise of our capacity to have a coherent set of psychological states.

In order to spell this story out in full detail, as noted above, we would have to provide a catalog of each and every principle of reason that governs the formation of our desires. Much of Williams's discussion is, we think, aimed at doing just this. For example, he tells us that another form of deliberative reasoning occurs when we gather knowledge of truths and, in the light of that knowledge, correct our desires. This can be thought of as another principle of reason which, indirectly, governs the formation of our desires. Consider a variation on the case just described, discussed explicitly by Williams, in which A desires to drink a gin and tonic, but where the stuff she takes to be gin is in fact petrol. If A were to engage in deliberative reasoning, in the sense of acquiring the knowledge that the stuff before her is petrol rather than gin, and if A conformed her desires to the means–end principle, she would not desire to drink the stuff before her mixed with tonic, as she would no longer have the relevant belief about means. In Williams's terms this is a case in which, under the pressure of principles of reason, the agent *subtracts from* her S.

Williams thinks that there are other principles of reason that govern the formation of desires as well, something he makes plain in the following passage:

> A clear example of practical reasoning is that leading to the conclusion that one has reason to φ because φ-ing would be the most convenient, economical, pleasant etc. way of satisfying some element in S, and this of course is controlled by other elements in S, if not necessarily in a very clear or determinate way. But there are much wider possibilities for deliberation, such as: thinking how the satisfaction of elements in S can be combined, e.g. by time ordering; where there is some irresoluble conflict among the elements of S, considering which one attaches most weight to . . . ; or, again, finding constitutive solutions, such as deciding what would make for an entertaining evening, granted that one wants entertainment. (Williams 1980: 104)

And later he tells us:

> More subtly, he may think he has reason to promote some development because he has not exercised his imagination about what it would be like if it came about. In his unaided deliberative reason, or encouraged by the persuasions of others, he may come to have some more concrete sense of what would be involved, and lose his desire for it, just as, positively, the imagination can create new possibilities and new desires. (Williams 1980: 104–5)

Williams's idea is presumably that these principles too give us the more independent grip on what it is that we believe when we believe that we have a reason. When A believes that she has a reason to φ what she believes is that she would be motivated to φ if she formed her desires under the pressure of all the principles of reason that there are: that is to say, *inter alia*, if she formed her desires in the light of all of the relevant information, if she exercised her imagination fully, if she considered how the various things she wants are effected by time-ordering, if she worked out the answers to various constitutive questions, and if her desires and means–end beliefs conformed to the means–end principle.

From here on we will assume that this is the proper way in which to interpret Williams's proposal that an agent, A, has an internal reason to ϕ only if she would be motivated to ϕ if she were to engage in deliberative reasoning. More specifically, Williams's idea is that we can specify what an individual, A, has internal reason to do in terms of what another individual, Å, desires to be done, where Å is simply A in the nearest possible world in which she has and exercises all of those capacities that ensure that her desires conform to all of the principles of reason that govern desires. In imagining Å, we thus imagine a transformation of A so that she is equipped with these knowledge-gathering and reasoning capacities: the halo represents the transformation. Williams's main task, in these terms, is to provide us with a list of principles that, as he sees things, are such principles of reason: that is, a complete specification of Å. Having said this, however, it should now also be clear that we could accept a proposal with the same general shape as Williams's without accepting that the list of principles he provides is indeed a list of principles of reason, and hence without accepting his specification of the nature of Å's halo.

Exemplars vs. advisers

A third clarification of Williams's proposal is required to fix the logical form of the desires that Å is supposed to have. The general idea, to repeat, is that A has internal reason to do what Å desires to be done. But we can think of Å's desire as being about what Å herself is to do in the circumstances of action that Å herself faces, or we can think of her desire as being about what A is to do in the circumstances of action that A faces. The first interpretation suggests that we specify A's reasons in terms of Å where Å is taken to be an exemplar, someone whose desires about what she (Å) is to do in her own (Å's own) circumstances A should try to emulate, or approximate, as best she can in her own (A's own) circumstances. The second suggests that we specify A's reasons in terms of Å where Å is taken to be an adviser, someone whose desires about what A is to do in the circumstances of action that she (A) faces A should take on in exactly the form in which Å has them (Smith 1995).

In order to see clearly the difference between these two quite different interpretations of the desires that Å might have, consider a variation on an example of Gary Watson's (Watson 1975). Imagine that A suffers a humiliating defeat in a game of squash. She is so angry with herself that she wants to smash her opponent in the face with her racquet. If she gets anywhere near him, this is exactly what she will do. Å, on the other hand, who has exercised her imagination and fully understands what it would be like to smash someone in the face with a squash racquet has no desire whatsoever to do this. What she desires herself to do in the circumstances of action that she (Å) faces is to walk right over and shake her opponent by the hand. This is, however, not something that she would want A to do in the circumstances of action that she (A) faces at all, given that A would follow up the handshake with a smash in the face. What Å desires A to do in the circumstances of action that she (A) faces is to walk off the court without saying a word and calm herself down, something which, let's suppose, A could indeed get herself to do. But, of course, walking off the court without saying a word and calming herself down is not something that Å desires herself (Å) to do in her own (Å) circumstances because, not being angry, she doesn't need to calm herself down. What does A have reason to do in this variation on Watson's example?

If we think of Å as an exemplar, then A has a reason to do what Å desires herself (Å) to do in her own (Å's own) circumstances. In other words, since Å desires to walk over and shake her opponent's hand, A too has a reason to walk over and shake her opponent's hand. Moreover, on the exemplar model, since Å has no desire at all to leave the court immediately without saying a word in her (Å's) circumstances, A has no reason at all to leave the court immediately and calm herself down. On the adviser model, by contrast, what A has reason to do is a matter of what Å would want A to do in her (A's) circumstances. In other words, on the advice model, A has no reason at all to walk over and shake her opponent's hand. Instead what she has reason to do is to leave the court without saying a word and to calm herself down.

With these two interpretations of Å's desire before us we must now ask which gives the best interpretation of Williams's concept of internal reasons. Williams himself doesn't explicitly acknowledge the distinction between these two interpretations, so the question is one that requires us to go beyond anything Williams says in his text. Our own view is that we should interpret his account of internal reasons in terms of the adviser model. The problem with the exemplar model is that it is hard to see the normative relevance of Å's desires about what she (Å) is to do in her (Å's) circumstances to what A has reason to do in her own (A's) completely different circumstances. The normative relevance of what Å wants A to do in her (A's) circumstances – the attraction of the adviser model – is, however, palpable. For the desire that Å has about what A is to do in her (A's) circumstances is the very best desire, from the point of view of reason, that one could have about what is to be done in the very circumstances of action that A faces.

It therefore seems to us that we should suppose that, according to Williams's formula, what A has internal reason to do in certain circumstances C is a matter of what an improved version of herself, Å, would desire A to do in those circumstances C. This is to interpret Å on the model of an adviser, not on the model of an exemplar. The transformation of A into Å is in turn provided, as before, by imagining what A would want if she had and exercised all of the capacities that ensure that her desires conform to principles of reason: that is to say, according to Williams, if she had all of the relevant information, if she exercised her imagination fully, if she considered how the various things she wants are effected by time-ordering, if she worked out the answers to various constitutive questions, and if she conformed her resultant desires and means–end beliefs to the means–end principle.

Recognition and response constraints

A fourth, and final, clarification concerns the constraint placed on the account of reasons, at least as Williams sees things, by the explanatory role of reasons. Here we return to issues of motivation. Very early on in "Internal and External Reasons" he tells us:

> If there are reasons for action, it must be that people sometimes act for those reasons, and if they do, their reasons must figure in some correct explanation of their action. (Williams 1980: 102)

As we understand it, this constraint tells us that, representing the fact that A has a reason to φ by a certain proposition p, then it must be the case that A could act because p. Now we have already seen how, in Williams's view, internal reasons could play such an explanatory role. For, as he sees things, we can come to believe that we have internal reasons, characterized in his preferred way, and, absent akrasia and the like, we can be motivated to act accordingly. Rational people – people who possess and exercise the capacity to have a coherent psychology – acquire desires to do what they believe they have internal reason to do. Nor should this be surprising. For, to repeat, when

A believes that Å desires that she φs in circumstances C, where Å is characterized as A herself, transformed so that she possesses and exercises all of the capacities that ensure that her desires conform to principles of reason, coherence does indeed seem to tell in favor of her acquiring the desire to φ in C (Smith 1999).

Williams elaborates further on this idea in his "Internal Reasons and the Obscurity of Blame" (Williams 1989) where his main aim is to get some purchase on what it is to have a reason by attending to the "close connection between blame and the agent's reasons" (Williams 1989: 41): that is, to the fact that when someone fails to act on a reason they thereby become liable for blame: "focused blame" as he puts it.

> Focused blame operates in the mode of "ought to have," which has a famous necessary connection with "could have." Focused blame will go by the board if "could have" is absent. The reason for this seems to be connected with the following consideration: if "ought to have" is appropriate afterwards in the modality of blame, then (roughly) "ought to" was appropriate at the time in the modality of advice. (Williams 1989: 40)

He immediately follows this remark up with a footnote:

> It is important, in exploring these connections, that we are indeed concerned with the modality of blame. In the case of an error that is not blamed, for instance because it was due to unforeseeable circumstances, "ought to have" may mean, at most, "could have; and it would have been better if he had." (Williams 1989: 45 n.7)

Williams's idea here seems to be that since reasons have to be capable of explaining the behavior of those whose reasons they are it follows not just that if A has a reason to act in a certain way then this has to be something that she could have done, but that acting in the way in question has to be something that she could have come to believe that she has reason to do. The information was available to her. Moreover, it also follows that, had she come to believe that that is so, she could have been motivated to act in the appropriate way. The desire was available to her. In a phrase, his view seems to be if A has a reason to φ then A must be actually capable of both recognizing and responding to this fact. Absent the possession of these recognitional and responsive capacities – that is, absent A's possession of these capacities in fact, not counterfactually – it simply isn't true that A has a reason to φ. The best we can say is that A could have φ-ed and that it would have been better if she had φ-ed. This, at any rate, seems to be Williams's suggestion (compare Pettit and Smith 1996).[2]

As we see things, reflection on the explanatory dimension of reasons puts a further constraint on Williams's proposal about internal reasons. So far the suggestion has been that what A has internal reason to do in certain circumstances C is a matter of what an improved version of herself, Å, would desire herself to do in those circumstances C, where this transformation of A into Å is provided by imagining what A would want if she had and exercised all of the capacities that ensure that her desires conform to the principles of reason. But it certainly seems possible that Å could desire that A φs in C and yet, due to A's own incapacities – remember, we are not supposing that A herself has and exercises all of the capacities that ensure that her desires conform to the principles of reason, only that Å has and exercises these capacities – A might actually be (actually be, not would be) incapable of coming to believe that this is so – that is, the recognition constraint might be violated. And it also seems possible that, even if A did come to believe that Å desires that A φs in C, due to A's own incapacities, A might actually be (again, actually be, not would be) incapable of acquiring a motive in the light of that belief – that is, the response constraint might be violated.

The gin and petrol case can be described in a way that brings out how the recognition constraint might be violated. Since, in this variation on the case, Å has all of the information that there is, it follows that Å knows that what A believes to be gin is in fact petrol. Consequently, we may suppose, Å is averse to A's drinking the stuff before her mixed with tonic. So far, then, we might think that A has a reason not to drink the stuff before her mixed with tonic. But, in the light of the recognition constraint, we can see that this may yet not be the case. The crucial further question is whether A is capable of coming to believe that this is what Å wants. If so, then perhaps A does indeed have a reason not to drink the stuff before her mixed with tonic. That will depend on whether the response constraint is met as well. But if not – that is, if A is incapable of coming to believe that this is what Å wants because, say, in order to acquire such a belief she would have to access the information that what she believes to be gin is in fact petrol, but the information that what she believes to be gin is petrol is unavailable to her – then it follows that it simply isn't the case that A has a reason not to drink the stuff before her mixed with tonic. In Williams's words, in a case like this we should suppose instead that though that A could fail to drink the stuff before her mixed with tonic, and though it would be good if she failed to do so, it isn't the case that she has a reason not to do so. It isn't the case that she has a reason not to do so because, being incapable of accessing this fact, we cannot blame her for failing to act on the reason.[3]

So much for how the recognitional constraint may be violated. Certain sorts of cases of depression, at least under certain assumptions about the way in which depression operates, provide examples where the response constraint is violated. Suppose that A is so depressed that she not only has no desire whatsoever to improve her life, but that her belief that Å desires that she (A) improves her life leaves her completely cold. The depression incapacitates her. Does A have a reason to improve her life in these circumstances? If we accept the response constraint on reasons then it follows she doesn't have a reason to improve her life. Since she is incapable of responding to her belief it follows that we cannot blame her for failing to act on what she believes her reason to be, notwithstanding the lack of coherence involved in her having the belief but lacking the desire. If she is literally incapable of acquiring a desire to improve her life – if no technique of self-control would get her to desire to do so – then the best that we can say is that it would be good for her to improve her life, not that she has a reason to do so.

What all of this suggests is that the recognition and response constraints have to be added as further constraints on internal reasons. We should therefore suppose that, according to Williams, for A to have an internal reason to φ in certain circumstances C two conditions have to be satisfied: (i) an improved version of herself, Å, would have to desire A to φ in those circumstances C, where this transformation of A into Å is in turn provided by imagining what A would want if she had and exercised all of the capacities that ensure that her desires conform to principles of reason: that is to say, according to Williams, if she had all of the relevant information, if she exercised her imagination fully, if she considered how the various things she wants are effected by time-ordering, if she worked out the answers to various constitutive questions, and if she conformed her resultant desires and means–end beliefs to the means–end principle; and (ii) A has to be capable of both recognizing and responding to the fact mentioned in (i).[4]

II   Williams's Claim that All Reasons are Internal Reasons

With this clarification of Williams's proposal about the nature of internal reasons before us, we are now in a position to ask whether it is plausible to suppose, as he does, that all reasons for action are internal reasons so defined. If we are right, then Williams's proposal in effect decomposes into three quite distinct parts:

(a)   There is the claim that an agent A has internal reason to φ in certain circumstances C only if Å wants A to φ in C, where Å has and exercises all of the capacities that ensure that her desires conform to principles of reason.

(b)   There is the further claim that A has an internal reason to φ in C only if A has – not would have, but has – the capacity to recognize and respond to the fact mentioned in (a).

(c)   There is Williams's description of the capacities possessed by someone who has and exercises all of the capacities that ensure that her desires conform to principles of reason: that is, his suggestion that the desires possessed by Å are those that A would have if she had all of the relevant information, if she exercised her imagination fully, if she considered how the various things she wants are effected by time-ordering, if she worked out the answers to various constitutive questions, and if she conformed her resultant desires and means–end beliefs to the means–end principle.

This means that someone could object to Williams's proposal by objecting to any one of the three distinct parts. We will consider them in reverse order.

Is claim (c) objectionable?

The most controversial part is claim (c): Williams's description of the capacities possessed by someone who has and exercises the capacities that ensure that her desires conform to principles of reason. It is here that his Humean leanings come to the fore, for the principles of reason implicit in his description are simply those that would be agreed to by those sympathetic with Hume's view of the relationship between reason and passion. As we understand it, it is this part of Williams's proposal to which both Brad Hooker and Christine Korsgaard object (Korsgaard 1986; Hooker 1987). Moreover, we think that their objections have considerable force.

It is striking that Williams nowhere in "Internal and External Reaons" argues that the following cannot be derived from principles of reason:

Reason requires that if A believes that B is another person, equally real, and A believes that B is in pain, and A believes that she can relieve B's pain by φ-ing, then A desires to φ.

Nor, as a result, does he argue that the capacities possessed by someone who has and exercises all of the capacities that ensure that her desires conform to principles of reason do not include a capacity to generate intrinsic desires in the presence of such beliefs in the manner described by this principle. Indeed, not only does Williams not give such an argument, he nowhere acknowledges the need to give such an argument.

The point that we are making here does not turn on the controversial claim that, contrary to Williams, this, or something much like it, is a principle of reason, or can be derived from principles of reason. We take no stand on this substantive issue. The point we are making turns rather on the fact that certain well-known theorists, both in the history of philosophy and in the contemporary literature, have insisted that this, or something much like it, is a principle of reason, or can be so derived. Thus, for example, Kant spends much of *The Metaphysics of Morals* trying to derive a principle much like the principle mentioned above from the fact that our willings must not be in any way contradictory (Kant 1786). More recently Thomas Nagel spends much of *The Possibility of Altruism* trying to derive a principle much like the principle mentioned from the fact that we each conceive of ourselves as one temporally extended deliberating agent among many (Nagel 1970). For Williams's characterization of the capacities that ensure that our desires conform to principles of reason to be compelling, he would therefore have to argue that views like Kant's and Nagel's are mistaken. Yet, to repeat, no such argument is either given or alluded to. He simply assumes that the rational principles governing desire formation require, at most, coherence with other desires.

Moreover, it seems to us that if we try charitably to read an argument to this effect into Williams's text, then the best that we can do is to supply a suppressed premise to the effect that the principles of reason, whatever they are, must wear their credentials as principles of reason on their sleeve: a principle of reason's status as a principle of reason must be uncontroversial, otherwise it isn't a principle of reason at all. We think that this is the feature that the principles on Williams's list all have in common: no one, or anyway no one sensible, would take issue with the claim that they are indeed principles of reason governing the formation of desires. But though this suppressed premise would, if true, make part (c) of Williams's proposal less objectionable, that doesn't show that the suppressed premise is itself plausible. Speaking for ourselves, we can see no merit in the suggestion that principles of reason are one and all uncontroversial.[5]

This leaves us with a further interpretative question. If we were to reject part (c) of Williams's proposal, then should we conclude that we thereby reject Williams's claim that all reasons are internal? In other words, is (c) strictly essential to the definition of internal reasons? If so, then it follows that we should believe, contrary to Williams, that there are external reasons. As we understand it, Brad Hooker assumes that this is so. This is why he suggests that theorists like Kant and Nagel should respond to Williams by pointing out that his argument against them turns on a persuasive definition of the term "deliberation": Williams's account of the capacities possessed by those who have and exercise all of the capacities that ensure that their desires conform to principles of reason. According to Hooker, these theorists should insist that, armed with a more plausible definition of the term "deliberation," and hence a more plausible description of the correlative capacities, we can see that there are indeed external reasons. Alternatively, if (c) is not strictly essential to the definition of internal reasons – if the crucial elements are parts (a) and (b), with part (c) simply being Williams registering, gratuitously, his own Humean leanings – then we should suppose that theorists like Kant and Nagel would have no objection to Williams's suggestion that all reasons are internal. As we understand it, this is Christine Korsgaard's view. She takes herself to agree with Williams that all reasons are internal, notwithstanding the fact that she disagrees with him about which principles are, and which principles are not, principles of reason governing the formation of desires.

We are not sure which of these options Williams himself would prefer. Our own view, however, is that to the extent that he is right that we can get an independent purchase on what it is to have a reason by attending to the twin facts that there is a "close connection between blame and the agent's reasons" (Williams 1989: 41) and that "blame will go by the board if 'could have' is absent" (Williams 1989: 40), he should prefer the second to the first (though see the discussion in the next section). For the possibility of blame, in the relevant sense, would seem to follow from our failure to believe or desire or do what we are capable of believing or desiring or doing as creatures who are bound by principles of reason that govern what we believe, desire and do. But in saying this we need take no stand on the precise content of these principles of reason.

Seen in this light, part (c) of Williams's proposal does just seem like a gratuitous registering of his own Humean leanings. What is crucial is parts (a) and (b): the suggestion that A has a reason to φ in circumstances C only if (a) an improved version of herself, Å, would desire that A φ's in circumstances C, where this transformation of A into Å is in turn provided by imagining what A would want if she had and exercised all of the capacities that ensure that her desires conform to principles of reason, whatever they are; and (b) A is capable of both recognizing and responding to the fact mentioned in (a).

Is claim (b) objectionable?

Next consider part (b) of Williams's proposal. There is, we think, inherent slippage in the concept of a capacity, and hence in the concept of blame. As we see things, this slippage leaves Williams's claim that all reasons are internal because of the close connections between reasons and blame, on the one hand, and blame and "could have," on the other, open to serious objection.

Consider the following two equations:

$$\text{Equation 1:} \quad x - 4 = 10$$

$$\text{Equation 2:} \quad \frac{34}{x^2 - 3x + 7} + 5 = 2x - 3$$

Though anyone with normal high school mathematical abilities is capable of solving for x in each, a failure to exercise these capacities in the one case, as against the other, would appear to warrant quite different attitudes with regard to blame. The reason is the mundane one that, given that a priori reasoning may be more or less difficult, having a capacity for a priori reasoning is one thing and exercising that capacity is quite another. Since solving for x in Equation 1 is clearly a good deal less difficult than solving for x in Equation 2 it therefore follows that, notwithstanding the fact that anyone with normal high school mathematical abilities has the capacity to solve for x in each of these equations, failing to exercise the capacity to solve for x in Equation 2 is at least not uncommon, whereas failing to exercise the capacity to solve for x in Equation 1 is rare.

This, in turn, means that while we might reasonably expect virtually everyone with normal high school mathematical abilities to solve for x in Equation 1 if they tried, we could not reasonably expect everyone with normal high school mathematical abilities to solve for x in Equation 2 if they tried. Of course, this is not to say that they shouldn't both succeed. Given that they could all solve for x in each of the equations, of course they should. It is rather to say that, as a matter of empirical fact, it is only to be expected that some people would fail in the one case but not in the other, and that their failure would be readily intelligible. They fail because of the difficulty of the task, not because they are incapable.

Relatedly, though both those with normal high school mathematical abilities who fail to solve for x in Equation 1 and Equation 2 fail to exercise capacities that they possess as creatures capable of priori reasoning, we would almost certainly baulk at calling those who fail to solve for x in Equation 2 irrational. The charge of irrationality would, however, seem to sit well with those with normal high school mathematical abilities who fail to solve for x in Equation 1. There is therefore a distinction to be made between failing to exercise such capacities as one possesses to make one's beliefs conform to principles of reason and being irrational.

Now consider the issue of blame. Is it appropriate to blame someone for failing to exercise reasoning capacities that they have even if we could not reasonably expect them to succeed? In other words, does blame require not just that people fail to exercise a capacity that they have that they should exercise, but also, in addition, that they fail to meet a commonly achieved standard? Does the difficulty of a task, notwithstanding an agent's capacities, affect the appropriateness of blame? If not, then we should blame anyone with normal high school mathematical abilities who fails to solve for x in both Equation 1 and Equation 2. If so – that is, if blame is only appropriate to the extent that people fail to meet some commonly achieved standard; if blame sits more happily alongside a charge of irrationality (Rosen 2002; Pettit 2001: ch.1) – then, though we should blame anyone with normal high school mathematical abilities who fails to solve for x in Equation 1, we should not blame them for failing to solve for x in Equation 2.[6]

Our own view, for what it is worth, is that this question cannot be answered without supplying more information about the context in which we are supposed to blame some particular person. But the mere fact that the question can be sensibly asked is, we think, enough to make trouble for Williams's claim that all reasons are internal reasons, given that reasons have a close connection with blame and blame has a close connection with "could have." Remember, condition (b) says that A has an internal reason to ϕ in circumstances C only if A is capable of both recognizing and responding to the fact (supposing it to be a fact) that an improved version of herself, Å, desires that A ϕs in those circumstances C, where this transformation of A into Å is in turn provided by imagining what A would want if she had and exercised all of the capacities that ensure that her desires conform to principles of reason. But the capacities to recognize and respond to such facts are, in crucial respects, a lot like mathematical abilities. Notwithstanding the fact that anyone with normal recognition and response capacities could recognize and respond to certain such facts, it might well be the case that two such facts differ in the following crucial respect: though it would be astonishing to find people with such recognition and response capacities who fail to recognize and respond to one such fact – a failure to do so would suggest gross irrationality – a non-trivial number of people with such capacities would fail to recognize and respond to the other because of the difficulty of the task.

For example, perhaps it is easy for A to form the belief that Å would want her to make herself happy (supposing that Å would want this). Virtually no one with normal recognition capacities would fail to recognize that that is so, given that it is so. A failure to recognize such a fact would signal gross irrationality. But perhaps it is very difficult for A to see that Å would want her to make huge sacrifices in her happiness in order to increase the amount of happiness enjoyed by others (supposing this to be so). That would require quite a lot of hard thought and reflection. Consequently, a non-trivial number of people with normal recognition capacities would fail to recognize that that is so, notwithstanding the fact (supposing it to be a fact) that it is so. The charge of irrationality would not sit happily, notwithstanding the fact there is a failure to exercise the reasoning capacities that they have.

Or perhaps it is easy for A to get herself to desire to make herself happy, having formed the belief that Å would want A to make herself happy. No one with normal response capacities – that is to say, no one with normal capacities for self-control (Pettit and Smith 1993a; Pettit and Smith

1993b) – would fail to have this desire, given that they have the belief. Failure to exercise self-control would signal an irrational failure of self-control. But perhaps it is very difficult for A to get herself to desire to make huge sacrifices in her own happiness in order to increase the amount of happiness enjoyed by others, having formed the belief that Å would want A to make huge sacrifices in her own happiness in order to increase the amount of happiness enjoyed by others. A non-trivial number of people with normal response capacities would fail to have this desire, notwithstanding the fact that they have the belief. The idea that there is an irrational failure of self-control in such cases might therefore not work so well, notwithstanding the fact that there is a failure to exercise such capacities for self-control as they have.

This, in turn, means that while we might reasonably expect virtually everyone with normal recognition and response capacities to recognize and respond to the fact (supposing it to be a fact) that their haloed counterparts would want them to make themselves happy, we might well not be able reasonably to expect everyone with such capacities to recognize and respond to the fact (supposing it to be a fact) that their haloed counterparts would want them to make huge sacrifices in their happiness in order to increase the amount of happiness enjoyed by others. But this, in turn, has the potential to affect who we blame. The issue, this time, is whether it is only appropriate to blame someone for failing to exercise their capacities to recognize and respond to facts about what their haloed counterparts want if we could reasonably expect them to succeed. If so – if the appropriateness of blame turns on the difficulty of the task – then, in our example, it is only appropriate to blame people who fail to make themselves happy. If not, then it is equally appropriate to blame people who fail to make themselves happy and those who fail to make huge sacrifices in their happiness in order to increase the amount of happiness enjoyed by others.

We now have a further interpretative question on our hands. Williams insists that there is a close connection between blame and an agent's reasons. His definition of internal reasons makes that more or less explicit by having agents' reasons be limited by their capacities for recognition and response. This is the role of part (b) of his proposal. But the inherent slippage in the concept of a capacity means that we need to know how part (b) is to be understood. No matter how we answer this question, we think that this leaves his claim that all reasons are internal open to serious objection.

At one extreme, if Williams insists that his definition of internal reasons limits the capacities for recognition and response to those it is reasonable to expect someone to exercise, then, we say, there is room for the external reasons theorist quite reasonably to insist that the concept of a reason places no such limitation on the capacities for recognition and response. At this extreme the upshot would be that, though Williams succeeds in defining a class of internal reasons, he fails to show that all reasons are internal. There are external reasons, namely, those that are limited by agents' capacities for recognition and response which are not, in turn, capacities that we reasonably expect them to exercise.

At the other extreme, if Williams insists that his definition of internal reasons does not limit the capacities for recognition and response to those that it is reasonable to expect someone to exercise, then we think that there is room for the external reasons theorist to take issue with Williams's insistence that there is the close connection between blame and an agent's reasons that he imagines. To be sure, the external reasons theorist might say, Williams has succeeded in defining the class of reasons which an agent has the capacity to recognize and respond to. These are reasons that satisfy both part (a) and part (b) of Williams's proposal. But, he might say, reasons satisfying both parts (a) and (b) of Williams's proposal form only a subclass of the total set of reasons. The total set of reasons include those that simply satisfy part (a): in other words, (a) is both necessary and sufficient for the existence of reasons as such. We can illustrate the plausibility of this claim if we reconsider the two examples given above of the ways in which the recognition and response condition constrains an agent's internal reasons.

Suppose that A is incapable of forming the belief that the stuff before her, which she believes to be gin, is in fact petrol. In order to recognize this fact she would have to be equipped with knowledge-gathering capacities that she doesn't actually have. As a result, she desires to drink the stuff before her mixed with tonic and no amount of the information-gathering of which she is capable would make that desire go away. Still, the external reasons theorist might say, if Å, who is equipped with these capacities and so does know that the stuff before her is petrol, would want her not to drink the stuff before her mixed with tonic, it follows that there is a sense in which she has a reason not to drink that stuff. The fact that it may take conversion, not rational persuasion, to get A to recognize her reasons – for it might take conversion, not rational persuasion, to equip A with the capacity to recognize the relevant facts – is neither here nor there. All that this means is that we cannot blame A for failing to act on her reason. But, the external reasons theorist might say, that is precisely the point: there is a kind of reason that we do not blame the agent for acting on.

Or suppose that A is so depressed that she not only has no desire whatsoever to improve her life, but that her belief that Å desires that she (A) improves her life leaves her completely cold. The depression incapacitates her. It removes her capacity for self-control: stops her being able to respond, appropriately, to the incoherence involved in her having the belief but lacking the desire. Does A have a reason to improve her life in these circumstances nonetheless? The external reasons theorist might insist that, in a sense, she does, simply in virtue of the fact that Å, who suffers no such incapacity, does want A to improve her life. The fact that it may take conversion, not rational persuasion, to get A to respond to her reasons – for it might take conversion, not rational persuasion, to equip A with the capacity for self-control – is neither here nor there. Again, all that this means is that we cannot blame A for failing to act on her reason. But that is no objection if the external reasons theorist's point is that that is a kind of reason that we do not blame the agent for acting on.

Of course, if an external reasons theorist were to argue in this way then Williams would no doubt press him to explain why these claims – claims that only satisfy part (a) of his proposal – should be thought of as reasons, and not as simply things that it would be good for the agent to do. But we think that the external reasons theorist has a principled response to this. For he could insist that they are reasons precisely because they are constrained by part (a) of Williams's proposal: that is, because they are the things which an agent would want herself to do if she had and exercised all of the capacities that ensure that her desires conform to principles of reason. Put another way, he could insist that they are reasons, not simply things that it would be good for the agent to do, because they are things that an agent would want herself to do from a viewpoint endorsed by reason itself. This, the external reasons theorist might say, and quite plausibly, is the crucial feature of reasons. They are things that it would be good-from-the-viewpoint-of-reason to do.

The upshot, at least as we see things, is that the inherent slippage in the concept of a capacity, as in part (b) of Williams's proposal, leaves his claim that all reasons are internal open to serious objection. Williams makes part (b) essential to his definition of an internal reason because, as he sees things, there is a close connection between blame and what an agent has reason to do, and because blame goes by the board if it isn't true that the agent could have acted as the reason requires. But it is open to the external reasons theorist to argue that the connection is nowhere near as close or as determinate as Williams needs it to be for his claim that there are no external reasons to have any serious plausibility. We have sketched various ways in which the external reasons theorist might make out his case on this score.

Is claim (a) objectionable?

Finally, let's consider part (a) of Williams's proposal: his suggestion that an agent A has internal reason to φ in certain circumstances C only if Å wants A to φ in C, where Å has and exercises all of the capacities that ensure that her desires conform to principles of reason. Is there room here for an objection to Williams's proposal that all reasons are internal? In other words, are there reasons that do not satisfy even this necessary condition on Williams's internal reasons? As we see things, this is where Williams's proposal is at its very strongest. In order to see why, it will help if we compare a close relative of his proposal, namely, Hume's sentimentalist analysis of moral judgment. Though Hume's analysis of moral judgment is extremely complicated – we ourselves are indebted to Sayre-McCord's treatment (1994) – for our purposes a bare bones account will suffice.

Hume famously argues that our moral judgments track our sentiments. But he also insists that they do not track just any old sentiment, as our sentiments include not just our moral sentiments, but also our "particular interests" (Hume 1740: 472): that is to say, our interests in our own weal and woe, as distinct from our interests in the weal and woe of others. As Hume sees things, our moral judgments abstract away from such particular interests. They track, instead, our sympathetic responses: the responses we have to the weal and woe of all affected. But nor, according to Hume, do our moral judgments simply track just any old sympathetic responses we have. Our sympathetic responses are, after all, variable "according to the present disposition of our mind" (Hume 1740: 582): we represent the weal and woe of some people more or less vividly than that of others, and our sympathetic responses vary accordingly. Rather, according to Hume, our moral judgments track our corrected sympathy, that is to say, the sympathetic responses we would have if we were to consider the weal and woe of each person affected equally vividly.

The similarities and differences between Hume's analysis of moral judgment and Williams's analysis of internal reasons should now be plain. Both insist that a feature of A's actions – in Hume's case, an action of a certain kind's being virtuous; in Williams's, an action of a certain kind's being one that the agent has reason to perform – can be understood in dispositional terms: specfically, in terms of what an idealized version of A, Å, would want. But whereas in Williams's analysis of internal reasons we idealize A by equipping her with all of the capacities required to ensure that her desires conform to principles of reason and then having her exercise those capacities, in Hume's analysis of moral judgment we idealize by requiring A to lose all of her interests in herself so that her reactions are determined solely by her sympathetic responses. Williams's idealization transforms A into Å^R, as Williams idealizes by requiring A to conform to ideals of reason (the "R" is for "reason" and is to be read as qualifying the kind of halo Å wears), whereas Hume's idealization transforms A into Å^{MH}, as Hume idealizes by requiring A to conform to certain moral ideals, at least as he conceives of these moral ideals (hence Å's halo is qualfied by an "MH" for "morality as conceived by Hume").

Once we see the general form that both Hume's and Williams's analyses have in common, we can see that similar analyses to Hume's could in fact be given of all sorts of concepts. For example, if, following Hume, facts about what Å^{MH} wants provide an analysis of the concept of what it would be good-from-the-standpoint-of-morality-as-conceived-by-Hume for someone to do, then it seems that facts about what $Å^E$ wants – here we equip A with the capacities required to act in a well-mannered way, hence the halo is qualified by an "E" for "etiquette" – provide an analysis of the concept of what it would be good-from-the-standpoint-of-etiquette for someone to do; facts about what $Å^B$ wants – in this case we equip A with the capacities required to act in ways that promote his biological fitness, hence the halo is qualified by a "B" for "biology" – provide an analysis of the concept of what it would be good-from-the-standpoint-of-biology for someone to do; and so on and so forth.[7]

Suppose someone were to suggest that Hume's analysis of what it would be virtuous for someone to do – or, for that matter, one of the analyses just given of what it would be good-from-the-standpoint-of-etiquette/biology/and the like to do – captures another concept of what one has reason to do. Would that suggestion have anything to recommend it? We think not. After all, Hume's idea that in analyzing the concept of what it would be virtuous for someone to do we must privilege our sympathetic responses has nothing whatsoever to do with norms of reason: as he sees things, there is not only nothing contrary to reason in A's having interests in her own weal and woe alongside her sympathetic responses, there would be nothing contrary to reason in A's having interests in her own weal and woe but having no sympathetic responses at all (Hume 1740: 416). The reason that we privilege A's sympathetic responses in analyzing the concept of what it would be virtuous for someone to do – at least according to Hume – is that what we are trying to analyze is a moral concept, and morality has everything to do with abstracting away from one's own interests and taking a more general view. The suggestion that Hume's analysis captures the concept of what one has reason to do – or, for that matter, the analyses just given of what it would be good-from-the-standpoint-of-etiquette/biology/and the like to do – thus simply obliterates a distinction that is there to be made.

We are now in a position to see the real force that lies behind Williams's idea that all reasons must satisfy part (a) of his analysis of internal reasons. For, if Williams is right, then the distinction between reason claims and claims about what it would be good for someone to do must, in effect, be made *within* a more general framework from within which we see a fundamental similarity between reason claims and claims about what it would be good for someone to do. Within this more general framework it is *the nature of the idealization* – that is, whether we characterize Å as someone whose desires meet certain norms of reason, or morality, or etiquette, or biology, or whatever – that is the only variable. The difference between a reason claim and a claim about what it would be good for someone to do is thus, in effect, the difference between a claim about what it would be good-from-the-standpoint-of-reason for someone to do and a claim about what it would good-from-the-standpoint-of-some-ideal-other-than-reason for someone to do. It therefore follows that part (a) of Williams's proposal must, in effect, be accepted by default. Only so can we make the distinction between reason claims and claims about what it would be good for someone to do.[8]

It is important to note that what we have just said does not beg any important questions. Suppose, for example, that we were to reject Williams's own account of the capacities possessed by someone who has the capacities required to ensure that her desires conform to principles of reason. Imagine, more specifically, that it is an open question whether we can derive principles of reason like those argued for by Kant and Nagel, and hence an open question whether there are corresponding capacities. In that case we would have to suppose, likewise, that it is an open question whether there is a reason for people to do what, in terms of Hume's analysis, it would be morally good for them to do; an open question whether what it would be good-from-the-standpoint-of-reason for them to do is what it would be good-from-the-standpoint-of-some-ideal-other-than-reason for people to do. Whether or not this is so turns on whether or not the privileging of sympathetic responses can be seen to follow, in some way or other, from certain principles of reason. We take no stand on this issue. For the crucial point that we have just made is rather a conceptual one, namely, that if Hume is right, then the concept of what it would be morally good for someone to do itself requires that we privilege sympathy. The privileging of sympathy does not need to follow from the requirement that our concerns not be contradictory, as Kant thinks, or the requirement that our concerns dovetail with our conception of ourselves as one temporally extended deliberating agent among many, as Nagel thinks. Indeed, if Hume is right, these requirements might have nothing to do with morality at all. But, to repeat, this leaves it open that Kant and Nagel might well be right, and hence that there is a reason for people to do what, in terms of Hume's analysis, it would be morally good for them to do.

To sum up, Williams's analysis of internal reasons divides into three main parts:

(a) There is the claim that an agent A has internal reason to φ in certain circumstances C only if Å wants A to φ in C, where Å has and exercises all of the capacities that ensure that her desires conform to principles of reason.

(b) There is the further claim that A has an internal reason to φ in C only if A has – not would have, but has – the capacity to recognize and respond to the fact just mentioned.

(c) There is Williams's description of the capacities possessed by someone who has and exercises all of the capacities that ensure that her desires conform to principles of reason: that is, his suggestion that the desires possessed by Å are those that A would have if she had all of the relevant information, if she exercised her imagination fully, if she considered how the various things she wants are effected by time-ordering, if she worked out the answers to various constitutive questions, and if she conformed her resultant desires and means–end beliefs to the means–end principle.

We have seen that very plausible objections can be made to Williams's claim that all reasons satisfy parts (b) and (c) of his analysis of internal reasons. To this extent it seems to us not just that Williams is wrong that all reasons are internal – there are external reasons, indeed, potentially, there are many different kinds of external reason – but that he himself does us the great service of making it clear how there can be such reasons: how external reasons differ from his internal reasons. However we have also seen that there is great force in his suggestion that all reasons satisfy part (a) of his analysis of internal reasons; great force in the idea that the difference between a reason claim and a claim about what it would be good for someone to do is, in effect, the difference between a claim about what it would be good-from-the-standpoint-of-reason for someone to do and a claim about what it would be good-from-the-standpoint-of-some-ideal-other-than-reason for someone to do.[9]

III McDowell's Analysis of External Reasons

Let's now turn to McDowell's own analysis of external reasons. To which part of Williams's suggestion that all reasons are internal reasons does he object? Does he take issue with the claim that all reasons satisfy (a) or (b) – with, of course, the word "internal" removed – or with claim (c)? We argue that the real difference is over part (a), but that this is not always clear, because McDowell fails to distinguish clearly enough between these three claims.

Is (c) true?

McDowell begins not by giving his own characterization of external reasons, but instead by asking how Williams thinks that external reasons should be characterized. As we later discover, he does this so as to make it clear that the kind of external reasons whose possibility he wishes to defend is different from the kind that he thinks Williams takes to be impossible.

> As Williams describes his position, the external reasons theorist must envisage a procedure of correct deliberation or reasoning which gives rise to a motivation, but which is not "controlled" by existing motivations, in the way that figures in the account of internal reasons; for, if the deliberation were thus "controlled" by existing motivations, the reason it brought to light would simply be an internal reason. So the external reasons theorist has to envisage the generation of a new motivation by reason in an exercise in which the directions it can take are not determined by the shape of the agent's prior motivations – an exercise that would be rationally compelling whatever motivations one started from. As Williams says, it is very hard to believe that there could be a kind of reasoning that was pure in this sense – owing none of its cogency to the specific shape of pre-existing motivations – but nevertheless motivationally efficacious. If the rational cogency of a piece of deliberation is in no way dependent on prior motivations, how can we comprehend it giving rise to a new motivation? (McDowell 1995: 71–2)

McDowell's focus in this passage is plainly on part (c) of Williams's analysis of internal reasons. From our point of view, there are two main points to make about this passage.

For one thing, it shows that, as McDowell reads "Internal and External Reasons," Williams's commitment to all reasons being internal is tied very closely to his Humean conception of the capacities possessed by someone who has and exercises all of the capacities that ensure that her desires conform to principles of reason. Thus, according to McDowell, Williams thinks that for reasons not to be internal, in his sense, we would have to suppose that there are principles of reason much like those that Kant and Nagel believe in. We gave an example of such a principle earlier on.

> Reason requires that if A believes that B is another person, equally real, and A believes that B is in pain, and A believes that she can relieve B's pain by ϕ-ing, then A desires to ϕ.

McDowell tells us that it is because Williams thinks that there are no such principles that he rejects the possibility of external reasons. However, for the reasons given above, we do not interpret Williams's paper in this way. We think that his own Humean views about the capacities possessed by someone who has and exercises all of the capacities that ensure that her desires conform to principles of reason is, in the end, best interpreted as an add-on in the context of his overall argument for the claim that all reasons are internal.

Williams's crucial point, to repeat, is that we can get an independent purchase on what it is to have a reason by attending to the close connection between blame and an agent's reasons and to the connection between blame and "could have." But the possibility of blame, in the relevant sense, follows from our failure to believe or desire or do what we are capable of believing or desiring or doing as creatures who are bound by principles of reason that govern what we believe, desire, and do. Williams's own Humean views about the precise content of these principles of reason is thus neither here nor there. This is why we think Korsgaard is right to suppose that she shares with Williams the view that all reasons are internal, notwithstanding the fact that, like Kant and Nagel, but unlike Williams, she thinks that there are principles of reason much like those described above.[10]

The passage just quoted from McDowell is remarkable for another reason as well. For it becomes clear in this passage that he basically agrees with Williams's own Humean views about the nature of the capacities possessed by someone who has and exercises all of the capacities that ensure that her desires conform to principles of reason. Indeed, he reiterates the point later on:

> [R]easoning aimed at generating new motivations will surely stand a chance of working only if it appeals to something in the audience's existing motivational makeup, in something like the way exploited in Williams's account of the internal interpretation. (McDowell 1995: 74)

In other words, we are to take it that McDowell and Williams agree that the desires possessed by $Å^R$ are those that A would have if she had all of the relevant information, if she exercised her imagination fully, if she considered how the various things she wants are effected by time-ordering, if she worked out the answers to various constitutive questions, and if she conformed her resultant desires and means–end beliefs to the means–end principle. His disagreements with Williams on this score are, as we will see, at most disagreements about the nature of desire. The upshot is thus that McDowell's own defense of the possibility of external reasons will not turn on his denying that all reasons satisfy part (c) of Williams's analysis.

Is (b) true of all reasons?

McDowell's next move is to sketch his own alternative account of external reasons:

> The external reasons theorist must suppose that the agent acquires the motivation by coming to believe the external reason statement. To be an external reason statement, that statement must have been true all along; in coming to believe it the agent must be coming to consider the matter aright. The crucial question is this: why must the external reasons theorist envisage this transition to considering the matter aright as being effected by *correct deliberation*? . . . The argument debars the external reasons theorist from supposing that there is no way to effect the transition except one that would not count as being swayed by reasons: for instance . . . , being persuaded by moving rhetoric, and, by implication . . . , inspiration and conversion. But what is the ground for this exclusion? (McDowell 1995: 72)

At first sight it looks like McDowell's challenge in this passage is not to part (a) of Williams's analysis – not to his claim that A has reason to φ in C only if $Å^R$ wants him to φ in C – but rather to his claim that all reasons have the feature picked out in part (b) of his analysis. In other words, McDowell seems to be asking why, taking (a) as read, we should suppose that, for a reason to be a reason, the person whose reason it is has to be capable of recognizing and responding to that reason. Why shouldn't we suppose, instead, that agents have reasons that they don't have the capacity to recognize and respond to, and that, in order to develop the capacity to recognize and respond to their reasons, they would have to undergo a conversion?

We have already seen how Williams would answer this challenge. As he sees things, if agents had reasons that they didn't have the capacity to recognize and respond to then we wouldn't be able to blame them for failing to act on their reasons. It is thus the close connection between reasons and blame, and between blame and "could have," that is supposed to convince us that all reasons satisfy part (b) of his analysis of internal reasons. So Williams would say. However, much as McDowell seems to be suggesting in the passage just quoted, we ourselves insisted above that this part of Williams's analysis isn't really very compelling. It is open to the external reasons theorist to argue that the connection between reasons and blame, and between blame and "could have," is nowhere near as close or as determinate as Williams needs it to be for the claim that all reasons satisfy part (b) of his analysis to have any serious plausibility. The external reasons theorist could then suggest, much as McDowell suggests, that it would take conversion for A to acquire the capacities to recognize and respond to her reasons. She may have to acquire information-gathering capacities, or perhaps capacities for rational self-control, that she doesn't actually have.

Is (a) true of all reasons?

But, having said all that, in fact we think that this is not the right way to interpret the passage just quoted from McDowell. McDowell expands on what he means by conversion in a passage that follows.

> If we think of ethical upbringing in a roughly Aristotelian way, as a process of habituation into suitable modes of behaviour, inextricably bound up with the inculcation of suitably related modes of thought, there is no mystery about how the process can be the acquisition, simultaneously, of a way of seeing things and of a collection of motivational directions or practical concerns, focussed and activated in particular cases by exercises of the way of seeing things. And if the upbringing has gone as it should, we shall want to say that the way of seeing things – the upshot, if you like, of a moulding of the agent's subjectivity – involves considering them aright, that is, having a correct conception of their actual layout. Here talking of being properly brought up and talking of considering things aright are two ways of giving expression to the same assessment: one that would be up for justification by ethical argument. (McDowell 1995: 73)

Remember, Williams's idea is that for A to have an internal reason to ϕ in certain circumstances C the following condition has to be satisfied:

(a)   an improved version of herself, $\mathring{A}^R$, would have to desire A to ϕ in those circumstances C, where the "R" signifies that we are to imagine the transformation of A into $\mathring{A}$ by imagining what A would want if she had and exercised all of the capacities that ensure that her desires conform to principles of reason.

As we see things, McDowell's suggestion in these passages is that there are reasons that do not satisfy (a). Regimented so as to make it easier to compare his suggestion with Williams's, McDowell's proposal is that what makes it true that A has such a reason to ϕ in certain circumstances C – an external reason, now, not an internal reason – is that an improved version of herself, $\mathring{A}^{PAU}$, desires that she ϕs in C, where this transformation of A into $\mathring{A}^{PAU}$ is provided by going to a possible world in which, having been properly brought up, A exercises her capacity to see that A is indeed in circumstances C: she forms a proper conception of those circumstances. The "PAU" here stands for a "proper Aristotelian upbringing." It signifies that we are to imagine the transformation of A into $\mathring{A}$ by imagining what A would want if she was properly brought up in the ways required to live a life recommended by Aristotelian ethics. The capacity to see that A is in C is thus meant to be a distinctive kind of capacity for perception or belief that is, at the same time, both a perception or belief that A is in C and a desire that A φs in C, a capacity that A acquires as a result of her proper Aristotelian upbringing.

Much of this should, of course, sound familiar. For McDowell here basically draws on claims about the nature of virtuous conduct for which he makes a well-known case in earlier work. What makes it possible for a virtuous agent to behave virtuously, he tells us in "Are Moral Requirements Hypothetical Imperatives?", is that she is capable of enjoying a distinctive kind of psychological state that is both belief-like and desire-like:

> [In] . . . urging behaviour one takes to be morally required, one finds oneself saying things like this: "You don't know what it means that someone is shy and sensitive." Conveying what a circumstance means in this loaded sense, is getting someone to see it in the special way in which a virtuous person would see it. In the attempt to do so, one exploits contrivances similar to those one exploits in other areas where the task is to back up the injunction "See it like this": helpful juxtapositions of cases, descriptions with carefully chosen terms and carefully placed emphasis, and the like . . . No such contrivances can be guaranteed success, in the sense that failure would show irrationality on the part of the audience. That, together with the importance of rhetorical skills to their successful deployment, sets them apart from the sorts of thing we typically regard as paradigms of argument. But these seem insufficient grounds for concluding that they are appeals to passion as opposed to reason: for concluding that "See it like this" is really a covert invitation to feel, quite over and above one's view of the facts, a desire which will combine with one's belief to recommend acting in the appropriate way. (McDowell 1978: 21–2)

McDowell admits that:

> Failure to see what a circumstance means, in the loaded sense, is of course, compatible with competence, by all ordinary tests, with the language used to describe the circumstance; that brings out how loaded the notion of meaning involved in the protest is. (McDowell 1978: 22)

But he thinks that this simply shows that the ordinary tests we have for individuating the agents' ways of thinking about their circumstances are inadequate:

> To preserve the distinction we should say that the relevant conceptions are not so much as possessed except by those whose wills are influenced appropriately (McDowell 1978: 23).

In other words, seeing things in the distinctive way in which a virtuous person sees them – believing what the virtuous person believes about the circumstances of action she contemplates – is having certain desires about how things turn out in those circumstances (see also McDowell 1979). To use J. E. J. Altham's neologism, the virtuous person is more accurately described not so much as having either beliefs or desires, but rather as having a hybrid kind of psychological state, a belief that is at one and the same time a desire, that is to say, a "besire" (Altham 1986).[11]

In the light of this reminder of McDowell's earlier work, let's now return to our schematic example and consider how he understands A's inability both to appreciate the fact that she is indeed in circumstances C and to desire that she φs in C. In "Are Moral Requirements Hypothetical Imperatives?" McDowell acknowledges that this kind of failure would not signal irrationality on an agent's behalf. However, as we saw in our earlier discussion of Williams on blame, the mere fact that a failure does not signal irrationality on an agent's behalf is consistent with its signaling a failure to exercise a capacity to ensure that her beliefs and desires conform to principles of reason. Such exercises can be more or less difficult, and the charge of irrationality sits most happily with the latter, rather than the former charge. In the passages just discussed from "Are Moral Requirements Hypothetical Imperatives?" McDowell effectively leaves this possibility open. A's inability both to appreciate the fact that she is indeed in circumstances C and to desire that she ϕs in C might well, for all that McDowell tells us in this early paper, signal a failure to exercise a capacity to ensure that her beliefs and desires conform to principles of reason notwithstanding the fact that it doesn't signal irrationality.

But in "Might There Be External Reasons?" McDowell effectively closes this possibility. The difference between A and Å^{PAU}, we now learn, is not that the latter has a capacity to ensure that her beliefs and desires conform to principles of reason that the former lacks: A and Å^{PAU} may well both have and exercise exactly the same capacities to imagine fully, to consider how the various things wanted are effected by time-ordering, to work out the answers to various constitutive questions, and to conform resultant desires and means–end beliefs to the means–end principle. These, you will recall, are the only capacities to ensure that beliefs and desires conform to principles of reason that McDowell acknowledges; in this he is of the same mind as Williams. The difference between them is that Å^{PAU}, in virtue of having been given a proper Aristotelian upbringing, has a capacity to see and so desire things that A, lacking that upbringing, doesn't have, but by having this capacity Å^{PAU} does not thereby conform to any requirement of reason, and by not having it A does not thereby violate any requirement of reason. Requirements of reason are silent about whether or not people are to see and so desire things in this way.

This too should sound all too familiar. For it turns out that McDowell's analysis of external reasons is, in crucial respects, exactly like Hume's analysis of what it is virtuous for someone to do. As we saw earlier, Hume thinks that in analyzing the concept of what it would be virtuous for A to do we must consider what Å^{MH} would want A to do, where Å^{MH} is a transformed version of A, namely, A in the possible world in which she has the sympathetic sentiments demanded by morality as Hume conceives of it (thus the "HM"). As is already clear, perhaps, we could just as easily state this in more McDowellian terms. In Hume's view it is virtuous for A to ϕ in C only if Å^{PHU} desires that A ϕs in C, where Å^{PHU} is a transformed version of A, namely, A in the possible world in which she has a proper Humean upbringing, one in which A is made sympathetic. McDowell, by contrast, thinks that A has external reason to ϕ in C only if Å^{PAU} wants A to ϕ in C, where Å^{PAU} is a transformed version of A, namely, A in the possible world in which she has a proper Aristotelian upbringing, one in which A is given capacities to see things in certain ways. But just as Hume thinks that this privileging of an upbringing that equips A with sympathy has nothing whatsoever to do with A's conforming her desires to principles of reason, as reason is silent about whether or not A should be brought up so as to be sympathetic, so McDowell thinks that the privileging of a proper Aristotelian upbringing has nothing whatsoever to do with A's conforming her desires to principles of reason, as reason is silent about whether or not A should end up having the desires that result from an Aristotelian upbringing.

McDowell makes the similarities and the differences between his own view and Hume's more or less explicit in his critique of psychologism: psychologism, in this context, is the view that deliberation is a "procedure for imposing coherence and practical determinacy on whatever collection of prior motivations one presents it with" (McDowell 1995: 79).

> The opposition to psychologism that I have described pictures practical predicaments as structured out of collections of values that are independent of any individual's motivational makeup, and this may

seem to reintroduce the threat of a weird metaphysic which I discounted earlier. But this is a mistake. One way to avoid such a metaphysic is to regard values as reflections or projections of psychological facts involving affect or sentiment, and such a position might indeed have difficulties in accepting the kind of transcendence I have envisaged. But in order to acknowledge the constitutive connection of values to human subjectivity, it is not obligatory to suppose that the genealogy of value can be unravelled, retrospectively, in such a way as to permit factoring out a contribution made by isolable facts about our individual psychology to the evaluable contours of our world. A sane subjectivism can allow that value transcends independently describable psychological fact. (McDowell 1995: 80)

Here McDowell shows that he accepts, in broad outline, Hume's sentimentalist projectivism. His disagreement with Hume lies not in the commitment to sentimentalist projectivism as such, but rather in the conception of the sentiments in terms of which his own preferred version of sentimentalist projectivism is constructed.

Whereas the story of Humean sentimentalist projectivism is told in terms of sympathy, where sympathy is independent of – that is, "can be unravelled" from – certain ways of seeing circumstances, McDowell's own preferred version of sentimentalist projectivism is told in terms of sentiments that are not, in this way, independent of ways of seeing. In our schematic regimentation of McDowell's view we registered this point by requiring that $Å^{PAU}$ both sees or believes that A is in C and desires that A ϕs in C, where her seeing or believing that A is in C is her desiring that A ϕs in C. The point is not just that someone incapable of conceiving of A's circumstances in the way in which $Å^{PAU}$ conceives of them cannot have the desire that $Å^{PAU}$ has about what is to be done. The point is rather that someone who does not desire that A ϕs in C thereby fails to see or believe that A is in C. It is in this way that McDowell's sentimentalist projectivism rests on the possibility of there being besires.

So far our concern has been to explain why McDowell thinks that there are reasons that do not satisfy the conditions Williams places on internal reasons. As we see things, McDowell's main challenge is to Williams's claim that all reasons satisfy claim (a): A may have reason to ϕ in C even though $Å^R$ doesn't desire that she ϕs in C, for what is required for A to have a reason to ϕ in C – an external reason to ϕ in C, not an internal reason – is that $Å^{PAU}$ desires that she ϕs in C. With this interpretation of McDowellian external reasons in mind, let's now ask how Williams should respond to McDowell's challenge.

Evaluation of McDowell's account of external reasons

We think that there are two main lines of response. The first lies in questioning the materials out of which McDowell constructs his account of external reasons. The second lies in questioning whether the account he constructs deserves to be called an account of reasons.

As we have seen, the external reasons McDowell purports to define require us to make sense of the possibility that there are beliefs that are desires; that is to say, there must be a coherent concept of a besire. But if the concept of a besire betrays some latent incoherence, then it follows that the very concept of McDowellian external reasons is itself incoherent. The crucial question is thus whether the idea that there are besires makes any real sense. Can we tell a coherent story about conceptions of circumstances which, as McDowell puts it, "are not so much as possessed except by those whose wills are influenced appropriately" (McDowell 1978: 23)? Or does our very telling of this story reveal that such conceptions are impossible? Interesting though it would be to pursue this line of objection further, however, we will not pause to consider it here. The coherence of the concept of a besire has been canvassed extensively elsewhere – suffice it to say that opinion is divided – and we feel that there is nothing new we could add to what we have already said (Smith 1987; Pettit 1987; Smith 1988; Collins 1988; Lewis 1988; Dancy 1993; Quinn 1993; Smith 1994: ch.4; Jackson and Pettit 1995; Lewis 1996; Mele 1996; Little 1997; Raz 1999: chs 2 and 3; Scanlon 1998: ch.1).

There is, though, a second and much more decisive line of response. Even if there are besires, the real question is why we should suppose that facts about what $\AA^{PAU}$ desires A to do constitute facts about what A has external reason to do rather than facts about what it would be good for A to do. Or, more precisely, why shouldn't we suppose that such facts constitute facts about what it would be good-from-the-standpoint-of-ethics-as -conceived-by-Aristotle for A to do? The crucial point here is the one that we made earlier in our discussion of the similarities between Williams's account of what an agent has internal reason to do and the analysis of what it is virtuous for someone to do offered by Hume's sentimentalist projectivism.

As we saw then, the real force behind Williams's idea that all reasons must satisfy part (a) of his analysis of internal reasons – the real force behind the claim that all reasons must be facts about what $\AA^{R}$ desires – lies in the fact that the distinction between reason claims and claims about what it would be good for someone to do must be made *within* a more general framework from within which we see a fundamental similarity between reason claims and claims about what it would be good for someone to do. Within this more general framework, the nature of the idealization is the only variable. Å may be characterized as someone whose desires meet certain norms of reason ($\AA^{R}$), or etiquette ($\AA^{E}$), or biology ($\AA^{B}$), or for that matter as someone who has had a proper upbringing as such an upbringing is conceived by Aristotle ($\AA^{PAU}$), or a proper upbringing as such an upbringing is conceived by Hume ($\AA^{PHU}$). If we have to distinguish the class of reasons, within this more general framework, from the class of facts about what it would be good for someone to do, then, it seems, identifying the class of reasons with the class of facts about what $\AA^{R}$ desires looks to be the only principled choice. Reasons must have to do with . . . having desires that meet norms of reason: what else?

Towards the end of "Might There Be External Reasons?," when McDowell takes himself to have "touched on what is, in one sense, the heart of the matter," he betrays his failure to appreciate this point, a failure that we think can be traced to his failure to distinguish Williams's analysis into its component parts, that is, (a), (b), and (c). He tells us:

> Williams's explicit argument has no deeper foundation than the assumption that the external reasons theorist wants to be entitled to find irrationality when someone is insensitive to the force of a supposed external reason; and, in its naked form, the assumption seems too transparently flimsy to be the real basis for his conclusion. It is too easy to drive a wedge between irrationality and insensitivity to reasons which are nevertheless there. (McDowell 1995: 81)

But while finding irrationality might be the key to Williams's view that all reasons satisfy part (b) of his analysis of internal reasons – and, as we have seen, even this is only so on a very strict interpretation of part (b) – it is by no means the key to his view that all reasons satisfy part (a) of the analysis of internal reasons. To repeat, the attraction of the suggestion that all reasons satisfy part (a), whether or not they also satisfy part (b) on any interpretation, lies in the fact that only so can we make a principled distinction between reason claims and claims about what it would be good for someone to do.[12]

Conclusion

It may be useful, in conclusion, to summarize the main philosophical points that we think emerge from our considerations:

(i)   Normative reasons, internal or external, should be identified by an amendment of Williams's claim (a). A has reason to φ in certain circumstances C, we might say, only if Å desires A to φ in C, where Å has and exercises all of the capacities that ensure that her desires conform to principles of reason. Otherwise put, A has a reason to φ in certain circumstances C only if it would be good-from-the-standpoint-of-reason for A to do so.

(ii)   Internal reasons should be identified more narrowly by reliance on Williams's claim (b). We might describe them as those normative reasons which A has the capacity to recognize and to which A has the capacity to respond. There are serious difficulties, however, in providing a measure of when those capacities are present and when therefore, as Williams suggests, blame might be appropriate.

(iii)   What it would be good-from-the-standpoint-of-reason for A to do, and what A in that sense has normative reason to do, is an open question. Williams assumes in his claim (c) that Hume offers us the best account of this, and McDowell goes along with him on that point. But the claim is disputable, and is disputed by figures like Kant and Nagel and Korsgaard.

(iv)   The category of what it would be good-from-the-standpoint-of-reason to do contrasts nicely with categories that replace "reason" by some other term like "morality" or "etiquette" or "biology," or more specifically by "Humean morality" or "Aristotelian morality" or whatever. What it would be good for A to do in C from such a perspective is what Å desires A to do in C, where Å is well brought up in that perspective.

(v)   The best interpretation of McDowell's argument against Williams's position leaves that argument vulnerable to an objection which Williams himself suggests. By the above criteria, what McDowell directs our attention to are not external normative reasons but rather considerations to do with what it would be good for an agent to do from the standpoint of Aristotelian morality.

(vi)   How significant is it that McDowell opts for an Aristotelian rather than, say, a Humean perspective? By his lights, very significant, since he insists that beliefs and desires do not neatly unravel in the standpoint of someone who is well brought up in Aristotelian terms.[13]

Notes

1   Note that the claim that it would be good for someone to act in a certain way, as used here, is synonymous with the claim that that person's acting in that way would be good. The locution "good for," as used in the present context, is thus not supposed to carry the implication that acting in the way in question would be to serve the agent's interests, or to contribute to his welfare.

2   In the terminology of our "Backgrounding Desire," (Pettit and Smith 1990), Williams here foregrounds the (alleged) fact that a certain consideration is a reason. Moreover, if to believe that one has a reason to φ in C is, as Williams supposes (in Williams 1980: 109), to believe that one would have desire that

one φs in C if one were to deliberate, then it follows that he thereby foregrounds (alleged) facts about one's counterfactual desires; compare Pettit and Smith (1997).

3   Importantly, note that it doesn't follow from what we have just said that A must, in such a case, have a reason to drink the stuff before her mixed with tonic. As we understand it, the recognition constraint comes into play after we have established what Å would want, where Å is imagined to have all the information that there is. (Reasons are, after all, supposed to be able to explain in favored cases, and explanation is factive.) Thus, what the recognition constraint tells us is that A has an internal reason to do only a subset of the things that Å desires that she does: specifically, she has a reason to do that subset of things that she could come to believe that Å desires that she does. But since imagining Å to have all of the information that there is, is to imagine her having no desire whatsoever that A drinks the stuff before her mixed with tonic, it therefore follows that A does not have a reason to drink the stuff before her mixed with tonic.

4   As further proof that the recognition and response constraint is at least implicit in Williams's original account of internal reasons consider the following passage, from Williams (1980: 103): "A may be ignorant of some fact such that if he did know it he would, in virtue of some element in S, be disposed to φ: we can say that he has a reason to φ, though he does not know it. For it to be the case that he actually has such a reason, however, it seems that the relevance of the unknown fact to his actions has to be fairly close and immediate; otherwise one merely says that A would have a reason to φ if he knew the fact. I shall not pursue the question of the conditions for saying the one thing or the other, but it must be closely connected with the question of when the ignorance forms part of the explanation of what A actually does."

5   We prefer an approach whereby the principles of reason are those whose endorsement would survive in a conversational practice: see Pettit and Smith (1996); Pettit (2001); and Pettit and Smith (2004).

6   Akeel Bilgrami pointed out to us that it cannot be simply assumed, as the previous discussion might suggest, that which capacities agents possess can be determined independently of whether or not we take them to be liable for blame. A live possibility must be that we inter-define the concepts of agents' capacities and their liability for blame. Our hope is that what we have said here is consistent with this possibility.

7   As Graham Macdonald pointed out to us, it might not be possible for agents to internalize all of these "good" claims. How might an agent dedicate himself to doing what it would be good-from-the-stand-point-of-biology to do, for example? But even if only some can be internalized, they all still provide a standard by which behavior can be evaluated from a third-person standpoint.

8   Another possible idealization, suggested to us by Peter Roeper, is the idealization formed by going to the possible world in which A fully exercises such capacities as she has to ensure that her desires conform to principles of reason, where these capacities might be very impoverished indeed: this is how the proposed idealization differs from the $\mathring{A}^R$ idealization. It is an interesting question whether facts about what A would want herself to do, under the proposed idealization, have any normative significance independent of whatever normative significance attaches to the fact that A could form beliefs about what $\mathring{A}^R$ would want her to do.

9   Of course, Williams's claim that all reasons are internal would be very plausible indeed if (a) were meant to be both necessary and sufficient for a reason's being internal. Our own view is that, when "Internal and External Reasons" first appeared, this was a very natural interpretation of his claim. Korsgaard interprets him in this way, and so explicitly says that, as she sees things, all reasons are internal even though not all reasons satisfy (b); see Korsgaard (1986: 13–14 n.9). One of us interpreted Williams in this way in earlier work; see Smith (1995). It is only when we read "Internal Reasons and the Obscurity of Blame" that the relevance of (b) comes to the fore.

10   Williams agrees too. As he puts it, "Somebody may say that every rational deliberator is committed to constraints of morality as much as to the requirements of truth or sound reasoning. But if this is so, then the constraints of morality are part of everybody's S, and every correct moral reason will be an

internal reason. But there has to be an argument for that conclusion. Someone who claims that the constraints of morality are themselves built into the notion of what it is to be a rational deliberator cannot get that conclusion for nothing." See Williams (1995: 37). His disagreement with Korsgaard turns on the fact that he can see no good reason for believing that there are any principles of reason like those that Kant and Nagel believe in; see also Williams (1995: 44 n.3).

11 It is important to see just how strong this claim is. The claim is not that there is a normative connection between certain beliefs and certain desires. As we have seen, this is a claim to which Williams himself seems committed, for he suggests, in effect, that coherence tells in favor of pairing the belief that one has a reason to φ with the desire to φ. The claim is rather the much stronger one that certain beliefs *are* desires: hence "besires."

12 It might be thought that this suggests an alternative interpretation of McDowell. Williams claims that what a subject has internal reason to do is what she would want herself to do if she had and exercised the capacity to rationally deliberate on the basis of all of the information that there is. But he implicitly assumes that we can characterize such information without deciding whether or not the subject has had a proper Aristotelian upbringing. McDowell's suggestion might be that we cannot leave this open – not, at any rate, if we take an interest in claims about what subjects have external reason to do. These are claims about the *reasons* such subjects have because their truth turns on what subjects would want after rationally deliberating, albeit on the basis of a more expansive class of information, information that they can appreciate only if they have had a proper Aristotelian upbringing. This is why they are external, rather than internal. But while this alternative might sound superficially different from the interpretation of McDowell we have offered in the text, it isn't really different. What is the normative force of the claim that we *should* rationally deliberate on the basis of information that we can access only if we have had a proper Aristotelian upbringing? It is not an ideal of reason that we have the wherewithal to access such information. The only force that can attach to saying that we should rationally deliberate on the basis of such information is thus that it would be good to do so – good from a perspective other than reason. But in that case the alternative interpretation reduces to the interpretation offered in the text.

13 We are extremely grateful for the many helpful comments we received when earlier versions of this paper were presented at the Australian National University, the University of Canterbury, and Columbia University. Special thanks are due to Akeel Bilgrami, Janice Dowell, Patricia Kitcher, Philip Kitcher, Cynthia Macdonald, Graham Macdonald, Peter Roeper, Gideon Rosen, and David Sobel.

References

Altham, J. E. J. 1986. "The Legacy of Emotivism," in G. Macdonald and C. Wright (eds.), *Fact, Science and Morality*, Oxford: Blackwell.

Collins, J. 1988. "Belief, Desire and Revision," *Mind* 97: 333–42.

Dancy, J. 1993. *Moral Reasons*, Oxford: Blackwell, 1993.

Hooker, B. W. 1987. "Williams' Argument against External Reasons," *Analysis* 44: 42–4.

Hume, D. 1740. *A Treatise of Human Nature*, Oxford: Clarendon Press, 1968.

Jackson, F. and Pettit, P. 1995. "Moral Functionalism and Moral Motivation," *Philosophical Quarterly* 45: 20–40.

Kant, I. 1786. *Groundwork of the Metaphysics of Morals*, London: Hutchinson and Company, 1948.

Korsgaard, C. 1986. "Skepticism about Practical Reason," *Journal of Philosophy* 83: 5–25.

Lewis, D. 1988. "Desire as Belief," *Mind* 97: 323–32.

Lewis, D. 1996. "Desire as Belief II," *Mind* 105: 303–13.

Little, M. 1997. "Virtue as Knowledge: Objections from the Philosophy of Mind," *Nous* 31: 59–79.

McDowell, J. 1978. "Are Moral Requirements Hypothetical Imperatives?", *Proceedings of the Aristotelian Society* Supplementary Volume 52: 13–29.

McDowell, J. 1979. "Virtue and Reason," *The Monist* 62: 331–50.

McDowell, J. 1995. "Might There Be External Reasons?", in J. E. J. Altham and R. Harrison (eds.), *World, Mind, and Ethics: Essays on the Ethical Philosophy of Bernard Williams*, Cambridge: Cambridge University Press, 68–85.

Mele, A. 1996: "Internalist Moral Cognitivism and Listlessness," *Ethics* 106: 727–53.

Nagel, T. 1970. *The Possibility of Altruism*, Princeton: Princeton University Press.

Pettit, P. 1987. "Humeans, Anti-Humeans and Motivation," *Mind* 96: 530–3.

Pettit, P. 2001. *A Theory of Freedom*, Oxford: Polity.

Pettit, P. and Smith, M. 1990. "Backgrounding Desire," *Philosophical Review* 99: 565–92

Pettit, P. and Smith, M. 1993a. "Practical Unreason," *Mind* 102: 53–79.

Pettit, P. and Smith, M. 1993b. "Brandt on Self-Control," in B. Hooker (ed.), *Rationality, Rules and Utility: New Essays on the Moral Philosophy of Richard B. Brandt*, Boulder, Colo.: Westview Press, 33–50.

Pettit, P. and Smith, M. 1996. "Freedom in Belief and Desire," *Journal of Philosophy* 93: 429–49.

Pettit, P. and Smith, M. 1997. "Parfit's P," in J. Dancy (ed.), *Reading Parfit*, Oxford: Blackwell, 71–95.

Pettit, P. and Smith, M. 2004. "The Truth in Deontology," in R. Jay. Wallace, P. Pettit, S. Scheffler, and M. Smith (eds.), *Reason and Value: Themes from the Moral Philosophy of Joseph Raz*, Oxford: Oxford University Press, 153–75.

Quinn, W. 1993. "Putting Rationality in its Place," in his *Morality and Action*, Cambridge: Cambridge University Press.

Raz, J. 1999. *Engaging Reason*, Oxford: Oxford University Press.

Rosen, G. 2002. "Culpability and Ignorance," *Proceedings of the Aristotelian Society* 103: 61–84.

Sayre-McCord, G. 1994. "On Why Hume's General Point of View Isn't Ideal – and Shouldn't Be," *Social Philosophy and Policy* 11: 202–28.

Scanlon, T. 1998. *What We Owe to Each Other*, Cambridge, Mass.: Harvard University Press.

Smith, M. 1987. "The Humean Theory of Motivation," *Mind* 96: 36–61.

Smith, M. 1988. "On Humeans, Anti-Humeans and Motivation: A Reply to Pettit," *Mind* 97: 589–95.

Smith, M. 1994. *The Moral Problem*, Oxford: Blackwell.

Smith, M. 1995. "Internal Reasons," *Philosophy and Phenomenological Research* 55: 109–31.

Smith, M. 1998. "The Possibility of Philosophy of Action," in J. Bransen and S. Cuypers (eds.), *Human Action, Deliberation and Causation*, Dordrecht: Kluwer Academic Publishers, 1998, 17–41.

Watson, G. 1975. "Free Agency." Reprinted in G. Watson (ed.), *Free Will*, Oxford: Oxford University Press, 1982, 96–110.

Williams, B. 1980. "Internal and External Reasons." Reprinted in his *Moral Luck*, Cambridge: Cambridge University Press, 1981.

Williams, B. 1989. "Internal Reasons and the Obscurity of Blame." Reprinted in his *Making Sense of Humanity*, Cambridge: Cambridge University Press, 1995.

Williams, B. 1995. "Replies," in J. E. J. Altham and R. Harrison (eds.), *World, Mind, and Ethics: Essays on the Ethical Philosophy of Bernard Williams*, Cambridge: Cambridge University Press, 1995, 185–224.

Woods, M. 1972. "Reasons for Action and Desire," *Proceedings of the Aristotelian Society*, Supplementary Volume 46: 189–201.

Response to Philip Pettit and Michael Smith

1 Pettit and Smith offer a "regimentation" of Williams that at best marginalizes his central point. Partly as a result, they are off target in their reading of my response to Williams. They conclude that Williams is fundamentally right against me. But the issue he raises, the issue I respond to, does not come into view in their chapter, so they are not in a position to adjudicate the dispute. This will take some explaining.

2   When Williams expounds his conception of the internal reasons interpretation of reason statements, he starts from what he calls "the sub-Humean model," according to which a subject has reason to do only what will be, or promote, the satisfaction of some element in her existing "subjective motivational set."[1] The sub-Humean model is too simple, and Williams moves to a conception according to which the reasons a subject has are limited to reasons she can come to see that she has as a result of deliberation. He gives an informal sketch of what he means by "deliberation." Deliberation starts from a subject's existing motivational set and is controlled by it, but leads to adding new motivational states or subtracting old ones.

Pettit and Smith read into Williams a conception of deliberation as "the quite general activity of forming desires under the pressure of principles of reason." There are at least two things wrong here.

3   First, introducing principles of reason is gratuitous. As an ingredient in a reading of Williams, it is out of line with his suspicion of a rationalistic conception of rationality, a conception that "requires in principle every decision to be based on grounds that can be discursively explained."[2]

It is true, and important, that Williams thinks deliberation can be done correctly, and when done correctly it leads to knowledge. Deliberation can bring a subject to realize that she has some reason she did not realize she had, or that she does not have some reason she thought she had. But it is tendentious to assume that it must be possible to spell out the conception of knowability in play here in terms of principles of reason, let alone what Pettit and Smith envisage, "a catalogue of each and every principle of reason that governs the formation of our desires."

As I said, Williams sketches various kinds of thing one can do in deliberation. Pettit and Smith read this as making a start on providing such a catalogue. Williams says deliberation can include "finding constitutive solutions, such as deciding what would make for an entertaining evening, granted that one wants entertainment" (104). Pettit and Smith take this to imply that for Williams it is a principle of reason governing the formation of desires that one must work out the answers to various constitutive questions.

Here the reading has led to foisting an absurdity on Williams. A principle of reason governing the formation of desires should help one answer questions about what desires one should have. But the principle Pettit and Smith attribute to Williams merely describes a form sometimes taken by problems about what desires one should have. I want an entertaining evening, but I do not know what particular activity my wanting entertainment gives me reason to engage in. It cannot help to tell me that reason requires me to work out the answer to my constitutive question. That is just a way to say what my problem is.

This is not an objection to Williams. It just brings out how far from Williams's thinking the "regimentation" is.

From here on, I shall often replace the talk of principles of reason with expressions of the idea on which it constitutes a tendentious gloss, the idea that deliberation is a route to knowledge.

4   To digress for a moment: I have spoken, on Williams's behalf, of deliberation leading to knowledge of what one has reason to do. I think it would be characteristic of Williams to conceive deliberation as addressed, in the first instance, to the question what to do.[3] But if one supposes one has resolved a question what to do by rational thinking, one must suppose one has arrived at a specification of something one has reason to do.[4] So in deliberating one figures out what one has reason to do.

Pettit and Smith make heavy weather over whether that description captures Williams's view of deliberation. They conclude that it does not, and this is part of why they attribute to him, as a supposedly necessary alternative, the conception of deliberation I am objecting to. But this reflects a misreading of two passages in Williams's paper.

The first is one in which Williams exploits the rhetorical question: "*What* is it that one comes to believe when he comes to believe that there is a reason for him to φ, if it is not the proposition, or something that entails the proposition, that if he deliberated rationally, he would be motivated to act appropriately?" (109). Pettit and Smith think Williams is posing a problem about the content of the belief that one has a reason, and suggesting that that content needs to be reformulated in terms of what deliberation aims at. And if we say deliberation aims at figuring out what one has reason to do, this does not yield a reformulation of the content of the belief that one has a reason.

But this makes nothing of the dialectical context of the rhetorical question. (It does not even accommodate the fact that the question is rhetorical.) Williams is expressing skepticism about whether beliefs with that content – a content that either is or entails the proposition that deliberation taking all the reasons there are into account would lead to an appropriate motivation – could be true even if, as the external reasons view requires, they are not reachable by the sort of deliberation the internal reasons view can countenance. (I shall come to the question what sort of deliberation that is.) The content is such as to require that acquiring such a belief would make a certain motivation rational for the subject; that is what the rhetorical question emphasizes. Williams's skepticism is about how the belief could have that connection with motivation, if the belief is not acquired through the sort of deliberation the internal reasons view can countenance. His thought is not that there is a problem about the content of the belief. His thought is that it is questionable whether there can be true beliefs that have that content but are not reachable by that sort of deliberation.

The second passage is one in which Williams explicitly grants that "believing that a particular consideration is a reason to act in a particular way provide[s], or indeed constitute[s], a motivation to act" (107). Amazingly, Pettit and Smith say: "Williams tells us here that, as he sees things, the belief that one has a reason is not a belief which brings motivation with it." That credits Williams with the negation of what he explicitly grants.

Pettit and Smith seem not to have understood Williams's proviso about akrasia. They think that in making it Williams is denying what they have just quoted him granting; they think he sees akrasia as a counterexample to the thesis that believing one has a reason brings motivation with it. But this reading, which makes Williams contradict what he has just explicitly granted, would seem necessary only if we assumed that an akratic subject has *no* motivation to act on the reason she believes she has but fails to act on. Williams's point in the proviso is that we should not make that assumption. The thesis that believing one has a reason brings motivation with it does not require a motivation that gets acted on. The view that beliefs about reasons provide, or even constitute, motivations to act, which Williams grants and indeed exploits in his argument against external reasons, must be understood so as to leave more needing to be said, if we are interested in how it is determined which of the motivations a subject has, reflecting her beliefs about reasons she has, she acts on.

5   The second thing wrong with the conception of deliberation that Pettit and Smith attribute to Williams is that it omits the continuing role of the subject's existing motivational set, in Wil-

liams's improvement on the sub-Humean model. Here we come to the heart of Williams's position.

The sub-Humean model gives the simplest conceivable picture of how existing motivational states might be seen as determining what a subject has reason to do. Now it is central to Williams's thinking that when he improves on the sub-Humean model, he does not abandon the idea that a subject's existing motivational states enter into determining what she has reason to do. He offers a more sophisticated account of how that determination is effected. As I said, he replaces the sub-Humean model with a sketch of deliberation as reasoning controlled by elements in the subject's motivational set, as it stands before she embarks on deliberation.

Pettit and Smith substitute for this a picture of a kind of reasoning specified entirely in terms of its aim, not in terms of its procedures. The aim is to equip one with desires that conform to "the principles of reason that govern the formation of desire". On this picture, unlike Williams's, there is no requirement that the motivational states a subject has at the beginning enter into determining the course deliberation can take. Pettit and Smith register that in Williams's view "each of us begins with a certain stock of desires." But in their account of what they think Williams means by "deliberation," the content of the stock of desires one begins with does not limit the deliberative procedures that are open to one. They purport to capture Williams's "basic idea" as the idea "that what we each have reason to do is a matter of what we would be motivated to do – that is, what we would desire that we do – if our [subjective motivational set] were added to and subtracted from under the pressure of all the principles of reason that there are." I have objected to the invocation of principles here, but that is not my present point. My point now is that in this reading of Williams the fact that we start with a motivational set is, in a crucial respect that involves a sharp contrast with Williams, inessential. In deliberation on the picture Pettit and Smith attribute to Williams, we consider what desires reason requires us to have. (That reformulates their representation of the "basic idea" without the tendentious appeal to principles.) Our motivational set when we ask what desires we should have figures in this picture only as what we add desires to or subtract them from when we arrive at an answer. It does not figure, as it does in Williams, in an account of the procedures for arriving at an answer.

6   The feature of Williams's thinking that I am insisting on is not completely absent from Pettit and Smith's reading. But the closest they come to acknowledging it is in the "quite distinct" part (c) of their "regimentation," which they frame as capturing an idiosyncratic view, on Williams's part, of "the capacities possessed by someone who has and exercises all of the capacities that ensure that her desires conform to principles of reason." They think this part of Williams's thinking is "a gratuitous registering of his own Humean leanings," inessential to the main thrust of his argument – "an add-on in the context of his overall argument for the claim that all reasons are internal." This is what I had in mind when I said they at best marginalize Williams's main point.

Williams's idea that rational thinking about what one has reason to do must be controlled by one's existing motivational set is precisely what gives bite to the limitation on reasons imposed by his thesis that there are only internal reasons. He acknowledges that his sketch of modes of deliberation leaves it "unclear what the limits are to what an agent might arrive at by rational deliberation from his existing [subjective motivational set]" (110). But he urges that that is as it should be. And the acknowledged indeterminacy does not imply that anything goes. The restriction to reasoning from existing motivations sets limits on true reason statements. Owen Wingrave's father, in the Henry James story Williams uses as an example, transgresses those limits. He cannot cite an existing motivation of Owen's that joining the army would satisfy, and he does not claim to be able to show that Owen should acquire a motivation to join the army, by an argument starting from Owen's existing motivations.

Contrast the account of deliberation that Pettit and Smith think captures Williams's "basic idea." Their picture gives no content to the idea of correctness in deliberation, apart from the idea that one's desires should conform to the principles of reason that govern the formation of desires. If we drop the tendentious introduction of principles, what we are left with is just that one's desires should be those that reason requires one to have (and perhaps also those that reason permits one to have). But Wingrave *père* surely thinks a desire to join the army is one that reason requires Owen to have. Even if we let Pettit and Smith insist on the formulation in terms of principles, there is nothing to prevent Wingrave *père* from framing what he says to Owen as a deliberation in their sense, turning on a principle of reason that requires one to construct one's life plans so as to follow family tradition. Of course Owen would dispute whether there is any such principle of reason. But Williams's account of deliberation, complete with the feature Pettit and Smith think should be segregated as a mere add-on, excludes Wingrave *père*'s stance – and thereby illustrates a real limit on reasons imposed by the restriction to internal reasons – on purely structural grounds, without any need to adjudicate such disputes.

If Wingrave *père* argues that reason requires Owen to join the army, while admitting that there is no deliberative route from some existing motivation of Owen's to the conclusion that Owen should join the army, he stands revealed, by Williams's lights, as trying to make an external reason statement, and hence as trying to say something excluded by the restriction to internal reasons. Whereas any limits on reasons one could generate within Pettit and Smith's framework would need to come from settling questions about what the principles of reason are, or – if we drop the tendentious invocation of principles – about what desires reason requires. On their picture Wingrave *père*'s statement is not straight off disqualified as a candidate for capturing an internal reason, even though Wingrave *père* admits that he cannot connect his argument with anything in Owen's existing motivational set. The only question Pettit and Smith's picture makes room for raising about the statement is whether it is true, and that depends only on whether reason really does require one to form one's desires so as to conform to family tradition. A distinctively internal interpretation of reason statements does no work here. In their picture, the idea of deliberation as a specific rational procedure does not pull any weight in determining what reasons agents can have. I think that means they simply miss Williams's point.

As I noted, Pettit and Smith think Williams's structural requirement on deliberation, that it must work from existing motivations, reflects gratuitous Humean leanings. If that were right, it might be a ground for regarding the requirement as unfortunate. (Though that would not undermine the point I have been insisting on, that this structural feature of Williams's conception is crucial for the way his account sets limits to reasons.) But in fact there is nothing especially Humean about the structural requirement. This emerges from Christine Korsgaard's response to Williams, which Pettit and Smith are unable to understand, because of the way they marginalize the significance Williams attaches to existing motivational states.

Korsgaard claims she can reveal the reasons for acting envisaged in broadly Kantian ethics as internal reasons in Williams's sense. Her claim is not that she can derive, say, the thesis that any agent has reason to respect the interests of others from "principles of reason." Staying with the same example, her claim is that she can display the thesis that a given agent has reason to respect the interests of others as the conclusion of deliberation that conforms to Williams's structural requirement – deliberation from some element in the agent's existing motivational set. (We can see this as an attempt to exploit the indeterminacy Williams acknowledges, in the limits set to internal reasons by his structural requirement.) Williams's dispute with Korsgaard is not, as Pettit and Smith say, over whether there are "principles of reason" that can be made to yield that kind of thesis about the reasons agents have. The dispute is over whether there is a deliberative route to the broadly Kantian conclusion, in a sense of "deliberative" that incorporates Williams's structural requirement – whether there is an argument that starts from something in the existing motivations of any subject capable of reflecting on what she has reason to do, and yields the conclusion that the agent has reason to respect the interests of others. Korsgaard says there is; Williams doubts it. Insisting that the structural requirement is integral to Williams's thinking leaves this dispute just as live as it should be. Korsgaard's claim is that she can respect the requirement and still arrive at a notably non-Humean conception of what reasons for acting people have. There is no basis for Pettit and Smith's recommendation to set the structural requirement aside as a dispensable Humean quirk on Williams's part.

7 I have so far ignored part (b) in Pettit and Smith's "regimentation." I think it is irrelevant to Williams's position, and hence to anything I want to say against him.

Williams limits the reasons a subject has to reasons she can come to realize that she has by deliberating. He sketches a picture of deliberation as a mode of rational thinking capable of improving a subject's thinking about what she has reason to do. Now consider a particular subject, A. Pettit and Smith read into Williams's thinking the idea of a subject, Å (A with a halo), who is "A in the nearest possible world in which she has and exercises all of those capacities that ensure that her desires conform to all of the principles of reason that govern desires." Here again there is the gratuitous invocation of principles, but again the point I want to make is different. Williams's appeal to deliberation, to restrict the reasons a subject has, requires only that on this or that occasion of deliberation a subject exercises (and so of course has) whatever capacity to recognize and be persuaded by good practical reasoning is needed for being convinced by the deliberation she is actually engaged in. The idea of a totality of capacities that would ensure that one's desires are conformable to reason – the capacities possessed by Pettit and Smith's Å – is not in the picture. Williams proposes a necessary condition for a subject to have a reason: there must be a deliberative way for that subject to come to appreciate that she has that reason. Pettit and Smith's play with Å would be to the point if Williams wanted a sufficient condition for a desire to be one that reason requires a subject to have.[5]

There is a rough structural match between the issues Pettit and Smith raise in connection with (b) and the issues that arise about Williams's restriction to internal reasons. Unsurprisingly, given the idealization that enters into characterizing Å, an unqualified use of the idea of what Å wants A to do in A's circumstances, to determine what reasons A has, would generate reasons that would be external in an obvious sense. A might be unable to recognize considerations that would weigh with Å, or unable to respond to them as Å would. So Pettit and Smith add a "quite distinct" recognition and response constraint, part (b) in their "regimentation" of Williams. Then they make trouble for Williams on the ground that "slippage" in the idea of capacities for recognition and response means that the original risk, that the reasons generated by the story about Å include reasons that would be external, is still a live one. But this to-and-fro simply does not impinge on Williams. His idea is that a subject has a reason only if there is a deliberative way she could come to see that she has it. It should be palpable that there is no need here for an *additional* constraint involving capacities for recognition and response. The "slippage" in the concept of capacity that Pettit and Smith talk about is just part of the indeterminacy Williams cheerfully acknowledges, in the limit that his restriction to internal reasons puts on what reason statements can be true. There is no problem here for Williams.[6]

8 Pettit and Smith find my response to Williams hard to interpret. They say this is because I "fail to distinguish clearly enough between" the three parts of their "regimentation." I have just explained why their (b) does not belong in a reading of Williams, and I argued earlier that when they relegate the importance Williams attaches to a deliberating subject's existing motivations to the supposedly dispensable (c), they marginalize the main point of Williams's paper. Williams poses a sharp challenge to the idea that there could be external reasons, and Pettit and Smith's "regimentation" has the effect that the challenge does not come into view. No wonder they find my attempt to respond to it hard to interpret.

A subject's internal reasons are reasons she can come to realize she has by deliberating from her existing motivations. The challenge is to say how there could be reason statements true of a subject but not conforming to that condition. In coming to believe she has a reason, the subject should acquire a motivation to act on it. With internal reason statements that is unproblematic; the subject can come to believe the reason statement by deliberating, which intelligibly generates a new motivation from motivations she already has. Williams's challenge is to say how the requirement can be met if the possibilities for acquiring the relevant belief that she has a reason do not include deliberating from existing motivations. (If they do, the reason is internal.) In having the new belief, the subject must be "considering the matter aright" (109); the belief must have been true before the subject acquired it, and thereby acquired the motivation. Williams takes this to imply that the belief, and the accompanying motivation, must be reachable by a rational procedure. So (p. 109)

> what has to hold for external reason statements to be true . . . is that the new motivation could be in some way rationally arrived at, granted the earlier motivations. Yet at the same time it must not bear to the earlier motivations the kind of rational relation which we considered in the earlier discussion of deliberation – for in that case an internal reason statement would have been true in the first place.

And Williams says: "I see no reason to suppose that these conditions could possibly be met." My response to this can be divided into two parts.

First, a concession. If it were right to assume that a new true belief to the effect that one has a reason, and the associated motivation, would need to be reachable by a rational procedure, this would be a convincing argument for the restriction to internal reasons. It is plausible that something on the lines of Williams's sketch of deliberation exhausts the possibilities for acquiring new motivations by rational thinking.

But, second, the assumption is tendentious. The transition to "considering the matter aright" need not be capable of being effected by deliberation. We can suppose that a transition would be a transition to considering the matter aright – to recognizing some reason one did not previously realize one had – even if there is no way for one to reason oneself into making it. Since the transition would be to considering the matter aright, the reason would be a reason one had all along. But in the kind of case we are envisaging, realization that one had it would not have been reachable by deliberation. So it would be an external reason. I exemplify this possibility by talking about a transition, not plausibly effectable by reasoning, to seeing situations as a properly brought up person would.

Unsurprisingly given their failure to grasp Williams's argument, Pettit and Smith do not understand this response to it.

9   They quote a passage in which I make the concession, and draw two conclusions from it.

The first is this: in making the concession, I am saying Williams's ground for rejecting the possibility of external reasons is that he thinks there are no principles of reason of the Kant/Nagel sort, which Pettit and Smith exemplify with a principle according to which reason requires rational agents to desire to relieve the pain of others.

Now I dare say Williams does disbelieve in such principles of reason. But that is not his point in restricting reasons to internal reasons, and nothing I say implies that it is. We can get this clear by returning to Korsgaard. Korsgaard claims that one can establish principles of reason of that sort by arguing – to stay with Pettit and Smith's example – that any subject capable of raising the question what she has reason to do has an internal reason, in Williams's sense, for relieving the pain of others; that is, a reason she can come to realize she has by deliberating from motivations she already has. In this claim, Korsgaard is accepting the restriction to deliberation from existing motivations. And Williams's rejection of external reasons does not by itself imply anything about the prospects for the kind of argument Korsgaard envisages. It is not external reasons that Korsgaard's argument is supposed to persuade us that there are. Williams's skepticism about Korsgaard's argument is skepticism about the cogency of an argument for the existence of certain internal reasons. His ground for rejecting external reasons is the quite different skepticism I have rehearsed, about the possibility of new rational motivations not reachable by deliberation from existing motivations. And my concession is to an ingredient in that skepticism. The concession, to repeat, is that he makes it plausible that the only way to acquire new motivations by reasoning is deliberation from existing motivations.

The second conclusion Pettit and Smith draw from my concession is this: I agree with Williams that "the desires possessed by $\mathring{A}^R$" – A idealized so as to have the desires she should have from the standpoint of reason – are restricted to the desires A could come to have by deliberation as Williams describes it, deliberation from existing motivations.

But this would grant Williams his rejection of external reasons. This reading of the concession leaves no room for the second part of my response to him. The desires A could come to have by deliberation from existing motivations are desires that would correspond to reasons A has on the internal interpretation, reasons A could come to see that she has by deliberation from existing motivations. My concession to Williams is that such desires are the only ones that can be intelligibly generated by reasoning. But when I object to Williams's argument against external reasons, it is simply a way of putting my point to say that those are not the only desires that would correspond to reasons A actually has. This contradicts the conclusion Pettit and Smith draw from my concession. Though, as I have explained, the idealizing apparatus is foreign to the issue Williams raises, I can put this claim of mine, which disappears in their reading of me, in their terms, by saying $\mathring{A}^R$ has desires over and above any desires A could come to have by deliberation from A's existing motivations.

Pettit and Smith search for something I disagree with in their "regimentation" of Williams, and conclude that it must be their (a). As I have explained, their idealizing in terms of $\mathring{A}$, and their talk of principles, make (a) as they formulate it a poor fit for anything Williams is committed to. But we can drop those elements, and what results is something like this: a subject has reason to φ only if a motivation that might be operative in her φ-ing would be included in the motivations she should have from the standpoint of reason. Or perhaps (Pettit and Smith sometimes use wording on these lines): only if it would be good from the standpoint of reason if she were to φ. I think something on those lines is truistic – not the core of a position that might impose substantive limits on the reasons a subject has, as Williams's position does. But, taking my disagreement about Williams's limits to be a disagreement about (a), Pettit and Smith cast me as objecting to that truism – as pleading for reasons a subject has such that conforming her desires to them is not required by reason. I think that is incoherent. It is certainly not what I urge.

In "Are Moral Requirements Hypothetical Imperatives?", as Pettit and Smith note, I open a gap between being irrational and failing to have one's beliefs and desires as they should be from the standpoint of reason. (Here again I have rephrased their way of putting things, to leave out the gratuitous assumption that "as they should be from the standpoint of reason" can be glossed in terms of conformity to principles.) They think I close this gap in the paper in which I respond to Williams. This reflects the same obliteration of my point.

Why do they think I close that gap? Starting from my supposed agreement with Williams about the capacities that would ensure that one's desires are as they should be from the standpoint of reason, they infer that according to me someone who does not see situations as a properly brought up person would "does not thereby violate any requirement of reason." So they take me to put forward a conception of external reasons as considerations that are reasons all right, but not such that failing to have one's motivations correspond to them is failing to have one's motivations in accordance with requirements of reason. This closes the gap because the claim (which I do make), that a person who does not see things as a properly brought up person would is not thereby shown to be irrational, can after all coincide with the claim they take me to make, that such a person violates no requirement of reason.

But this makes no contact with what I argue. As I said a moment ago, the conception of external reasons Pettit and Smith attribute to me – as reasons that are not such that reason requires one to be responsive to them – strikes me as incoherent. There is no good inference from anything I say to their conclusion that according to me there is no violation of requirements of reason in failing to see things as a properly brought up person would. As I have explained, I do not agree with Williams about the capacities that would ensure that one's desires are as they should be from the standpoint of reason. Exactly not; that would be agreeing that there can only be internal reasons. When I invoke the idea of a properly brought up person, my point is to claim that such a person sees, and responds to, reasons for acting that there really are. It is just another way of making that claim to say that if someone does not have motivations that are responsive to those reasons, her motivations are not as they should be from the standpoint of reason. I do not think it makes sense to effect a separation between the idea of having one's motivations as they should be from the standpoint of reason and the idea of having one's motivations responsive to whatever reasons there are. But if it is because someone has not been properly brought up that she does not have her motivations as they should be from the standpoint of reason, the failure does not imply irrationality. This contrasts with flouting reasons that one is in a position to appreciate. So there is exactly the gap I open in the earlier paper. (I reiterate the point in section V of the paper Pettit and Smith discuss.)

Taking me to deny the connection between failing to respond to reasons and failing to conform to requirements of reason, Pettit and Smith think I would acknowledge that for some action to be such that going in for it would be good from the standpoint of a properly brought up person is not thereby for it to be such that going in for it would be good from the standpoint of reason. Of course this makes me a patsy for the accusation that I try to sell, as external reasons, what are (even by my own lights) merely considerations in the light of which it would be good, from a standpoint other than that of reason, for someone to act in some specified way. That is the basis of their verdict on the dispute between Williams and me. But there is nothing well-founded here. The point of invoking the idea of a properly brought up person is to claim that her upbringing has left her able to see and respond to reasons for acting that there are. I think that implies, by way of the connection Pettit and Smith wrongly think I reject, that what it is good for such a person to do in the light of how she sees situations is thereby something it is good for her to do from the standpoint of reason.[7] The distinction between reason claims and claims about what it would be good for someone to do, from some standpoint that is not guaranteed to coincide with the standpoint of reason, is a fine distinction, but it does not tell against me.

If the reasons for acting that a properly brought up person purports to discern really are reasons, and if there need be no way for someone who has not been properly brought up to reason herself into seeing situations as a properly brought up person would, it follows that Williams is wrong to suppose new rational motivations would have to be acquirable by reasoning from existing motivations. And it is that view that drives Williams's argument against external reasons. Perhaps there is room for dispute about whether the reasons a properly brought up person purports to discern really are reasons, though to me it seems that that claim just spells out part of the content of the idea of a properly brought up person. (Disputes between different substantive conceptions of what it takes to have been properly brought up are not to the point here. What matters is only that the idea has application.) One thing that would clearly be illicit, in resisting my objection to Williams, would be to argue that these supposed reasons are not reasons on the ground that there cannot be external reasons; that would allow Williams's argument to rely on the conclusion it aims at. Maybe there are more respectable grounds for resistance. But Pettit and Smith offer none. Since they do not understand what Williams's argument is, and, partly in consequence, do not understand what my objection to it is, they are, as I said at the beginning, not in a position to judge that my objection leaves Williams's argument unscathed. What is at issue in the dispute between Williams and me does not come into view in their chapter.

Notes and References

1 "Internal and External Reasons," in Williams's *Moral Luck*, Cambridge: Cambridge University Press, 1981. Page references in my text will be to this printing of the paper.
2 *Ethics and the Limits of Philosophy*, London: Fontana/Collins, 1985, 18.
3 See, e.g., *Ethics and the Limits of Philosophy*, 18.
4 This leaves room for a kind of case in which one cannot resolve the question what to do by deliberation, at least the first time around, and one decides what to do by, say, the spin of a coin. (The first time around. Perhaps one then takes oneself to have reason to do whatever the spin of the coin directs one to do, and that conclusion could be represented as the result of adding a deliberative step to the first, inconclusive deliberation.)
5 Pettit and Smith know that Williams is only interested in a necessary condition, but in their exploitation of Å they seem to forget this.
6 The material about exemplars and advisers is similarly irrelevant to Williams, since Å is. Pettit and Smith say "Williams himself doesn't explicitly acknowledge the distinction between these two interpretations." But the exemplar and adviser interpretations are not competing interpretations of anything Williams says, and he has no need to be helped out by going beyond his text.
7 That this might be what I am urging almost comes into view in Pettit and Smith's final note. But they consider only a back-to-front counterpart of the idea. I do not claim that it is because it is somehow independently rational to take into account the considerations that properly brought up people are responsive to that those considerations count as reasons. It is because they are, anyway, reasons that it is rational to take them into account in deliberation.

8

Aristotle's Use of Prudential Concepts

T. H. Irwin

I

John McDowell's first essay on Aristotle's ethics raises some basic questions about Aristotle's aims and argument: What is the point of Aristotle's appeal to happiness as a final good?[1] How does this appeal introduce an appeal to nature? What sort of foundation, justification, explanation, or understanding of ethics does he hope to derive from an appeal to happiness and nature? These questions recur in his later essays on Greek ethics.

I had hoped to have space in this paper to discuss all of these essays, but I found that the first of them raised enough issues for one paper. Many teachers of Aristotle's *Ethics* recommend McDowell's essay as basic reading on its topic. It fully deserves this recommendation; and so I hope that a discussion of it will help to throw some further light on the questions that it raises. Though this essay is over twenty years old, McDowell's later papers do not reject its main argument, and so we may fairly take it to underlie his general outlook on Aristotle's ethics.[2]

McDowell takes his discussions of Aristotle, and of Greek ethics in general, to mark some important contrasts between Greek and modern assumptions:

> My main aim in these papers is to counteract a way in which, as I see it, modern prejudices about rationality tend to distort our understanding of Greek ethics. When a Greek thinker says something to the effect that a life of virtue is a life in accordance with reason, modern commentators tend to suppose he must mean that such a life can be recommended as worth going in for, with the recommendation not needing to appeal to habituated propensities to be attracted towards, and recoil from actions of different kinds – the features of a person's make-up that figure, for instance, in Aristotle's discussion of virtue of character. This reflects a dualism between reason and the more evidently "natural" aspects of character (vii–viii).

His aim is to free our interpretation of Aristotle from distorting influences that arise from modern prejudices. From "Two Sorts of Naturalism" we learn that the main sources of these prejudices are the outlook of modern science (as we tend to understand it) and the metaphysics, epistemology, and moral philosophy of Hume.

McDowell explains the appeal of erroneous (as he believes) interpretations of Aristotle by citing the influence of modern prejudices. Is his explanation correct? Or can we defend interpretations opposed to his even if we do not rely on the modern prejudices? To answer these questions, we need to see where he thinks the modern prejudices influence his opponents' views of Aristotle.

II

McDowell discusses the role of happiness in the *Ethics* because he believes other interpreters have been wrong about the significance of eudaemonism for Aristotle's general approach to ethics. We may begin, then, by recalling some passages where Aristotle comments on the importance of his appeal to happiness.

Near the beginning of the *EN* Aristotle says why it is important to find an account of the final good.

> Will not the knowledge of it, then, have a great influence on life? Shall we not, like archers who have a mark to aim at, be more likely to hit upon what is right? If so, we must try, in outline at least, to determine what it is, and of which of the sciences or capacities it is the object. (1094a22–6)[3]

This claim suggests one constraint on an adequate interpretation of the role of happiness. Knowledge of it should make a practical difference, by giving us a mark to aim at. Aristotle believes that failure to have our lives organized with reference to some end is "a sign of much folly" (*EE* 1214b10–11).[4]

How might we expect the relevant organization to help us? Aristotle argues that our first task is to distinguish the relative status of different goods.

> Then above all we must first define to ourselves without hurry or carelessness in which of our belongings the happy life is lodged, and what are the indispensable conditions of its attainment . . . For herein is the cause of the disputes about happy living, its nature and causes; for some take to be elements in happiness what are merely its indispensable conditions. (*EE* 1214b11–27)[5]

This passage offers a suggestion about the practical benefit to be gained from knowledge of the final good. It should contribute essentially to knowledge of which goods are non-instrumental and parts of happiness (*merê tês eudaimonias*, *EE* 1214b26–7).

These remarks suggest that grasping the character of happiness[6] is itself a basis for organizing our lives correctly. Aristotle does not simply say that the lives of people who grasp the character of happiness are well organized. That might be true if the good organization and the grasp of happiness both rested on some further condition, and the grasp of happiness were merely a coincidental result of the further condition. But Aristotle implies that the grasp of happiness, in its own right, shows us how to organize our lives correctly.

To make this point a little more concrete, let us consider a form of argument that would establish some connexion between happiness and a well-ordered life, but would not justify Aristotle's claim about the importance of grasping happiness. We might argue as follows. (1) We can learn about the virtues without any antecedent understanding of happiness. (2) Once we learn about the virtues we will know how to organize our lives well. (3) This knowledge gives us knowledge of happiness. (4) Therefore we organize our lives well if we know about happiness. According to this form of argument, Aristotle would be right to connect knowledge of happiness with good order in our lives, but he would be wrong about the nature of the connexion; for the connexion would be purely incidental, a result of the knowledge that really matters for the good order of our lives.

If I understand McDowell correctly, he attributes to Aristotle an argument of the form I have just described. I have tried to show that this is not the form of argument we ought to expect from Aristotle, given his initial remarks about happiness. But it may still be the form of argument he actually offers. We may now consider McDowell's reasons for believing this is the form of Aristotle's argument.

III

To see what we learn from an appeal to happiness, McDowell observes that "the concept of *eudaimonia* is in some sense a prudential concept" (14). Hence the force of an appeal to happiness depends on our interpretation of the relevant prudential concepts (good for me, my welfare, my interest, gain or loss for me, and so on). In identifying something with my happiness we imply that it is good for me, promotes my interest, and so on. In taking the question "What is happiness?" to be the basic question in ethics, Aristotle claims that questions about my own interest are basic questions. But before we draw any rash conclusions about the consequences of this claim, we ought to understand Aristotle's use of the prudential concepts connected with the concept of happiness. In McDowell's view, misunderstanding of his use of these concepts has led interpreters astray.

Aristotle's account of happiness, according to McDowell, identifies happiness with a life of morally virtuous activity.[7]

> When Aristotle says that activity in accordance with excellence is *eudaimonia*, what he says can be paraphrased as the claim that two prima facie different interpretations of phrases like "doing well" coincide in their extension: doing well (sc. in accordance with excellence, living as a good man would) is doing well (sc. as one would wish: living in one's best interest). (14f.)

The crucial question, then, is to understand how the identification of happiness with activity is in accordance with excellence.

To explain Aristotle's account of happiness, McDowell offers two accounts of the formula "activity in accordance with excellence is *eudaimonia*":

(1) The reductive account. We may "make our way into the equation at the right-hand side" (15), by relying on some prior idea of the most desirable life.[8] We claim that life in accord with moral excellence satisfies this prior idea of the most desirable life. Hence Aristotle's formula means: activity in accordance with virtue is identical to happiness (as we antecedently understand it).

(2) The moralizing account. We enter the equation at the left-hand side, claiming that our conception of excellence determines our conception of *eudaimonia*. We claim that our prior conception of moral excellence determines the judgments about our good, interest, welfare, and so on that form our judgments about happiness. Hence Aristotle's formula means: activity in accordance with moral virtue (as we antecedently understand it) is identical to the life that (from the moral point of view) we correctly count as happy.

My labels for these two accounts are not McDowell's, but I believe they convey one of his points in distinguishing them. The first account is reductive in so far as it begins by fixing our assumptions about prudence and reduces the "benefit" or "good" or "advantage" of morality to something that counts as good or beneficial by the measure of these antecedent assumptions. The second account is a moralizing account in so far as it measures advantage and gain by standards derived from the reasons that count for the virtuous person.

These two accounts of Aristotle's formula rely on two different employments of prudential concepts, which McDowell calls the "ordinary" and the "derivative" employment. The reductive account relies on the ordinary use, whereas the moralizing account relies on the derivative use.

McDowell has more to say about the derivative use than about the ordinary use. He claims that the virtuous person uses prudential concepts in this special way.

> if someone really embraces a specific conception of human excellence, however grounded, then that will of itself equip him to understand special employments of the typical notions of "prudential" reasoning . . . according to which (for instance) no payoff from flouting a requirement of excellence . . . can count as a genuine advantage; and, conversely, no sacrifice necessitated by the life of excellence, however desirable what one misses may be . . . can count as a genuine loss. (16f.)

For a temperate person, missing the pleasure that a temperate person has to forgo is, given the circumstances, no loss.

McDowell calls the virtuous person's use of "gain," "loss," "benefit," "harm," and so on, a derivative use of these concepts. One's use of them is guided not by a point of view external to the virtuous person's conception of loss and gain, but by the virtuous person's own conception. Virtuous people's conception of loss and gain is controlled by their conception of reasons for acting.

> Now for any way of employing the notion of a reason, we can make sense of a derivative way of employing the "prudential" notions, controlled by such formal inter-definitions as that a benefit is what one has reason to pursue and a harm is what one has reason to avoid . . . even though the attractiveness of the missed pleasure would have been a reason to pursue it if one could have done so without flouting a requirement of excellence, nevertheless in the circumstances that reason is silenced. And if one misses something that one had no reason to pursue, that is no loss. (17f.)

To claim that acting in accord with virtue is identical to happiness is to claim that virtuous action never involves any loss.

Since McDowell considers only these two accounts of Aristotle's definition of happiness, one may reasonably take him to assume that no other account deserves consideration. I do not accept this assumption. But for the moment I will attend only to his two options, and consider why he believes they throw light on Aristotle's claims about happiness.

IV

What is the "derivative" use of prudential concepts derived from?[9] It is "controlled by such formal inter-definitions as that a benefit is what one has reason to pursue and a harm is what one has reason to avoid" (17). This description does not imply that the use is derivative. For one might suppose that the ordinary use is also controlled by formal inter-definitions including those that McDowell offers as examples. He does not say that the formal inter-definitions he mentions are exhaustive; indeed he suggests that they are not (since he says "such . . . as"). Perhaps he means that the ordinary use is controlled by different inter-definitions (in addition to those he mentions, which seem to be common to the ordinary and the derivative uses). But he does not say what these different inter-definitions are.

I conjecture that McDowell takes the derivative use to be derived from the common-sense use or "ordinary use." Further, I conjecture that the ordinary use includes the assumptions underlying the reductive account of Aristotle's definition of happiness. This account of the definitional identity-statement ("activity in accordance with excellence is *eudaimonia*") helps us to "make our way into the equation at the right-hand side" (15), by appeal to some prior idea of the most desirable life. This idea is prior in so far as judgments about the desirable life are uninfluenced by one's moral judgments. These judgments about the desirable life rest on "independent canons of desirability."

> The requisite idea of the most desirable life must involve canons of desirability [1] acceptable to all parties in the disputes, and [2] intelligible, in advance of adopting one of the disputed theses, to someone wondering what sort of life he should lead. Such prior and independent canons of desirability would presumably need to be [3] constructed somehow out of the content of desires any human being can be expected to have: thus, desires conceived as manifestations of a fairly stable and universal human nature, susceptible of investigation independently of adopting one of the disputed theses about *eudaimonia*. (15; reference numbers added.)

The ordinary use of prudential concepts, then rests on these canons of desirability. In this use, we assume that what is good for a person is good in so far as it meets the prior canons of desirability.[10]

If McDowell intends this connexion between the ordinary use of prudential concepts and the prior canons of desirability, we can understand why he thinks the second account of Aristotle's formula involves a different use of the prudential concepts; for it rejects the prior canons of desirability.

Even if my conjecture captures McDowell's reason for believing in two uses of prudential concepts, involving the acceptance and rejection of prior canons of desirability, it casts no light, so far, on why he thinks the second use is derived from the first. I therefore conjecture that he takes the derivation to be psychological (rather than conceptual or explanatory), simply because the first use, in his view, is the ordinary one. We tend to take for granted a use that assumes prior canons of desirability. The second use is less familiar to us, and we need to understand it by abstraction from the first; while it relies on some formal inter-definitions that it shares with the first use,[11] it rejects the assumption about prior canons of desirability.

I am not sure I am right to suppose that McDowell takes the ordinary use of prudential concepts to rely on the prior canons of desirability. For he believes that these canons of desirability are Humean, in so far as they rely on some construction of the desirable from the universally desired. Though he does not mention Humean views when he first introduces the prior canons of desirability (15), he mentions them later (21) as the source of these canons.[12] One might suppose that they reflect one of the modern prejudices that McDowell takes to distort many people's interpretation of Aristotle.

If this were McDowell's view of the prior canons of desirability, it would be surprising if he believed that they underlie not only our ordinary use of prudential concepts, but also one of Aristotle's uses of them. For in allowing this he would allow that the relevant canons of desirability do not simply reflect inappropriate Humean assumptions, but actually capture part of common sense, and part of Aristotle's treatment of the prudential concepts.

Though this is a reasonable doubt about my interpretation of McDowell's position, I cannot think of a plausible alternative. Unless this is what he has in mind, we cannot easily form any clear view of the ordinary use of prudential concepts, as he conceives it. I will therefore proceed on the assumption that I have correctly understood his views on the ordinary use.

V

Why should we suppose that Aristotle employs prudential concepts in both the ways we have described?

McDowell believes that some of Aristotle's remarks about the relation between happiness and external goods presuppose these two different uses. (1) We find the ordinary use in Aristotle's "common-sense inclination to say . . . that external goods make a life more satisfactory." According to this use, a life of exercises of excellence that suffers great misfortunes "would have been better if the fates had been kinder."[13] (2) We find the derivative use in "Aristotle's contention that a person's *eudaimonia* is his own doing, not conferred by fate or other people." According to this view, "a life of exercises of excellence, being – as *eudaimonia* is – self-sufficient, can contain no ground for regret in spite of great ill fortune." When we find remarks similar to those in (1), allowing that happiness is in some way vulnerable to fortune, we should (in McDowell's view) attribute the first use to Aristotle; when we find remarks similar to those in (2), making happiness invulnerable in certain ways, we should attribute the second use to him.

Why should we not attribute a single use to Aristotle throughout? I take McDowell to argue that if Aristotle maintained a single use of the prudential concepts, he would be committed to a contradiction, because he would accept all of the following:

(1)   A life of exercise of excellence is self-sufficient.
(2)   A self-sufficient life can contain no ground for regret in spite of great ill fortune.
(3)   A life of exercise of excellence that suffers great ill fortunes would have been better if the fates had been kinder.
(4)   Therefore a life of exercise of excellence that suffers great ill fortune contains grounds for regret, because of the ill fortune.

Since (2) and (4) are inconsistent, Aristotle's position would be inconsistent if he maintained a single use of the concepts.

Aristotle avoids the inconsistency, however, if we distinguish an ordinary and a derivative use of "good." (3) is true if "better" has the ordinary use, but (2) would conflict with (4) only if "better" had the derivative use. Once we distinguish the two uses, we see that (2) implies that a life of excellence could not have been "better," but only in the derivative sense of "better." Hence (2) and (4) are consistent. The argument that attributes an inconsistency to Aristotle fails, because it involves an equivocation. Once the two senses of the relevant terms are distinguished, the appearance of inconsistency disappears.

How clear is Aristotle about all this? McDowell suggests that Aristotle may not see clearly that the two uses are needed to make his position consistent. For McDowell sees some "strains" in Aristotle's remarks.

> There seems to be no obstacle to allowing this derivative employment of the "prudential" concepts to occur side by side with a more ordinary employment – except that there is a risk of confusing them. (18)

> ...the strains in Aristotle's treatment...can be plausibly explained in terms of an intelligible tendency to slide between the derivative employment and a more ordinary conception of prudence. (18)

If Aristotle had clearly distinguished the two uses of prudential concepts, he could assert claims (1)–(4) without any strain. Hence McDowell does not seem to believe that Aristotle is clear on these points. He speaks of distinguishing "on Aristotle's behalf" two "measures of desirability or satisfactoriness" resulting from the two uses of the prudential concepts. Probably, then, McDowell believes that the "strains" and "slide" in Aristotle's discussion result from the lack of a clear grasp of the double use of prudential concepts.

We can now apply this point about Aristotle's lack of clarity to McDowell's suggestions about the two accounts of Aristotle's definition of happiness.[14] McDowell offers two interpretative suggestions. (a) Aristotle does not accept the reductive account of the definition of happiness. (b) He intends the moralizing account of the definition. Since the moralizing account relies on the derivative use of prudential concepts, Aristotle accepts this derivative use.

McDowell, however, qualifies his defense of (a) and (b). If Aristotle's use shows the "strains" and "slide" described by McDowell, he does not clearly grasp the derivative use. Hence he does not clearly intend the second account of his definition. McDowell, therefore, suggests that Aristotle has an imperfect grasp of the two uses of the prudential concepts. Some of his claims about happiness and external goods are more plausible (according to McDowell) if they rely on the derivative use, while others are more plausible if they rely on the ordinary use. But the "strains" and "slide" suggest that he does not clearly grasp the two uses, and therefore does not clearly intend the moralizing account of the definition of happiness.

How plausible are these claims about Aristotle? We can examine them by considering three questions. Does Aristotle rely on the double use of prudential concepts? Does his discussion of virtue and external goods involve any "strains" or "slide"? Is the double use relevant to his definition of happiness?

VI

Before discussing whether McDowell is right to allege any "strains" or "slide" in Aristotle, we should notice an ambiguity in the claims about "silencing."[15] (1) As McDowell first introduces silencing, it is "local" silencing, referring to features of particular situations. He speaks of "occasions" and "circumstances" that suggest decisions about what to do here and now.[16] One thinks of a brave person deciding to sacrifice her life; as she sees it (according to McDowell), the fact that she will be dead is no reason at all, here and now, for failing to act bravely, or for regretting the need to sacrifice one's life. (2) But when he cites evidence of this attitude in Aristotle, he speaks only of a "life of excellence" containing no ground for regret (18). Similarly, in "Eudaimonism and Realism," he speaks of "the life of a virtuous person" (210). This is a doctrine of "global" silencing.

These two ways of considering silencing and absence of regret lead to sharply different conclusions. In particular, the second explanation of silencing does not imply the first. One might argue that in a virtuous person's life as a whole, there is nothing to regret, because the various losses that one suffers on particular occasions do not constitute any reason, even a reason that can be overridden, for choosing a different kind of life. According to this doctrine of global silencing, one cannot infer that if one suffers losses on particular occasions these losses necessarily constitute a reason for not choosing a life that includes them.

But one can maintain this global doctrine of silencing while rejecting local silencing; one may still believe that the virtuous person loses something on particular occasions, and that there are reasons, on those occasions, for not doing the virtuous action. The virtuous person's view is not that she loses nothing on particular occasions when she acts bravely or temperately, but that her losses on particular occasions do not constitute any reason for choosing a different sort of life.

If, therefore, McDowell only cites evidence of Aristotle's belief in global silencing, he offers no evidence of Aristotle's belief in local silencing. But he attributes a doctrine of local silencing to Aristotle. If we distinguish a choice of lives from a choice of actions on particular occasions, we need not follow McDowell in attributing a doctrine of local silencing to Aristotle.

VII

We may now return to the main question, about whether Aristotle believes in global silencing. McDowell ascribes this belief to him because of the derivative use of prudential concepts. He also supposes that Aristotle "slides" between the derivative and the ordinary use of these concepts. Does the text provide evidence of both uses of the relevant prudential concepts?[17]

For the moment I will assume, following McDowell, that Aristotle sometimes uses prudential concepts in the "ordinary" way that McDowell describes. What is the evidence for the derivative use?

McDowell argues on Aristotle's behalf. (1) Happiness is self-sufficient. (2) Activity in accordance with excellence is identical to happiness. (3) Therefore "a life of exercises of excellence" is self-sufficient. The argument is valid, and Aristotle certainly accepts the first step. To show that he accepts the second, McDowell cites a passage (1097b22–1098a20) in which Aristotle presents his account of happiness. We may usefully consider that passage more closely.

Aristotle describes his account as an outline, to answer the request (1097b22–4) for a clearer account of what the best good is.

> if this is the case, human good turns out to be activity of soul in accordance with virtue, and if there are more than one virtue, in accordance with the best and most complete. But we must add "in a complete life." For one swallow does not make a summer, nor does one day; and so too one day, or a short time, does not make a man blessed and happy. Let this serve as an outline of the good; for we must presumably first sketch it roughly, and then later fill in the details. (1098a16–22)

McDowell does not mention the two clauses (a) "in accordance with the best and most complete virtue,"[18] and (b) "in a complete life." The two clauses are parts of Aristotle's account of the good, since "Let this serve as an outline" comes after them, signaling that they complete the outline account of the good.

These two clauses make a significant difference to the account of happiness. The first clause shows that not just any virtue, but the best and most complete virtue, must be identified before we have identified happiness. The second clause shows that happiness requires a complete life, which at least includes more than one day or a short time.[19]

If, therefore, Aristotle believes happiness is self-sufficient, he does not imply that a life of activity in accordance with virtue is self-sufficient; he implies that activity in accord with the best and most complete virtue in a complete life is self-sufficient.

To see why the parts of Aristotle's account that McDowell omits make a difference, we need to ask what Aristotle means by "complete life." In i.7 he gives an outline (1098a18–22), and he clarifies "complete life" only by mentioning an appropriate length of life. But later he clarifies the conditions for a complete life:

> neither will he [sc. the happy person] be moved from his happy state easily or by any ordinary mis-adventures, but only by many great ones, nor, if he has had many great misadventures, will he recover his happiness in a short time, but if at all, only in a long and complete one in which he has achieved many fine things.[20] Why then should we not say that he is happy who is active in accordance with complete virtue and is sufficiently equipped with external goods, not for some chance period but throughout a complete life? (1101a9–16)

Aristotle is discussing the conditions in which a person who is happy can lose and then regain happiness. Since he envisages the possibility of being first happy, then not happy, and then happy again, he cannot take a "complete life" to be an entire lifetime; each of the two periods in which the agent is happy must be long enough to be suitable for a complete life. The explanation "in which he has achieved many fine things" suggests that a complete life is a period that is long enough for these.

McDowell's argument from the self-sufficiency of happiness is therefore unsuccessful. Aristotle identifies happiness not with virtuous activity, but with activity in accord with the best and most complete virtue in a complete life. Hence the self-sufficiency of happiness does not imply the self-sufficiency of virtuous activity or of a life of virtuous activity.

VIII

McDowell's second reason for attributing the derivative use of prudential concepts to Aristotle rests on a claim about regret. He argues that since a life of exercise of excellence is self-sufficient, it "can contain no ground for regret in spite of great ill fortune" (18). If Aristotle indeed suggests that such a life is free of regret, perhaps we should doubt our previous conclusion that he does not take the virtuous life to be self-sufficient. What, then, is the evidence to show that Aristotle believes the virtuous life to be free of regret?

McDowell cites without comment a passage from i.10, just after Aristotle has mentioned the virtuous person's magnanimous attitude in misfortune.

> If activities are, as we said, what gives life its character,[21] no happy man can become miserable; for he will never do the acts that are hateful and mean. For the man who is truly good and wise, we think, bears all the chances of life becomingly and always makes the best of circumstances, as a good general makes the best military use of the army at his command and a good shoemaker makes the best shoes out of the hides that are given him; and so with all other craftsmen. And if this is the case, the happy man can never become miserable; though he will not reach blessedness, if he meet with fortunes like those of Priam.

McDowell does not say how this passage bears on regret. But he may have in mind the claim that the happy person can never become miserable. Does this claim imply freedom from regret?

The answer depends on what Aristotle means in this context by "miserable" (*athlios*).[22] He probably means the contrary state to happiness, rather than the mere negation of happiness.[23] The miserable condition belongs to vicious people; their condition is not only to be condemned but also to be abhorred and avoided. At any rate, misery is a desperate condition; we can avoid the degradation of the vicious person without being free of regret in our lives. The mere fact that we regret (for instance) some decisions we made, or the way some things turned out, does not throw us into the condition that Aristotle describes as miserable.

But even if this passage does not support McDowell's claim that the virtuous life is free of regret, another passage may seem to help.[24] Here Aristotle discusses the attitude that virtuous people take to themselves and to their choices and actions:

> And such a man wishes to live with himself; for he does so with pleasure, since the memories of his past acts are delightful and his hopes for the future are good, and therefore pleasant. His mind is well stored too with subjects of contemplation. And he grieves and rejoices, more than any other, with himself; for the same thing is always painful, and the same thing always pleasant, and not one thing at one time and another at another, since practically speaking he is a person without regret (*ametamelêtos*).[25] (1166a23–9)

This passage occurs in a difficult discussion of the difference between virtuous and vicious people.[26] It give us some idea of what makes the virtuous person "free of regret" or "free of repentance" (*ametamelêtos*). Aristotle appeals to the constancy of a virtuous person's plans and preferences, and argues that this constancy ensures the relevant freedom from regret.

What sort of freedom from regret might be expected to follow from the virtuous person's outlook? It is helpful to consider two sorts of regret. (1) I might regret what I did because I wish that I had acted in different circumstances, or that I had known something I did not know, or things had turned out differently. In this respect, a surgeon might regret that she had to amputate the leg of a young athlete who had been injured in a road accident, or a general might regret that he had given an order just before he unexpectedly received information that would have changed his mind, or I might regret building a house on a spot where it was struck by lightning. (2) I might regret my decision because it was thoughtless or negligent or callous or blameworthy in some other way.

What sort of regret does the virtuous person avoid? It is difficult to see how the features that Aristotle ascribes, in this passage, to the virtuous character could explain the absence of the first sort of regret. But they help to explain the absence of the second kind of regret (often called "remorse"). Virtuous people care most about carrying out the appropriate plans. This is their steady aim; and if they are virtuous, they steadily act on their aim. They do not wish that, in the circumstances as they could reasonably be expected to see them, they had deliberated differently. Still, they might wish that something had been different in the circumstances or the outcome. Aristotle does not claim that virtuous people will never wish that external circumstances or results had been different. He claims only that they will have nothing to blame themselves for. They are free of the second kind of regret, but not thereby free of the first kind.

This is only a rough sketch of a distinction that is difficult to draw precisely and in detail. But if I have captured Aristotle's point about regret, the absence of regret (of the second kind) in the virtuous person's life does not ensure that such a life is self-sufficient and lacking in nothing. Hence – to return to McDowell's argument – Aristotle's claims about regret do not show that he takes a life of virtuous activity to be sufficient for happiness.

In order to show that the virtuous person is free of the first kind of regret, we would have to take Aristotle to mean that whenever a virtuous person makes the virtuous choice, there is nothing to be said for any alternative or for any of its results. This would be close to McDowell's views about local silencing, but would be even more extreme. McDowell seems to treat local silencing as a feature of situations viewed prospectively; he suggests that if I am faced with a choice between a brave and a cowardly action, the fact that the brave action threatens me with unpopularity and resentment is no reason at all, in this situation, for hesitating about it. It does not follow, however, that if I had to act in ways that provoked unpopularity and resentment, that is no reason for retrospective regret (of the first kind). In order to exclude retrospective regret, silencing must apply to the retrospective as well as the prospective point of view. This extreme thesis about silencing goes beyond the thesis that McDowell ascribes to Aristotle.

We have no reason to find the extreme thesis about silencing in this passage about the virtuous person's freedom from regret. The passage does not commit Aristotle to any thesis about silencing. He refers only to the second kind of regret. Hence this passage does not show that the virtuous person's life is self-sufficient and therefore happy. Since Aristotle does not claim this about the virtuous person's life, he does not appeal to a derivative use of prudential concepts.

IX

McDowell offers a third argument to show that Aristotle relies on this derivative use. He cites "Aristotle's contention that a person's *eudaimonia* is his own doing, not conferred by fate or other people." To show that this is Aristotle's contention, he appeals to one passage in the *EN*:[27]

> It [sc. happiness] will also on this view be very generally shared; for all who are not maimed as regards their potentiality for virtue may win it by a certain kind of study and care. But if it is better to be happy thus than by chance, it is reasonable that the facts should be so, . . . To entrust to chance what is greatest and most noble would be a very defective arrangement. (1099b18–25)

A similar view of happiness appears in Aristotle's criticism of the view that finds happiness in being honored by others.

> But it seems too superficial to be what we are looking for, since it is thought to depend on those who bestow honour rather than on him who receives it, but the good we divine to be something of our own and not easily taken from us. (1095b23–6)[28]

Here also Aristotle rejects the view that happiness could be primarily the gift of people or circumstances external to us, and insists that it must be our own (*oikeion*).

We might wonder how this claim can be reconciled with Aristotle's belief that external circumstances are relevant to happiness. Aristotle himself tries to clarify this question, in explaining how virtuous actions are "controlling" or "decisive" (*kuriai*) in happiness.

> Success or failure in life does not depend on these [sc. fortunes], but human life, as we said, needs these added,[29] whereas virtuous activities or their contraries control happiness or the contrary.[30] (1100b8–11)

What controls an effect is not, in Aristotle's view, sufficient by itself for the effect. In saying that human life needs good fortune added to virtuous activities, he asserts that virtuous activities alone are not sufficient for happiness. Nonetheless they are the controlling or decisive element, not merely one of the individually necessary conditions that are jointly sufficient for happiness.

This conception of the relation between virtuous actions and external goods explains why Aristotle says we intuitively believe that the good is something of our own and hard to take away (*dusaphaireton*). He does not say it cannot be taken away. Though happy people are not easily shaken by ill fortune, they are shaken by serious ill fortune.

These passages do not support McDowell's view that Aristotle relies on the derivative use of prudential concepts in order to maintain that the virtuous person never suffers any loss by acting virtuously. Aristotle's understanding of the claim that happiness is "one's own" makes happiness subject to ill fortune; he does not suggest that a virtuous person will regard virtuous action as involving no loss. All of his remarks about happiness are consistent with the ordinary use of prudential concepts, according to which a virtuous person's life is not happy if it suffers serious ill fortune.

These observations on the relevant texts suggest that "The Role of *Eudaimonia*" gives insufficient reason for finding the double use of prudential concepts in Aristotle's remarks on happiness. But in "Eudaimonism and Realism," McDowell returns to this issue, and alludes to some of the evidence I have discussed:

> There are passages where he [sc. Aristotle] seems to be trying to insist that eudaimonia is an agent's own achievement rather than a gift of chance. . . . Factors outside an agent's control can make it impossible to live the life of a virtuous person . . . as perhaps in cases like that of Priam (1100a5–9). But chance goods can surely make a life more desirable, in some obvious sense, otherwise than through their effect on what it is possible for the agent to achieve by his own efforts, and the ranking of lives as more or less desirable that is operative here ought not to be relevant to their assessment in terms of eudaimonia. (210f.)

McDowell distinguishes two ways in which fortune can affect one's life. (1) It may make it impossible to live as a virtuous person would. (2) It may make life more or less desirable without making it impossible to live as a virtuous person would. McDowell claims that the second sort of effect does not affect the assessment of one's life in terms of *eudaimonia*.

We may test this claim by considering the passage that almost immediately follows Aristotle's claim that virtuous actions control happiness. He considers the ways in which fortune is relevant:

> Now many events happen by chance, and events differing in importance; small pieces of good fortune or of its opposite clearly do not weigh down the scales of life one way or the other, but a multitude of great events if they turn out well will make life more blessed (for they themselves are such as to add adornment to life, and his way of dealing with them proves to be fine and good), while if they turn out ill they crush and maim blessedness; for they both bring pain with them and hinder many activities. (1100b22–30)

Good fortune can make a happy life happier both because the gifts of fortune "adorn" life and because the good person deals with them virtuously. Hence Aristotle does not confine evaluation in terms of happiness to virtuous action and the conditions for it; he also takes the further adornments to add to happiness.

He has already affirmed the importance of external conditions that are not simply instruments for virtuous actions:

> Yet evidently, as we said, it [sc. happiness] needs the external goods as well; for it is impossible, or not easy, to do fine acts without the proper equipment. In many actions we use friends and riches and political power as instruments; and there are some things the lack of which spoils blessedness, as good birth, goodly children, beauty; for the man who is very ugly in appearance or ill-born or solitary and childless is not really the sort to be happy,[31] still less perhaps if he had thoroughly bad children or friends or had lost good children or friends by death. As we said, then, happiness seems to need this sort of prosperity in addition. (1099a31–b7)[32]

The second class of external goods ("the lack of which spoils blessedness") are not used as "instruments" (*organa*), but they nonetheless count as "equipment" (*chorêgia*).[33] Evaluation of a life with reference to happiness legitimately includes consideration of external conditions that are non-instrumentally related to virtuous action.

Aristotle does not take this acknowledgment of the role of external goods to conflict with his claims about virtuous actions. Virtue is, in one respect, decisive for the character of a person's life, even in adverse external circumstances:

> Yet even in these [sc. misfortunes] the fine shines through, when a man bears with resignation many great misfortunes, not through insensibility to pain but through nobility and magnanimity. If, as we said, activities control life, no blessed man can become miserable; for he will never do the acts that are hateful and mean. For the man who is truly good and wise, we think, bears all the chances of life becomingly and always does the finest things in the circumstances, as a good general makes the best military use of the army at his command and a good shoemaker makes the finest shoes out of the hides that are given him; and so with all other craftsmen. And if this is the case, the happy man can never become miserable; though he will not be blessed, if he meets with fortunes like those of Priam.[34] (1100b30–1101a8)

The virtuous person can no longer do the actions he could do in favorable circumstances. But he still acts finely, because he does the finest actions he can do in unfavorable circumstances; he therefore avoids being miserable, even though he has lost his happiness.

McDowell does not show, therefore, that Aristotle takes chance goods to be irrelevant to the assessment of lives in terms of *eudaimonia*. For they can make a happy person happier (if they are added) and they can make a happy person no longer happy (if they are taken away). Aristotle implies that questions about happiness are not settled simply by considering the "kind of desirability that Aristotle thinks is correctly captured by rightly applying the concept of the noble."[35]

A complication, however, needs to be considered. The interpretation I have offered presupposes that Aristotle uses "happy" and "blessed" interchangeably in this passage. Several interpreters accept this presupposition, but it might be questioned, and one might wonder whether a distinction in sense would support McDowell's claim about Aristotle.[36] A distinction that would help him would say this: (1) We are happy as long as we can live a life of acting virtuously. But (2) we are blessed if and only if we also have the further external goods that make life more desirable without being relevant to its assessment in terms of *eudaimonia*.

This distinction does not fit Aristotle. We might try to say that though added good fortune makes one more blessed, it does not make one happier, and that misfortunes that "crush and maim blessedness" do not crush and maim happiness. But Aristotle does not draw this distinction in his discussion of Priam's misfortunes. McDowell correctly suggests that Priam's misfortunes interfere with the life of virtuous activity; hence one would expect Aristotle to say that they prevent happiness. But in fact he says they prevent blessedness (1101a7–8). If McDowell is right about Aristotle's view, this remark is significantly weaker than the one Aristotle ought to make (namely, that they prevent happiness).

To see whether Aristotle intends the distinction between "happy" and "blessed" that is relevant to McDowell's claims, we may look at the next passage. After saying that the happy person will not be blessed if he suffers Priam's misfortunes, Aristotle continues:

> Nor, again, is he many-coloured and changeable; for neither will he be moved from his happiness easily or by any ordinary misadventures, but only by many great ones, nor, if he has had many great misadventures, will he become happy again in a short time, but if at all, only in a long and complete one in which he has attained many splendid successes. (1101a8–13)[37]

This passage explains the sense in which virtuous activity makes happiness stable. Though it prevents happiness from being shaken by relatively small misfortunes, it still allows happiness to be shaken by large misfortunes. The large misfortunes that were previously said to destroy blessedness are now said to destroy happiness.

These passages suggest that Aristotle does not distinguish "blessed" and "happy" in a way that would support McDowell's thesis about the different types of desirability and their different bearing on happiness.

X

If Aristotle does not rely on the derivative use of prudential concepts, does it follow that he relies on their ordinary use? Do McDowell's two uses exhaust the plausible options? Let us remind ourselves of the conception of prudential value that underlies the ordinary use.

The ordinary use involves canons of desirability that are: (1) acceptable to all parties in the disputes; (2) intelligible, in advance of adopting one of the disputed theses, to someone wondering what sort of life he should lead; (3) constructed out of the content of desires any human being can be expected to have, and thus manifestations of a fairly stable and universal human nature, susceptible of investigation independently of adopting one of the disputed theses about *eudaimonia*.[38]

These three conditions seem to be separable. In particular, we might doubt whether all canons satisfying the first two conditions must also satisfy the third. Why should antecedently acceptable and intelligible canons be constructed out of the content of desires?

Perhaps McDowell believes that since some people believe that the desirable must be constructed out of the content of desires, the only universally acceptable canons of desirability are those that meet the third condition. If this is the reason that persuades him that the three conditions are inseparable, he seems to understand "acceptable to" as "likely to be accepted by." On this understanding, the ordinary use of prudential concepts rests on canons that are likely to be accepted when they are proposed and understood.

We might try an alternative set of conditions. We might say that the relevant canons must be: (1a) acceptable, in the sense of being such that everyone has reason to accept them, and (2a) intelligible to everyone, in the sense that everyone can be brought to understand them, in advance of accepting the disputed claims about the nature of happiness. We need not insist that the relevant canons must be constructed out of universal desires.

To show that Aristotle relies on the "ordinary" use of prudential concepts, we would have to show that he appeals to canons of desirability constructed from universal desires. McDowell suggests that the ordinary use of prudential concepts underlies the judgment that "a life of exercise of excellence that suffers great misfortunes would have been better if the fates had been kinder."[39] But does this judgment about goodness rely on any construction from universal desires? One might appeal instead to Aristotle's views about the connexion between the good and the realization of human capacities. If he believes that misfortune interferes with the realization of these capacities, he is entitled to infer that misfortune is bad for human beings. The inference does not depend on any assumption about universal human desires. The canons of desirability underlying the claim about capacities might satisfy conditions (1a) and (2a) rather than conditions (1)–(3).

McDowell's derivative use is not the only plausible alternative to the ordinary use. McDowell is right to suggest that some of Aristotle's claims would be difficult to accept if he were relying exclusively on the ordinary use.

> The exercise of temperance will on occasion require sacrificing the opportunity of some otherwise attractive gratification of appetite. According to the way of employing the prudential notions that is appropriate to the position I considered in §12, that means that to live the life of excellence will be, on such an occasion, to incur a loss; and Aristotle's equation, on the interpretation I considered in §12, could be maintained in the face of such occasions only by claiming that acting temperately would involve a gain (in terms of the independent standards of gain and loss appropriate to the position of §12) sufficient to outweigh that loss. In suitably described cases any such claim would be implausible to the extent of being fantastic. (17)

If Aristotle claims it is always better for us to be virtuous, no matter what the cost, and "better" is assessed by the ordinary use, his claim is implausible.[40]

But if we concede this point to him, should we accept his alternative? McDowell takes Aristotle to rely on silencing:

> the thesis is not that the missed chance of pleasure is an admitted loss, compensated for, however, by a counterbalancing gain; but, rather, that in the circumstances . . . missing the pleasure is no loss at all. (17)

To see whether silencing is the only option or the best option if we reject the interpretation relying on the ordinary use, we should compare two claims. (1) Virtuous people do not lose something and gain a counterbalancing good, as judged according to the ordinary use. (2) They do not lose something and gain a counterbalancing good. McDowell has given good reasons for attributing the first claim to Aristotle. But the doctrine of silencing requires the second claim as well. I don't see a good reason to suppose that Aristotle accepts the second claim as well as the first.

To make this issue a little more specific, let us assume that Aristotle's use of prudential concepts is not the ordinary use described by McDowell (involving the three conditions listed above), but the alternative use I described (involving only the first two conditions). And let us suppose, very crudely, that Aristotle appeals to the realization of human capacities as the basis for judgments about goodness and happiness. By that standard, is it "implausible to the extent of being fantastic" to claim that the virtuous person suffers some loss but gains a compensating good? I don't see that it is obviously so implausible. Whether or not it is ultimately implausible depends on what we can say about attempts to explain judgments about goodness and happiness by reference to the realization of human capacities. I have not tried, in this chapter, to evaluate attempts at such an explanation. I simply remark that McDowell's essay gives us no reason to believe that these attempts are likely to fail.

XI

Having mentioned this issue about human capacities, I want to touch on a series of further questions that I can't pursue in detail here. The third condition in McDowell's "prior canons of desirability" requires the relevant canons to be "(a) constructed out of the content of desires any human being can be expected to have, and thus (b) manifestations of a fairly stable and universal human nature, (c) susceptible of investigation independently of adopting one of the disputed theses about *eudaimonia*" (15). The three elements in this third condition raise a question about their connexion. Could we, for instance, maintain (b) and (c) without (a)? We might try to distinguish "Humean naturalism," maintaining all three elements, from "non-Humean naturalism," rejecting (a). It is not clear in this paper where McDowell stands on the plausibility of a naturalist position that rejects the specifically Humean element in (a).

McDowell speaks of human nature as a subject of some sort of "independent" investigation. He explains the relevant sort of independence as independence of one of the disputed theses about *eudaimonia*. But in challenging this way of looking at human nature, he also speaks of an "independent, 'value-free' investigation of human nature" (19). How does value-freedom enter the argument? Is it an additional constraint that not all "independent" investigations of human nature need satisfy? Or is it a consequence of the relevant sort of independence?

We could show that independence and value-freedom are necessarily connected if we argued as follows:

(1) An independent investigation must be independent of adopting any disputed thesis about *eudaimonia*.

(2) All value judgments depend on adopting a disputed thesis about *eudaimonia*.

(3) Hence no value judgments are independent of adopting a disputed thesis about *eudaimonia*.

(4) Hence any investigation that is independent of adopting any disputed thesis about *eudaimonia* must also be value-free.

Neither the second nor the third step is plausible. We might believe that not all facts about goods for human beings and about goodness in human beings would be as they are if *eudaimonia* were not what it is. But it does not follow that we are entitled to rely on judgments about goods or goodness only if we have already adopted a disputed thesis about *eudaimonia*. Even if we concede (contrary to fact) that all values involve goods or goodness and that the only relevant value judgments are those about human beings, we may still be entitled to make some value judgments without having first adopted a disputed thesis about *eudaimonia*.

Hence we should not agree that if an investigation of human nature is independent of adoption of a disputed thesis about happiness, it is a value-free investigation. McDowell does not invite us to consider all the options that are worth considering.

If I had more space I would examine McDowell's fuller remarks about naturalism in some of his other papers. Instead of doing that, however, I will simply conclude by expressing gratitude for the stimulus and provocation offered by McDowell's work. He not only raises important questions himself, but also helps the reflective reader to raise further questions that bring us closer to an understanding of some basic issues in Aristotle's approach to ethics.

Notes

1   In the rest of this paper I will use *eudaimonia* and "happiness" interchangeably. I am not taking a position on whether this conventional translation is seriously misleading.

2   All the references to McDowell's essays cite pages of *Mind, Value, and Reality*, Cambridge, Mass.: Harvard University Press, 1998, except that I also draw on "Eudaimonism and Realism in Aristotle's Ethics," in R. Heinaman (ed.), *Aristotle and Moral Realism*, London: UCL Press, 1995, 201–18.

3   Following McDowell's practice, I quote from W. D. Ross's translation, Oxford: Oxford University Press, 1925. I will correct it only when the correction matters for present purposes. I also refer to translations (or translations with notes) of the *EN* by M. Ostwald, Indianapolis: Bobbs-Merrill, 1962; T. H. Irwin, Indianapolis: Hackett, 2nd edn, 1999; R. Crisp, Cambridge: Cambridge University Press, 2000; and C. J. Rowe and S. W. Broadie, Oxford: Oxford University Press, 2001. I have occasionally cited commentaries on the *EN* by G. Ramsauer, Leipzig: Teubner, 1878; J. A. Stewart, Oxford: Oxford University Press, 1892; and R. A. Gauthier and J. Y. Jolif, Louvain: Publications Universitaires, 2nd edn., 1970. I have given only a very few references to secondary literature on the *EN*.

4   McDowell comments on this and the preceding passage at 9.

5   Translation by J. Solomon, Oxford: Oxford University Press, 1915.

6   For present purposes I am ignoring any differences between the concepts of *eudaimonia* and *to agathon*.

7   I will not discuss McDowell's reasons for introducing morality into the discussion. See 15ff.

8   See the passage quoted above in section IV.

9   First he speaks of "special employments of the typical notions of 'prudential' reasoning" (end of 16). He speaks of a "derivative employment of the 'prudential' notions" at 17 (last paragraph).

10 I say "prior" rather than "prior and independent" (as McDowell says), on the assumption that priority (in a given respect) implies independence (in that respect).

11 McDowell does not say this. But I see no reason to deny that the specific formal inter-definitions that he mentions hold for the first employment of prudential concepts. See section III above.

12 "But the philosophical framework I have in mind purports to justify that demand directly, by way of the Humean thesis that a genuine reason for acting owes its rational cogency ultimately to the fact that the action for which it is a reason will satisfy an unmotivated desire . . . Given that thesis, an account of practical rationality . . . cannot but be on the lines of the position of §12: that is, in terms of the maximizing of some bundle of goods recognizable as such from outside any of the disputed positions about excellence." (21).

13 These quotations are all taken from 18.

14 See section III above.

15 See the passage quoted in section III above.

16 See 17f., and esp. 18 n.24. McDowell refers to "Virtue and Reason," where he says: "Here and now the risk to life and limb is not seen as any reason for removing himself" (56).

17 The relevant questions about Aristotle's treatment of happiness and external goods have been extensively discussed in the years since McDowell's "Role of *Eudaimonia*," but since he does not change his view

(as far as I can see) in his later "Eudaimonism and Realism" (210f.), I will therefore take both papers to describe his position, and confine myself to the issues that they raise.

Among contributions to discussion of happiness and fortune see J. M. Cooper, "Aristotle on the Goods of Fortune," *Philosophical Review* 94 (1985): 173–96, repr. in *Reason and Emotion*, Princeton: Princeton University Press, 1999; T. H. Irwin, "Permanent Happiness," *Oxford Studies in Ancient Philosophy* 3 (1985): 89–124, esp. 94n.; S. A. White, *Sovereign Virtue*, Stanford: Stanford University Press, 1992. D. Wiggins, "Eudaimonism and Realism: A Reply," in *Aristotle and Modern Moral Realism* (see n.2 above), 227ff., alludes to these issues.

18 I am assuming that Aristotle believes the protasis "if there are more than one virtue" is satisfied.

19 This passage alone does not tell us whether these two clauses mark independent conditions on happiness. An answer to this question depends on whether activity in accord with the best and most complete virtue can exist without a complete life that (at least) lasts for the right length of time. If we cannot have the relevant activity without a complete life, the second clause makes clear an implication of the first.

20 Ross's rendering, "attained many splendid successes," conceals the presence of "*kalon*" in the Greek.

21 This would be better rendered as "If activities . . . control (*kuriai*) life." On "controlling" see section IX above.

22 Ostwald, Irwin, and Rowe agree with Ross in using "miserable." Crisp prefers "wretched."

23 See Irwin, *EN* 339.

24 McDowell does not cite this passage, and so may not disagree with my claim that it fails to support his contention about regret.

25 I have substituted Rowe's rendering of the last clause for Ross's "he has, so to speak, nothing to repent of." Ostwald, Irwin, and Crisp also use "regret" here. Ross's use of "so to speak" for *hôs eipein* is misleading. The point of the Greek phrase (here as usual) is to apologize for an exaggeration (hence Irwin and Rowe use "practically"), not for a surprising form of words.

26 I have discussed it further in *EN* ad loc., and in "Vice and Reason," *Journal of Ethics* 5 (2001): 73–97.

27 He also cites *Politics* 1323b24–9; *EE* 1215a12–19.

28 Ross's version, altered.

29 Ross: "as mere additions."

30 Ross: "while virtuous activities or their opposites are what constitute happiness or the reverse." (Ostwald also uses "constitute.") This exaggerates the force of *kuriai*, as do Stewart and Gauthier ad loc. Ramsauer ad loc. captures Aristotle's point. Crisp translates "what really matters"; Rowe renders "responsible for"; either rendering is better than Ross's.

31 I have followed Crisp's rendering of *ou panu eudaimonikos*. Ross has "not very likely to be happy." Other examples of *eudaimonikos* in Aristotle suggest that the sense is "suitable for happiness." Hence we might say that these people are not good candidates for being happy.

32 Ross's version, altered.

33 See Irwin, "Permanent happiness," 95.

34 Ross's version, altered.

35 "Noble" is McDowell's rendering of "*kalon*."

36 Broadie ad 1101a16–21 suggests that *makarios* and *eudaimôn* are interchangeable until 1101a16, or perhaps until 1101a7. White, *Sovereign Virtue*, 100, takes *makarios* to differ in sense from *eudaimôn* in 1101a7 (though his explanation of 1101a16ff. at 99 n.15 seems to make this explanation of a7 less probable).

37 Ross's version, altered.

38 These criteria are taken from the passage quoted in section IV above.

39 This was claim (3) in section V above.

40 It is difficult to reach a decision, however, without a more precise idea of the particular sort of construction that is being considered.

Response to T. H. Irwin

1   Irwin is so gracious about my work on Aristotle that it may seem churlish to take issue with his reservations about it. But I do want to say some things in my defense. If he were right to find the paper he discusses questionable in the ways he does, I think it would not deserve the praise he gives it.

2   A great deal turns on the thesis that *eudaimonia* is activity in accordance with excellence or virtue, which I attribute to Aristotle.[1] Irwin resists this attribution. He objects (in his section VII) that I omit two things: Aristotle's qualification, "and if there are more than one virtue, in accordance with the best and most complete" (*Nicomachean Ethics* 1098a17–18), and his remark that we must add "in a complete life" (1098a18). But I cannot see that these omissions matter for my claims about the role of the concept of *eudaimonia* in Aristotle's thinking.[2]

As for the first point, I take it that the qualification prepares the way for Book X, where Aristotle identifies the highest *eudaimonia* with a life of contemplation. On a second reading of *NE*, knowing how it is going to end, we already know Aristotle is going to make that move when we try to understand his formula at i.7. But in the main body of *NE* Aristotle focuses on ordinarily human virtues. And they should not drop out of the picture when we consider what he is saying *eudaimonia* is at i.7 – even if we have to anticipate that the *eudaimonia* that would be specified by Aristotle's formula, understood so that the scope of "virtue" includes virtues other than those exercised in contemplation, will turn out to be only a second best, something "merely human" as opposed to something that engages a feature of our make-up in respect of which we approximate to the condition of gods. Including virtues other than "the best and most complete" seems to be required if we are to make room for how, at the beginning of i.13, a version of the thesis of i.7 serves as a pretext for embarking on the treatment of virtue *in general* that occupies most of the rest of the work. In the version at i.13, which must be meant to pick up the formulation at i.7, there had better not be a suggestion that activity in accordance with some virtues, those that are not "the best and most complete," does not count.[3] So it seems harmless to ignore the qualification, except when Book X is explicitly our topic.

As for the second point, it can be put by saying that what is in the first instance up for assessment as exemplifying *eudaimonia* or not is a complete life. And however that is to be understood in detail, I cannot see that it threatens to undermine Aristotle's commitment to this: in judging whether a life – a complete life, by all means – exemplifies *eudaimonia*, all we need to consider is whether it is made up of activity in accordance with virtue. The point about the need for a complete life does not imply that, for assessments of *eudaimonia*, any consideration about lives matters apart from whether they are made up of activity in accordance with virtue – the bit of Aristotle's "outline" that I single out.

According to Aristotle's substantive view about the nature of ordinary human virtue, and hence about the nature of *eudaimonia*, activity in accordance with at least ordinary human virtue is activity for the sake of the noble, activity whose point is captured by the concept of the noble. And this brings us at least close to a thesis of mine that Irwin resists: that when Aristotle implies that a life of virtuous activity is a maximally desirable life (as he does, according to me, by identifying it with *eudaimonia*, given the prudential character of the concept of *eudaimonia*), the kind of desirability in question need not be other than the kind of desirability one finds in an action when one takes its being noble to be a sufficient reason for going in for it.

3 I use the term "silencing" only in connection with what Irwin calls "local" silencing. My claim in this connection is that in situations that call for action in accordance with a virtue, the attractions of alternative courses of action are (correctly) seen by a fully virtuous person as, here and now, not constituting any reason for pursuing them. I attribute this view to Aristotle on the ground that it makes sense of his distinction between virtue and mere continence.[4] (Or perhaps a generalization of that distinction. Aristotle formulates the distinction in relation to temperance in particular.) The distinction implies that a fully virtuous person is not attracted to, not tempted by, alternative courses of action. In the case of temperance, there are alternatives that promise pleasure. The prospect of pleasure can rationally generate motivational impulses, but in circumstances in which temperance is called for, its power to do so is neutralized by the temperate person's view of what matters about the situation. If that were not so – if there were conflicting motivational impulses one had to overcome in order to act as a temperate person would – then the best one could achieve would be continent action.

Aristotle says *eudaimonia* conforms to a requirement the good must meet, that of being self-sufficient: on its own such as to make life desirable and lacking in nothing. In the passage Irwin considers in his section VI, I aim to bring out a satisfying mesh between that claim and the thesis of "local" silencing. According to my reading, *eudaimonia* is (a life made up of) activity in accordance with excellence. That is the reading I began by defending, against Irwin's complaints about my omissions from the passage I find the thesis expressed in. Now "local" silencing provides a way to make sense of Aristotle's holding that such a life is self-sufficient. A life made up of actions in accordance with excellence would lack something, in the area of (the relevant kind of) desirability, only if the attractions of courses of action not pursued in it were reasons for pursuing them. But according to the thesis of "local" silencing they are not, so it does not lack anything in the relevant sense.

Irwin objects that "global" silencing, the idea that a certain life contains no ground for regret, does not imply "local" silencing, the idea that when virtue requires some action the attractions of alternatives do not constitute reasons in favor of them. He envisages a position that rejects "local" silencing, holding that missing the payoffs of alternatives is a loss, but endorses "global" silencing, on the ground that such losses are not a reason for choosing a different kind of life. But this complaint gets my dialectic backwards. As I have just formulated it, the mesh I envisage consists in an implication in the other direction, from "local" silencing – which, as I say, is independently justified by its capacity to make sense of what Aristotle says about continence – to Aristotle's claim that *eudaimonia* is self-sufficient.

I interpret that claim in a way that diverges from what Irwin makes of "global" silencing. As I said, Irwin thinks one can accept "global" silencing while rejecting "local" silencing. That would require a conceptual separation between reasons for choosing a life and reasons for engaging in the activities that constitute it. But as I read Aristotle's thesis that the life of *eudaimonia* is lacking in no relevant desirability, it involves no such separation. Saying that the life of *eudaimonia* is lacking in no relevant desirability is just another way of saying that, in the circumstances in which they are undertaken, the actions that make up that life are not undertaken in the face of reasons to do anything else.

If the "global" thesis and the "local" thesis are just two ways of saying the same thing, there is, after all, the implication from "global" to "local" that Irwin resists, working with a different interpretation of the "global" thesis. But the way to appreciate the interpretation is as I did a few paragraphs back, through the implication in the other direction.

When I say that for Aristotle "a life of exercises of excellence . . . can contain no ground for regret in spite of great ill fortune" (18), I mean that as simply a rewording of Aristotle's explicit claim that *eudaimonia* is self-sufficient. The rewording is licensed, in my reading, by the fact that according to me Aristotle identifies *eudaimonia* with (a life of) exercises of excellence.

Irwin rejects the identification, on the insufficient grounds I dealt with at the beginning. On that basis he rejects my view that it is the virtuous life that Aristotle is attributing self-sufficiency to when he says *eudaimonia* is self-sufficient.

It should be clear that what is at issue between us, over whether there is a conception of grounds for regret on which Aristotle thinks a life of exercises of excellence contains no such grounds, turns on the status of the identification. When I cite 1100b33–1101a8 in a footnote (18 n.26), I do not mean to be citing independent evidence that Aristotle takes the virtuous life to be, in some relevant sense, free of regret, as Irwin's discussion in his section VIII implies. Irwin is surely right that the passage on its own could not license reading Aristotle that way, but that is irrelevant. What does license reading him that way is the self-sufficiency claim, in the context of the identification that Irwin refuses to credit to Aristotle, I think on insufficient grounds. My point in citing 1100b33–1101a8 is that it works with the sort of conception of desirability in a life that is needed for the self-sufficiency thesis as I understand it. Aristotle's thoughts in this passage presuppose that a life is less satisfactory just by including acts that are "hateful and mean" and more satisfactory just by including acts in which one "bears the chances of life becomingly." The measure of desirability in play here would not be applicable by someone who did not value and disvalue actions in the way characteristic of a virtuous person.

4   In his section II, Irwin attributes to me a reading that makes it wrong for Aristotle to claim that knowledge of *eudaimonia* would itself be a basis for good organization of one's life. On the reading Irwin attributes to me, knowledge of virtue "without any antecedent understanding of" *eudaimonia* enables one to know how to organize one's life well, which in turn affords knowledge of *eudaimonia*. So there is a connection between good order in one's life and knowledge of *eudaimonia*, but it is "purely incidental, a result of the knowledge that really matters for the good order of our lives." Irwin uses this, in effect, to set up a presumption against my reading, on the ground that it makes Aristotle out to be wrong about the role of *eudaimonia* in his own thinking.

Now this might be telling if it were not for the fact that I see Aristotle as identifying *eudaimonia* with activity in accordance with virtue. It is true that on my view coming to know what virtue requires does not involve an *antecedent* understanding of *eudaimonia*. (At any rate not of what *eudaimonia* substantively amounts to. Perhaps one can have an abstract grasp of the concept in advance of acquiring the substantive practical knowledge one acquires when one acquires virtue.) But if *eudaimonia* is activity in accordance with virtue, acquiring virtue in the strict sense of vi.13 – which includes acquiring the practical knowledge that enables us to order our lives well – *is* acquiring understanding of *eudaimonia*. Knowing which human traits are virtues *is* knowing what *eudaimonia* requires; it is not just knowledge from which knowledge of what *eudaimonia* requires can be derived. So the knowledge that matters for organizing our lives can be described indifferently as knowledge of virtue and as knowledge of *eudaimonia*, and Irwin is wrong to claim that according to my reading the connection between *eudaimonia* and good order in our lives is "purely incidental."

Irwin knows I take Aristotle to equate *eudaimonia* with activity in accordance with virtue; he takes issue with the reading later in his chapter, in a passage I have already dealt with. So it is strange that here in his section II he suggests I attribute to Aristotle an argument that contrives to represent the connection of *eudaimonia* with the knowledge we need for organizing our lives as merely incidental, but which has that effect only because it ignores the equation. This makes me wonder if Irwin understands the equation I mean to attribute to Aristotle. Even in saying what he takes me to be committed to, he allows himself to work with a conception in which "happiness" is at best a consequence of acting in accordance with virtue, whereas the thought I attribute to Aristotle is that acting in accordance with virtue is what *eudaimonia* is.

It may be another indication of this that Irwin places an expression of the concept of *eudaimonia* determinately on the right-hand side, the prudential side, of the conceptual equation for which I contrast two interpretations, the interpretations Irwin labels "reductive" and "moralizing."[5] It is really the whole point of my reading that the concept of *eudaimonia* straddles the two sides; it is a concept of doing well in which "well" means both "in accordance with virtue" and "as one would prefer," not exclusively or primarily the latter, as Irwin's wording of the equation suggests.

5   In his section IV, Irwin makes heavy weather of my talk of two ways of using prudential concepts. I call the use that my Aristotle needs, for his thesis that a life of virtuous activity is self-sufficient, "derivative." Irwin wonders what it is derivative from, and he conjectures that I think it is derivative from the ordinary use of prudential concepts. And, with some hesitation, he takes me to hold that the ordinary use of prudential concepts is determined by the "canons of desirability" I consider on p. 15 of my paper – canons of desirability that might seem suited for resolving disputes about which life is best for human beings, of the sort that might arise between people who value justice and so forth, on the one hand, and people who value a supposedly clear-sighted pursuit of personal advantage, on the other.

He is wrong on both these points.

First, he himself, in his preceding section (section III), has wording that captures the much simpler point I mean to make by talking of a derivative use of prudential concepts. He writes on my behalf of measuring advantage or gain "by standards *derived* from the reasons that count for the virtuous person" (my emphasis). And later he says, again on my behalf, that the conception of loss and gain that is relevant to how virtuous people can be seen as counting a life of virtuous activity as maximally worth going in for "is controlled by their conception of reasons for acting." Here he already has the answer to his question, "Derivative from what?", and it is not the conjectural answer he offers in the next section. The derivative use of prudential concepts is derivative in that the standards of desirability operative in it are derived from the valuations that are internal to a specific conception of human excellence.

Second, Irwin's hesitation about taking me to gloss the ordinary use of prudential concepts in terms of those "canons of desirability" – which, as he remarks, are Humean – is well placed. The idea of universally acceptable "canons of desirability" figures in my thinking, not as an inevitable accompaniment of using prudential concepts in a more ordinary way than one in which their use is controlled by a virtuous person's conception of reasons for acting, but as something that will seem to be required if one supposes that a substantive specification of what it is to act in accordance with virtue can be certified to be correct, in a way that should be convincing even to people who start with a different conception of virtue, on the ground that a life made up of such actions would be maximally desirable. Those "canons of desirability" come into the picture only in the context of the "reductive" reading of the equation between a life of activity in accordance with virtue and a life that is maximally desirable. Since I do not attribute the equation to Aristotle on the "reductive" reading, I do not imply that any of Aristotle's uses of prudential concepts are controlled by that Humean picture. I do not take the ordinary use of prudential concepts to need any special explanation. When I contrast the derivative use and a more ordinary employment, my point is just to contrast the derivative way of using prudential concepts with one in which how they are to be applied is not controlled by a conception of reasons for acting that is determined by a conception of virtue.

As far as I can see, this shows that the main body of Irwin's section X is irrelevant to any claim of mine. But I want to comment on his suggestion that Aristotle might invoke the idea that a life of *eudaimonia* realizes human capacities. Something like that idea does seem plausibly Aristotelian. But it is a way of putting one of my points to say that the realization of human capacities does not need to figure in Aristotle's thinking in the way Irwin suggests, as "the *basis* for judgments about goodness and happiness" (my emphasis). That would require a conception according to which one could determine which capacities are properly human in advance of determining which human traits are virtues. (See my discussion of the claim that "the life of exercises of excellence is the life that most fully actualizes the potentialities that constitute human nature," at p. 19 of the paper Irwin considers.) It does seem to me fantastic to imagine that a proponent of a position like that of Callicles in Plato's *Gorgias* could be shown, by exploiting an idea of advantage grounded in a conception of human capacities of that kind, a conception that could be accepted even by someone who was thus radically out of sympathy with conventional ethical thinking, that the disadvantages he sees in conventionally virtuous behavior are outweighed by compensating gains.

Irwin is right, in his section XI, that I go too quickly from the idea that a foundational investigation of human capacities would need to be prior to the ethical to the idea that it would need to be value-free. But this does no damage to my main claim: that Aristotle can be read in such a way that he has interesting things to say about the desirability of the virtuous life, without pointing in the direction of that supposedly foundational appeal to human nature.

Notes and References

1   Irwin says I take Aristotle to identify *eudaimonia* with a life of *morally* virtuous activity. This is a misreading. In the paper Irwin is discussing, I acknowledge that some of the character traits Aristotle identifies as virtues are not intelligibly objects of distinctively moral admiration. In fact I find it plausible that Aristotle does not so much as have the concept of a distinctively moral mode of evaluation. Aristotle's concept of virtue of character ("ethical virtue") is not a concept of moral virtue. But apart from some verbal infelicities I do not think this makes any difference to the substance of Irwin's discussion.

2   In "Some Issues in Aristotle's Moral Psychology," in *Mind, Value, and Reality*, Cambridge, Mass.: Harvard University Press, 1998, I do discuss both these features of Aristotle's "outline."

3   i.13 begins "Since happiness is an activity of soul in accordance with perfect virtue, we must consider the nature of virtue; for perhaps we shall thus see better the nature of happiness." (The word Ross translates with "perfect" here is the word that figures in the superlative, represented by "most complete" in Ross's translation, at 1098a17–18. But here it had better not imply the exclusion of some virtues, or the remark would not serve to introduce the discussion of virtue in general, as it does.)

4   See "Virtue and Reason," cited in n.24 (p. 18) of the paper Irwin focuses on. My earliest presentation of the idea is in "Are Moral Requirements Hypothetical Imperatives?", now reprinted in *Mind, Value, and Reality*.

5   "Moralizing" is a bad label; see n.1 above. But that does not matter here.

9

Julius Caesar and George Berkeley Play Leapfrog

Simon Blackburn

I

Some twenty years ago I voiced reservations about John McDowell's embrace of a spatial metaphor, whereby we should expand our idea of the "space" occupied by the mind, locating its boundaries far outside the skin, way into the world.[1] I thought at the time that the spatial metaphor was a flourish McDowell had been betrayed into, particularly by some of the terminology of his dispute with Dummett over "manifestation." But over the years it began to be clear that it was more than that, being one of several metaphors that figure centrally in his extensive and influential meditations on the relationship between ourselves and our world. Indeed, the best thumbnail description of his aim would be to show that the world is not "blankly external" to the mind, and this description uses the metaphor. So the reservation went unheeded, and years later the metaphor and its cousins occupied large parts of *Mind and World*,[2] which is the principal text I shall consider here, although they liberally sprinkle other writings as well. I shall use this opportunity to try to sensitize others to my reasons for discomfort.

My discomfort equally concerns the metaphor of the two spaces, the space of reasons and the space of causes, or, as McDowell prefers to put it, the contrast between the space of reasons and the "realm of law."

Why should one worry about these two metaphors? I think we should acknowledge immediately that they do some sterling work in McDowell's criticism of others. Quine, for instance, makes the same mistake that, according to T. H. Green, Locke and Hume made, of conflating data in the sense of brute causal impingements from without, and data in the sense of basic reasons for beliefs.[3] This can be put by saying that he confuses denizens in the space of reason with those in the space of causes. Davidson makes the mistake of avoiding pure coherentism only by a global assurance that (from without) you will be seen as possessing mostly true beliefs, although God knows what their content will be. This is no substitute for wanting beliefs known true by local attention to the way of the world. Rorty jettisons too much of what makes the space of reasons what it is, giving us only a substitute that, because of its avoidance of representation and truth, is essentially mindless. These criticisms are compelling, and what is right about them can be indicated in part by use of the metaphor.

Yet there is danger at hand, because a metaphor can pave the way for inferences, inviting us to frame problems one way rather than another. A metaphor can blind us to possibilities, including the possibilities that give us philosophical control of an area. For that matter a metaphor can also make it easy to demonize those who do not see the subject in quite the same way. And I believe the spatial metaphors put us in peril of framing issues in a misleading and ultimately unsustainable way, a way that disappears with a more complete emancipation from a false view of the mind. So, as I read it, while much of *Mind and World* is written in terms of these metaphors, including its positive theses, they fit badly with what is best in the book. They show that McDowell is not as free of the presuppositions of an old and discredited philosophy of mind as his own animadversions on that philosophy would lead the innocent to believe.

I believe that this accounts for the sense some readers must surely have, that somehow in the course of the work, rather large rabbits are pulled out of a rather small hat. For then, not wanting to devalue the hat, seduced by the metaphors and perhaps by the almost sacerdotal progress of McDowell's persuasive prose, the unwary reader sees no option but to confess that it must indeed hold these rabbits.

The best parts I am referring to, as well as the criticisms of other major players already mentioned, are the Austinian or Strawsonian parts, seeking to substitute a better theory of perception and its objects for anything modeled on old-fashioned sense-datum theory. The rabbits include the metaphysical inflation, railing against the bald and shallow metaphysics of the scientific world view. They include the dismissal of the standpoint of the "cosmic exile" or "sideways views" from which we attempt to understand ourselves as parts of a natural world. They include the doctrine that when we evaluate things we simply display a sensitivity to the values things have. And above all, perhaps, they include the doctrine of "disjunctivitis," or the denial of a highest common psychological factor between cases where we perceive things rightly and cases where we do not.

So what we have, I shall argue, is an admirable adherence to modern views about perception, made to deliver ambitious results, but only via allegiance to a way of framing the issues that are undermined in part by those views themselves, properly understood.

II

Early in *Mind and World* we are introduced to the Sellarsian concept of the space of reasons, and made to face up to the idea that only conceptual items, things within that space, are capable of justifying or being justified. The idea of the Given is the enemy, and:

> The idea of the Given is the idea that the space of reasons, the space of justifications or warrants, extends more widely than the conceptual sphere. The extra extent of the space of reasons is supposed to allow it to incorporate non-conceptual impacts from outside the realm of thought. But we cannot really understand the relations in virtue of which a judgement is warranted except as relations within the space of concepts: relations such as implication or probabilification, which hold between potential exercises of conceptual capacities. The attempt to extend the scope of justificatory relations outside the conceptual sphere cannot do what it is supposed to do. (p. 7)

McDowell goes on to elaborate:

> What we wanted was a reassurance that when we use our concepts in judgement, our freedom – our spontaneity in the exercise of our understanding – is constrained from outside thought, and constrained in a way that we can appeal to in displaying the judgements as justified. But when we make out that the space of reasons is more extensive than the conceptual sphere, so that it can incorporate extra conceptual impingements from the world, the result is a picture in which constraint from outside

is exerted at the outer boundary of the expanded space of reasons, in what we are committed to depicting as a brute impact from the exterior. (p. 8)

McDowell goes on to talk of an "alien force," the causal impact of the world, operating outside the control of our spontaneity, or reason or judgment. In a well-known footnote, he compares the result of such an impact to that of being deposited somewhere by a tornado, giving us an event that might exculpate us (if, for instance, the question arose of whether we are somewhere we have any right to be), but that cannot be said to justify us, or give us reason for being where we are.

This enables McDowell both to set up a problem and give his solution to it. The problem is to stop the exercise of judgment from being entirely self-contained, disengaged from a reality outside the mind. In this picture it would be the play of what, in Kantian terms, would be concepts without intuitions, or concepts without responsiveness to anything other than themselves, in a self-contained dance of inferences. McDowell fears that Davidson has fallen into the trap of presenting a picture in which our thinking is thus self-contained, or only rescued by the inadequate global subterfuge indicated above, and it is frequently raised as a charge against his colleague Robert Brandom. It is as if a thought only maintains friendly relations with other thoughts, and never with things outside the realm of thought. This would be a version of idealism, and while it may be mischievous to say that it might remind us of Berkeley, it is sufficiently similar to his doctrine that an idea can only resemble (have representational relations with) another idea to explain one part of my title.[4] Of course, this is consistent with McDowell's point that the real problem is not one of epistemology, but is "transcendental," in that what in Berkeley purport to be ideas, or in Davidson purport to be thoughts, in this scenario would fail to be ideas or thoughts at all.

McDowell wants to rescue us from the oscillation between this threat of idealism, on the one hand, in which, as he nicely puts it, thought (or, better, fake thought, something that is only the façade of thought) spins frictionlessly in the void, and, on the other hand, the lame solution represented by the Myth of the Given, whereby impingements from outside the space of reasons nevertheless anchor that balloon nicely to the world. His own proposal is what he calls the "unboundedness of the conceptual." An independent reality does exercise control over our thinking, and this control is rational control. But it can only do this because it is itself in some sense "conceptual." The bad picture is one of an:

> outer boundary around the sphere of the conceptual, with a reality outside the boundary impinging inward on the system. Any impingements across such an outer boundary could only be causal, and not rational. (34)

Since experience, or what McDowell likes to call receptivity, certainly gives us rational control over what we believe, it is itself to be regarded as a kind of judgment, a judgment that typically discloses how things stand.

Thus begin McDowell's battles with writers such as Evans and Peacocke, who have found it necessary to notice a "non-conceptual" element within experience. According to McDowell, Evans, for example, falls for the myth of the given, by first acknowledging a non-conceptual element in experience (the kind of modification of consciousness that we might share with animals, for instance), and then trying to see the non-conceptual part as standing in some rational relationship to whatever judgment expresses what we experience.[5]

This is a very interesting issue, and has probably prompted most of the reactions to *Mind and World*. But whatever its intrinsic interest, it is not actually central to the theory of mind and world,

and by McDowell's own lights we ought to be able to put it to one side. We can see this by thinking for a moment of the Davidsonian coherentist slogan that nothing can count as a reason for
holding a belief except another belief. What strikes us as uncomfortable about that slogan is not
the presence or absence of various non-conceptual elements in experience. As McDowell initially
and rightly emphasizes, we are made uncomfortable by the absence of rational links to the world.
If experience is introduced to allay this discomfort, it had better not figure as just another *belief.*
And neither can it figure as just more belief, only tricked out with something else: modifications
of experience, such as sensations or qualia or the rest. So far as establishing contact with the world
goes, these would simply function as decorations, having at best a causal role in making us believe
things. Davidson's slogan would still rule. The question of sensation, a component of experience
that we may well share with brute animals, is not fundamental. It simply would not matter whether
consciousness included such stuff. If it could only function causally, it would be as if we were
victims of an incessant succession of belief-inducting injections, and we would still be left with
idealism or coherentism. It wouldn't matter in the least if the injections also felt one way or another.
To sum up, what is missing is not the idea of experience as belief plus an add-on of sensation or
feeling or anything non-conceptual, for no add-on would do the work of showing that in experience beliefs are formed in ways, whatever they may be, that make them more likely to be true. It
is clear that no phenomenal extra, intrinsic to the experience itself, could do that.

If non-conceptual content is not thought of in this way, because the idea of genuine content is
played up beyond anything recognizable as mere sensation, then it has a very narrow path to find,
being neither phenomenologically self-standing as sensations and qualia might be, nor articulable
by the agent as the reason for a belief (since that would make it conceptual again). It is indeed hard
to see what it could be, and for the purpose of this chapter I am happy to let McDowell's rejection
of it stand (I am not here bothered by the problem of animal thought). It is, of course, an entirely
different matter whether an episode of perceiving something, say for a definite duration, is to be
assimilated to a different event, such as believing something for the same duration. Sidelining the
word "content" does not mean sidelining perceptual events, nor dismissing everything that is distinctive about perception, distinguishing it from the simple arrivals and departures of beliefs.[6]

III

Should we then avoid extending "the scope of justificatory relations outside the conceptual sphere?"
I think it is too unclear what this means for us to judge. Let us consider an everyday observation.
Mary has come to believe that there is butter in the fridge. How? Suppose that she saw it. She
went and looked, and there was the butter. What justifies her belief? Most obviously, *that* she saw
it. Here we can agree with Strawson, Evans, and nearly all contemporary philosophers, that her
doing so is necessarily but a tiny exercise of a vast set of dispositions. Mary has learned to interpret
what she sees. She has learned how far she can see. She has some practiced confidence (she gets
butter right) and surrounding modesties (she cannot tell contraband butter from legitimate butter,
or Jersey from Guernsey, just at sight). She knows in the same way how to find out if there is
butter in the fridge, a car in the garage, or a cat in the garden, and she knows that if there was
butter in the fridge a few minutes ago and nobody in the room, then it is probably there now, that
if it can be seen from one angle it can be seen from others, that it has a life of its own when she
departs, and she can tell if other things are in the fridge and if the butter is in other places, and
so on and so on.

So when we say that Mary is justified because the butter was there and she saw it, are we taking justificatory relations "outside the conceptual sphere"? We are taking them as far as the butter and the fridge. Mary is certainly justified, and by that plenipotent way of earning the title, namely that she got the right result, and did so by exercising an activity exactly adapted to getting the right result, and that she knew to be so adapted. She would not be displaying confidence about the butter had she not gone and looked; she does not find herself in the grip of strange and inexplicable beliefs on such matters, and she gets things right markedly more often when she does go and look. We might say that Mary is abundantly justified, leaving it open how much of this abundance she could jettison while still being justified.

McDowell does not of course deny any of the common-sense thoughts about observation. Indeed, it is part of his project to establish them. But he thinks he can only do so by firmly placing the facts about butter, cars, and cats "within" the conceptual sphere. More precisely, the very things that Mary knows – that the butter is in the fridge and so on – are those to be enfolded in the sphere or space of concepts. So, in turn, the question now becomes where we know what is referred to by such clauses, and hence what it means to think of their referents as being in some space or another.

One might hazard that it is a fact that is referred to, and McDowell often describes himself as insisting that the mind reaches as far as facts. And we can say that it is the fact that butter is in the fridge, together with the other things I have mentioned, that justifies Mary. But facts are queer referents, queer enough not even to be regarded as referents by many philosophers (including Strawson). They are not spatial entities. If they were, as Wittgenstein remarked, they could move around, but they cannot. Some of their queerness as referents comes out if we consider again the central sentence of the first quotation from McDowell that I gave: "But we cannot really understand the relations in virtue of which a judgement is warranted except as relations within the space of concepts: relations such as implication or probabilification, which hold between potential exercises of conceptual capacities." That the butter is in the fridge is a potential exercise of conceptual capacities? Surely not. That the butter is in the fridge might be, for instance, a reasonable matter for gratitude or source of amazement, but it is not a potential exercise of a conceptual capacity for which one is then grateful or at which one is amazed. That the butter is in the fridge may put us at risk of getting fatter. But it is not the exercise of a conceptual capacity that puts us at such risk.

So do we recoil to the allegedly sole alternative, so that "that the butter is in the fridge" becomes tornado-like, brute, alien, merely a provider of "impacts from the exterior"? Not if we refuse to work in terms of the spatial metaphor. There are of course a number of things that make this language inappropriate to Mary. One is that her activities as an observer – her goings and lookings – are intelligently directed. She knows what she is doing, and what she is doing is exactly what is needed to discover what she wants to know. Mary is in control, precisely unlike someone deposited here and there by tornadoes. Like Julius Caesar, she comes, she sees, and she conquers. What she conquers is her ignorance of where the butter is, or of what is in the fridge.

A related thing to say is that when we describe Mary, we are not confined to listing the onset of her beliefs, as we might be if we were making the diary of the mental life of a delusive paranoid. This is one thing that is jarring about Davidson's slogan. It makes it sound as though a sufficient list of her beliefs, made independently of any concern with how they were formed, would tell us everything we need to know about Mary's status as a reasonable person. But this is quite wrong. We applaud Mary as reasonable only because we know, as she does, not only that beliefs were formed, but why they were formed.

The butter is firmly within the realm of law, and that the butter is in the fridge might be so as well (if we were worried about both butter and fridges being human artifacts we could change the example). Things like butter have a chemical constitution, shape, size, weight, and mass and behave in predictable ways. That is why we can see them. The butter impinges on Mary, and if she is a typical fridge-gazer, it will generate an impact from the exterior, from outside her boundaries, in fact from about three or four feet away from her. But then many things "within" the realm of law seem to be understood by us, and so in some sense at any rate fall "within" the sphere of our concepts. Otherwise we could not talk about them.

Minimalists about truth and facts will deny that "that the butter is in the fridge" has a referent at all. Others think it does. Some will hold that it refers to a proposition, others that sometimes it splits into a demonstrative, and the production of a saying which is then demonstrated.[7] Others again, including Davidson, celebrate the notorious slingshot argument, as showing that all facts collapse into one. I can afford to remain agnostic about that. All I am denying is that any referent we may devise for it is an appropriate candidate for spatial imagery. Indeed, if we were to adopt McDowell's spatial imagery, we might say that Mary's receptivity is within the sphere of her spontaneity, meaning that the way she makes observations is something over which she exercises rational control. But then we might equally find ourselves saying that her spontaneity is within the sphere of her receptivity, meaning that the way she thinks about things is responsive to what she observes. Perhaps we want to be able to say both these things, but the metaphor of spaces and spheres then gets in the way. It leaves us with the uncomfortable image of my title. One moment Julius Caesar – our information-gathering techniques and activities exercised in the realm of law – is on top; the next moment George Berkeley – the fact that all this is understood by us, and can be made to appear to be just one more element in our system of beliefs – gains the ascendance, and so it goes on.[8]

The problem here is that McDowell does not succeed in cementing the idea of an observation firmly into the idea of *activities* within the world, *techniques* of discovery and manipulation which are possible to us only as situated within the same spatial and causal world as the things which concern us, the realm of law.

Nothing we have said about Mary take what she saw outside the realm of law. But neither do they take Mary. Mary's belief that butter is in the fridge is certainly one on which she can exercise reason. At the limit, if she has excellent reason for doubting that such a thing could be, she will doubt the evidence of her senses. But without the dualistic metaphors (realm of spontaneity versus realm of law; space of reasons versus space of causes) this should not worry us. Philosophers enamoured of the scientific world view never denied that Mary would be complex, able to juggle observations against memory or testimony or other ancillary evidences. The baldest of scientific metaphysics will accommodate Mary, or, if it will not, it will be because of some other way in which intentionality escapes the realm of law, and that other way is not yet on the table.

IV

The butter caused Mary's belief. Had it not been there, reflecting light or doing other buttery things, Mary would not have formed her confidence that it was there. We know of this causal relationship, which is why we can use it to effect changes in Mary's belief. If we know she will be worried about having butter over Christmas, we can reassure her best by putting the butter where she will lay eyes on it.

I do not want to charge McDowell with ignoring such platitudes, although I believe that some have taken the oneness of mind and world to exclude any conceptual linkage between causation and observation.[9] But it is fair to worry whether causation is entirely central to McDowell's thinking. Could the notion of spontaneity take its leading role if it were? There is nothing spontaneous in any ordinary sense about Mary's coming into awareness of the butter, however many conceptual abilities are in play as she does so. But for ancillary evidence that causation may need to make its voice heard more loudly, I should like to turn briefly to a different work.

In his paper "Non-Cognitivism and Rule Following" McDowell introduces his interpretation of the rule-following considerations.[10] In particular he discusses their significance for the issue of objectivity in moral philosophy, by quoting what he ringingly endorses as a marvelous passage from Stanley Cavell:

> We learn and teach words in certain contexts, and then we are expected, and expect others, to be able to project them into further contexts. Nothing insures that this projection will take place (in particular, not the grasping of universals nor the grasping of books of rules), just as nothing insures that we will make, and understand, the same projections. That on the whole we do is a matter of our sharing routes of interest and feeling, senses of humour and of significance and of fulfillment, of what is outrageous, of what is similar to what else, what a rebuke, what forgiveness, of when an utterance is an assertion, when an appeal, when an explanation – all the whirl of organism Wittgenstein calls "forms of life." Human speech and activity, sanity and community, rest upon nothing more, but nothing less, than this. It is a vision as simple as it is difficult, and as difficult as it is (and because it is) terrifying.[11]

It is, I think, a little surprising to find this passage as an icon for a philosophy so hostile to attempts to gain "sideways-on" views of ourselves. In this passage Cavell manages to tell us rather a lot from what might seem to be an external or sideways-on standpoint on our language and thought. He tells us both what language does "rest upon," and what it does not. Perhaps this is not in the relevant sense to be thought of as taking up a sideways-on viewpoint. But that merely raises the question of what then is to be tarred with that particular brush.

But before we return to that, while we are worrying about causation there is a different problem. Consider the things upon which language is said to rest here: routes of interest and feeling, senses of humor and so on. All of the things Cavell cites are reasonably called aspects of human nature. Cavell simply ignores any aspects of the world apart from human nature. He might have mentioned the properties and powers of things, or the existence of causal laws or substances or space or time. For one would have thought at the very least that our language rests upon the surroundings in which we find ourselves and live our lives, just as firmly as it rests upon us ourselves. But natural kinds are absent, and with them causal powers and the influence of those powers. The "realm of law" is just not invited.

This omission is not just an accident or an oversight. For the vision that Cavell talks of at the climax of his account is "terrifying" *only* because of the absence of the world. Suppose instead Cavell had said that we teach and learn words in connection with kinds of things; people catch on to which kinds of things these are; nothing logically guarantees that they will, but their shared natures make it very likely that they will, and human speech and activity rest on nothing more nor less than that, together of course with our senses of humor and the rest. There is no vertiginous vision, and nothing terrifying there. The vertigo we are invited to suffer (and the thrill of suffering it) depend entirely on the absence of anything to anchor us, and the resulting image of ourselves as either spinning in a void, or at best in a world entirely of our own making. And although it is incidental to this chapter I myself doubt if this purely anthropocentric emphasis is faithful to Wittgenstein. On p. 230 of the *Investigations*, Wittgenstein says "Our interest certainly includes the correspondence between concepts and very general facts of nature." I do not hear Wittgenstein intending anything vertiginous.

But Cavell's neglect is explicable. He will not seem to have neglected anything important when Berkeley is on top. The things Julius Caesar stands for – placing ourselves, manipulating things, exploiting what we know of the ways things work – are not denied. They are just assimilated to other conceptual exercises, such as the making of inferences, or the popping of new ideas into the mind. Hence, they do not deserve separate mention.

This becomes important when we remember that Strawson, McDowell, and practically all philosophers for the last half-century have emphasized both the non-inferential nature of observation and the range of things we can properly be said to observe. Things do not come to us as raw stimuli tagged in some empiricist language: what Quine himself called the fancifully fanciless medium of unvarnished news. Instead, an observation is more like the first thought that comes into our head. It is this that enables McDowell to bring into the *geisteswissenschaften* the equivalent of the collapse of the observation-theory distinction in the *naturwissenschaften*. The well-trained natural scientist, at home with his instruments, sees the nebula, the mitochondria, or the electrical field. The human being, with a second-nature properly developed, sees or hears the meaning of another's words, the intention of their action, or the villainy or innocence of their demeanour. In neither case is there any conscious inference, so in each case we can talk unblushingly of observation.

If we put together the Berkeleian turn represented by Cavell, and Strawson's generosity, the way is open to our deeming ourselves to observe more or less what we like: the past, the future, norms, forces, counterfactual truths, the meaning of the Constitution or Picasso's intentions, and, if we are so minded, the grace of God or impending doom.

V

I said that Mary knew why she came to believe that there was butter in the fridge, and so do we. Possibly, neither Mary nor we made any conscious inference, although of course it is also possible that we did. But why would that be an interesting question? Observation is a source of authority, but it makes little difference to Mary's authority whether she had to make an inference, or whether a training and a habituation meant that the first thought that came into her head already gave her its conclusion. Her inference, had she needed to make one, might have been unwarranted. But then her training and habituation might have warped her mind as well. Indeed we might have thought that Cavell himself, as well as boycotting reality, goes out of his way to invite a certain pessimism about the credentials of observation. At any rate virtually all the features of human nature that he cites are very clearly empirically variable. On the face of it they would be of more service to a Kuhn or a Foucault than to the project of recovering an Aristotelian innocence. If we are denied a sideways look at ourselves, the result, in cases of ideology and ethics, would be not so much confidence that our particular *bildung* has resulted in an unbounded openness of world to mind, as fear that it has trapped us so firmly within our paradigms or our *episteme* that we no longer recognize our prison as a confinement. If we are deaf to the threat of skepticism or relativism at this point, it will not so much seem like an exercise of Aristotelian innocence or magnificence, as an exercise of, well, deafness.[12]

If we put agency and causation back in the center of the picture, we can say some more things than this. We can in principle discover which of Mary's subconscious or subdoxastic systems was involved with the observation she made, and we can talk of the links between the ways such systems work, and the truth or falsity that Mary enunciates. Suppose, for instance, Mary hears the sarcasm in someone's voice. We can ask what caused her so to hear him. We might get the plonking reply that it was the sarcasm (in one terminology, this is called a modest reply, but it is at least as natural to hear it as incipiently self-congratulatory). But we might also get a more informative reply: the contours of his intonation, or the fact that he avoided this word, or stressed that one. And in turn these factors can be expanded or detailed further, and we could build up a picture of Mary's reliability as a detector of sarcasm. We might find, for instance, that in some contexts she is very good, but in others fails to notice sarcasm, or invents it where it does not exist. She might be good amongst her peers, but get thrown completely by the accents of a different class or place.

If she possesses more than a rudimentary self-consciousness, Mary will herself be able to conduct this thinking, and test her own diagnosis of sarcasm. Children manage to learn that not everybody who sounds slightly different is mocking them. Of course, as we measure ourselves, we also use our own judgments, but that is quite in order, provided that there is enough independent confirmation or disconfirmation of what we spontaneously judged to give us a handle on the nature of our spontaneous judgment and its reliability.

This independence, of course, can only be granted up to a certain point. Mary, or people observing her, can come upon the question of whether such-and-such an intonation is a reliable sign of sarcasm, but they cannot answer it independently of *any* use of *some* indication of sarcasm. There are currently suggestions that microscopic muscular changes around the eyes betoken dishonesty, and that while only gifted human observers are sensitive to these cues, machines could be developed that register them much more reliably. Well and good, but we need (and of course, have) less subtle manifestations of dishonesty against which to calibrate the gifted observers, or the machines.

Quine and Rorty have said things like this:

> An observation sentence is one which all speakers of the language give the same verdict when given the same concurrent stimulation. To put the point negatively, an observation sentence is one that is not sensitive to differences in past experience within the speech community.[13]

An observation is, in effect, what enough other people will accept as an authoritative first thought to pop into your head in one circumstance or another. McDowell is right to guard against the democratic air of this. There is such a thing as the development of sensitivity, or the trained observer or *phronimos* who may indeed observe things that other people cannot. But once we bring causation back into the picture, we see that the authority of the trained observer is not, as it were, self-standing. His or her credentials are established, and in difficult cases, either in science or in human life, there are procedures for querying them, and procedures for self-checking that an intelligent agent can use. These procedures take us back to less theoretical or less ambitious conceptions of what made the agents give the verdict they did, and the links between the situation described in those terms, and the situation as interpreted in the original terms.

It is possible then to distinguish two different cases. Sometimes, but not always, the procedures can start from asking what was actually seen or heard in stripped down terms, less ambitious terms than the subject first used. We have the lawyer's injunction to "just stick to the facts". Some cases always fit such a request. The first thought in the subject's head may have been "impending rain", but we can request an answer to what was observed that sticks to the present. "That it is going to rain" can be seen or felt, but only because something else is seen or felt. This in no way implies that the thought that it is about to rain is the conclusion of an inference: our natural belief formation can be more automatic, and just as rational as anything deserving the name of inference. Ethical observation also conforms to this model. In Harman's famous example, in one sense the first thought in the spectators' minds may have been "what a dreadful thing to do", but there is a stripped down report that they are also able to give: "first they caught the cat, then they got the gasoline." Furthermore, spectators who were genuinely unable to give that second report would be highly suspect as moralists. It is not a signal of good moralists that they find the thought that something was a dreadful thing to do popping into their heads without their having anything to say about why (there are fascinating contrasts here with aesthetics, arising from the strong justificatory demands that good moralizing has to meet). In fact, a sufficient inability to retreat will disqualify the subject from being properly regarded as a moralist at all. In McDowell's own phrase, he will just begin to seem to be somebody who on occasion sounds off.

In other cases however the subject may have nowhere to which to retreat, while the interlocutor does. The subject just heard the melody or the sarcasm or saw the benevolence or the beauty, and asked by the lawyer to stick to exactly what was seen or heard, is at a loss. It does not follow that the interlocutor has nowhere to which to retreat. He or she can discover what else it was about the situation that prompted the subject's verdict, just as the artist may know what shapes and shadings to create to prompt the seeing of the drawing as a picture of a sneer or a smile, or the investigator might discover what the conjuror did in order that the audience saw him produce an egg from his ear.

Finally there are cases of what we might call bare receptivity. Here, neither the subject nor any investigator can retreat to a stripped down story. Suppose, for instance, the subject saw a straight black line on a white page. Faced with the demand to tell exactly what he saw, there is unlikely to be anything further he can say. And in an ordinary case there is unlikely to be anything else an investigator can say either: there is no story of the kind "this is how it was done" except that it was done by a straight black line on a white page. Of course, there will be further things to know about the retina and the optic nerve and the visual cortex. But these form no part of normal self-reflective practice. They are not used in everyday procedures. It does not follow that they should be banished from philosophy, of course, and the theory of secondary qualities hinges very importantly on knowing just how they get in. But for the present purpose what is telling, and what surely motivated traditional philosophy of science and traditional moral and mental epistemology alike at this point, is that even if we are receptive to quarks, duties and other minds, we are surely not barely receptive to them.

The point of these thoughts about observation and judgment is not to reintroduce some version of the idea that anything to which we are not barely receptive is the result of inference, or even to reintroduce an observation/theory distinction. The point is just that in cases where we are not barely receptive to one or another feature of things, there is available an ordinary "sideways-on" perspective on what we do. It is this sideways-on perspective, a refinement of common-sense, that motivates worries about the enchanted world which McDowell takes to be "disclosed" to us. Of course, the worries will not be felt by anyone secure enough in her own sense of her own receptivity not to raise any questions. The believer feels within herself the working of divine grace, and her confrères think she does too. They never have to raise the question of whether this is the operation of bare receptivity, and neither do we, unless of course we want to understand things better.

Properly read, even Cavell does not have us stop before these thoughts, since he leaves it quite possible that the confidence that we have observed in our own souls of the working of divine grace is the function of some other element of our whirl of life: our self-importance or our resentment or imperial will to power, for instance, after which it will be impossible to think of it as a simple openness of mind to world.

VI

The spatial metaphor more or less forces the allied doctrine of "disjunctivitis" upon us, and it is a tribute to McDowell's strength of mind that he has been able to accept it. In its industrial-strength version disjunctivitis is the view that there is nothing fundamental in common, no "highest common factor" between someone whose mind embraces a fact, and someone whose mind does not. One mind has a bit in it (the referent of the "that" clause, construed as telling of the fact that is "within" the mind) and the other does not. Their minds are unlike, as unlike as a nest with an egg in it and a nest without one. And there is nothing else to say about how they are similar, except in the most general terms: that each satisfies the disjunction of being either genuinely faced with a fact, or not (each either has an egg in it, or is empty). The quietist potential of this doctrine is apparent: either you embrace the facts or you do not, and if you do you owe no explanation – indeed there simply is no explanation – of your doing that starts, as it were, from anywhere psychologically or metaphysically further back.

Disjunctivists might be thought to hold that there is no such thing as false belief. For if there is nothing in common, no highest common factor, between minds perceiving (containing, reaching as far as, disclosed to by) a fact, and failed minds appeared to in such a way that they take the same thing to be a fact when it is not, then how can there be anything in common between minds believing something to be a fact when it is, and those other failures believing it to be a fact when it is not? For some reason however, and in spite of the general trend to assimilate perception to belief, the doctrine is usually confined to perceptual experience.

If we avoid the spatial metaphor for the mind, will anything motivate disjunctivitis? Indeed, can we so much as believe that we *understand* the doctrine, without a fatal distortion of the whole philosophy of mind?

Mary and twin-Mary can equally be told by their experience that there is butter in front of them, when one is faced with butter, and the other only with fool's butter (margarine, perhaps). Third twin-Mary further out in modal space, who is faced with nothing, but is having her optic nerve stimulated by the mad scientist, is equally being told by her experience that there is butter in front of her. But, according to this version of disjunctivitis, there is no more in common between these sisters than between Mary and anyone else who is not faced with butter: a twin facing an elephant, or another sky-diving for instance.

What could motivate this view? Some things certainly will not. The position that experience is intrinsically or fundamentally "presentational" will not. This is the doctrine that an experience could not be what it is did it not present things to us as being one way or another. But each of these sisters is being told, by her experience, how things stand, and each can absorb what they are told and factor it into their other beliefs and desires.[14] In other words, each can behave rationally as a result. This is what made it so unappealing to deny that one using a term empty of reference, as one of these three would be doing if she said "Lo, that butter is rancid," is thereby denied the status of thinking anything, while the other two qualify. In fact this last claim is a pure example of the spatial way of thinking in action: here an empty demonstrative is diagnosed as leaving a hole in a complex called "content" – a hole in the head, as it were.

A second fear that we can discount is that if we admit a commonality between our Marys, we will be ignoring Austin's or Sellars's claim for the priority of "is" over "appears." Not at all, for we can give the veridical case priority in all kinds of ways. Alexander Bain said that a belief was a preparation for action, so we might try the idea that it appearing to one as if there is butter there is a state disposing one to readiness for actions that, given one's desires, would be successful if and only if there is butter in the environment. This kind of suggestion, crude though it may be, accords with Sellars's priority for it approaches "appears" only in terms of "is." And it is only a suggestion, for there would be many other similar approaches.

Another fear that should be put aside is that unless we embrace disjunctivitis, the old grim problems of Cartesian epistemology will once more overwhelm us.[15] The idea will be that to defeat these problems Mary will need to strip what she is allowed to know down to some subjective core that she shares with her siblings, and enter on the forlorn attempt to regain the whole sphere of empirical knowledge from just such a string of subjective cores. But this is in no way implied by agreeing to what we have said about Mary and her siblings. The world is presented as being a certain way, the same way, to each of them. Two are mistaken. But this does not mean that they are never justified in taking their experience at face value. Nor does it mean that they ever gain anything except confusion by attempting to subject all their experience, en bloc, to a process of Cartesian doubt. We can admit a shared psychological state between a Mary who remembers childhood abuse, and another who is the victim of induced false memory syndrome, without falling into a pit in which memory is regarded as intrinsically untrustworthy, or only otherwise by the grace of God. We can admit shared beliefs between those who believe truly and those who believe falsely, without making a single step to thinking that our beliefs together form a set of presences from which we vainly try to infer facts about the world.

Such an idea may well sound absurd in the case of beliefs, but it is no more absurd than the fear that the "highest common factor" must be thought of in terms of the presence of a proxy: mental butter, perhaps something like an extremely thin slice of butter or an "extremely thin colored picture" of ordinary butter.[16] To think that is just to reapply the bad old spatial metaphor. The sisters, we have said, are each in the same state of experiencing the world as having butter before them. This is the highest common factor. There is simply no reason to think of this "state" as reified, a Tractarian configuration in which mind contains some sinister thing which in one of the cases is a fact, but in two of the cases fails to be, and so is nothing of this world but only something "in the head."

In the grip of the spatial metaphor, one might uncritically find oneself heaping scorn on those who reject disjunctivitis. They will be leaving facts blankly external to minds. They will be denying transparency of mind to world. They will be condemned to failure of understanding altogether, to darkness within. But shake off the grip, and all is well. People finding an interesting commonality between Mary and her twins are as commonsensical as those finding an interesting commonality between believing that it is Mary in the room when it is Mary, and believing that it is Mary when it is her indistinguishable twin Mary.

It is interesting that in a discussion of McDowell on this matter, Hilary Putnam in effect interprets this as being McDowell's own point.[17] According to Putnam, McDowell would of course admit to the highest common factor I talked of (let us call it the highest common *feature*): the fact that each of them is being told by their experience that there is butter in front of them. According to Putnam, McDowell's point is simply to exorcise the tendency to think of this shared feature in terms of the presence of a proxy, a mental object or intermediate thing. He thus sees McDowell as simply following the Jamesian, or Austinian, path of distinguishing sharply between a quality of being "in" an experience intentionally (it is how the experience presents things as being) and of it being something else, a proxy, described adjectivally. This is not an industrial-strength disjunctivitis, but a pussy-cat disjunctivitis, telling us to avoid thinking of the highest common feature spatially.

Often, McDowell's own language is indeed interpretable either way. For example, he identifies the highest common factor conception as:

> The idea that even when things go well, cognitively speaking, our subjective position can only be something common between such cases and cases in which things do not go well. (p. 113)

But that description of an idea straddles the harmless, indeed essential, things we have said about Mary and her twins, and the harmful spatialization of it that suggests the idea of a proxy. It is indeterminate from this whether McDowell intended a denial of the apparently harmless and essential things, which certainly makes the doctrine of disjunctivitis radical, but also quite unacceptable, or only a denial of something like old-fashioned sense-data, which leave it quite innocuous. My claim is that McDowell does not bring the difference into focus and does not speak unambiguously precisely because of the power of the spatial metaphor in his thought. It means that whenever subjectivity becomes the topic the fear of the mind as retreating "within" takes over, and then the harmless and essential things to say about delusive perception and false belief get caught up in the panic.

I said above that even taking oneself to understand the doctrine of disjunctivitis already implies a contaminated philosophy of mind, and it may still not be apparent why this is so. Well, what could be meant by saying that those who have experience as of butter being present when it is not, and those who have experience as of butter being present when it is (I almost wrote, those who have the same experience when it is) share no single state of mind? Quite apart from the phantom fears that motivate the doctrine, what can we make of the doctrine itself? It is admitted that Mary and twin-Mary and third twin-Mary are in indistinguishable states (if the butter flickered into margarine and back, or was miraculously substituted by proximate or distal stimuli of just the right kind, Mary or her twins could not tell). So there are *lots* of descriptions that apply equally to them, such as the one about action derived from Alexander Bain. Their functioning, and their dispositions such as their preparations for agency, are identical, insofar as these are functions of how things appear. So what is not identical?

The only answer is their "mental states," conceived as these would be by a spatially contaminated philosophy of mind (it does not matter how obese this mind has become, for the image is still fatal). These "mental states" are reified states like structures, occupying a region that either contains something or does not. And then it is indeed possible to think that Mary has a real egg in her nest, twin-Mary only a cuckoo's egg, and third twin-Mary has nothing there at all. Their inner spaces differ, just because its boundaries now extend so far.

McDowell on Putnam's interpretation ought, therefore, to be counseling us firmly *against* the blandishments of disjunctivitis. There is nothing to be said for it once the spatial metaphor is abandoned. And McDowell's embrace of the doctrine undermines any claim to be free of the ghosts of the past. But even if Putnam were right our interpretations would agree about this, that one of the results of *Mind and World* – and it is not a negligible result – should be an even more profound mistrust of the spatial metaphors which alarm me by presenting themselves so much as crucial parts of its argument, and of its solution to the problem of relating world and mind.

Notes and References

1   S. Blackburn, "Knowledge, Truth and Reliability," Henrietta Hertz lecture to the British Academy, 1984, esp. fn. Reprinted in *Essays in Quasi-Realism*, Oxford: Oxford University Press, 1993, esp. 43–4.

2   J. McDowell, *Mind and World*, Cambridge, Mass.: Harvard University Press, 1994.

3   T. H. Green, Introduction to David Hume (ed.), *A Treatise of Human Nature*, London: Green & Grose, Longman's, 1874.

4   More pedantically, the parallel is that Berkeley makes it impossible that an idea should have rational relationships with anything except another idea, just as Davidson makes it impossible that a belief or concept should have rational relations with anything except another belief or concept. The moral of quite popular transcendental arguments, such as that of Putnam's brain-in-a-vat thought experiment, would be that this means that in the absence of a common-sense world, we could not be the subjects of genuine ideas or concepts at all. With these arguments in place, the idea is not so much one of thought spinning frictionlessly in the void, as of what purports to be thought not really being thought at all. I am indebted to Mark de Silva for conversation on this point.

5   There is a scholarly question about whether it is fair to criticize Evans for falling for the Myth of the Given. Sellars's own attack on the myth takes as a premise a distinction between the materials of sense and the inputs to the processes of reason. It presupposes, therefore, that the sensory experiences and the conceptualizations are not the same thing, as indeed he says repeatedly, for instance between sections 25 and 32 of *Empiricism and the Philosophy of Mind*. We should also remember that Sellars thought there were two mind–body problems. One was understanding how sensory qualities can be in brains, and the other was understanding how thoughts can be in brains. Sellars is not a monist about the contents of consciousness. In his own attack on the myth Sellars was primarily concerned to deny that sensations can play the role of empiricist foundations for belief, so the question is whether Evans thinks that they do.

6   To take just one instance: the arrivals and departures of experience command attention in the way that arrivals and departures of beliefs need not. The enjoyment of experiences is episodic whereas the having of a belief is not.

7   D. Davidson, "On Saying That," *Synthèse* 19 (1968). Reprinted in *Inquiries into Truth and Interpretation*, 2nd edn, Oxford: Clarendon Press, 2001.

8   There is an echo here of the "just more theory" debate between David Lewis (here representing the Julius Caesar tendency) and Hilary Putnam. See H. Putnam, "Models and Reality," in his *Realism and Reason*, Cambridge: Cambridge University Press, 1983, 1–26; D. Lewis, "Putnam's Paradox," *Australasian Journal of Philosophy* 62 (1984): 221–36; B. Taylor, "Just More Theory," *Australasian Journal of Philosophy* 69 (1991): 152–66.

9   P. Snowdon, "The Objects of Perceptual Appearance," *Proceedings of the Aristotelian Society*, Supplementary Volume 64 (1990): 121–50.

10 J. McDowell, "Non-Cognitivism and Rule-Following," in S. Holtzman and C. Leich (eds.), *Wittgenstein: To Follow a Rule*, London: Routledge, 1981, 141–62.

11 S. Cavell, *Must We Mean What We Say?*, New York: Charles Scribner, 1969, 52.

12 This is where we can feel the attractions of Rorty's attempt simply to abandon any notion of representation at all. I do the same in the case of ethics, but not across the board.

13 W. V. Quine, "Epistemology Naturalised," in his *Ontological Relativity and Other Essays*, New York: Columbia University Press, 1969, 86.

14 If we are fastidious about the dangers of metaphor, we will worry about the locution of "being told" something by their experience. All that I want is that this is the understanding of what they are faced with, that is all-but-irresistibly borne in upon them by what they see, and we can add for basic cases that they have no retreat to a less demanding conception of what they are faced with.

15 This especially grips McDowell on pp. 111–13.

16 This phrase parodying sense-datum theory comes from John Wisdom.

17 H. Putnam, *The Threefold Cord Mind, Body, and World*, New York: Columbia University Press, 2000, 152.

Response to Simon Blackburn

1 Long ago Blackburn warned me against overindulging in spatial metaphors about minds. The warning went unheeded, and now he thinks my fondness for talk of how widely the mind extends, and for the cognate metaphor of the space of reasons, has had damaging effects, which detract from the admittedly good bits in my more recent work.

But Blackburn's earlier reservation, against my proposal that we set the mind's boundaries, so to speak, outside those that enclose its embodied owner, was based on a failure to take the point of the proposal.[1] And the same is true of his present discomforts.

2 In my *Mind and World*,[2] I work with a contrast between the space of reasons (an image I borrow from Sellars) and the realm of law. Beginning in his second paragraph, Blackburn assumes that this is merely my preferred way of describing a contrast between the space of reasons and the space of causes. But I do not set off the space of reasons by distinguishing it from something describable as the space of causes. In fact I explicitly protest (71 n.2) against Richard Rorty's doing that, in contexts in which Rorty is aiming to capture the point of Sellars's idea that the space of reasons is special. This means that the main thrust of Blackburn's reflections about Mary and the butter is unthreatening to me.

When Sellars says we should conceive knowledge as a position in the space of reasons, he is attacking the Myth of the Given. Part of his point is that we must not confuse *brutely* causal impingements on believers with justifications for belief. This is a thought Blackburn finds already expressed in T. H. Green's treatment of Locke and Hume, and applauds me for restating. It would be quite another matter to suppose *no* causal connections between judgments and their subject matter can be epistemologically significant – as if a relation's belonging to the space of causes (not a locution of mine, as I have noted) would exclude its belonging to the space of reasons. Nothing in Sellars, or in the use I make of Sellars, rules out the idea that sensory experience links observational judgments to their subject matter both causally and, thereby, in a way that is relevant to the justification of the judgments. And that is just how things are with Blackburn's Mary. Causal relations between the butter and Mary obviously matter to Mary's acquisition of knowledge that there is butter in the fridge. And that obvious fact is not threatened by anything in the way I exploit the image of the space of reasons. Observation is possible for us only because we are causally related to the things we observe. Blackburn thinks I have a problem acknowledging that, but this is because he foists on me a conception of a space of causes that is foreign to me.

The point of the distinction I do rely on, between the space of reasons and the realm of law, is not to separate rational from causal understandings of phenomena. On the contrary, I follow Davidson in holding that rational understanding can *be* causal understanding.[3] The point of the contrast with the realm of law is, rather, to bring out how special a kind of understanding we acquire when we see something in a subject's life, say acting or coming to have a belief, in the light of a conception of the subject as aspiring to live up to the requirements of rationality. The contrast with the realm of law is meant to bring space-of-reasons understanding into focus by contrasting it with the kind of understanding we get when we see something as simply a case of how events regularly unfold. Not all causal understanding involves seeing something as simply a case of how events regularly unfold. Some causal understanding – specifically, the causal understanding yielded by explanations in terms of reasons for believing or acting – is space-of-reasons understanding. Attempting to live up to the requirements of rationality can be, for instance, opening oneself to causal influences from objects, as one does in observing how things are. And the contrast I exploit, which is not the contrast Blackburn saddles me with, does not threaten that obvious fact.

Of course, as Blackburn triumphantly points out, the fact that the butter is in the fridge is not a potential exercise of conceptual capacities on anyone's part. But equally obviously, it is only as *taken in* by Mary that the fact has the relevance it has to her justification for believing that the butter is in the fridge. Its sheer obtaining, unobserved by her, would not enable us to recognize her belief as justified. My claim is, in the first instance, that the taking in must be a matter of conceptual capacities at work, if it is to figure as it does in the warrant for Mary's belief. At least for the purposes of this paper (see the end of his section I), Blackburn does not dispute that. And if it is granted, we can hardly go on to suppose that what is taken in is outside the reach of those conceptual capacities.

In this last remark I use the spatial imagery that Blackburn thinks is so dangerous. As I have insisted, I have no problem acknowledging that Mary's possibilities for acquiring observational knowledge about the butter depend on causal relations between it and her. Once that misunderstanding is cleared away, I see no reason to suppose this use of spatial imagery puts me at the top of a slippery slope with trouble at its foot.

3 Blackburn urges that questions about a non-conceptual element in experience are irrelevant to my main concerns. He seems to think the conception of a non-conceptual element that I attack is one in which sensation or feeling figures as a phenomenologically characterized supplementation, a "what it is like" element added to experience conceived as onset of belief. But that is not my target at all. What I attack is a position according to which, first, an experiencing subject takes in how things are, or at least seems to take in how things are, so that experience can be relevant to one's credentials in believing that things are that way; but, second, the way experience has its content – the way experience purports to reveal that things are thus and so – is not, at any rate not wholly, to be understood in terms of actualization of conceptual capacities. It is utterly central to my concerns to urge, against this, that a taking in of how things are that can be relevant to one's rational status in believing that they are that way must be conceptual.

That is not at all to say, as Blackburn suggests, that according to me experience "is itself to be regarded as a kind of judgment." At one point he says, as if to correct me, that "there is nothing spontaneous in any ordinary sense about Mary's coming into awareness of the butter." But that is exactly my point when I talk about the actualization of conceptual capacities in receptivity. The capacities belong to spontaneity in that they *can* be used in responsible cognitive activity, para-digmatically judging. But in experience they come into operation outside our control.

4 Blackburn ends his reflections about Mary by saying she can be accommodated by "the baldest of scientific metaphysics."

I suspect this belongs with his claim that my use of spatial imagery leads to a "dismissal of the standpoint of the 'cosmic exile' or 'sideways view' from which we attempt to understand ourselves as parts of a natural world." This blanket claim runs two different things together. My skepticism about sideways-on views belongs in quite specific philosophical contexts. They have nothing to do with a refusal to acknowledge that, for instance, Mary's possibilities for observational knowledge depend on connections that are suitable for scientific investigation. It is quite wrong to read the skepticism about sideways-on views, in the specific contexts in which I express it, as implying the idiotic idea that once we have decided to place things in the space of reasons, we are precluded from aspiring to understandings that exploit the terms of a restrictive ("bald") naturalism – as if being interested in, say, speech acts as meaningful performances precluded being interested in, say, how certain complex musculature enables us to produce articulate vocal sounds. Naturalistic understandings, in that sense, are just fine. If it were true that I dismiss all attempts to understand ourselves as parts of the natural world, it might be understandable if someone reacted by claiming – exaggerating in the opposite direction – that such understandings can do everything for us. That is the only way I can begin to make sense of Blackburn's implication here: that simply insisting on the relevance of the causal facts about Mary is enough to warrant claiming that a bald scientific metaphysics will accommodate whatever can be said about her in intentionality-involving terms.

What Blackburn actually says is this: "The baldest of scientific metaphysics will accommodate Mary, or if it will not, it will be because of some other way in which intentionality escapes the realm of law, and that other way is not yet on the table." But the way intentionality "escapes the realm of law" is just the way Sellars explains in terms of the image of the space of reasons, and the obvious facts about Mary's causal situation in the world cannot dislodge this thought from the place on the table that I have given it.

5 Blackburn misses the thrust of the passage I applauded from Cavell. Of course he is right that Wittgenstein does not intend his readers to be suffering from vertigo when they finish reading his book. But for there to be a point in the reflections about rule-following, Wittgenstein's thought must be that there is a pervasive *risk* of falling into the paradox of *Philosophical Investigations* §201. And the risk is what is beautifully captured in the passage from Cavell.

No doubt at some level it is correct to say, as Blackburn does, that "our language rests upon the surroundings in which we find ourselves and live our lives, just as firmly as it rests upon us ourselves." But if someone is puzzled about how it is possible for us to catch on to kinds, in the way Wittgenstein makes vivid, it cannot be any help – before we have dislodged the temptation to suppose the necessary projection can only be a leap in the dark – to reaffirm that there are kinds for us to catch on to. In fact the threat of vertigo is fully alive if, as Blackburn's putatively reassuring story has it, the best we can have is a *likelihood* that we have all caught on to the same kinds.

Blackburn uses his animadversions on the Cavell passage as a pretext for linking my supposedly insufficient acknowledgment of the importance of causation with a doctrine he attributes to me to the effect that in evaluation "we *simply* display a sensitivity to the values things have," with the sensitivity conceived as "a *simple* openness of mind to world." (I have added the emphasis.) But the note of simplicity here fits nothing in my thinking.

As I see things, all receptivity, of the relevant sort, is conceptually shaped. Depending on the structure of the conceptual capacities in question, this makes more or less space for the sort of finer-grained story Blackburn plausibly tells in connection with the ability to detect sarcasm. That ability is a pretty good model for the ability to detect instances of the subtler sorts of values, or disvalues, as I conceive that ability.

Of course, as Blackburn insists, if we want to suppose that what we are dealing with is an ability to *detect* something, we are vulnerable to arguments purporting to show that the supposedly detected something is not there to be detected, but a figment of groundless traditional modes of thinking, or power relations that distort discourse, or whatever. We had better not think in terms of detection unless we are confident that we are entitled to reject such arguments. But unless we think some specific argument of that kind works in some area to undermine the idea of a capacity to get things right (as Blackburn and I do in the case of divine grace, and as he and I do not in the case of, say, injustice), we have no reason to avoid thinking of the capacity as a capacity to detect something. The sheer fact that a finer-grained story can be told, so that the candidate for being a capacity to detect something is not a *simple* openness of mind to world, is not by itself a reason to be suspicious of the idea that the capacity really is a capacity for detection. Blackburn implies that we have to choose between a general suspicion of detection talk, on the one hand, and a picture in which values (and so forth) are available to a bare unreflective receptivity, on the other. That is quite wrong. It gives suspicion of detection talk an undeserved general cachet, whereas its respectability depends entirely on whatever specific grounds are to be had in this or that case.[4]

6   Finally, Blackburn has simply not understood the disjunctive conception of perceptual experience, at least in the version I have recommended.

He attributes to me the bizarre thesis that there is nothing in common between someone who perceives that things are thus and so and someone to whom it merely seems that she perceives that things are thus and so. In fact it is boringly obvious that there is something in common between the cases. The locution "seems" and its kin are precisely suited to capture the common feature. In Blackburn's example, both Mary and her twin are subjects to whom it looks as if (i.e., it visually appears that) there is butter in the fridge.

My point is not to deny that there is a highest common factor between such cases. The highest common factor would be something on these lines: what would be specified by a maximal account of what is shared between Mary and her twin, an account that leaves out nothing that is true of both of them.

My claim is not that there is no highest common factor, but that a highest common factor does not exhaust the epistemological significance of experience, in a case in which someone perceives that things are thus and so, as Mary does and her twin does not. There is a pervasive temptation to suppose that the epistemic credentials a subject acquires through perceptual experience can never be more than a highest common factor between cases in which the experiencing is perceiving that things are thus and so and cases in which the experiencing is having it merely appear to one that things are thus and so. That would imply that the epistemic credentials yielded by experience can never be better than they are in cases of mere appearance. To resist this is not to hold that Mary does not share a psychological state with her twin. It is to insist that crediting her with a psychological state she shares with her twin does not capture what her experience contributes to her epistemic standing. If we say no more about her than what we can equally say about her twin, we omit the fact that she sees that there is butter in the fridge. If we suppose that a psychological state she shares with her twin exhausts the contribution of her experience to her epistemic standing, we are obliged to reconstruct the fact that she sees that there is butter in the fridge as an amalgam of what her experience supposedly yields, the highest common factor, and something additional to that, and I claim that that yields no workable conception of how it can be knowledge that she has. I find it helpful to say "external" where I have just said "additional," but the case against this conception of seeing how things are does not turn on such spatial imagery.

Blackburn suggests that if it is not a denial of the obvious commonality between, for instance, Mary and her twin, the disjunctive conception can only be a familiar rejection of a sense-datum picture of perception. But the thought rejected by the disjunctive conception, the thought that perceptual situations that are indistinguishable from the point of view of the subject cannot differ in the epistemic credentials provided by experience, has a persistent power to seem compelling. Its attractions can survive even if we are not at all tempted to think vision yields extremely thin colored pictures of worldly states of affairs, to echo the wonderful wording for a certain conception of sense-data that Blackburn quotes from John Wisdom.

To put forward the disjunctive conception is not yet to diagnose what is wrong with the thought that subjective indistinguishability implies sameness in epistemic import. It is merely to deny that thought. But, so far from being a crazy outcome of over-indulgence in spatial imagery, it is, for all Blackburn says, a necessary first step toward a satisfying epistemology of knowledge acquired through perceptual experience.

Notes and References

1   I explained this in some of the footnotes to "Knowledge and the Internal" and "Knowledge by Hearsay," now reprinted in my *Meaning, Knowledge, and Reality*, Cambridge, Mass.: Harvard University Press, 1998. See especially n.15 in the former, at p. 406. Since Blackburn does not restate his earlier objection, I shall not go over the point again here.

2   Cambridge, Mass.: Harvard University Press, 1994, and 1996.

3   See "Actions, Reasons, and Causes," in Davidson's *Essays on Actions and Events*, Oxford: Clarendon Press, 1980, 3–19.

4   For a bit more on this, see my "Projection and Truth in Ethics," in my *Mind, Value, and Reality*, Cambridge, Mass.: Harvard University Press, 1998.

10

The Two Natures: Another Dogma?

Graham Macdonald

I Introduction

It is fair to say that the latter part of twentieth-century analytic philosophy was dominated by what could be called "the naturalist turn," the influence of which was felt particularly in philosophy of mind. Here naturalism took the form of a demand: render all theories of, say, reference, or intentionality, or, more generally, rationality, consistent with what science tells us about our place in the natural world – or else cast them into the flames. This demand is further elaborated when "science" and "consistent with" are made more determinate. Given the task is to naturalize the mind, "science" gets qualified as "natural science," and "consistent with" is usually taken to be "reducible to." This latter notion has been taken to require property-identity, this being the modern variant on Nagel's original stipulation that there must be bridge laws connecting the relevant terms of the reduced and reducing theory.

There is a familiar problem, however, with the stipulation that only the natural sciences are to count if the proposed reduction is to do its ontologically purifying (and so naturalizing) work. For how do we decide what counts as a natural science? The problem encountered in answering this question is that it will be seen as merely stipulative if we simply name the privileged sciences, say physics and chemistry, leaving any other contenders out in the cold. The distinction "natural/non-natural" must be explained, not just decreed, otherwise the motivation behind the naturalist's project will be obscure. This leads to the second, related, problem, a variant of "Hempel's Dilemma":[1] if we count only those sciences we presently recognize as natural, then we advantage present knowledge over future discovery. Nothing will count as natural that is not known now, surely a *reductio* of the method of favoring the present over the future. And as we cannot know what the future will bring, not so favoring the present will leave us toothless; the requirement to use only the theories of a natural science leaves us ignorant as to how to satisfy the requirement.

In what follows I wish to, indirectly, pursue this topic whilst also, more directly, pursuing John McDowell's rejection of this naturalizing project. McDowell has stood out in bold relief in recent philosophy for resisting the siren call of science, arguing for an alternative naturalism, one that sees only a limited role for the natural sciences. What connects McDowell's rejection of what I will call "one-nature" naturalism (abbreviated to "N1" in what follows) to my previous theme is just the obvious thought that any rejection of N1 must itself be predicated on an understanding of what a natural science is. My suggestion is that McDowell's two-nature naturalism (hereafter "N2") will be seen to be absorbable by (natural) science if we have a suitably realistic idea of what a natural science could be. Second nature will turn out to be just nature, pure and simple. McDowell, though, has explicitly rejected this suggestion, but before examining his reasons for doing so I turn to characterizing in more detail his rejection of N1 and espousal of N2.

II Nature Divided

There are different ways in which one might argue for the essentially non-scientific nature of our account of being minded. One would be ontological, arguing for the essentially non-physical nature of the mind, and hence the impossibility of capturing its essence in terms appropriate to the natural sciences. McDowell does not pursue this route, although what he says has echoes in such ontological arguments. McDowell prefers to focus on what he takes to be distinctive about being a reasoning being, that such reasoning is essentially norm-governed, and that it yields accounts of human action that are not predictive. Propositional attitudes "figure in a kind of explanation that is *sui generis*" (1998b: 332): they occur within a space of reasons that cannot be captured in the realm of law. The "concepts of the propositional attitudes have their proper home in explanations in which things are made intelligible by being revealed to be, or approximate to being, as they rationally ought to be." This contrasts with a style of explanation in which one makes things intelligible "by representing their coming into being as a particular instance of how things generally tend to happen" (1998b: 328). This is the contrast between the space of reasons and the realm of law. The former, as we shall see, is part of second nature, the latter being first nature.

It is important for McDowell that reasoning beings acquire their rational capacities through becoming language-users: only linguistic creatures can be reasoners.[2] This has attracted considerable criticism, especially from those who wish to defend the idea that there can be non-conceptual representations figuring in justifications of our perceptual knowledge. One feature of this criticism is relevant here, and that is the thought that permitting such non-conceptual content to figure in our own epistemological domain renders our cognitive capacities "more continuous with" those of non-linguistic creatures, for whom all knowledge will be non-conceptually based. Now McDowell does not have any problem with attributing to non-linguistic creatures a capacity to be, as he puts it, "on to things" in their environment. "Non-human animals can have knowledge; the cat's awareness of the prey is genuinely a case of awareness of the prey . . . need not be part of the role of the image of the space of reasons to secure for us the very idea of being on to things."[3] The claim is just that this kind of knowledge is not provided by the workings of reason, the processes of which go beyond the minimal idea of just "being on to things." To be subject to the pull of reason one must be capable of reflecting on what one takes to be a reason. One must be capable of critical thought, this involving the ability to reflect on the grounds for one's belief or action, to evaluate one's evidence, to scrutinize beliefs for coherence, have reasoned beliefs about the consequences of our actions, and so on. Without this capacity for critical reflection the pull of a reason will become just the power of a cause, and so not have any justificatory force. And this critical capacity can only be exercised by those who have conceptual resources, which, it is claimed, requires the possession of language.

It is also not the case that McDowell thinks that the space of reasons is disconnected from the realm of law. Being at home in the space of reasons "could not float free of potentialities that belong to a normal human organism. This gives enough of a foothold in the realm of law to satisfy any proper respect for modern natural science" (McDowell 1994: 84). But the realm of law is essentially non-normative, so cannot be understood as containing the space of reasons. This does not have the consequence that reasoning is not part of nature, as McDowell insists that the realm of law does not exhaust what is natural, so normativity is not excluded from nature.

At first blush it would appear the nature invoked here, the nature that includes norms, is one that McDowell thinks lies not only outside the realm of law, but also outside the domain of science, which is why it is "second nature":

Acquiring command of a language, which is coming to inhabit the logical space of reasons, is acquiring a second nature. Given that the space of reasons is special . . . ideas of phenomena that are manifestations of a second nature acquired in acquiring command of a language do not, as such, fit in the logical space of natural-scientific understanding. But there is no reason why that should rule out seeing those phenomena as manifestations of nature, since the nature in question can be a second nature. Actualizations of conceptual capacities, which as such belong in the logical space of reasons, can be natural in a different sense from the one that figures in the admittedly well-drawn contrast with the logical space of reasons.[4]

At least two questions immediately come to mind. First, what is the conception of science in play here? Second, wherein lies the incompatibility between understanding some phenomena in a "natural-scientific" way and an understanding that relies on rational norms? The first question is relevant because it appears that McDowell, in separating out the domain of law from the space of reasons, is identifying natural science with the domain of law, and so concluding that phenomena that are manifestations of rationality are not understandable by natural science. And it would be just such an identification (of natural science with the domain of law) that explains the rejection of any natural-scientific understanding of rational processes, the domain of natural law being norm-free, that of rationality being norm-governed. The defender of one-nature naturalism, then, can reject the idea that all natural-scientific understanding must exploit only law-based explanation, leaving it open whether an alternative form of explanation can capture the norms of rationality whilst still being a natural-scientific explanation.

Just such an alternative has, of course, been advanced by assorted teleosemanticists, who claim that the functional explanations to be found in biology are neither law-dependent nor norm-free. If they are right, and given the status of biology as a natural science, it could appear that McDowell's rejection of a natural-scientific understanding of rationality is predicated on too narrow a conception of natural science. Now McDowell has rejected the accusation that his anti-naturalism (N1) is based on a misconception of the scope of natural science, and in fact complicates the neat division between the realm of law and the space of reasons by allowing that non-human (non-rational) animals also enjoy a second nature, one not capturable by a law-based understanding. There is already a disunity in the realm of the non-human natural:

the idea of second nature belongs on both sides of the distinction I am chiefly concerned with, between what can be made intelligible by placement in the space of reasons and everything else. The distinction cannot be equated with a division between first and second nature. But, no doubt predictably, I want to sidestep the demand for a substantial unification. . . . I think the only unity there needs to be in the idea of the natural, as it applies, on the one hand, to the intelligibility of physical and merely biological phenomena (themselves needing to be differentiated for some purposes . . .), and, on the other, to the intelligibility of rational activity, is captured by a contrast with the idea of the supernatural – the spooky or the occult. I need only the bare invocation of *Bildung* – not . . . a detailed story about how what happens in *Bildung* connects with phenomena characterizable in terms of conformity to natural law – in order to bring out an analogy between the acquisiton of responsiveness to reasons and, for instance, the accquisition of secondary sexual characteristics. Both of these developments are . . . part of "the normal maturation of human beings." That should be enough to reassure us that, for all the *sui generis* character of responsiveness to reasons, there is nothing spooky about it, and that is all that I need from the idea of second nature. (McDowell 1999: 99)

So now we have two divisions, that between the space of reasons and everything else, and that between first and second nature. The relation between these divisions can be articulated as: (a) the realm of law; (b) second nature, this being split into (b₁) the second nature enjoyed by both human and non-human animals,[5] and (b₂) the second nature enjoyed only by rational beings. But the picture becomes somewhat more complicated when we look at the distinction between a "natural-scientific understanding" of phenomena and that which resists such an understanding – the space of reasons. The complication is that a natural reading of McDowell's claims about the inability of a natural scientific understanding to accommodate manifestations of rationality is that that understanding is limited to law-based explanation, whereas in the quotation above he seems to be including "merely biological phenomena" within the compass of such a scientific understanding. One who defends the distinctiveness of functional explanations in biology will cavil at this suggested limitation of scientific explanation to law-based explanation.

A reasonable interpretation of McDowell's position, though, will be one recognizing that the primary division he stresses is that between an understanding that depends on the norms of rationality and those explanations that do not, these latter including both law-based and function-based explanations. And it is surely plausible that the "merely biological phenomena" will be amenable to a natural-scientific understanding, so this must now be taken to be less restricted than previously thought, given that it now includes explanations of phenomena that are exercises of functional capacities. But although I think this is the most reasonable interpretation of McDowell's position, it leaves one with a puzzle. Second nature is to be found on both sides of the main divide, both in non-rational and rational animals. Are we to say that some manifestations of second nature are explainable by natural science whereas others (those that exhibit the marks of rationality) are not, or is the position that all manifestations of second nature, both in human and non-human animals, are not so explicable?

The first option is suggested by the thought that the second nature of non-human animals does seem cognizable in scientific terms; it is part of the science of animal behavior to study, and explain, the emergence of instinctual and learned behavior in the life of individual animals. The second option, however, renders the distinction between first and second nature more philosophically attractive – it makes for a clearer picture about what is, and what is not, within the ambit of a natural scientific understanding.

Exegetically I would say that the emphasis placed by McDowell on the role of the rational ideal in our understanding of one another, and the difference this marks between ourselves and other animals, makes the first option more likely. But whichever option is chosen, the question will remain: why, if one includes the biological within the ambit of science (as McDowell clearly does), is second nature (either restricted to humans or not) not scientifically explicable? And if the first option is the one taken, the question can be put in a more pointed way: why is the *analogy* McDowell sees between human and non-human maturation insufficiently close for both to be legitimate subjects for scientific inquiry? The teleosemanticist sees the resemblance as more than analogical; the same principles, she will say, are at work in both the human and non-human cases, resulting in the same *form* of explanation for both.

Confronted with the teleosemanticist's ambitions for the now enlarged realm of (natural) science, my suspicion is that an anti-naturalist's objection to its proposed application to manifestations of rationality will be much the same as McDowell's objection to the understanding of such manifestations provided by law-dependent explanations: the kind of normativity displayed in rational behavior is not the same as that expressed in the "merely" biological phenomena that are grist to the teleosemanticist's mill. I do not know if McDowell has addressed the teleosemanticist's line of thought directly, but in what follows I want to persuade him that the resources available to the teleosemanticist are wider than often thought, and so have the potential to considerably soften the sharp distinction he draws between what is and what is not amenable to being understood by natural science. In the process of doing this, however, a non-orthodox version of teleosemantics will be defended.

III   A Non-Reductive Naturalism

In the brief characterization of the naturalist's project offered in section I it was asserted that naturalism requires the reduction of mental properties to "properly scientific" properties. However one brand of naturalism, teleosemantics, makes much of the non-reducibility of bio-functional properties to physical or chemical properties. This non-reducibility is a result of how functional properties are constituted. Functions arise as a result of a selection process operating on a varied and replicating population, the environment of that population favoring the possession of some properties at the expense of others. The favored properties are those whose effects directly or indirectly facilitate the reproduction of the bearers of the properties, increasing the ratio of instances of the favored properties in succeeding generations. The new instances of these properties are then said to have acquired a function – the function of doing whatever it was that previous (ancestral) instances of the property did in enhancing the reproductive capacity of their bearers, thus contributing to the increased production of instances of the favored property in future generations.

This story makes the functionality of instances of functional properties dependent on their particular histories, so two instances of a single physical property (i.e. typed as one property for the purposes of physics or chemistry) may differ with regards to function if those instances have different histories. Temporally "local" supervenience does not hold, so one can have homogeneity of the physical (same physical type) with heterogeneity of the functional. In addition, because the bio-function of a property is determined by what its prior instances *did*, what it effected to enhance – for example, its bearer's reproductive capacity – such a function is constituted by that effect. Hence two properties typed differently for the purposes of physics or chemistry may be co-typed for bio-functional purposes, provided that they produce the same effect and possess sufficiently similar histories. Here we have heterogeneity of the physical with sameness of functional type.

So both of these features of bio-functional properties militate against their reduction to physical or chemical properties. Now there is a tension in the position of the teleosemanticist who celebrates this non-reducibility whilst at the same time insisting on the reducibility of intentional properties; it is a virtue, it appears, for bio-functional properties to be non-reducible, but not a virtue for intentional properties. This tension will not be pursued here, as I wish to defend a particular kind of non-reductionist teleosemantics.[6]

"Normal" reductions require the identification of reduced and reducing properties, and it is usual for these properties to have been discerned independently of one another and *then* found to be identical.[7] If the teleosemantic program were reductionist in this sense what one would expect to find is the identification of various intentional or semantic properties with previously recognized biological properties. When one reads the relevant literature, though, whether it be Dretske, Millikan, or Papineau, one does not find this happening; there is no discussion of putative biological-psychological property identities. And it is patent that no such identifications occur when one specifies the content of a belief state via a particular type of function that that state has. Rather, what is going on is the application of a well-understood key theoretical notion ("function") from another ('reputable') discipline to facilitate the characterization and organization of the data in a supposedly different domain.

It is common coin that functionality provides a principled means of taxonomizing biological data;[8] using the same general notion of function to codify mental properties can lead to the *incorporation* of the mental into the biological – they possess, one could say, the same "kindhood." The style of reduction one finds here, if reduction it is, should be called "reduction by kind." In this case it is achieved by expanding the biological domain to include psychological traits, these now being seen as owing their character and organization to the same key feature operating within biology. One consequence of this approach is that the kinds will in the first instance be located within what Richard Boyd calls a "disciplinary matrix," which includes a very general account of the way in which the properties of the kinds referred to by the discipline are determined, or how they are related to each other. In the case under discussion, the most general account of the type of property with which we are concerned, biological properties, begins with noting that such properties look as though they are there to serve a purpose. To avoid accidental "brute" purposiveness, this is then coupled with the further thought that such purpose-serving properties owe their existence to having been designed for their goal-oriented roles. This very general idea then becomes more specific as it is given more substance by incorporating into it the role of natural selection plus the other shaping mechanisms that are responsible for these kind-properties. As Boyd notes, implicit in the very general specification of these properties will be an idea of the type of explanation appropriate for members of the kind, and it is to be expected that divergent kinds will be associated with different explanatory practices. The fundamental idea is that the principles governing taxonomies are entangled with the explanatory aims of different sciences – and the way we explain complex adaptations, it turns out, is different from that of explaining causal regularities.[9]

A consequence of this way of looking at the emergence and characterization of natural kinds is that kind-reduction will be effected when the very general account of the type of property invoked by a discipline is replaced by a different understanding of that type of property. The suggestion here is that what teleosemanticists propose is that one understand the most general definition of intentional mental kinds on the same lines by which one understands the general definition of biological kinds. That is, one is invited to see the mental properties as belonging to functional kinds, with such functional kinds now subsuming both mental and biological kinds. As in other types of reduction, the recognition of mental properties as functional properties may well require a revision of our previous understanding of the nature of these mental properties.

IV Norms and Function

Given this (perhaps unorthodox) understanding of the teleosemantic program, it is clear that any assessment of its prospects will have to examine the ability of functions to capture the previous understanding of the fundamental nature of the properties in question. The opponent of this particular naturalizing project may well object that the functional norms generated by the selection processes are so different from the rational norms constituting intentional properties that there is simply no hope that they could capture such rational norms. This objection may, though, rest on a mistaken appreciation of the scope of functionality.

Defenders of the historical (etiological) view of functions sketched above say that some descendant traits are there because instances of those traits in ancestors had reproduction-enhancing effects. But note that nothing has yet been said concerning the details of how reproduction is achieved, or how selection operates. This is just an abstract account of how functions come to be.

For example, behavioral reinforcement is a form of selective regime that is independent of natural selection.[10] In natural selection differential reproduction is the selector, and reproduction is via the chromosome-copying mechanism that retains the genetic information of the ancestor. In learning we have differential reinforcement, and memory is essential to the retentive process. But this process presupposes that there are means by which the behavior can be shaped by rewards and sanctions. Sentience can function in this manner, guiding us into patterns of behaving. One of the founding fathers of evolutionary epistemology, Donald Campbell, pointed this out many years ago. He talked of the significance of what he called vicarious selection processes:

> the nutritiousness of foods represents an external criterion of direct survival relevance. It is represented in us by approximately appropriate internal selective criteria of taste buds and associated pleasure and pain mechanisms, which become the predominately effective selective criteria in our choosing of foods. The adaptive appropriateness of these vicarious criteria are to past ecologies, and if the environment has markedly changed, the vicarious selective system may operate in ways irrelevant to current adaptiveness.[11]

The structure being suggested here is that one can have various selective regimes operating, perhaps originally nested, which may pull apart, giving rise to differing patterns of behavior, some of which can be the result of a (vicarious) selection process which produces results at variance with those required by natural selection. It is clear that there will be different types of explanation appropriate, depending upon which type of selection process we wish to concentrate. And one important feature of secondary selection is that the functional norm generated will be dependent on what the selector is. Take pain as one such secondary selector, selecting out behaviors that provide painful experiences for the agents. Actions managing to avoid pain will be functioning well according to this selector, those producing pain will not. At a different level, of course, the avoidance of pain may sometimes be bad for an agent, that "badness" bringing into play yet another norm. In Campbell's opinion, animals (including us) are stuffed full of what he called "Blind Variation and Selection Systems" (BVSS), all contributing to an organism's successful negotiation of its environment. On this view there can be a profusion of functions, with attendant norms, having their source in a variety of selection processes.

So the teleosemanticist has available to her the resources to account for a plethora of functions and a variety of norms, all generated from distinctive selection processes. One could go further and investigate those functions that, although based on selection processes, to some extent "float free" from their base, and which permit a teleosemanticist to account for what Millikan calls "useless content,"[12] but enough has been said to encourage the thought that functional norms *may* have the power to illuminate rational norms. Before looking at one final objection to this endeavor I want to provide further evidence that McDowell's "second nature" has striking affinities to the realm of functions.

V   Functions, Reason, and History

We have seen how the history behind the production of, say, a representation-producing mechanism may be relevant to a specification of the function of those representations and to the norms appropriate for the appraisal of the aptness of that content in a certain environment. The relevance of that history to functional identity has provoked what is known as the "swampman" objection:

two people physically type-identical (and in the same environment) may differ functionally because one may have the appropriate history that the other lacks. And if intentional content is dependent on function, then the physical type-identity is not sufficient to ensure identity of intentional content. This supposedly counterintuitive result is seen by some as a decisive objection to all accounts of content that have such a historical dimension.

Now I do not want to address this objection here, except to say that most theories of content would struggle to pass what I would call the "instantaneous" test. Most (plausible) accounts of intentional content require some interaction with the environment, physical or social, in order for the intentional state to have the content it does. Content that emerges spontaneously is fishy, and this is particularly so if the content is part of a system of concepts that engage with the world in a reliable way. The instantaneous emergence of a system of semantically evaluable items is surely magical, and it should be taken as an objection to any account of intentional content if it allows it.

Now one of the philosophers who may be seen as influencing McDowell's rejection of naturalism does allow for history to play a role in determining intentional normativity. It is one of the interesting facets of Wittgenstein's discussion of the normativity of mathematics and language that he endorses the importance of history, in particular the history that invokes training, such training producing the pattern of appropriate responses. "Our children are not only given practice in calculation, but are also trained to adopt a particular attitude towards a mistake in calculating. . . . What I am saying comes to this, that mathematics is normative." (*Remarks on the Foundations of Mathematics*, p. 425). See also *Philosophical Investigations*, 198: "What has the expression of a rule – say a sign post – got to do with my actions? What sort of connexion is there here? Well, perhaps this one: I have been trained to react to this sign in a particular way, and now I do so react to it."

What is fascinating here is that it is training (and learning) that provides the necessary selectionist history drawn upon by the teleosemanticist. It is not too fanciful to extend Wittgenstein's brief remarks, and say that the post is the sign that it is (it has the content we assign to it) *because* we have been trained to react to it in particular ways. And McDowell does stress the importance of "initiation," "social practice," and "tradition" in the acquisition of our second natures, all of which can be fitted into the extended teleosemanticist picture. In *Mind and World* he says:

A rational animal could not have acquired the conceptual capacities in whose possession its rationality consists except by being initiated into a social practice. (McDowell 1994: 104–5)

He insists that one could not simply credit individuals with a sense of how the space of reasons is laid out "without the benefit of anything like my appeal to initiation into a shared language and thereby a tradition" (185–6). And he also (implicitly) affirms the importance of history to the possession of reason (and hence conceptual content), claiming that "it is not even clearly intelligible to suppose a creature might be born at home in the space of reasons" (125).

It shouldn't really be surprising that the extended teleosemantic approach is one that is sympathetic to that favored by Wittgensteinians. Both emphasize the importance of training, in an appropriate environment, for the shaping of our responses, such a shaping endowing those responses with a normative dimension. Both emphasize the importance of "use" in the determination of intentional content, the teleosemanticist in terms that make the "consumer" of a representation an essential feature in the account of the content guiding the consumer's responses, or actions. And for both an essential, but often unstated, part of the background is the thought that what underlies commonality of responses to the environment is a common human nature.[13]

What may be of concern to somebody sympathetic to the Wittgensteinian approach, though, is that Wittgenstein was opposed to those projects that attempted *theoretical* explanations of our mental capacities, seeing in such accounts a misplaced desire to posit internal mechanisms causally responsible for our behavior. Such a desire is seen as a materialist version of the Cartesian assumption that the life of the mind is to be found "inside" the head. Now the desire to find such inner mechanisms may be appropriate in cases where what we want are "straight" causal explanations of phenomena, the idea being that such causal attributions are validated by finding mechanisms responsible for the perceived correlations. But functional explanation is not "straight" causal explanation; it is not in the business of recording causal regularities, and hence can be validated independently of the discovery of "internal" mechanisms. No doubt the discovery of such mechanisms is useful and illuminating, helping us to see how the functional properties do what they do, but those mechanisms won't confirm for us the *functionality* of the properties. Only the relevant history will do that.[14]

What I am calling the Wittgensteinian objection is sometimes put in an epistemological form: given that functionality is dependent on a certain type of (selectionist) history, it may be thought that it must be a requirement on our recognition of intentional content that we not only know the relevant history, but that we also be familiar with the theory of natural selection. If this were true then the requirement would be in tension, to say the least, with the apparent ease with which we recognize intentional content. But many features wear their functionality on their face; it is pretty clear what eyes are meant to do. In those cases where the designs of nature dazzle us, we do not need the history to know what the designed items are for, what their purpose is. Nor do we need to know about natural selection: pre-Darwinians were right to recognize such design, but they were wrong in the account they gave of how it came to be. The same capacity to be "instantly," pre-theoretically, recognizable is possessed, most of the time, by intentional content; we do not require that a theory be known before we can recognize the intention in an action, nor the meaning of a speaker's words. But not even the teleosemanticist would say that we are required to know about selection, or the history that determines the meaning to be what it is, before we can recognize that meaning. What may well be required is immersion in the same set of traditions, and participation in the same set of social practices, in which that meaning gains its "life." What will be insisted on is that that immersion be seen in terms of training and learning, and that is what seems to be involved in McDowell's invocation of a second nature.

VI   Only an Analogy?

What has been suggested above is that, on a certain broad understanding of teleosemantic naturalism, the notion of a "second" nature, one that plays a large part in McDowell's rejection of N1, can be accommodated within the one nature that the "scientific" naturalist recognizes. Essentially, the (now suitably armed) defender of N1 can draw upon an extended account of what can be included within N1, in particular by drawing attention to the role of "friction" (selection) in the development of our conceptual capacities, such "friction" consisting of a combination of training, learning, and felt experience.

This suggestion takes us back to our earlier worries about what gets to be included in the "science" that both the defender and critic of N1 take as their starting points. An unsophisticated scientific naturalism will limit the relevant sciences to physics and chemistry, and it would appear that McDowell accepts this limitation in the contrast he draws between the realm of laws and the space of reasons. This appearance would, however, be misleading, as McDowell explicitly rejects the idea that a more sophisticated conception of science renders the distinction between the realm of laws and the space of reasons otiose. He says:

> I need a less monolithic conception of the kind of explanation that is to be contrasted with placement in the space of reasons. But I believe the *"sui generis"* claim retains its plausibility in the context of a less primitive conception of the (not particularly unified) kind of explanation that is characteristic of the natural sciences. And that is why I continue to think my relaxed Platonism can be genuinely distinguished from a scientifically inspired naturalism, however sophisticated. ("Responses," in McDowell 1999: 103–4)

And his claim that he needs only the *analogy* between "the acquisition of responsiveness to reasons and, for instance, the acquisition of secondary sexual characteristics" suggests that he has already taken into account the kind of extended teleosemantic naturalism presented above in his continued affirmation of the *sui generis* nature of the space of reasons. Now I think that the case for understanding what belongs to second nature as being formed by processes that are *of the same type* as those that figure in the formation of "ordinary" functional properties is pretty strong, so the difference that is seen as crucial, the difference making the space of reasons *sui generis*, must be found elsewhere. My understanding of McDowell's position is that second nature, being common to human and non-human animals, is insufficient to characterize the distinctive features of rationality. That is, whilst it is true that our possession of rational capacities requires the kind of history sketched above, one common to all functional features, what the history delivers in the case of rationality is a capacity whose exercise is governed by norms not capturable by "mere" functionality. So we are driven back to the position that it is the novelty of these norms that is the source of the skepticism concerning N1.

That this is the source of the rejection of N1 may be so obvious that a reader may wonder why it has taken us so long to get there. The point in dragging it out has been to make it as difficult as possible to contrast rational norms (whatever they may be) with functional norms; that contrast can be made too easily if a caricatured version of functional norms serves as one part of the contrasted pair. What one finds is a crude rejection of a teleosemantic position along the lines of "There is more to the rationality of action than the propagation of one's genes." The point of the discussion of the extended teleosemantic position argued for above was to show that there are many types of functional norms generated by the variety of processes that give rise to them. There are "multi-level" selection processes, each spawning a norm appropriate to that selector.[15]

It has also been worthwhile stressing the (close) similarities between the processes called upon by McDowell in his account of second nature and those historical processes included in "first" nature. At times he relies on the "non-spookiness" of these processes to vindicate his claim that there is nothing "spookily" non-natural about the space of reasons, even though it is *sui generis*. But if the processes in the one case, that of "first" nature, result only in the production of functional norms, then there is still some work to do to show that the different norms of rationality are *not* mysteriously non-natural. The end effect, I hope, is to create a burden of proof for the defender of N2: to show that rational norms are distinct from any functional norm generated by a relevant history.

One potentially interesting way to discharge the burden would be to stress the difference made by metacognition; we are able to reflect on not only the contents of our beliefs, say, but also on the means by which these contents came to be believed by us, this enabling us to assess these means as providing reliable or unreliable paths to the truth. Metacognition also supplies us with the ability to assess our goals and so to reject some as unworthy, pursuing what we take to be the virtuous path. Taking this line is consistent with McDowell's claim that non-human animals can have knowledge – be "on to things" – whilst not operating within the space of reasons: "it need not be part of the role of the image of the space of reasons to secure for us the very idea of being on to things. The knowledge that Sellars's remark distinctively fits comes into view when what are *already* ways of being on to things . . . are taken up into the ambit of the space of reasons" (2002: 104).

If one does not add anything to this, however, the enlightened N1 champion will claim victory on the grounds that metacognition is something enjoyed by non-human animals, and can be made sense of using only the resources available to (suitably extended) natural science. At the very least, it will be claimed, whether this is true or not cannot be settled a priori, it being a matter for science itself to appraise. And it does seem plausible that if *cognition* is scientifically explicable, then so too will metacognition be, it just being another form of cognition. It would appear, then, that something further is required in order to make a stronger case for the *sui generis* status of the space of reasons.

The further, tempting, thought may well be that it is this reflective capacity that supports our ability to choose one action rather than another, and to assess one content as more believable than another. With choice goes freedom, and, it may be argued, we have to be sensitive to rational norms in a way that floats free of functionality, dependent as that is on history.

I say this is tempting because I find it so. It would vindicate a venerable philosophical tradition that sees us as unique in virtue of our capacity to reason, that capacity presupposing that we can reason about reason, that we can evaluate our choices in the light of reason, and so freely act. It does, however, place a lot of weight on being clear as to what this freedom consists in. What McDowell says about it is (untypically) cautious, cleaving as he does to a Davidsonian compatibilism:

> An occurrence conforms to natural law, if it does, under a description. The idea of conformity to laws is the idea of a framework of characterizations that can fit occurrences, characterizations under which they stand revealed as instances of the operation of law. Placing spontaneity in nature is insisting that some natural occurrences are describable in terms that function in a *sui generis* way, which displays those occurrences as intelligible otherwise than as conforming to law. . . . But this raises no question about our entitlement to conceive nature as a realm of law in the sense of containing law-governed occurrences. (McDowell 1999: 101–2)

And the pertinent question is one he puts himself: "How genuine a space for spontaneity is provided by this formal move? . . . how can [actions] count as free simply on the ground that they are also susceptible to other descriptions under which they are not subsumable under law?" (McDowell 1999: 102). The dilemma is that, on the one hand, appealing just to the different descriptions we have available seems too weak a defense of genuine freedom, but, on the other hand, rescuing freedom by rejecting the universality of natural law will produce the kind of dualism in nature that McDowell wishes to avoid.[16]

If my diagnosis concerning the source of distinctiveness of rational norms is correct, rather a lot depends on how this dilemma gets resolved. The whole case for resisting "one nature" naturalism rests on rescuing a robust-enough notion of freedom without alienating ourselves from nature. How it gets resolved also raises issues central to our self-understanding of what philosophers can do, and what the nature of philosophy is. If one does think, as I do (and McDowell suggests he does), that mere difference in description is too weak a foundation for freedom, then one may be inclined to trade predicates for properties, founding freedom on the distinctive nature of mental properties. The problem will then be to explain how this property-distinctiveness is consistent with universal law, or "closed" physical causation, or whatever rules the roost in the physical domain. This can be done, but what is required is some heavy-duty metaphysics.[17] It is not clear to me that McDowell's inclination to "quietism," to seeing philosophical problems as arising from mistaken assumptions, will allow him to see the metaphysical move as in any way attractive, given that that move is proposed as a substantial solution to a genuine problem. But if not that move, then what?

VII Concluding Thoughts

In this chapter I have been trying to put pressure on McDowell's insistence that defending N1 is a doomed enterprise – doomed because we have to recognize that the space of reasons is not one that can be brought within the domain of any science. The strategy has been to provide a non-orthodox (because non-reductionist) account of the teleosemantic project, and then to elaborate on the variety of processes that can give rise to the central working part in that project, functionality. Given that many of these processes are of the same type as those required for the formation of our second natures, the question arises as to what, in principle, makes rationality elude the reach of science. One possible answer was briefly canvassed: that the internal connection between acting rationally and acting freely made for the impossibility of a scientific understanding of that action, qua rational. The question was then posed: how do we make sense of this freedom, given the presumption of universal law? Is heavy-duty metaphysics required?

A final thought, arising from the way the debate between naturalists and their opponents has been conducted, leads us back to our original musings about the nature of the science invoked in the naturalism wars. McDowell has suggested that when one finds a philosophical impasse, two opposed positions hammering away at each other without discernible progress being made, then one should look behind the entrenched positions and examine the assumptions fueling the debate. In this case, both naturalists and their opponents make much of the science/non-science distinction, and both seem to agree that rational explanations ("understandings") of phenomena are not scientific explanations. The question is whether this distinction can carry the weight placed on it. It is not that either party to the dispute will disagree about whether the *application* of a rational understanding requires empirical knowledge. Given this, how much hangs on the further claims regarding the scientific or non-scientific nature of rational explanation? Perhaps this distinction is just one more empiricist dogma.

Notes

1 Carl Hempel put forward his version of this dilemma, using the physics/non-physics dichotomy, in "Reduction: Ontological and Linguistic Facets," in S. Morgenbesser, P. Suppes, and M. White (eds.), *Philosophy, Science, and Method*, 1969, 179–99.

2 "Acquiring command of a language, which is coming to inhabit the logical space of reasons, is acquiring a second nature. Given that the space of reasons is special . . . ideas of phenomena that are manifestations of a second nature acquired in acquiring command of a language do not, as such, fit in the logical space of natural-scientific understanding." (M. Willaschek (ed.), "Experiencing the World," in *John*

McDowell: Reason and Nature, 1999, 3–17.) Also: "A rational animal could not have acquired the conceptual capacities in whose possession its rationality consists except by being initiated into a social practice," in J. McDowell, "Knowledge and the Internal Revisited," 2002, 93–117.

3   "Knowledge and the Internal Revisited," 104–5.

4   M. Willaschek (ed.), "Experiencing the World," in *John McDowell: Reason and Nature,* 1999, 7.

5   The inclusion of human animals in (b₁) is my interpretation, but it is fairly clear that McDowell would endorse it.

6   R. Millikan, particularly in *Language, Thought, and Other Biological Categories,* 1984, has characterized her program as being reductionist, but for the reasons given above I think that is a misconstrual of what is going on in her project.

7   Eliminative reductions are not being considered here; these "normal" reductions have been called *conservative* reductions.

8   What is contested is not only the specific interpretation of "function" (see n.3), but also how much weight functional organization has in comparison to other organizing principles. For a discussion of this latter debate, see K. Neander's discussion in "Types of Trait: The Importance of Functional Homologues," in Ariew, Cummins, and Perlman (eds.), 2002.

9   This echoes Davidson's strategy in his argument for non-reductive physicalism in his seminal "Mental Events" (Davidson 1980).

10 In what follows I will be using the expression "natural selection" to mean only that process of variable genetic reproduction which evolutionary biologists refer to in their explanations of species modifications.

11 D. T. Campbell, "Variation and Retention in Socio-Cultural Evolution," in Barringer, Blanksten, and Mack (eds.), 1965, 33.

12 See Millikan, "Useless Content," forthcoming. Millikan discusses ways in which the various functions may generate diverse, even clashing, goals in "Cross-Purposes," ch.1 of her *Varieties of Meaning: The 2002 Jean Nicod Lectures,* 2004.

13 McDowell notes that "sparse teaching" can suffice to make somebody sensitive to a rule, and so able to "go on" appropriately on future occasions. He explains the efficacy of such sparse teaching by our possession of a common human nature (and common forms of life). See "Virtue and Reason," in *Mind, Value, and Reality,* 1998b, 65.

14 See also: "It is an insight on Searle's part that intentionality is a biological phenomenon . . . but intentionality needs to be understood in the context of an organism's life in the world; we cannot understand it, or even keep it in view, if we try to think of it in the context of the brain's life inside the head" (McDowell, "Singular Thought and the Extent of Inner Space," 1986, 167 n.59). The teleosemantic perspective prides itself on viewing the person as essentially "in the world."

15 This has been emphasized recently by R. Millikan; see her *Varieties of Meaning: The 2002 Jean Nicod Lectures,* 2004.

16 He notes one can reject the claim that all events are subsumable under law, but that leaves open the question as to how the law-governed and the free are related, "especially given how plausible it is that natural law holds sway at least over the sub-personal machinery that underlies our ability to act and think." (McDowell 1999), 102.

17 See C. and G. Macdonald, "The Metaphysics of Mental Causation," and C. Macdonald, *Mind – Body Identity Theories,* 1989.

References

Ariew, A., Cummins, R., and Perlman, M. (eds.) 2002. *Functions,* Oxford: Oxford University Press.
Campbell, D. 1965. "Variation and Retention in Socio-Cultural Evolution," in H. R. Barringer, G. I. Blanksten, and R. W. Mack (eds.), *Social Change in Developing Areas,* Mass.: Schenkman Publishing Co.

Davidson, D. 1980. *Essays On Actions and Events*, Oxford: Clarendon Press.

Hempel, C. 1969. "Reduction: Ontological and Linguistic Facets," in S. Morgenbesser, P. Suppes, and M. White (eds.). 1969. *Philosophy, Science, and Method*, New York: St Martin's Press, 179–99.

Macdonald, C. 1989. *Mind – Body Identity Theories*, London: Routledge.

McDowell, J. 1986. "Singular Thought and the Extent of Inner Space," in P. Pettit and J. McDowell, *Subject, Thought, and Context*, Oxford: Blackwell.

McDowell, J. 1994. *Mind and World*, Cambridge, Mass.: Harvard University Press.

McDowell, J. 1995. "Knowledge and the Internal," *Philosophy and Phenomenological Research* LV/4.

McDowell, J. 1998a. *Meaning, Knowledge, and Reality*, Cambridge, Mass.: Harvard University Press.

McDowell, J. 1998b. *Mind, Value, and Reality*, Cambridge, Mass.: Harvard University Press.

McDowell, J. 1999. "Experiencing the World" and "Responses," in M. Willaschek (ed.), 1999.

McDowell, J. 2002. "Knowledge and the Internal Revisited," *Philosophy and Phenomenological Research* lxiv: 97–105.

Millikan, R. 1984. *Language, Thought, and other Biological Categories*, Cambridge, Mass.: MIT Press.

Millikan, R. 2004. *Varieties of Meaning: The 2002 Jean Nicod lectures*, Cambridge, Mass.: MIT Press.

Millikan, R. (forthcoming). "Useless Content," in G. Macdonald and D. Papineau *Teleosemantics*, Oxford: Oxford University Press.

Morgenbesser, S., Suppes, P., and White, M. (eds.). 1969. *Philosophy, Science, and Method*, New York: St Martin's Press.

Neander, K. 2002. "Types of Traits: The Importance of Functional Homologues," in A. Ariew, R. Cummins, and M. Perlman (eds.), 2002.

Willaschek, M. (ed.) 1999. *John McDowell: Reason and Nature*, Munster: Lit Verlag.

Wittgenstein, L. 1958. *Philosophical Investigations*, ed. R. Rhees and G. E. Anscombe, trans. G. E. Anscombe, Oxford: Blackwell.

Wittgenstein, L. 1967. *Remarks on the Foundations of Language*, ed. G. H. von Wright, R. Rhees, and G. E. Anscombe, trans. G. E. Anscombe, Oxford: Blackwell.

Response to Graham Macdonald

1 I try to isolate a special space-of-reasons kind of intelligibility – a kind of intelligibility we find in phenomena when we explain them in a way that turns on the idea of responsiveness to reasons as such – partly by contrasting it with a different kind of intelligibility. I should not have suggested, as I did in *Mind and World*, that the image of the realm of law fits the whole extent of the kind of intelligibility I want to contrast with space-of-reasons intelligibility. I am glad Macdonald quotes a passage, from a previous set of responses to critics, in which I try to correct the suggestion. I hope his mentioning the correction will give it more currency. But I think he makes unnecessarily heavy weather over interpreting what he quotes me as saying.

As he sees, the division I chiefly care about is between space-of-reasons intelligibility and any intelligibility that is not of that kind. (This needs to be restricted to intelligibility possessed by phenomena: that is, states or occurrences in empirically knowable reality. The restriction excludes, for instance, the intelligibility of truths of pure mathematics, which belongs to neither of my two kinds. That should not disrupt what I intend by the exhaustive division of kinds of intelligibility.)

What I acknowledge in the passage Macdonald quotes is that the idea of subsuming phenomena under natural law does not fit the intelligibility of many phenomena that are, as I put it there, merely biological. The point of the qualification "merely" is to leave room for a sense in which exercises of rationality on the part of human beings are biological phenomena. They are occurrences in the lives of human animals. But they are not *merely* biological, since their intelligibility is of the space-of-reasons variety.

Now clearly when I grant that the intelligibility of the merely biological need not be a matter of subsumability under law, I do not imply that merely biological phenomena are intelligible in a space-of-reasons way, a way that turns on responsiveness to reasons as such. I can still summarily describe the kind of intelligibility I want to contrast with space-of-reasons intelligibility as the kind of intelligibility revealed by explanations in natural science. The point is that natural-scientific intelligibility has more to it than subsumability under natural law. Macdonald gives a fine account of how the concept of function frames the kind of understanding characteristically achieved in biology, and I can appropriate that as putting in place a variety of indisputably scientific intelligibility that should not be assimilated to subsumability under natural law. So the intelligibility of the realm of law should have figured as at best exemplary of the kind of intelligibility I want to contrast with space-of-reasons intelligibility, not as coextensive with the contrasting kind of intelligibility.

The other point I make in the passage Macdonald quotes is that second nature straddles the division I chiefly care about. That is to say that some second-natural phenomena are intelligible in a space-of-reasons way, whereas some are not: for instance, the performances of a trained dog.

I cannot see why Macdonald thinks this leaves open, as an exegetical option, that according to me second-natural phenomena as such are outside the scope of natural-scientific understanding. What puts some intelligibility outside the reach of natural science, according to me, is still the fact that it turns on responsiveness to reasons as such. The point of saying that second nature straddles the main division is to note that it is only some second-natural phenomena that I am claiming natural science cannot accommodate, on the ground that their intelligibility is of the special space-of-reasons kind. In the passage Macdonald quotes, I abandon a monolithic space-of-law conception of natural-scientific intelligibity – the kind of intelligibility I continue to contrast with space-of-reasons intelligibility – in order to make room for a better picture of the surely natural-scientific intelligibility of the merely biological. The merely biological, as opposed to the phenomena in human lives that are within the scope of space-of-reasons understanding, clearly includes the second-natural dispositions and performances of trained dogs. So there is no go in the idea that I might be suggesting that the second-natural as such, on both sides of my main division, is not subject to natural-scientific understanding. That is not just the less likely of two possible readings of me, as Macdonald has it. It is simply excluded.

2   I reject a naturalism that identifies what is natural with what can be understood by the methods of natural science. In section 1 of this response I have been considering Macdonald's reading of my attempt to improve on the crude idea that natural-scientific understanding is exclusively a matter of subsuming phenomena under natural laws. But even with a less monolithic conception of natural science, I go on holding that phenomena intelligible in a way that centers on the idea of subjects who aspire to conform to rational norms are outside the scope of a naturalism of natural science. The point of my appeal to the idea of second nature is to insist that excluding these phenomena from the scope of natural-scientific intelligibility does not imply that they are not natural phenomena.

Now Macdonald thinks this stance lands me with a burden of proof, to show that a sufficiently sophisticated exploitation of the concept of function, as it figures in framing biological understanding, cannot accommodate the explanatory potential of appeals to rationality. But I reject this view of the dialectical situation.

For there to be a burden of proof where Macdonald places it, a naturalism of natural science would need to be the default position, the position that wins the day unless it can be shown to be unacceptable. Only so would resistance to it incur the onus Macdonald wants me to shoulder, the obligation to prove that the resources of natural science cannot extend to the intelligibility of exercises of rationality. But now that we have things set up in these terms, I can say this: what I aim to show is that there is nothing but a scientistic prejudice in the view that a naturalism of natural science has that default status – the view that the very idea of what is natural can be taken to be definable in terms of natural science, unless it can be proved that natural science cannot accommodate exercises of rationality.

A better candidate for being the default view, the view that should stand unless it can be shown to be wrong, is the "venerable philosophical tradition" that Macdonald admits he finds tempting. According to this tradition, human beings are unique among living things – outside the reach of the sort of understanding achievable by a scientific biology – in virtue of the freedom that belongs with our responsiveness to reasons as such.

There is a temptation to think this tradition can be dislodged from its default acceptability, on the ground of a supposed implication: that the phenomena whose specialness the tradition insists on are outside the scope of the natural, and hence unnatural or supernatural. My point is to consider and reject that temptation. I claim that the concept of second nature accommodates the phenomena in question, without any requirement that their intelligibility be shown to be a case of the sort of intelligibility that the natural sciences find in phenomena. And that gives the lie to the idea that the venerable tradition, with its denial that these phenomena are scientifically intelligible, implies that they are extra-natural.

The point is not at all to pretend to be able to show that the project of bringing rationality within the scope of natural-scientific intelligibility is impossible. The point is that starting from a naturalism that consists only in the thought that we should not countenance unnatural or supernatural phenomena unless it turns out to be unavoidable, we can derive no motivation at all for engaging in the project. It is perfectly feasible, at any rate so far as these considerations go, to let the venerable tradition stand. The point about the project is not that we are in a position to know it cannot be executed, but that these considerations show that it has no motivation except a bare faith in the universal scope of the natural sciences. That leaves it at least arguable that the venerable tradition is a more intellectually respectable starting point for reflection about rationality. It has more going for it than groundless confidence in science does.

3   I have no distaste for metaphysics as such. After all, the thought that rational animals are unique among living things in being free – the central thesis of the venerable tradition – is in an obvious sense a metaphysical thought.

Macdonald thinks I need heavy-duty metaphysics to sustain that thought. But this reflects the fact that he thinks I am committed to a Davidsonian compatibilism. Given that, he thinks I need to show how the freedom exemplified in some events can be consistent with their being subject to "universal law, or 'closed' physical causation, or whatever rules the roost in the physical domain."

But this is a misreading.

In the passage Macdonald takes to show my adherence to a Davidsonian compatibilism, my point is simply this: when I insist that, since nature includes second nature, it can embrace events that display the freedom implied by Kantian talk of spontaneity, I do not imply that there is *no* room in nature, so conceived, for conformity to law. (It is obvious that there is no such implication. But pointing that out was relevant, in the dialectical context of the response to criticism that Macdonald is quoting from.) The point is that conformity to law is not absent from nature as I recommend conceiving it. The point is not that *all* events that are natural, in the sense I am indicating, exemplify conformity to law (or some substitute: "whatever rules the roost in the physical domain"). So far as this goes, it could be that some events that are natural in the sense in question exemplify conformity to law (or an improved substitute), while others – those that display the freedom of exercises of rationality – do not.

As I go on to remark (in a bit of the passage that Macdonald omits), when I claim that to place spontaneity in nature is not to exclude conformity to law from nature, I am, so far, skirting issues raised by the thesis that *everything* that happens in nature is subsumable under natural law. I am certainly not indicating that I accept that thesis, as Macdonald apparently thinks.

Davidsonian compatibilism accepts some such thesis. Davidsonian compatibilism purports to vindicate a place for freedom in nature by claiming that some of the events in nature, all of which are supposedly subsumable under law under some descriptions, are also describable in ways that depict them as exercises of rationality and hence free.

I query whether this can be a satisfactory vindication of freedom. Here Macdonald takes me to be posing a problem for myself, given that, as he thinks, I am committed to the Davidsonian strategy for vindicating freedom. That is why he thinks I need that heavy-duty metaphysics. But when I raise that query, I mean to be expressing a skepticism about the Davidsonian strategy. Macdonald says "rescuing freedom by rejecting the universality of natural law will produce the kind of dualism in nature that McDowell wishes to avoid." On the contrary, that is exactly how I think freedom should be vindicated.

It is useful to reserve the label "dualism" for sources of philosophical trouble. On this usage, a contrast is not necessarily a dualism. I see no problem about rejecting the Davidsonian monism according to which, though some of what happens in nature is describable in terms of exercises of rationality, all of what happens in nature – including those events, which under other descriptions manifest freedom – is describable in terms of "whatever rules the roost in physics." I am quite happy to suppose there are two kinds of happenings in nature: those that are subsumable under natural law, and those that are not subsumable under natural law, because freedom is operative in them. That is a distinction, not a dualism, and I have no wish to avoid it.

This is not a line I am taking for the first time here, just to avoid trouble from Macdonald. In my paper "Functionalism and Anomalous Monism,"[1] I suggest a skepticism about Davidson's monism. As I note there, Davidson's monism, which is a monism of events, cannot be defended as a necessary means to avoid Cartesian dualism. Cartesian dualism is a dualism of substances, not of kinds of event. In Ryle's instructive caricature, Cartesian dualism depicts minds as para-material substances. If we hold that some events in human lives have no description that brings them within the scope of any science of matter, that does not imply that they take place in a para-material substance. It does not imply that the composition of a human being includes something just like a kind of stuff except that it is not material. That is a dualism, and we must avoid it. But it is not implied by the differentiation of kinds of events that I envisage.

As Macdonald notes, I acknowledge that if we hold that some events, those that manifest human freedom, are not subsumable under natural law, that leaves us needing to say more about how events that manifest freedom are related to events that are subsumable under natural law. In fact it would be better to formulate this consequential task in terms of the less monolithic conception of what it takes for events to be within the scope of natural-scientific intelligibility that was my concern in section 1 above. The question is how events that manifest freedom are related to events that are intelligible by the methods of natural science. And that is a good question. Exercises of human freedom cannot be simply independent of the workings of our (literally) internal organization, which are surely scientifically explicable.

But of course to acknowledge that there is more to be said if we take a certain line is not, just as such, to identify a reason against taking it. I think this conception of a remaining task yields a fine account of the intellectual interest that attaches to the scientific investigation of the machinery of mindedness, as I put it in the Introduction to *Mind and World* (pp. xxi–ii).

Note and Reference

1 Reprinted in *Mind, Value, and Reality*, Cambridge, Mass.: Harvard University Press, 1998.

Index